D0007393

Definite Descriptions *A Reader*

edited by Gary Ostertag

Definite Descriptions

econ

Definite Descriptions / A Reader

edited by Gary Ostertag

A Bradford Book
The MIT Press
Cambridge, Massachusetts
London, England

This book was set in Times New Roman on the Monotype "Prism Plus" Post-Script Imagesetter by Asco Trade Typesetting Ltd., Hong Kong.

Printed and bound in the United States of America.

Library of Congress Cataloging-in-Publication Data

Definite descriptions : a reader / edited by Gary Ostertag.
   p. cm.
"A Bradford book."
Includes bibliographical references and index.
ISBN 0-262-65049-5 (alk. paper)
   1. Language and languages—Philosophy. 2. Description
(Philosophy) 3. Definiteness (Linguistics) 4. Reference
(Linguistics) I. Ostertag, Gary.
P106.D426   1998
401—dc21   97-47000
                                  CIP

For Eileen

Contents

Definite Descriptions

Preface

The theory of descriptions provides a useful entry point into the philosophy of language: The literature is self-contained and comparatively accessible, and the relevant topics reappear in other areas of the philosophy of language, including areas of current research. The present anthology is concerned both to introduce students to the philosophy of language via the theory of descriptions, and to provide scholars access to some of the central contributions to the latter. Of course, even the reader with substantial knowledge of the tradition may gain something. The hope is that, placed in their proper dialectical environment, the reader will perceive important trends and themes in the selections that would not otherwise have been apparent.

It is regrettable that the best work in the tradition comprises more articles than can be included in a reasonably sized volume. Many excellent papers—some of them indisputably classics—had to be omitted. I regret especially the omission of papers by William K. Blackburn, Marga Reimer, Nathan Salmon, and Wilfrid Sellars—papers that, to my mind, have played an essential role in shaping the current debate between the Russellian and the referentialist. I have consoled myself with the thought that an anthology of this sort is not a "greatest hits" package: Its goal is to acquaint the reader with a set of philosophical problems and attempted resolutions. In any case, the reader who has made her way through this book will surely turn to the authors mentioned to fill in missing stages of the dialectic.

Another regret is that I have not adequately represented an important new trend relevant to the theory of descriptions. This is the study of descriptive, or E-type, pronouns—a study initiated by Peter Geach and Barbara Partee and whose current significance owes much to the work of Gareth Evans. The literature on descriptive pronouns is a topic worthy of

an anthology in its own right. Indeed, this is what prompted my decision
not to include a representative sampling of the various approaches.
Moreover, much of the literature is exceedingly technical and thus inappropriate for an anthology attempting to be self-contained. The interested reader should consult the bibliography for the relevant literature.

There are many people to thank for helpful suggestions, advice, time,
and interest in the project. Thanks to Phil Bricker, Russell Dale, Ed
Gettier, Eileen O'Neill, and Stephen Schiffer, who provided valuable
comments on the introduction, and to Arnold Koslow, Stephen Neale,
Mark Sainsbury, and an anonymous referee, who made a number of
helpful suggestions concerning the selections. Thanks go as well to my
editor, Amy Brand, for her patient and expert help throughout, and to my
copy editor, Judy Feldmann, for her meticulous care in handling the
manuscript. The Philosophy Department at New York University is to be
thanked for allowing me to be a visiting scholar for the academic years
1996–1997 and 1997–1998.

Without the continued support and advice of Stephen Schiffer, this
project would have ended where it began—as a projected table of contents. It was Stephen's immediate response—something to the effect of
"I'm amazed that no one has ever thought of it before"—that made me
realize that the project was indeed a valuable one. His encouragement has
been absolutely crucial to me. I am also lucky to have had Russell Dale's
enthusiastic support. My countless conversations with Russell, as well
as his own work on the theory of meaning, have forced me to rethink
a number of key issues in the philosophy of language. Russell also
helped with the proofreading, for which I am grateful. And thanks to my
parents, Rosemarie and Bernhard Ostertag, for their encouragement and
generosity.

Finally, there is my muse, Eileen O'Neill, who provided essential
philosophical input, feedback, and much-needed distraction (the latter
with the help of two unbelievably demanding Persian cats). Her own work
in the history of philosophy inspired me to look to the historical roots
of my research, and to attempt to make sense of it within a larger context.
Her companionship has made philosophical discourse, and much else in
life, an absolute joy. This one is for her.

Introduction

I Origins

In October 1905, Bertrand Russell published, within months of its conception, his first statement of the theory of descriptions. The period was a tumultuous one in Russell's life,[1] but whatever his distractions, he managed to attain a clarity and originality of thought that has rarely been matched in the philosophical writing of the twentieth century. At the time, Russell was becoming increasingly uncomfortable with the extreme realism of his earlier work, *The Principles of Mathematics*, and with the work of the Austrian metaphysician, Alexius Meinong, whose views Russell had endorsed. In *The Principles*, Russell felt compelled to admit nonexistent entities into his ontology to function as the referents of nondenoting terms, such as "Apollo" and "Priam." Similarly, Meinong acknowledged impossibilia, which allegedly functioned as the "denotations" of descriptions such as "the round square" and "the golden mountain." By early 1905, Russell's temperament had shifted. In a review of a paper by the Scottish logician Hugh MacColl, Russell, armed with the Frege-inspired distinction between the meaning of an expression and its denotation, renounced the ontological commitments of *The Principles*. He was now in the grip of the "robust sense of reality" that was to inform his subsequent writings.[2]

By June of the same year, Russell had come upon the theory of descriptions. According to his new view, definite descriptions do not refer, nor can they be said to have meaning (or sense) in the way in which referring expressions may be said to have meaning (or sense). Rather, like other denoting phrases (e.g., "all women," "some women" and "no women"), they are devices of quantification. As such, they cannot be assigned semantical values directly or "in isolation." Their contribution to the meanings of sentences in which they occur can only be captured by providing a representation of the entire context. Here Russell broke new ground: In the response to MacColl he had maintained that the propositional contribution of a definite description is a "complex concept" (which he elsewhere refers to as a "denoting concept")—something that can be assigned to a description in isolation. His new doctrine abandoned this view.

To understand the change in Russell's thought, it is important to note something that is often overlooked, which is that Russell was not concerned exclusively with definite descriptions in "On Denoting." His concern was to solve the more general problem of providing a uniform treatment of denoting phrases. This is evident from his delineation of the subject matter in the first sentence:

By a "denoting phrase" I mean a phrase such as any one of the following: a man, some man, any man, every man, all men, the present King of England, the centre of mass of the Solar System at the first instance of the twentieth century, the revolution of the earth round the sun, the revolution of the sun round the earth.

It is also significant that, in a letter to the mathematician and Leibniz scholar Louis Couturat, dated July 23, 1905, Russell referred to the article (as yet unwritten) under the title "On Denoting Phrases."[3] In the paper, we find a solution to a problem that had eluded Russell in *The Principles*. This problem is whether quantified noun phrases are semantically structured.[4] "If u be a class-concept," he asked, "is the concept 'all u's' analyzable into two constituents *all* and u, or is it a new concept, defined by a certain relation to u, and no more complex than u itself?"[5] Russell continued:

"All men" and "all numbers" have in common the fact that they both have a certain relation to a class-concept, namely *man* and *number* respectively. But it is very difficult to isolate any further element of *allness* which both share, unless we take as this element the mere fact that both are concepts of classes. It would seem, then, that "all u's" is not validly analyzable into *all* and u, and that language, in this case as in some others, is a misleading guide. The same remark will apply to *every, any, some, a*, and *the*. (*Principles*, p. 72–73)

The problem is that expressions such as "all men" and "all numbers," while syntactically complex, do not seem amenable to a semantic analysis, although they seem, for all that, semantically complex.[6] If we take Russell to have been concerned with providing a compositional meaning theory for a certain fragment of English—a theory that assigns meanings to arbitrarily selected sentences from this fragment—the worry becomes clear. It seems that a speaker who understands the expressions "all" and "logicist" can provide an interpretation of a sentence in which the expression "all logicists" occurs—for example, "All logicists admire Russell" —without having previously encountered that expression (assuming the remaining expressions are familiar). This fact is inexplicable if we cannot isolate what it is that "all logicists" and, for example, "all formalists" have in common.

"On Denoting" addresses precisely this worry, providing an analysis of the relevant expressions, or, more accurately, of the contexts in which they occur. The crucial feature of this analysis is the doctrine of contextual definition, or "meaning in use":

> *Everything, nothing,* and *something* are not assumed to have any meaning in isolation, but a meaning is assigned to *every* proposition in which they occur. This is the principle of the theory of denoting I wish to advocate: that denoting phrases never have meaning in themselves, but that every proposition in whose verbal expression they occur has meaning.

The analysis takes the following concept as primitive: the propositional function $C(x)$ is always true.[7] For current purposes, we can equate this with the metalinguistic claim that the predicate "$C(x)$" is satisfied by, or true of, every object in the relevant domain. This primitive, together with a stock of logical connectives enabling him to create complex propositional functions, allows Russell to provide the basis for a compositional analysis of a number of quantified sentence forms. "Everything is C"— in Russell's notation "C(everything)"—is analyzed directly as: "$C(x)$" is true of all objects in the domain. Similarly, "Nothing is C"—or "C(nothing)"—is analyzed as: "It-is-not-the-case-that-$C(x)$" is true of all objects in the domain. Assuming the now standard conditional analysis of universal generalizations, he arrives at the following analysis of "All men are mortal": "If x is human, then x is mortal" is true of all objects in the domain. Treatments for the other quantified noun phrases ("no men," "some men," and "every man") follow. Russell then turns to definite descriptions, which are "by far the most interesting and difficult of denoting phrases." This difficulty notwithstanding, the analysis of descriptions is fully stated within two paragraphs. The remainder of the paper is devoted to its defense and to attacks on Meinongian and Fregean alternatives.

An important feature of Russell's discussion in "On Denoting" is the centrality accorded the Principle of Acquaintance, which states that a proposition cannot be understood unless one has immediate acquaintance with its constituents. The Principle of Acquaintance is important in that it represents an attempt to provide a criterion for our grasping or understanding a proposition. Russell's previous theory, according to which denoting phrases such as "some men" express denoting concepts, failed to meet the constraint imposed by this principle. Russell had held that the denoting concept expressed by "some men" is a constituent of the proposition expressed by, for example, "Some men are logicists." Coupled with the Principle of Acquaintance, this theory implies that understanding the proposition that some men are logicists requires acquaintance with the denoting concept itself. But this suggestion is absurd.

"On Denoting" represents a change in Russell's views on propositional constituency. For Russell circa *The Principles*, any object, of whatever ontological grade, may function as a propositional constituent (or "term," in Russell's phrase). And to be a constituent (or term) of a proposition is to be what that proposition is about. Thus, on this view, the proposition that Leibniz was a determinist contains Leibniz as a constituent. As Russell saw, however, denoting phrases present a prima facie problem for the aboutness-as-constituency view. For if mere constituency amounts to aboutness, then "I met a man" will be as much about the denoting concept, *a man*, as "I met Jones" is about the man, Jones. The denoting concept *a man* is, after all, as much a constituent of the proposition expressed by "I met a man" as Jones is a constituent of the proposition expressed by "I met Jones." But, as Russell wrote of the former proposition:

the proposition is not about *a man*: this is a concept which does not walk the streets, but lives in the shadowy limbo of the logic books. What I meant was a thing, not a concept, an actual man with a tailor and a bank-account or a public house and a drunken wife. (*Principles*, p. 53)

The problems posed by denoting phrases were solved by Russell's method of paraphrasing the entire context in which a denoting phrase occurs. The latter method allowed Russell to comply with the Principle of Acquaintance: Every constituent of the paraphrase is one with which a speaker can be acquainted. The method also avoided the problem denoting phrases posed to the aboutness-as-constituency view:

One interesting result of the theory of denoting is this: when there is anything with which we do not have immediate acquaintance, but only definition by denoting phrases, then the propositions in which this thing is introduced by means of a denoting phrase do not really contain this thing as a constituent, but contain instead the constituents expressed by the several words of the denoting phrase. Thus in every proposition that we can apprehend ... all the constituents are really entities with which we have immediate acquaintance.

Thus, in one stroke, three problems—concerning the logical complexity of denoting phrases, their challenge to the analysis of aboutness in terms of constituency, and their failure to comply with the Principle of Acquaintance—are resolved. Russell continued to refine his analysis of denoting phrases in the years leading to *Principia Mathematica*. In particular, he attended to issues concerning scope and he avoided explicit mention of propositional-function expressions in the analysis of denoting phrases. Nonetheless, the essential features of the analysis were set by the publication of "On Denoting."[8]

There is a common misconception that the change in philosophical temperament that resulted in Russell's break with Meinong was due to Russell's discovery of the theory of descriptions. Quine, for example, writes that the break with Meinong was "no simple change of heart; it hinged on his discovery of a means of dispensing with [Meinong's] unwelcome objects."[9] The suggestion is that the discovery of a method for eliminating apparent singular terms preceded the doctrinal shift. In fact, Russell's response to Hugh MacColl, mentioned above, shows this suggestion to be false (as does the letter to Meinong mentioned in note 2): The break with Meinong preceded the discovery of the theory of descriptions. In the response to MacColl, Russell took definite descriptions to be "complex concepts," which may or may not denote. This was the view that he associated with Frege and which would come under heavy attack in "On Denoting" (appearing, as it turned out, in the subsequent issue of *Mind*). For example, Russell wrote that "The present King of France" is a "complex concept denoting nothing":

The phrase intends to point out an individual, but fails to do so: it does not point out an unreal individual, but no individual at all. The same explanation applies to mythical personages, Apollo, Priam, etc. These words have a *meaning*, which can be found by looking them up in a classical dictionary; but they have not a *denotation*: there is no entity, real, or imaginary, which they point out. ("The Existential Import of Propositions," p. 100)

The passage exhibits both Russell's newfound ontological conservatism as well as his confidence, however fleeting, that the Frege-inspired distinction between the meaning of a singular term and its denotation would enable him to avoid Meinong's jungle. Interestingly, Russell himself was partly to blame for the common impression that the theory of descriptions was the immediate result of his "desire to avoid Meinong's unduly populous realm of being."[10] As he would write in *My Philosophical Development*:

Meinong ... pointed out that one can make statements in which the logical subject
is "the golden mountain" although no golden mountain exists. He argued, if you
say that the golden mountain does not exist, it is obvious that there is something
that you are saying does not exist—namely the golden mountain; therefore the
golden mountain must subsist in some shadowy Platonic world of being, for otherwise your statement that the golden mountain does not exist would have no
meaning. I confess that, until I hit upon the theory of descriptions, this argument
seemed to me convincing. (p. 64)

The final claim is false: the argument ceased to be convincing to Russell
well before he discovered the theory of descriptions. The meaning–
denotation distinction provided a way for him to explain the meaningful-
ness of "The golden mountain does not exist" without being forced to
postulate "shadowy" entities. What prompted the theory of descriptions
was not his disenchantment with Meinong, but rather with a cluster of
issues concerning denoting phrases.

One element of this cluster was the "inextricable tangle" of section 3 of
"On Denoting." I will not say much here about this problem. It concerns
the view that the meaning of a denoting phrase—something that can be
assigned to such a phrase in isolation—fixes its denotation. As Russell
rightly pointed out, the relation between "The author of *Waverly*" and its
denotation, Scott, is "not merely linguistic through the phrase: there must
be a logical relation involved, which we express by saying that the meaning denotes the denotation." We can relate Russell's claim here to the
concern for a compositional analysis of quantified noun phrases generally.
Unlike a name, "The author of *Waverly*" is not directly assigned a denotation by linguistic convention; its denotation is determined by its components and their mode of combination. (This is what Russell means by
saying that "there must be a logical relation involved.")[11] Yet, as Russell
attempted to show, preserving the desired connection between meaning
and denotation is impossible without collapsing the distinction between
the two.

II Definite Descriptions in *Principia Mathematica*

Principia Mathematica presents the formal development of the theory
of descriptions. As we shall see, the version of the theory in *Principia*
is superior to that presented in "On Denoting" in its handling of scope
ambiguities. Another improvement is that in *Principia*, Russell abandoned
the metalinguistic analysis of denoting phrases he had developed in "On
Denoting." Whereas Russell previously had held that "The *F* is *G*" ex-

presses a proposition about the propositional functions Fx, Gx and $Fy \supset y = x$, he now assigned it (more accurately, assigned its formal counterpart $G(\imath x)Fx$) quite a different proposition. The metalinguistic analysis evidently came to strike Russell as unsatisfactory and is, in any case, inadequate. Except for unusual cases, description sentences are not about expressions. The view suggested by (*14.01) (see below) is that a sentence of the form *The F is G* expresses a proposition that is true at a possible world w just in case exactly one thing is F at w and anything that is F at w is G at w, and false otherwise. While the apparatus of possible worlds is foreign to the *Principia*, this is the interpretation of (*14.01) that constitutes Russell's theory as it is currently understood. There is little doubt that if Russell were to have used the apparatus, he would have accepted the interpretation.

In the language of *Principia*, a definite description possesses the surface grammar of a singular term, and thus would seem amenable to an analysis according to which it can be assigned a meaning "in isolation." In fact, Russell claimed that a definite description is an "incomplete symbol" and can only be defined contextually. Whereas to assign a meaning to a singular term is to assign it a referent (and perhaps a sense as well), to assign a meaning to a description is to assign meaning to the entire context in which it occurs. In addition, the resulting representation of the context's meaning will contain no constituent corresponding to the description itself.

Russell's remarks about descriptions apply equally to both natural language descriptions and to descriptions in the formal language of *Principia*. He analyzed the English sentence (1a) as (1b):

(1a) The present King of France is bald.

(1b) There is exactly one present King of France, and anything that is at present King of France is bald.

In the formal language of *Principia*, (1a) and (1b) correspond, respectively, to:

(1a′) $B(\imath x)Fx$

(1b′) $\exists x(\forall y(Fy \equiv y = x) \bullet Bx)$

(1b′) is equivalent to the following, which is somewhat easier to interpret:

$\exists x(Fx \bullet \forall y(Fy \supset y = x) \bullet Bx)$

As we can see, neither (1b) nor its formal counterparts contain a constituent corresponding to the relevant description.

The key propositions of *Principia* allowing for the elimination of descriptions are (*14.01) and (*14.02):

(*14.01) $[(\imath x)\Phi x]\ \Psi(\imath x)\Phi x = \exists x(\forall y(\Phi y \equiv y = x) \bullet \Psi x)$

(*14.02) $E!(\imath x)\Phi x = \exists x \forall y(\Phi y \equiv y = x)$

Together, these definitions (note the equals sign) provide an elimination procedure for descriptions. (*14.02) concerns the special context of existence claims; (*14.01) suffices for all other contexts. I have omitted Russell's convention of using dots to indicate scope, in favor of parentheses. The iota phrase in brackets prefixed to the left-hand side of (*14.01) indicates the scope of the definite description, which is the sentence to which it is immediately adjoined.[12]

What (*14.01) states is, in effect, that a sentence "$\Psi(\imath x)\Phi x$," in which the definite description "$(\imath x)\Phi x$" takes wide scope, is equivalent to the formula that claims that there exists exactly one object satisfying "Φx" and that anything satisfying "Φx" satisfies "Ψx." (*14.02) states that the claim that the Φ exists (i.e., "$E!(\imath x)\Phi x$") is equivalent to the formula asserting the existence of exactly one object satisfying "Φx."

As Russell showed, these definitions provide two distinct readings of the following sentence:

(2) $\Psi(\imath x)\Phi x \supset p$

One reading of (2) is that *the thing that is Φ is such that: it is Ψ only if p*; the other reading is that *the thing that is Φ is Ψ, only if p*. These are clearly different propositions, with different truth conditions. The first implies that there is a unique Φ (i.e., it implies "$E!(\imath x)\Phi x$"); the second does not. Using Russell's notation, the first reading is represented by (2a) (where the scope of the description is the sentence (2)), whereas the second reading is represented by (2b) (where the scope of the description is simply "$\Psi(\imath x)\Phi x$"):

(2a) $[(\imath x)\Phi x]\ (\Psi(\imath x)\Phi x \supset p)$

(2b) $[(\imath x)\Phi x]\ \Psi(\imath x)\Phi x \supset p$

For reference, the expansions of (2a) and (2b) are (2a$'$) and (2b$'$), respectively:

(2a$'$) $\exists x(\forall y(\Phi y \equiv y = x) \bullet (\Psi x \supset p))$

(2b$'$) $\exists x(\forall y(\Phi y \equiv y = x) \bullet \Psi x) \supset p$

An iota phrase takes wide scope with respect to a sentence S just in case its scope is S itself; it takes narrow scope with respect to S just in case it is within the scope of the main logical operator of S. In (2a), then, the iota phrase takes wide scope, as its scope is (2); whereas in (2b), it takes narrow scope, as its scope is only the antecedent of (2). Another example where scope indicators are necessary is (3):

(3) $\neg \Psi(\iota x)\Phi x$

This is ambiguous between the following two readings:

(3a) $\exists x(\forall y(\Phi y \equiv y = x) \bullet \neg \Psi x)$

(3b) $\neg \exists x(\forall y(\Phi y \equiv y = x) \bullet \Psi x)$

(Quasi-English parallels to (3a) and (3b) would be "something is uniquely Φ and not Ψ" and "it's not the case that something is both Ψ and uniquely Φ," respectively.) Once again, Russell's notation saves the day:

(3a') $[(\iota x)\Phi x] \neg \{\Psi(\iota x)\Phi x\}$

(3b') $\neg \{[(\iota x)\Phi x]\Psi(\iota x)\Phi x\}$

The scope of the negation in (3a') is within the scope of the iota phrase, which takes wide scope; these scope relations are inverted in (3b'), where the iota phrase is within the scope of the negation sign.[13]

Recently, a uniform method of representing quantified noun phrases—Russell's "denoting phrases"—has emerged. On this view, quantified noun phrases are represented as the concatenation of a determiner (a member of the category including "all," "no," "some," "a," "most," etc.) and a predicate (e.g., "Men (x)"), resulting in an expression exemplifying the following syntactic form: "[Some x: Men (x)]." Combining such expressions with a predicate produces a sentence (or complex predicate). For example, "[Some x: Men (x)]" can combine with "Mortal (x)" to produce "[Some x: Men (x)] (Mortal (x))"—in English, "Some men are mortal." Russellians, such as Stephen Neale, have adopted this method of representing quantified sentences and have seen it as the basis for classifying descriptions within the same category as "all men," "no men," "some men," etc. One consequence of this assimilation is that scope indicators are no longer necessary. On the new notation, (3a') and (3b') correspond to (3a'') and (3b''), respectively:

(3a'') [the x: Φx] $(\neg \Psi x)$

(3b'') $\neg$[the x: Φx] (Ψx)

The larger project, of which the introduction of restricted quantifiers is a part, is to connect Russell's theory with an important research program in syntax. Syntacticians, working in a framework derived from Noam Chomsky's Government and Binding theory, have located a level of the syntactic representation of sentences where all anaphoric relations (e.g., between quantifier and pronoun) are made explicit.[14] This level is referred to as "LF" (for "Logical Form"). LF represents quantified noun phrases (including *wh*-phrases such as "which men") as restricted quantifiers. This has suggested to certain philosophers, such as Stephen Neale and James Higginbotham, that LF is the level of syntactic representation at which *semantic* interpretation occurs. This is for two reasons: First, as indicated, LF is a medium where scope relations are explicit. This makes LF appropriate for semantic interpretation, since all structural ambiguities will have been resolved at this level of representation. In addition, the use of restricted quantification in LF provides the semanticist with a medium that serves as input for a semantic theory—for example, a theory that will provide an assignment of truth conditions to all well-formed LF structures. No further translation, for example, from LF to first-order logic, is then necessary.

While the use of restricted quantification has been advocated by some Russellians, it is not an essential component of that view. What *is* essential is the thesis, stated above, that *the F is G* is true at *w* just in case the unique *F* at *w* is *G* at *w*, and false otherwise. In section IV, we turn to a challenge to this thesis.

III Contemporary Significance

Russell's theory was famously characterized by Frank Ramsey as a "paradigm of philosophy." While Ramsey's remark is widely quoted, the irony it contains is rarely appreciated.[15] What made Ramsey's remark true seventy years ago is not what makes it true today. For Ramsey, Russell's theory was a paradigm of philosophical *analysis*.[16] On the method of analysis, language is taken to be the proper object of philosophical investigation.[17] Moreover, the method is sensitive to the constraint, articulated by Frege, that grammatical structure should not be taken as a guide to logical or semantic structure.[18] The theory of descriptions showed the power of this methodology. It allowed certain venerable problems—for example, the problems of nonexistence and of informativeness—to be successfully resolved by looking beyond the grammatical clothing of the relevant linguistic contexts, into their "logical form." And it provided a deep insight into logical form that was, until then, unnoticed: certain apparent singular terms are, in fact, devices of quantification. This discovery allowed Russell to draw a sharp distinction between those propositions expressed by sentences containing singular terms (e.g., "He is smoking") and those propositions expressed by sentences containing descriptions (e.g., "The man in the corner is smoking"). Propositions of the first class are object-dependent: specification of their truth conditions necessarily involves reference to a specific object. Propositions of the second class are object-independent: Their truth conditions can be specified without reference to any particular individual. Finally, the comprehensiveness of Russell and Whitehead's formalism in *Principia Mathematica*, which showed explicitly how contexts containing these apparent singular terms could be disposed of in favor of contexts in which only the familiar logical particles are present, was also taken to be a reflection of the power of the method of analysis.

Yet, the theory of descriptions, as it is applied in the work of contemporary logicians, linguists, and philosophers, can no longer be taken to constitute a paradigm of analysis. Let me suggest a number of contrasts between the significance of the theory when its full impact was first felt, and its significance for contemporary theorists.

(1) First, the study of natural language quantification has given a new dimension to the idea that descriptions, on Russell's theory, are devices of quantification and not of reference. The description "the poet" is now taken by many researchers to be, as are "all poets," "some poets," and "no poets," a restricted quantifier (or, in some formal languages, a generalized quantifier; see note 6). Yet, since syntacticians take these expressions to belong to the grammatical category *quantified noun phrase*, this interpretation of Russell's theory parts ways with the idea that the grammatical form of descriptions does not reveal their logical form. Moreover, this revision of Russell's theory was neither arbitrary nor guided by concerns extrinsic to philosophical semantics. On the contrary, it was occasioned, in part,[19] by a philosophical project that gained prominence in the 1950s and became, arguably, the central issue in the philosophy of language for the next quarter-century: the task of constructing an adequate meaning-theory for natural languages. Briefly, a meaning-theory for a given language L will consist in the assignment, to each indicative sentence S of L, of a property Φ, such that grasping that S has Φ would constitute understanding S. Armed with such a theory, one

would be able to determine for any sentence S of L what a speaker said when she uttered S. (Here the *saying* relation is a relation that obtains between a speaker and the literal meaning of a sentence.) There were various conceptions of how this project should be pursued. Following the suggestions of Donald Davidson, certain philosophers argued that the form a theory of meaning should take is a theory of truth. That is, the role of a meaning-theory would be performed by a theory that assigns, to each sentence of the relevant language, the conditions under which that sentence is true. Yet, whatever the conception of how a meaning-theory should be constructed, the goal was invariably the same: to provide an account of how a speaker could come to understand sentences that she has never previously encountered. Since Russell's theory ascribed to sentences containing descriptions a logical form that it took substantial ingenuity to uncover, it was not well poised to explain how it is that ordinary speakers can assign meanings (or truth conditions) to such sentences. What was a virtue of the theory in Ramsey's eyes—namely, its marked departure from surface grammar—proved an embarrassment in the new environment.[20]

(2) Another contrast concerns the epistemological role of the theory of descriptions. Russell wedded the theory of descriptions to a sense-datum epistemology.[21] On Russell's view, only objects of immediate acquaintance can be named. Since ordinary proper names do not name such objects, he reasoned, they must in reality be disguised descriptions. While many contemporary philosophers are sympathetic with Russell's view that we can only refer to objects with which we are acquainted, they do not mean by "acquainted" *immediately acquainted*. Thus middle-sized objects are within the range of the acquaintance relation. This dramatically limits the need—and thus the scope—of the theory of descriptions in epistemological discussions.[22]

(3) Finally, there is the issue of the role of philosophy of language vis-à-vis philosophy as a whole. Philosophy of language has been "first philosophy" for most of this century, in much the way that metaphysics had been first philosophy from Aristotle until the rise of analysis. The source of this emphasis is often located with the writings of Frege. For example, Michael Dummett writes in a famous passage:

Only with Frege was the proper object of philosophy finally established: namely, first, that the goal of philosophy is the analysis of the structure of *thought*; secondly, that the study of *thought* is to be sharply distinguished from the psychological process of *thinking*; and, finally, that the only proper method for analyzing thought consists in the analysis of language.[23]

Dummett makes explicit a view shared by many. Indeed, even those, such as Quine and Wittgenstein, who denied that linguistic analysis could yield substantive a priori knowledge never disputed the centrality of language to philosophy. Whatever the merits of the view Dummett states above, few today are optimistic that analysis can provide substantive metaphysical knowledge. However, the demise of philosophical analysis has not steered philosophers away from the study of language. Nonetheless, the interest does not derive from an underlying picture that unifies the various areas of linguistic research.[24] While the problems of meaning, reference, representation, and truth (to name but a few) retain their pull, it remains the case that philosophy of language is but one form of philosophical inquiry among many, with no claim to priority.

As I have suggested, these three contrasts point to an irony in Ramsey's characterization of the theory of descriptions—or, more accurately, to an irony in the fact that this characterization is often repeated by philosophers of language. The theory of descriptions is a paradigm of philosophy precisely because it has caught the attention of philosophers for reasons that are, to a large extent, extrinsic to the way it was originally conceived. It has steered a course which from one perspective seemed inevitable. But a closer look suggests that what seemed inevitable was in fact largely accidental. Indeed, we have seen that it was Russell himself who made the first opportunistic use of his own theory, claiming that it was "the desire to avoid Meinong's unduly populous realm of being" that occasioned the theory. The textual facts tell otherwise: As we now know, Russell had found a way to avoid Meinong's ontological jungle at least a half-year prior to his discovery of the theory of descriptions. Nonetheless, in misrepresenting his own intentions, Russell inaugurated a venerable tradition—a tradition whose contribution to contemporary philosophy is immeasurable.

IV Referential and Attributive Uses of Descriptions

Contemporary interest in the theory of descriptions emerged from the various responses to Keith Donnellan's distinction between referential and attributive uses of definite descriptions. This distinction was almost immediately dismissed as a pragmatic phenomenon by advocates of Russell, such as Paul Grice (see chapter 9) and Saul Kripke (see chapter 11).[25] But coeval developments in the theory of reference, fueled in part by Donnellan's distinction, led many to think otherwise.

Roughly, a description "the F" is used referentially in an utterance of "the F is G" when there is some object o such that it is the speaker's primary intention to communicate the (object-dependent) proposition that o is G. (See chapter 14, section 14.5, for a more precise formulation.[26] On the other hand, a description "the F" is used attributively in an utterance of "the F is G" when it is the speaker's primary intention to communicate the (object-independent) proposition that exactly one thing is F, and whatever is F is G. The attributive use of definite descriptions is essentially the use of descriptions that conforms to Russell's theory; the referential use, in contrast, is the use that fails to conform to Russell's theory.[27]

One theme that is prominent in a number of the selections that follow concerns the question whether Russell's theory can accommodate the referential use of definite descriptions. Even those who maintain, with Russell, that descriptions are devices of quantification and not reference nonetheless acknowledge that descriptions are often *used* referentially.[28] As an example of such usage, consider the utterance of (1) below in a situation where a man appears to be drinking a martini. (The example is Donnellan's.)

(1) The man drinking a martini is drunk.

In such a situation, I may utter (1) with the primary intention of informing my audience that a given man, say Smith, is drunk. Evidence that this was my primary intention could be supplied by considering the relevance, to the truth of what I intended to communicate, of the following: Smith was in fact drinking mineral water, although there was one (unobserved) man drinking a martini, who was sober. Surely, there is a sense in which the truth of what I intended to communicate is not challenged by the discovery of this fact. For what I intended to communicate was that Smith is drunk, and it is not relevant to this claim that Smith is drinking mineral water, nor is it relevant that some other man happens to be sober.[29] (The discovery is, of course, relevant to what I said in uttering (1), according to Russell's theory.)

This reasoning has been taken to be the basis of an argument for the claim that descriptions can function semantically as referential singular terms. Following Neale, we may call the argument just sketched "the argument from misdescription." As indicated, it is not open to dispute that what the speaker intended to communicate in uttering (1) is a proposition that contains Smith as a constituent: its truth is wholly determined by whether or not Smith is drunk. Employing terminology introduced in the previous section, we can say that the speaker intended to communicate an object-dependent proposition—a proposition the specification of whose truth conditions requires reference to an individual, in this case, Smith.

Let us stipulate that what a speaker *A says* in uttering *S* is the proposition that *A*'s use of *S* "expresses" *relative to the context of utterance.*[30] And let us stipulate that what *A means* in uttering *S* is the proposition that *A* is primarily concerned to communicate in uttering *S*.

Given this distinction, due to Grice, a reasonably precise characterization of the dialectical situation is possible. The Russellian can consistently maintain [R] even while acknowledging the referential use of definite descriptions.

[R] The object-dependent proposition that the speaker *meant* in uttering (1)—namely, that Smith is drunk—is not to be identified with what the speaker *said* in uttering (1).

The Russellian is committed to the idea that sentences exemplifying (1) can only be used to *say* that the unique martini-drinking man is drunk. But this does not preclude her from recognizing that it is often a speaker's primary intention, in uttering such sentences, to convey something object-dependent.

Let us call the view that claims that our speaker in uttering (1) *says* that Smith is drunk the *referential thesis*. According to an interpretation of the referential thesis suggested by philosophers such as Christopher Peacocke, Michael Devitt, and Howard Wettstein, a "referentially used description functions semantically as a demonstrative."[31] That is to say, a referentially used description "the F," as it occurs in an utterance *u*, introduces its referent, and only its referent, into the proposition expressed by *u*.

While Russellians often claim that it is the burden of the referentialist to establish that the referential use of definite descriptions is semantically significant, the referentialist claims that, in fact, the burden resides with the Russellian. The referentialist appeals to a "direct intuition" (Schiffer) that certain uses of "The *F* is *G*" have, as their semantic content, a proposition of the form "α is *G*" (where "α" is a term of direct reference). To use Christopher Peacocke's terminology, this amounts to the claim that the "entity-invoking" use of a description is semantically referential.

How legitimate is the referentialist's appeal to the direct intuition that the entity-invoking use of "The *F* is *G*" expresses an object-dependent proposition? The following response is available. The Russellian can maintain that intuition is not an infallible guide. It may well be that the referentialist mistakenly identifies what a speaker means in a referential use of "The F is G" with what she says. At best, intuition can serve as a guide to what a speaker *typically means* when uttering a given form of expression in a certain class of contexts; it cannot decide that what the speaker means in those contexts is the semantic content of her utterance. While it may be conceded that the inference from "a speaker typically means p in uttering S in such-and-such contexts" to "a speaker says p in uttering S in such-and-such contexts" has a prima facie plausibility, it is nonetheless invalid, for it may be challenged by general, methodological considerations. It is, for example, undeniable that in a typical utterance of "John woke up and had a cigarette" the speaker meant *that John woke up and had a cigarette some time after waking up.* Yet, it is rather implausible to take this fact as necessitating the hypothesis that what a speaker says in uttering "John woke up and had a cigarette" is the italicized proposition. The reason that it is implausible is that it takes the mere fact that an expression (here, "and") exemplifies distinct patterns of use to constitute conclusive evidence for attributing distinct senses to that expression. Since these uses can be explained by appeal to general principles governing conversation—principles that have an independent justification —there is no reason to complicate the semantics of the expression in question.[32]

To challenge the Russellian successfully, the referentialist must point to a decisive intuition that what the utterance of (1) says is true. Unfortunately, we see that no such intuition exists. In fact, a well-known method for evaluating semantic claims suggests that, if anything, what the utterance says is precisely what the Russellian claims it says. I now consider an argument appealing to the method in question.

The method runs as follows. We take a *context of utterance* to be a region of reality at which an utterance is interpreted. For example, let the context of Al Gore's utterance "I am in New York" be New York City, May 23, 1997. We thus interpret the utterance, according to the semantic rules of English, as *saying* that Al Gore is in New York. Using Kaplan's terminology, we may say that the context serves to "generate" a proposition.[33] A *circumstance of evaluation* is, like a context, a region of reality (perhaps an entire possible world); but it is a region of reality at which propositions are *evaluated*, not *generated*. Unlike contexts, circumstances of evaluation do not require elements such as agents or addressees. Thus what Al Gore said in uttering "I am in New York" determines the value *true* at an arbitrary circumstance of evaluation E just in case Al Gore is in New York at E. Note that the truth-value of that proposition at E does not hinge on whether or not Gore is the designated agent of E or even on whether or not E has an agent. What Gore said could be true at a circumstance of evaluation at which Gore is sleeping.

Let us now apply this method. Consider an utterance u of (2) by A at the following context: Jones, although innocent, is on trial for Smith's murder; his behavior at the trial is noticeably odd.

(2) Smith's murderer is insane.

Now evaluate *what A said* by u at a world w_1 at which there are no murders and thus at which murderers are nonexistent. Is this content true or false? Howard Wettstein maintains that what A said in uttering u is true at w_1. However, the Russellian Nathan Salmon denies this, arguing that *what A said* is false at w_1:

[Wettstein] must maintain that the sentence "The murderer is insane," as used on this occasion, is true with respect to any possible world in which Jones is insane, even if Smith is alive and well, Jones is no murderer at all, and in fact, no murders are committed by anyone, anywhere. It is clear, however, that the *sentence* "The murderer is insane" is not true with respect to such a world, and indeed, it is clear that the phrase "the murderer" does not denote anyone, not even Jones, with respect to such a world.[34]

In response to Salmon's criticism, Wettstein claims that it "depends crucially on the assumption that sentences (as used on particular occasions), are what we evaluate with respect to counterfactual circumstances."[35] If, instead, we assume that what is to be evaluated at a circumstance of evaluation is a proposition, Salmon's criticisms fail. To show this, Wettstein has us consider the sentence (3), uttered at a context C, at which the intended referent is male.

(3) She is a professional tennis player.

Consider a world w_2 at which no women exist. On Salmon's view (claims Wettstein), the *sentence* (3), as used at C, is false at w_2. Nonetheless, this does not show that the *proposition* expressed by (3) as used at C is false at w_2. For, Wettstein claims, the question of the truth of (3) at C is entirely irrelevant to the question of the truth, at w_2, of the proposition expressed by (3) at C. He continues:

Similarly, it is a mistake to ask whether the sentence [(2)], as used on the occasion in question, would be true or false in a world in which there are no murderers. I am not committed to any answer whatever to that question in virtue of my view about referentially used descriptions. I am committed to the view that the *singular proposition* determined in the context in question is true in a possible world just in case Jones, the actual murderer, is insane at that world, whether or not he (or anyone else) committed a murder in that world. This, however, does not seem objectionable once we become clear that the object of such counterfactual evaluation is not a piece of language (as used on a certain occasion) but a content, in this case a singular proposition.[36]

(For current purposes, we can use "singular proposition" and "object-dependent proposition" interchangeably.) The strategy here is clear: Provide an example of the use of a sentence S, where S is false at a given circumstance of evaluation E but where its use nonetheless expresses (or asserts) a proposition that is true at E. If, indeed, such an example can be provided, then Wettstein will have shown the ball to be squarely in the Russellian's court. Note that it is important that the example concern a demonstrative, since Wettstein is maintaining that descriptions, in their referential use, are essentially demonstratives. By providing an example in which an infelicitous use of a demonstrative sentence nonetheless "determines" (in Wettstein's terminology) a true proposition at a world at which nothing answers to the demonstrative, Wettstein shows the following: The use of (2) in question may be infelicitous and yet fully compatible with its "determining" a true proposition at a world at which nothing answers to the description it contains. This would show (or, at least, make very plausible) that, in general, an utterance of "The F is G" may be infelicitous and, for all that, may still "determine" a true proposition.

This response is weak, however, as it conflates the Gricean distinction between what is said by an utterance and what is meant by it. Wettstein wants to claim that the truth at w_2 of (3) as used at C is irrelevant to the truth at w_2 of the proposition "determined" by (3) at C. Presumably, this means that while (3) as used at C may not be true at w_2, the proposition determined by (3) at C would be true at w_2. Here, "determine" may be interpreted as standing for a semantic relation—one that obtains among a sentence S, a context C, and a proposition p just in case p is what S says at C. Or it may stand for a pragmatic relation—one that obtains among a sentence S, a context C, and a proposition p just in case p is what S means at C. If "determines" is of the latter sort, Wettstein has not engaged the Russellian, for the Russellian does not deny that what the speaker *meant* in uttering (2) was the object-dependent (or singular) proposition that Jones is insane. As stated previously, that descriptions are sometimes *used* referentially is not at issue. Yet, if "determines" stands for a semantic relation, then Wettstein's suggestion that the truth of the *sentences* (2) and (3) is irrelevant to the truth of the propositions expressed is just false. There is a very tight relationship between a sentence S interpreted relative to a context C and the proposition (literally) expressed by that sentence— in fact, the proposition expressed is a function of S and C. Consequently, the truth of a sentence at a context is, contra Wettstein, entirely relevant to the truth of the proposition expressed by the sentence at the context. To suppose otherwise would be to assume that the proposition expressed by a sentence at a context was partly determined by an additional element —that it is a function of S, C, and an unknown third parameter—but this idea is difficult to take seriously.

Thus Wettstein's argument fails to challenge the Russellian. To establish this, though, it is not necessary to assume, as Salmon does, that there is a clear intuition of the falsity of (2) at the murderer-less world w_1. To avoid Wettstein's conclusion, it is sufficient to adhere to the more conservative strategy of maintaining that the relevant utterance of (2) is *not true* at w_1. This is, indeed, what Grice, Kripke, and Neale recommend. As Neale writes,

The problem with [the argument from misdescription] is that it relies on the existence of a clear intuition that the proposition expressed is still true despite the fact that neither Jones nor anyone else satisfies the description "Smith's murderer." But this is simply not so. We feel an uneasy tension when presented with such cases.... After all, the description [that the speaker used *failed to fit* the person [that the speaker] wanted to "talk about," and to that extent the speech act was defective. (chapter 14, p. 339)

As Neale goes on to point out, the Russellian, armed with the Gricean distinction between what is said and what is meant, can explain how the object-dependent proposition *that Jones is insane* got generated by the utterance of (2) at C. She can also go some distance in explaining our intuition, on being apprised of the facts, that the utterance was "defective": it said something that was ultimately irrelevant to the conversational interests of speaker and audience.

V   Incompleteness

The argument from misdescription is thus inconclusive. There is, however, a stronger challenge to Russellianism. This is (again following Neale) the "argument from incompleteness." Consider an utterance u of (4) at a context C:

(4) The table is covered with books.

There is no question that u is potentially true even in worlds in excess of one table. Yet, on a naïve interpretation of Russell's theory, u must be false at any world at which there is not exactly one table. On that interpretation, it is true just in case there is exactly one table and anything that is a table is covered with books. One obvious solution to this problem runs as follows. Take the utterance to be elliptical for a completing sentence S, where S would be equivalent at C to u. Following Neale, we will refer to this approach as the *explicit* approach. Thus we might say that u is elliptical for (5):

(5) The table that John bought yesterday is covered with books.

A problem for the explicit approach is that the notion of ellipsis appealed to is not the one familiar from syntactic theory. There are syntactic rules that relate an ellipsis, such as "Mary thanked everyone that Susan did," to the sentence for which it is elliptical: "Mary thanked everyone that Susan thanked." But it seems clear that whatever the relation is that holds between (4) and (5), it is not syntactic.[37] Yet, even if we pass over this worry, we are faced with another, perhaps more serious objection, stated by Howard Wettstein (chapter 12) and Stephen Schiffer (chapter 15).

Wettstein suggests that there is, typically, no nonarbitrary way to complete sentences containing incomplete descriptions. That is, in general, a context will not supply a unique completion. Let me introduce the following terminology to help us characterize the phenomenon in question: Let a *candidate completion* be a completion of an utterance of a description sentence that is truth-conditionally equivalent to our intuitive truth-conditional assessment of the sentence as uttered. Now consider u. It is clear that many candidate completions, no two of which are synonymous, may be raised to conversational salience by such an utterance. (Wettstein's sample completions are: "the table in room 209 of Camden Hall at t_1," "the table at which the author of *The Persistence of Objects* is sitting at t_1"). But each completion would result in a different descriptive proposition's being assigned to (4). As Wettstein asks, "The question now arises, which of these more complete (or Russellian) descriptions (or conjunction of descriptions) is *the correct one*, the one that actually captures what the speaker intended by his use of the definite description 'the table'?"

Wettstein poses two difficulties for a Russellian response. The first is epistemological. Even if we assume that the speaker had intended a definite completion of the description in question, the audience would not typically be in a position to determine what that completion is. The second response goes further, denying that there is a fact of the matter concerning the correct completion: Often the speaker may have no determinate intention with respect to any particular completion. If asked, the speaker might respond that he did indeed intend to speak about the table, but that he did not intend to have it thought of as, for example, the table in room 209 of Camden Hall at t_1, or the table at which the author of *The Persistence of Objects* was sitting at t_1. Yet, if the speaker himself cannot specify what he meant—cannot paraphrase what it is he attempted to convey in additional descriptive terms—then it seems unlikely that there could have been anything descriptive that he did mean. Thus Wettstein's conclusion:

It now becomes difficult to attach sense to the idea that one of these Russellian descriptions could be correct. Surely it is implausible in the extreme to suppose that in fact one of these descriptions captures what the speaker intended but that we cannot, even with the help of the speaker himself, come to know what description that is. (p. 263)

Stephen Schiffer (chapter 15) expresses a similar worry about the ability of the context to supply a unique description or individual concept. He imagines a hypothetical speaker who utters the sentence: "I'll be damned! The guy's drunk." According to the explicit approach, the speaker asserts a proposition of the form "The male Φ is drunk"—where Φ is a property that completes the description. But in such a context it is likely that speaker and audience share, and know themselves to share, a number of descriptions uniquely specifying the relevant individual. He writes:

Imagining myself as your audience, I do not see how I could have identified any one individual concept, however complex, as *the one* which figured into the proposition that you asserted. And yet it would seem that I understood your utterance perfectly well. (p. 376)

Let us call the problem presented by Wettstein and Schiffer—that in a typical use of an incomplete description, neither speaker nor hearer are capable of identifying a unique completion—the *identification problem*. It would be premature to take the identification problem as presenting a decisive case against the explicit approach. One line of response is to deny, for example, that the hypothesized utterance u of (4) is in fact semantically determinate. It might be the case that, for each candidate completion Φ of u, u indeterminately means *that the Φ table is covered* *with books.* On this view, there is no unique proposition that I meant in uttering *u*, but there are a number of propositions that I *indeterminately meant* in uttering *u*.[38] Alternatively, we may say that there is a proposition that I *determinately meant* in uttering *u*, but that this proposition is itself indeterminate. This would locate the indeterminacy within the content of *u*, and not within the intention with which *u* was uttered. I don't think much of importance turns on which formulation we choose. For reasons that will become clear shortly, I will stick with the latter formulation.

The indeterminacy proposal has its most plausible application in the case of vagueness. If I sincerely and literally utter "John is bald," I say something whose meaning, according to our intuitive assessment, is indeterminate. While it is compatible with a number of possible sharpenings of its meaning (e.g., "John has absolutely no hair"), the sentence does not select one such sharpening over any other. Following Kit Fine, we may define the truth of a vague sentence *S* in terms of the truth of the set of relevant sharpenings, or "precisifications," of *S*.[39] That is (roughly): *S* is *true* just in case it is true for all (relevant) precisifications, *false* if false for all (relevant) precisifications, and *neither true nor false* otherwise.

The Russellian who espouses the indeterminacy proposal sees an analogy between incomplete description sentences, such as (4), and vague sentences, such as "John is bald." The analogy seems strained, however. Given a vague sentence, there is a clear intuition of indeterminacy. For example, in "John is bald," it is apparent that there are a number of possible sharpenings of "bald," each compatible with the speaker's intentions, yet none of which is singled out by the utterance. In contrast, there is no similar intuition surrounding the hypothesized utterance of (4). On the contrary, the utterance appears to have perfectly determinate content.

Perhaps to refute this proposal it is not enough to rely on the observation that (4) *appears* to have determinate content—or, at the very least, that it does not appear to *lack* determinate content. One way for the indeterminacy theorist, as I shall call her, to challenge the claim that *u* has determinate content is to show that what was said by *u* fails to have a definite truth-value at a given circumstance of evaluation. This challenge appeals to the reasonable assumption that, if an utterance has determinate content, then it has determinate possible-worlds truth conditions. (It also appeals to the truism that a proposition has determinate possible-worlds truth-conditions at an arbitrarily selected circumstance of evaluation.) Thus the indeterminacy theorist needs to show that we have no clear intuition, at certain circumstances of evaluation, whether what u says is true or not. That we lacked a clear intuition as to the truth of what was said at such a circumstance would cast doubt on the idea that something determinate was said in the first place. As we might expect, this is true of the proposition expressed by an utterance of "John is bald." If John has absolutely no hair, the sentence will be true. But we may imagine circumstances at which John is in the penumbral region between bald and its counterextension; here there will be no decisive intuition concerning its truth.

If u is similarly indeterminate, then there must exist circumstances for which the question of the truth of u could receive no determinate answer. Imagine a circumstance of evaluation E at which only one of the candidate completions of u denotes uniquely and thus at which nothing is both *the table* in room 209 of Camden Hall at t_1 and *the table* at which the author of *The Persistence of Objects* is sitting at t_1. (E.g., imagine that there is more than one table in room 209 of Camden Hall at t_1.) Is u true at E? If we assume that the explicit approach gives the correct account of u, there is no definite answer to this question. Perhaps the following example is more telling: Imagine that the person who appears at public meetings as the President of the United States, and whose image, voice, etc. is universally held to belong to the President, is not in fact the person who was elected to office and who now makes executive decisions. Would my actual utterance of "The President is a Democrat" be true in such a circumstance—assuming that, at the circumstance in question, both the person who makes appearances for the president, as well as the elected official, are Democrats? Again, it seems that we would be incapable of giving a definite answer. This, moreover, would comport with the predictions of the indeterminacy theorist. (Recall that she claims that u would express an indeterminate proposition.) Thus, if the strategy recently proposed is acceptable, we have evidence for the semantic indeterminacy of u.[40]

Nonetheless, even if some version of the explicit approach is adopted—indeterminist, or otherwise—a problem remains. For the explicit approach to be successful, it must be shown that what u actually *says* is what (5), or some other completion, says. But it is entirely possible that u only presupposes (5). Perhaps, (5) expresses a proposition that I must have believed (and that I have assumed my audience to believe) in order to have meant what I did in uttering (4), and that it is not, in fact, what I *said* in uttering (4). The Russellian has the option of simply stipulating that (5), or some other completion, captures what I said when I uttered what I did, but this has, besides its arbitrariness, the following unwelcome consequence. Consider (6):

(6) That table is covered with books.

The relation that the actual utterance u of (4) bears to the proposition p expressed by (2) is a relation that a counterfactual utterance u^* of (3) must also bear to p. (For example, if we say that u presupposes p, we will be forced to say of u^* that it presupposes p.) Thus, if we follow the Russellian in maintaining that u says p, then we must, on pain of being arbitrary, maintain that u^* says p as well.

This consequence should make the Russellian uncomfortable. For it is integral to Russellianism that it make a sharp distinction between the content of sentences exemplifying (6) and those exemplifying (4). Neale speaks for all Russellians when he writes:

[A] sentence of the form "that F is G" is semantically very different from a sentence of the form "the F is G." An utterance of the former expresses an object-dependent proposition; an utterance of the latter expresses an object-independent proposition. (chapter 14, p. 317)

We can see now that the Russellian faces an unattractive dilemma: Either she must abandon the view that sentences containing descriptions are "semantically very different" from those containing demonstratives, or she must make a semantic distinction between the two that seems to have no basis in usage.[41]

Finally, it should be mentioned that unless the Russellian can provide an account of what was said in uttering u, she cannot succeed in providing an explanation of how it is that the speaker meant, in uttering u, that o (in our example, the relevant table) is G. For the standard "pragmatic" account of how a speaker imparts or implicates a proposition p in uttering S appeals to the knowledge, shared (and known to be shared) by speaker and audience, that S means a proposition q distinct from, but contextually related to, p. (See Neale, chapter 14, pp. 324–326.) From this shared knowledge, together with plausible assumptions concerning conversational principles and mutual expectations, it can be shown that in uttering S the speaker's primary intention was to convey q, and not p. Yet, it remains unclear whether the Russellian can succeed in telling us what the literal content of the utterance is. As we have seen, the candidate for the literal content of u may in truth be merely a presupposition of u. Thus it cannot be assumed to be a foregone conclusion that a Gricean explanation of what is meant is available, as it requires that the Russellian tell this part of the story. If the Russellian fails to do this, she will have no response to the challenge posed by the referentialist.

VI   Descriptions as Quantifiers

Neale has made the following methodological remark:

Whenever we find some phenomenon associated with the use of definite descriptions, we should look for corresponding phenomena associated with other quantifiers. (chapter 14, p. 342)

This remark seems especially relevant when assessing the significance of the identification problem for Russell's theory. According to Neale, once we take into consideration that descriptions are, on Russell's view, quantifiers, the problem of incompleteness should no longer be seen as a threat. The reason is that incompleteness occurs with as much frequency with respect to quantifiers constructed from "every," "all," and "no" as it does with respect to definite descriptions. And there is no question that these quantifiers cannot, except in very special circumstances, be interpreted referentially. But, since the inference from incompleteness to referentiality fails in the case of natural language quantifiers generally, there is no reason to think that it should succeed in the particular case of definite descriptions.

Consider an utterance of the following sentence:

(7) Everyone passed the exam.

If I utter this in certain contexts—for example, after a final exam—I will not intend to be taken as saying that everyone in existence passed the exam; nor will my audience interpret me that way. What is meant is that everyone that is Φ passed the exam, where "Φ" is a conversationally salient completion. We thus have an instance of the identification problem. Notice, however, that the utterance in question does not plausibly admit of a referential interpretation. But, if the identification problem does not force a referential interpretation of "everyone" as it occurs in the utterance of (7), how, it may be asked, can it force a referential interpretation of "the table" as it occurs in the utterance u discussed in the previous section?

Although pointed, this question raises some worries. First, Neale's defense against the referentialist is only as strong as the claim that descriptions are quantifiers. If the referentialist has reasons for doubting the latter, then she need not accept Neale's response. Moreover, there are reasons for questioning this claim. As Marga Reimer points out, it is a mark of quantified sentences that they can be used in response to questions of the form "How many Fs G-ed?"[42] For example, in response to "How many children danced?" any of the following would be appropriate: "Some children danced," "Finitely many children danced," "More children than adults danced," and "Most children danced." Yet, "*The child danced*" seems decidedly inappropriate. This is prima facie evidence against the assimilation of "the F" to quantified noun phrases.[43]

Another challenge, voiced by Reimer and by Jason Stanley and Timothy Williamson,[44] concerns the equivalence of "the F is G" to its Russellian expansion, "exactly one thing is F, and all Fs are G." This challenge is clearest in the context of an alternative approach to the problem of incompleteness: the *implicit* approach. On the implicit approach, quantifiers, including descriptions, are interpreted relative to a contextually definite domain of objects. For example, the utterance of (7) above might be interpreted relative to the domain consisting of persons who completed a given test. Similarly, an utterance of "the table is covered with books" might be interpreted relative to a domain containing the single table that is currently the focus of the speaker's attention.

This proposal faces the following objection. I utter at C "The record is scratched." Let us assume that the domain relevant to determining what I said is the set of records that we are currently listening to. A Russellian like Neale must claim that what I said is equivalent to what I would have said, at an otherwise identical context C*, by "exactly one thing is a record and every record is scratched." Yet, it seems implausible that the latter utterance should be equivalent to the former. To see this, consider the fact that an utterance of "the dog is barking" will generally be interpreted relative to a very small domain, whereas an utterance of "*every dog is barking*" will be assigned a larger domain.[45] Moreover, as Reimer notes, the domain implicitly referred to by the Russellian expansion of a description sentence is typically more inclusive than the domain implicitly referred to by the sentence itself. This shows that not only is it *possible* that a sentence and its Russellian expansion turn out to be nonequivalent when uttered at appropriately similar contexts—it is to be expected.

The significance of this point should not be underestimated. For if the equivalence cannot be assumed, then there is a real sense in which a theory that treats "the F" as a quantifier (and that acknowledges the context-sensitivity of quantifier interpretation) is not Russell's theory of descriptions. As Reimer notes, it is essential to that theory that a description sentence (at a context) and its expansion (at a relevantly similar context) say one and the same thing. The upshot seems to be that recognizing the context-sensitivity of descriptions forces a departure from Russell's theory. Notice, however, that it does not force a departure from the thesis that descriptions are quantifiers. This leads to an interesting outcome: If we follow Neale's methodological suggestion (i.e., that when examining a phenomenon associated with descriptions, we look to other quantifiers), we will avoid the argument from incompleteness only by abandoning Russell's theory of descriptions. The observation that descriptions often require, as do quantifiers generally, contextual supplementation—either by way of specification of an implicitly referred to domain, or by way of provision of completing predicates—allows us to avoid the argument from incompleteness, or, at least, to shift the burden of proof to the referentialist. But now it appears that this very feature presents an obstacle to the acceptance of Russell's theory. In a nutshell, the defense of Russell that appeals to Neale's methodological principle, requires, ultimately, a rejection of Russell's theory.

This poses a dilemma for the advocate of the view that descriptions are quantifiers. If we depart from Russell's theory (while retaining the view that descriptions are quantifiers), we will be forced to take subject-predicate sentences containing descriptions as semantically primitive. One consequence of this is that the standard Russellian entailments of "the *F* is *G*" will no longer hold. Another deeper consequence is that we will no longer have an *analysis* of "the *F*." On the other hand, if we retain Russell's theory and deny that context has any effect on the interpretation of descriptions, then we will have no capacity to accommodate incompleteness.

In sum, it seems that the following three theses cannot be maintained simultaneously:

(i) Definite descriptions are quantifiers.

(ii) Quantifiers are context-sensitive expressions.

(iii) A sentence containing a description is equivalent to its Russellian expansion.

Descriptions, like quantifiers generally, are context-sensitive expressions. Yet, the most plausible quantificational treatment of descriptions fails to comport with the assumption of their context-sensitivity. Perhaps the most reasonable strategy for the Russellian is to finesse (iii). One way to do this would be to claim that the alleged evidence against (iii) is not decisive, as it is not clearly semantic in nature. That is, the Russellian may claim that it is a pragmatic fact about "the F" that it is interpreted as taking a more restricted domain than "every F." If "The F is G" and "Every F is G" are both uttered in circumstances that differ only in respect of the words uttered, they should, strictly and literally speaking, be taken to be implicitly referring to the same domain. Similarly, if "The F is G" and "Exactly one thing is F, and every F is G" are uttered at appropriately similar circumstances, they should be interpreted as making literal reference to one and the same domain.

This is a promising strategy; nevertheless, it raises questions. For it attributes both a literal as well as a "pragmatic" reference to quantifiers. What the strategy claims is that when we assign the relevant quantifiers their literal references, the equivalence between "the F is G" at C and its expansion at a similar context C^* holds; when we assign the relevant quantifiers their pragmatic references, the equivalence will typically fail. The strategy goes on to claim that the objector mistakenly conflates these distinct references. The problem, however, is that there is no independent motivation for the claim that quantified sentences make two forms of implicit reference. Aside from a desire to preserve the Russellian equivalence at any cost, there seems to be no reason to suppose that the "pragmatic reference" of a quantifier expression is anything but its literal reference. And if not, then the Russellian is without an adequate defense.

In conclusion, it is interesting to note that we are now in a situation not unlike the one Russell faced in *The Principles*. Once we accept what now seems inevitable—that definite descriptions are context-sensitive expressions—we are no longer in possession of an account of how the meaning of the quantifier phrase "the F" is determined by the meanings of its constituents. Nor are we in possession of an account of how the meaning of the quantified *sentence* "the F is G" is determined by the meanings of *its* constituents.

Conclusion

The selections that follow pursue a number of interlocking themes. In this Introduction, I have touched on only a few of these. I have merely provided a preliminary overview, one that is, of necessity, only partial. I have emphasized certain debates to the exclusion of others that are, arguably, of equal importance. The goal has been to provide the reader with enough of a sense of the terrain to begin profitably reading the selections. An exhaustive, balanced survey would take a book-length study, and must wait for another time. For a recent, comprehensive discussion of definite descriptions from the perspective of a semantic theory of English, the interested reader may wish to consult Larson and Segal's *Knowledge of Meaning.*[46]

Notes

1. This is not an exaggeration. See Alasdair Urquhart's engrossing "G. F. Stout and the Theory of Descriptions" (Urquhart, 1994 95), for the details. (All citations in section 1 are listed in the "Origins" section of the bibliography.)

2. In fact, Russell's views had changed some time during the previous year. In a letter to Meinong, dated December 15, 1904, Russell wrote: "I have always believed up till now that every object must in some sense be, and I find it difficult to admit nonexistent objects. In such a case as that of the golden mountain or the round square one must distinguish between sense and reference (to speak with Frege): the sense is an object and has being, but the reference is no object." This letter is quoted in Kremer (1994), who also provided the translation. I have benefited greatly from Kremer's discussion of "On Denoting," as well as from Cartwright (1987), Coffa (1991), Hylton (1990a), (1990b), and Makin (1996).

3. Urquhart, op cit.

4. By "quantified noun phrase," I mean, roughly, the class of expressions Russell intended to capture by "denoting phrase."

5. For current purposes, a "class concept" can be taken to be an expression that has a class as its extension.

6. The element of *all-ness* that here eludes Russell was subsequently given a satisfactory analysis by generalized quantifier theory. Generalized quantifier theory is concerned with the semantic contribution of determiners—expressions such as "all," "some," and "no"—to quantifier phrases. It assigns compositional structure to quantifier phrases, but does so in a way that the Russell of *The Principles* would have found more attractive than would the Russell of "On Denoting," as it assigns a "meaning" to determiners and thereby avoids contextual definition (see below). "All men" is analyzed as *the set of sets containing all men*; "some men" is analyzed as *the set of sets containing some men,* etc. (The italicized phrases are represented set-theoretically; thus there is no circularity in the analysis.) The role of the determiner is then characterized as a function from a set (here, the set of men) to a generalized quantifier. For example, the function $[\![all]\!]$ (to adopt the standard notation) applied to the set of men yields, as value, the set of sets containing all men, whereas the function $[\![some]\!]$ applied to the set of men yields, as value, the set of sets containing at least one man. This analysis yields a treatment of quantified sentences that is truth-conditionally adequate. See further the entries under Barwise and Cooper (1981) and Chierchia and McConnell-Ginet (1990) in the *Descriptions as Quantifiers* section of the bibliography.

7. A propositional function is a function from objects to propositions: when we assign an object o to the variable "x" in the propositional function $C(x)$ we get the proposition that "$C(x)$" is true of o. Note that at this stage Russell takes propositional functions to be linguistic entities.

Another basic element of the analysis, which I cannot discuss here, is the variable.

8. The central contrast between the two approaches is that the emphasis in *Principia* is on unrestricted quantifiers, such as "everything" and "something." This leads to a treatment of descriptions that sets them apart from other quantified noun phrases. Even though the quantified noun phrases "every man" and "some men" disappear under analysis in *Principia*, they differ from "the man" in that they admit of an analysis in which their determiners are retained. Thus "every man is mortal" is analyzed as: "*Everything* is such that, if it is a man, then it is mortal." Similarly, "some man is mortal" becomes: "*Something* is such that it is a man and it is mortal." (Of course, the analysis occurs in the formal language of the *Principia*, not in English, but that does not bear on the point at issue.) Yet, "the man is mortal" cannot be analyzed in terms of "*the thing* is such that ..." In this sense, "the" is like the determiner "most": "Most men" cannot be analyzed in terms of "*most things* are such that...." (On the latter point, see David Wiggins, "'Most' and 'All': Some Comments on a Familiar Programme, and on the Logical Form of Quantified Sentences," in Mark Platts (ed.), *Reference, Truth, and Reality*, London: Routledge and Kegan Paul, 1980, pp. 318–346.)

9. Quine (1966), p. 292 (page reference is to the reprint). The historical error is remarkably resilient. Despite a decade of Russell scholarship attempting to correct it, certain writers persist in recapitulating the official story. A recent example is A. C. Grayling, *Russell* (New York: Oxford University Press, 1996), pp. 33–34.

10. Russell (1944), p. 13.

11. The idea, as well as the phraseology, already occurs in *Principles*, p. 52.

12. Note that a sentence of the form "E!t" asserts that t exists.

13. In "Descriptions" (chapter 3 of this anthology), Russell eschews talk of scope in favor of talk of "occurrences" of descriptions in S. A description δ has a *primary* occurrence in S just in case there is a predicate "Φx" such that S is the result of substituting δ for "x" in "Φx." Alternatively, δ has *secondary* occurrence when "the result of substituting the description for x in Φx gives only part of the proposition [sentence] concerned." It seems fair to say that he intended that a description taking wide scope with respect to S would have primary occurrence in S, whereas a description taking narrow scope with respect to S would have a secondary occurrence in S. (See also chapter 1, pp. 44–45.)

14. Noam Chomsky, *Lectures on Government and Binding* (Dordrecht: Foris, 1981); Robert May, *Logical Form* (Cambridge, Mass. The MIT Press, 1985).

15. An exception is Makin, op cit.

16. For an early discussion of the significance of Ramsey's remark, see G. E. Moore, "The Theory of Descriptions," in Schilpp (1944), pp. 177–224.

17. This aspect of the method of analysis was clear to Russell even before he wrote *The Principles*. In *The Philosophy of Leibniz* (London: George Allen & Unwin, 1937), first published in 1900, he wrote: "That all sound philosophy should begin with an analysis of propositions is a truth too evident, perhaps, to demand a proof" (p. 8).

18. This Fregean constraint is not present in *The Principles*, where Russell writes: "Although a grammatical distinction cannot be uncritically assumed to correspond to a genuine philosophical difference, yet the one is *prima facie* evidence of the other, and may often be usefully employed as a source of discovery.... On the whole, grammar seems to me to bring us much nearer to the correct logic than the current opinions of philosophers; and in what follows, grammar, though not our master, will yet be taken as our guide" (*Principles*, p. 42).

19. Another motivation, from within the theory of syntax, has already been mentioned.

20. On this contrast, see Neale's discussion in chapter 4, p. 89–90.

21. This aspect of the theory of descriptions does not emerge in the selections from Russell's writings that follow. See *The Problems of Philosophy* (New York: Oxford University Press, 1912) and "Lectures on Logical Atomism" in David Pears (ed.) *The Philosophy of Logical Atomism* (La Salle, Ill.: Open Court, 1985).

22. See John McDowell, "Singular Thought and the Extent of Inner Space" in P. Pettit and J. McDowell (eds.) *Subject, Thought and Context* (New York: Oxford University Press, 1986), for a contemporary assessment of Russell's views.

23. "Can Analytical Philosophy be Systematic and Ought it to Be?" in *Truth and other Enigmas*, Cambridge, Mass.: Harvard University Press, 1979, p. 458; see also p. 442, first paragraph. For a more recent discussion of these issues, see the introduction to Dummett's *The Logical Basis of Metaphysics*, Cambridge, Mass.: Harvard University Press, 1991.

24. Philosophy of language divorced from this unifying framework is what Richard Rorty has called "pure philosophy of language." See his *Philosophy and the Mirror of Nature* (Princeton: Princeton University Press, 1979), pp. 257–266.

25. Note that, while the Kripke selection was originally published in 1977, an early hint of the overall strategy pursued there is to be found in footnote 3 to his *Naming and Necessity* (Cambridge, Mass.: Harvard University Press, 1980, at p. 25), transcribed from lectures delivered in January, 1970, and first published in 1972.

26. There have been numerous attempts at formulating an adequate account of the referential use of definite descriptions. Donnellan, for example, suggests that a description δ is used referentially when its use presupposes that a given individual—not just some individual or other—satisfies δ. (He subsequently criticized this formulation.) Cleaned up, this suggests that δ is used referentially by A just in case there is some individual o such that A takes it to be commonly accepted between himself and his audience that o satisfies δ. The problem with this account is that it appears to preclude the possibility of a description's being used attributively

when the relevant presupposition holds. It seems possible, however, that I can attributively utter "The murderer should be convicted" even though I take it to be known that Jones uniquely satisfies "the murderer." (See chapter 14, section 14.5.) Another account identifies the referential–attributive distinction with the *de re–de dicto* distinction, still another with the wide scope–narrow scope distinction. Kripke, in chapter 11, neatly disposes of the latter two.

27. More precisely: the attributive use conforms to Russell's theory insofar as the proposition a speaker conveys in an attributive use of "The *F* is *G*" is true at precisely those worlds at which the Russellian analysis of "The *F* is *G*" is true. (Here I ignore issues raised by *incomplete* attributive uses.) This qualification allows the singular-term analysis of definite descriptions to accommodate the attributive use of definite descriptions. (For such analyses, see chapters 5 through 7.)

28. Note that one who holds that descriptions are singular-terms is not required to accept the claim that what we are calling the referential use of definite descriptions is semantically noteworthy. For the latter use, if it is taken to reflect a genuinely semantic aspect of descriptions, requires the singular-term theorist to recognize two distinct modes of reference for descriptions; and the singular-term theorist has just as much reason for objecting to this as the Russellian has for objecting to the claim that descriptions are ambiguous between referential and quantificational senses.

29. This use was first noted by the Port-Royal grammarians, Antoine Arnauld and Pierre Nicole, who spoke of the "equivocal universality" of such uses of descriptions:

What is ... remarkable about these complex terms is that some actually are determined to a single individual, but still retain a certain equivocal universality, which could be called equivocation by error. In these cases everyone has agreed that this term signifies just one unique thing, but for lack of identifying what this unique thing really is, some apply it to one thing and others to another (Antoine Arnauld and Pierre Nicole, *The Art of Thinking*, ed. and trans. by Jill Vance Buroker [New York: Cambridge University Press, 1996, p. 46; written between 1662 and 1683].)

The example they give is the expression "the true religion." While this description refers, on their view, to the Catholic faith alone, it cannot be assumed that a speaker, in uttering "The prince was zealous about the true religion," is indeed referring to that faith: "For if he were a Protestant, it would mean the Protestant religion; if he were an Arab Moslem who spoke this way about his prince, it would mean the Moslem religion; and we would judge that it was the Catholic religion only if we knew that the [speaker] was Catholic."

The suggestion is that a speaker can refer to a faith by using the description "the true religion," even though the faith in question is not, in fact, the denotation of that description. This seems precisely the phenomenon that Donnellan and others noticed three centuries later.

(Gina Fisch-Freedman kindly shared her translation of this passage with me before Buroker's became available; she also provided helpful comments on my interpretation.)

30. The emphasized condition ensures that what *A says* in uttering "I'm late" in context *C* differs from what *B* says when uttering the same sentence in a distinct context *C**. What *A* says is that *A* is late, what *B* says is that *B* is late.

31. See Peacocke (chapter 10), Kripke (chapter 11), Wettstein (chapter 12), and Devitt, "Donnellan's Distinction," *Midwest Studies in Philosophy VI* (1981), 511–524. The quotation is from Wettstein, "The Semantic Significance of the Referential –Attributive Distinction," *Philosophical Studies* 44 (1983), pp. 187–194, p. 188.

32. I here allude to Grice's work on conversation; chapters 9, 11, and 14 contain an application of the general approach. See also Grice's *Studies in the Way of Words* (Cambridge, Mass.: Harvard University Press, 1989). For important recent criticisms of Grice's approach, see the contributions of Carston and Récanati to Stephen Davis (ed.) *Pragmatics* (New York, Oxford University Press, 1990).

33. See David Kaplan, "Demonstratives," in Joseph Almog *et al.*, eds. *Themes from Kaplan* (New York: Oxford University Press, 1989). While the terminology is Kaplan's, the two-stage method of evaluation was first suggested by Robert Stalnaker in "Pragmatics," in Donald Davidson and Gilbert Harman (eds.), *Semantics of Natural Language* (Dordrecht: D. Reidel, 1972, pp. 176–186). See also Almog's "Naming without Necessity," *Journal of Philosophy* 83 (1986), pp. 210–242.

34. Nathan Salmon, "Assertion and Incomplete Definite Descriptions," *Philosophical Studies* 42 (1982), pp. 37–46, at pp. 42–43; my emphasis.

35. Wettstein, op cit.

36. Wettstein, ibid., p. 192.

37. This point is made in Kent Bach, *Thought and Reference* (New York: Oxford University Press, 1978), pp. 73–74.

38. This is, in fact, Schiffer's suggestion; see chapter 15, and William K. Blackburn's important paper, "Wettstein on Definite Descriptions," *Philosophical Studies* 53 (1988), 263–278.

39. Kit Fine, "Vagueness, Truth, and Logic," *Synthese* 30 (1975), pp. 265–300.

40. The argument in this paragraph derives from Brian Loar, "The Semantics of Singular Terms," *Philosophical Studies* 30 (1976), pp. 353–377.

41. For a closely related dilemma, see Schiffer's discussion in chapter 15, pp. 378–385.

42. "Incomplete Descriptions," *Erkenntnis* 37 (1992), 347–363, at p. 360.

43. I don't mean to imply that Reimer's test is decisive. In any case, there is syntactic evidence in the other direction as well. Robert Fiengo and Robert May, in *Indices and Identity* (Cambridge, Mass.: The MIT Press, 1994), pp. 242 and *passim*, suggest the following "diagnostic for quantification": An expression Q is a quantified noun phrase just in case it can be inserted into the following sentence form and not produce nonsense:

Dulles suspected Q that Angleton did.

Expressions such as "three spies," "some spies," and "many spies" can each be inserted into the position marked by Q; significantly, so can a definite description such as "the spy."

44. Jason Stanley and Timothy Williamson, "Quantifiers and Context Dependence," *Analysis* 55.4 (1995), pp. 291–295.

45. Richard Larson and Gabriel Segal, *Knowledge of Meaning* (Cambridge, Mass. The MIT Press, 1995), pp. 333–334.

46. Several paragraphs of this introduction are based on my paper "A Score-keeping Error," originally published in *Philosophical Studies* 52 (1998). They are reprinted with kind permission of Kluwer Academic Publishers.

Chapter 1

On Denoting   Bertrand Russell

By a "denoting phrase" I mean a phrase such as any one of the following:
a man, some man, any man, every man, all men, the present King of
England, the present King of France, the centre of mass of the Solar
System at the first instant of the twentieth century, the revolution of the
earth round the sun, the revolution of the sun round the earth. Thus a
phrase is denoting solely in virtue of its *form*. We may distinguish three
cases: (1) A phrase may be denoting, and yet not denote anything; e.g. "the
present King of France." (2) A phrase may denote one definite object; e.g.
"the present King of England" denotes a certain man. (3) A phrase may
denote ambiguously; e.g. "a man" denotes not many men, but an ambiguous man. The interpretation of such phrases is a matter of considerable
difficulty; indeed, it is very hard to frame any theory not susceptible of
formal refutation. All the difficulties with which I am acquainted are met,
so far as I can discover, by the theory which I am about to explain.

   The subject of denoting is of very great importance not only in logic
and mathematics, but also in theory of knowledge. For example, we know
that the centre of mass of the Solar System at a definite instant is some
definite point, and we can affirm a number of propositions about it; but
we have no immediate *acquaintance* with this point, which is only known
to us by description. The distinction between *acquaintance* and *knowledge
about* is the distinction between the things we have presentations of, and
the things we only reach by means of denoting phrases. It often happens
that we know that a certain phrase denotes unambiguously, although we
have no acquaintance with what it denotes; this occurs in the above case
of the centre of mass. In perception we have acquaintance with the objects

From *Mind* 14 (1905) (New Series), pp. 479–493.

of perception, and in thought we have acquaintance with objects of a more abstract logical character; but we do not necessarily have acquaintance with the objects denoted by phrases composed of words with whose meanings we are acquainted. To take a very important instance: There seems no reason to believe that we are ever acquainted with other people's minds, seeing that these are not directly perceived; hence what we know about them is obtained through denoting. All thinking has to start from acquaintance: but it succeeds in thinking *about* many things with which we have no acquaintance.

The course of my argument will be as follows. I shall begin by stating the theory I intend to advocate[1]; I shall then discuss the theories of Frege and Meinong, showing why neither of them satisfies me; then I shall give the grounds in favour of my theory; and finally I shall briefly indicate the philosophical consequences of my theory.

My theory, briefly, is as follows. I take the notion of the *variable* as fundamental; I use "$C(x)$" to mean a proposition[2] in which x is a constituent, where x, the variable, is essentially and wholly undetermined. Then we can consider the two notions "$C(x)$ is always true" and "$C(x)$ is sometimes true."[3] Then *everything* and *nothing* and *something* (which are the most primitive of denoting phrases) are to be interpreted as follows:

C(everything) means "$C(x)$ is always true";

C(nothing) means "'$C(x)$ is false' is always true";

C(something) means "It is false that '$C(x)$ is false' is always true."[4]

Here the notion "$C(x)$ is always true" is taken as ultimate and indefinable, and the others are defined by means of it. *Everything*, *nothing*, and *something* are not assumed to have any meaning in isolation, but a meaning is assigned to *every* proposition in which they occur. This is the principle of the theory of denoting I wish to advocate: that denoting phrases never have any meaning in themselves, but that every proposition in whose verbal expression they occur has a meaning. The difficulties concerning denoting are, I believe, all the result of a wrong analysis of propositions whose verbal expressions contain denoting phrases. The proper analysis, if I am not mistaken, may be further set forth as follows.

Suppose now we wish to interpret the proposition, "I met a man." If this is true, I met some definite man; but that is not what I affirm. What I affirm is, according to the theory I advocate:

"'I met x, and x is human' is not always false."

Generally, defining the class of men as the class of objects having the predicate *human*, we say that:

"C (a man)" means " 'C(x) and x is human' is not always false."

This leaves "a man," by itself, wholly destitute of meaning, but gives a meaning to every proposition in whose verbal expression "a man" occurs.

Consider next the proposition "all men are mortal." This proposition[5] is really hypothetical and states that *if* anything is a man, it is mortal. That is, it states that if x is a man, x is mortal, whatever x may be. Hence, substituting "x is human" for "x is a man," we find:

"All men are mortal" means " 'If x is human, x is mortal' is always true."

This is what is expressed in symbolic logic by saying that "all men are mortal" means " 'x is human' implies 'x is mortal' for all values of x." More generally, we say:

"C (all men)" means " 'If x is human, then C(x) is true' is always true."

Similarly

"C (no men)" means " 'If x is human, then C(x) is false' is always true."

"C (some men)" will means the same as "C (a man),"[6] and

"C (a man)" means "It is false that 'C(x) and x is human' is always false."

"C (every man)" will means the same as "C (all men)."

It remains to interpret phrases containing *the*. These are by far the most interesting and difficult of denoting phrases. Take as an instance "the father of Charles II was executed." This asserts that there was an x who was the father of Charles II and was executed. Now *the*, when it is strictly used, involves uniqueness; we do, it is true, speak of "*the* son of So-and-so" even when So-and-so has several sons, but it would be more correct to say "*a* son of So-and-so." Thus for our purposes we take *the* as involving uniqueness. Thus when we say "x was *the* father of Charles II" we not only assert that x had a certain relation to Charles II, but also that nothing else had this relation. The relation in question, without the assumption of uniqueness, and without any denoting phrases, is expressed by "x begat Charles II." To get an equivalent of "x was the father of Charles II," we must add, 'If y is other than x, y did not beget Charles II," or, what is equivalent, "If y begat Charles II, y is identical with x." Hence "x is the father of Charles II" becomes "x begat Charles II; and 'if y begat Charles II, y is identical with x' is always true of y."

Thus "the father of Charles II was executed" becomes:

"It is not always false of x that x begat Charles II and that x was executed and that 'if y begat Charles II, y is identical with x' is always true of y."

This may seem a somewhat incredible interpretation; but I am not at present giving reasons, I am merely *stating* the theory.

To interpret "C (the father of Charles II)," where C stands for any statement about him, we have only to substitute $C(x)$ for "x was executed" in the above. Observe that, according to the above interpretation, whatever statement C may be, "C (the father of Charles II)" implies:

"It is not always false of x that 'if y begat Charles II, y is identical with x' is always true of y,"

which is what is expressed in common language by "Charles II had one father and no more." Consequently if this condition fails, *every* proposition of the form "C (the father of Charles II)" is false. Thus, e.g. every proposition of the form "C (the present King of France)" is false. This is a great advantage in the present theory. I shall show later that it is not contrary to the law of contradiction, as might be at first supposed.

The above gives a reduction of all propositions in which denoting phrases occur to forms in which no such phrases occur. Why it is imperative to effect such a reduction, the subsequent discussion will endeavour to show.

The evidence for the above theory is derived from the difficulties which seem unavoidable if we regard denoting phrases as standing for genuine constituents of the propositions in whose verbal expressions they occur. Of the possible theories which admit such constituents the simplest is that of Meinong.[7] This theory regards any grammatically correct denoting phrase as standing for an *object*. Thus "the present King of France," "the round square," etc., are supposed to be genuine objects. It is admitted that such objects do not *subsist*, but nevertheless they are supposed to be objects. This is in itself a difficult view; but the chief objection is that such objects, admittedly, are apt to infringe the law of contradiction. It is contended, for example, that the existent present King of France exists, and also does not exist; that the round square is round, and also not round; etc. But this is intolerable; and if any theory can be found to avoid this result, it is surely to be preferred.

The above breach of the law of contradiction is avoided by Frege's theory. He distinguishes, in a denoting phrase, two elements, which we may call the *meaning* and the *denotation*.[8] Thus "the centre of mass of the Solar System at the beginning of the twentieth century" is highly complex in *meaning*, but its *denotation* is a certain point, which is simple. The Solar System, the twentieth century, etc., are constituents of the *meaning*; but the *denotation* has no constituents at all.[9] One advantage of this distinction is that it shows why it is often worth while to assert identity. If we say "Scott is the author of *Waverley*," we assert an identity of denotation with a difference of meaning. I shall, however, not repeat the grounds in favour of this theory, as I have urged its claims elsewhere (*loc. cit.*), and am now concerned to dispute those claims.

One of the first difficulties that confront us, when we adopt the view that denoting phrases *express* a meaning and *denote* a denotation,[10] concerns the cases in which the denotation appears to be absent. If we say "the King of England is bald," that is, it would seem, not a statement about the complex *meaning* "the King of England," but about the actual man denoted by the meaning. But now consider "the King of France is bald." By parity of form, this also ought to be about the denotation of the phrase "the King of France." But this phrase, though it has a *meaning* provided "the King of England" has a meaning, has certainly no denotation, at least in any obvious sense. Hence one would suppose that "the King of France is bald" ought to be nonsense; but it is not nonsense, since it is plainly false. Or again consider such a proposition as the following: "If u is a class which has only one member, then that one member is a member of u," or, as we may state it, "If u is a unit class, *the u* is a *u*." This proposition ought to be *always* true, since the conclusion is true whenever the hypothesis is true. But "the u" is a denoting phrase, and it is the denotation, not the meaning, that is said to be a u. Now if u is *not* a unit class, "the u" seems to denote nothing; hence our proposition would seem to become nonsense as soon as u is not a unit class.

Now it is plain that such propositions do *not* become nonsense merely because their hypotheses are false. The King in *The Tempest* might say, "If Ferdinand is not drowned, Ferdinand is my only son." Now "my only son" is a denoting phrase, which, on the face of it, has a denotation when, and only when, I have exactly one son. But the above statement would nevertheless have remained true if Ferdinand had been in fact drowned. Thus we must either provide a denotation in cases in which it is at first sight absent, or we must abandon the view that the denotation is what is concerned in propositions which contain denoting phrases. The latter is the course that I advocate. The former course may be taken, as by

Meinong, by admitting objects which do not subsist, and denying that they obey the law of contradiction; this, however, is to be avoided if possible. Another way of taking the same course (so far as our present alternative is concerned) is adopted by Frege, who provides by definition some purely conventional denotation for the cases in which otherwise there would be none. Thus "the King of France," is to denote the null-class; "the only son of Mr So-and-so" (who has a fine family of ten), is to denote the class of all his sons; and so on. But this procedure, though it may not lead to actual logical error, is plainly artificial, and does not give an exact analysis of the matter. Thus if we allow that denoting phrases, in general, have the two sides of meaning and denotation, the cases where there seems to be no denotation cause difficulties both on the assumption that there really is a denotation and on the assumption that there really is none.

A logical theory may be tested by its capacity for dealing with puzzles, and it is a wholesome plan, in thinking about logic, to stock the mind with as many puzzles as possible, since these serve much the same purpose as is served by experiments in physical science. I shall therefore state three puzzles which a theory as to denoting ought to be able to solve; and I shall show later that my theory solves them.

1. If a is identical with b, whatever is true of the one is true of the other, and either may be substituted for the other in any proposition without altering the truth or falsehood of that proposition. Now George IV wished to know whether Scott was the author of *Waverley*; and in fact Scott *was* the author of *Waverley*. Hence we may substitute *Scott* for *the author of Waverley*, and thereby prove that George IV wished to know whether Scott was Scott. Yet an interest in the law of identity can hardly be attributed to the first gentleman of Europe.

2. By the law of excluded middle, either "A is B" or "A is not B" must be true. Hence either "the present King of France is bald" or "the present King of France is not bald" must be true. Yet if we enumerated the things that are bald, and then the things that are not bald, we should not find the present King of France in either list. Hegelians, who love a synthesis, will probably conclude that he wears a wig.

3. Consider the proposition "A differs from B." If this is true, there is a difference between A and B, which fact may be expressed in the form "the difference between A and B subsists." But if it is false that A differs from B, then there is no difference between A and B, which fact may be expressed

in the form "the difference between A and B does not subsist." But how can a non-entity be the subject of a proposition? "I think, therefore I am" is no more evident than "I am the subject of a proposition, therefore I am," provided "I am" is taken to assert subsistence or being,[11] not existence. Hence, it would appear, it must always be self-contradictory to deny the being of anything; but we have seen, in connexion with Meinong, that to admit being also sometimes leads to contradictions. Thus if A and B do not differ, to suppose either that there is, or that there is not, such an object as "the difference between A and B" seems equally impossible.

The relation of the meaning to the denotation involves certain rather curious difficulties, which seem in themselves sufficient to prove that the theory which leads to such difficulties must be wrong.

When we wish to speak about the *meaning* of a denoting phrase, as opposed to its *denotation*, the natural mode of doing so is by inverted commas. Thus we say:

The centre of mass of the Solar System is a point, not a denoting complex;

"The centre of mass of the Solar System" is a denoting complex, not a point.

Or again,

The first line of Gray's *Elegy* states a proposition.

"The first line of Gray's *Elegy*" does not state a proposition.

Thus taking any denoting phrase, say C, we wish to consider the relation between C and "C," where the difference of the two is of the kind exemplified in the above two instances.

We say, to begin with, that when C occurs it is the *denotation* that we are speaking about; but when "C" occurs, it is the *meaning*. Now the relation of meaning and denotation is not merely linguistic through the phrase: there must be a logical relation involved, which we express by saying that the meaning denotes the denotation. But the difficulty which confronts us is that we cannot succeed in *both* preserving the connexion of meaning and denotation *and* preventing them from being one and the same; also that the meaning cannot be got at except by means of denoting phrases. This happens as follows.

The one phrase C was to have both meaning and denotation. But if we speak of "the meaning of C," that gives us the meaning (if any) of the denotation. "The meaning of the first line of Gray's *Elegy*" is the same as

"The meaning of 'The curfew tolls the knell of parting day,'" and is not the same as 'The meaning of 'the first line of Gray's *Elegy*.'" Thus in order to get the meaning we want, we must speak not of "the meaning of C," but of "the meaning of 'C,'" which is the same as "C" by itself. Similarly "the denotation of C" does not mean the denotation we want, but means something which, if it denotes at all, denotes what is denoted by the denotation we want. For example, let "C" be "the denoting complex occurring in the second of the above instance." Then C = "the first line of Gray's *Elegy*," and the denotation of C = The curfew tolls the knell of parting day. But what we *meant* to have as the denotation was "the first line of Gray's *Elegy*." Thus we have failed to get what we wanted.

The difficulty in speaking of the meaning of a denoting complex may be stated thus: The moment we put the complex in a proposition, the proposition is about the denotation; and if we make a proposition in which the subject is "the meaning of C," then the subject is the meaning (if any) of the denotation, which was not intended. This leads us to say that, when we distinguish meaning and denotation, we must be dealing with the meaning: the meaning has denotation and is a complex, and there is not something other than the meaning, which can be called the complex, and be said to *have* both meaning and denotation. The right phrase, on the view in question, is that some meanings have denotations.

But this only makes our difficulty in speaking of meanings more evident. For suppose C is our complex; then we are to say that C *is* the meaning of the complex. Nevertheless, whenever C occurs without inverted commas, what is said is not true of the meaning, but only of the denotation, as when we say: The centre of mass of the Solar System is a point. Thus to speak of C itself, i.e. to make a proposition about the meaning, our subject must not be C, but something which denotes C. Thus "C," which is what we use when we want to speak of the meaning, must be not the meaning, but something which denotes the meaning. And C must not be a constituent of this complex (as it is of "the meaning of C"); for if C occurs in the complex, it will be its denotation, not its meaning, that will occur, and there is no backward road from denotations to meanings, because every object can be denoted by an infinite number of different denoting phrases.

Thus it would seem that "C" and C are different entities, such that "C" denotes C; but this cannot be an explanation, because the relation of "C" to C remains wholly mysterious; and where are we to find the denoting complex "C" which is to denote C? Moreover, when C occurs in a proposition, it is not *only* the denotation that occurs (as we shall see in the next paragraph); yet, on the view in question, C is only the denotation, the meaning being wholly relegated to "C." This is an inextricable tangle, and seems to prove that the whole distinction of meaning and denotation has been wrongly conceived.

That the meaning is relevant when a denoting phrase occurs in a proposition is formally proved by the puzzle about the author of *Waverley*. The proposition "Scott was the author of *Waverley*" has a property not possessed by "Scott was Scott," namely the property that George IV wished to know whether it was true. Thus the two are not identical propositions; hence the meaning of "the author of *Waverley*" must be relevant as well as the denotation, if we adhere to the point of view to which this distinction belongs. Yet, as we have just seen, so long as we adhere to this point of view, we are compelled to hold that only the denotation can be relevant. Thus the point of view in question must be abandoned.

It remains to show how all the puzzles we have been considering are solved by the theory explained at the beginning of this article.

According to the view which I advocate, a denoting phrase is essentially *part* of a sentence, and does not, like most single words, have any significance on its own account. If I say "Scott was a man," that is a statement of the form "x was a man," and it has "Scott" for its subject. But if I say "the author of *Waverley* was a man," that is not a statement of the form "x was a man," and does not have "the author of *Waverley*" for its subject. Abbreviating the statement made at the beginning of this article, we may put, in place of "the author of *Waverley* was a man," the following: "One and only one entity wrote *Waverley*, and that one was a man." (This is not so strictly what is meant as what was said earlier; but it is easier to follow.) And speaking generally, suppose we wish to say that the author of *Waverley* had the property ϕ, what we wish to say is equivalent to "One and only one entity wrote *Waverley*, and that one had the property ϕ."

The explanation of *denotation* is now as follows. Every proposition in which "the author of *Waverley*" occurs being explained as above, the proposition "Scott was the author of *Waverley*" (i.e. "Scott was identical with the author of *Waverley*") becomes "One and only one entity wrote *Waverley*, and Scott was identical with that one"; or, reverting to the wholly explicit form: "It is not always false of x that x wrote *Waverley*, that it is always true of y that if y wrote *Waverley* y is identical with x, and that Scott is identical with x." Thus if "C" is a denoting phrase, it may happen that there is one entity x (there cannot be more than one) for which the proposition "x is identical with C" is true, this proposition being interpreted as above. We may then say that the entity x is the denotation of the phrase "C." Thus Scott is the denotation of "the author of *Waverley*." The "C" in inverted commas will be merely the *phrase*, not anything that can be called the *meaning*. The phrase *per se* has no meaning, because in any proposition in which it occurs the proposition, fully expressed, does not contain the phrase, which has been broken up.

The puzzle about George IV's curiosity is now seen to have a very simple solution. The proposition "Scott was the author of *Waverley*," which was written out in its unabbreviated form in the preceding paragraph, does not contain any constituent "the author of *Waverley*" for which we could substitute "Scott." This does not interfere with the truth of inferences resulting from making what is *verbally* the substitution of "Scott" for "the author of *Waverley*," so long as "the author of *Waverley*" has what I call a *primary* occurrence in the proposition considered. The difference of primary and secondary occurrences of denoting phrases is as follows:

When we say: "George IV wished to know whether so-and-so," or when we say "So-and-so is surprising" or "So-and-so is true," etc., the "so-and-so" must be a proposition. Suppose now that "so-and-so" contains a denoting phrase. We may either eliminate this denoting phrase from the subordinate proposition "so-and-so," or from the whole proposition in which "so-and-so" is a mere constituent. Different propositions result according to which we do. I have heard of a touchy owner of a yacht to whom a guest, on first seeing it remarked, "I thought your yacht was larger than it is"; and the owner replied, "No, my yacht is not larger than it is." What the guest meant was, "The size that I thought your yacht was is greater than the size your yacht is"; the meaning attributed to him is, "I thought the size of your yacht was greater than the size of your yacht." To return to George IV and *Waverley*, when we say, "George IV wished to know whether Scott was the author of *Waverley*," we normally mean "George IV wished to know whether one and only one man wrote *Waverley* and Scott was that man"; but we *may* also mean: "One and only one man wrote *Waverley*, and George IV wished to know whether Scott was that man." In the latter, "the author of *Waverley*" has a *primary* occurrence; in the former, a *secondary*. The latter might be expressed by "George IV wished to know, concerning the man who in fact wrote *Waverley*, whether he was Scott." This would be true, for example, if George IV had seen Scott at a distance, and had asked "Is that Scott?" A *secondary* occurrence of a denoting phrase may be defined as one in which the phrase occurs in a proposition p which is a mere constituent of the proposition we are considering, and the substitution for the denoting phrase is to be effected in p, not in the whole proposition concerned. The ambiguity as between primary and secondary occurrences is hard to avoid in language; but it does no harm if we are on our guard against it. In symbolic logic it is of course easily avoided.

The distinction of primary and secondary occurrences also enables us to deal with the question whether the present King of France is bald or not bald, and generally with the logical status of denoting phrases that denote nothing. If "C" is a denoting phrase, say "the term having the property F," then

"C has the property ϕ" means "one and only one term has the property F, and that one has the property ϕ."[12]

If now the property F belongs to no terms, or to several, it follows that "C has the property ϕ" is false for *all* values of ϕ. Thus "the present King of France is bald" is certainly false; and "the present King of France is not bald" is false if it means

"There is an entity which is now King of France and is not bald,"

but is true if it means

"It is false that there is an entity which is now King of France and is bald."

That is, "the King of France is not bald" is false if the occurrence of "the King of France" is *primary*, and true if it is *secondary*. Thus all propositions in which "the King of France" has a primary occurrence are false; the denials of such propositions are true, but in them "the King of France" has a secondary occurrence. Thus we escape the conclusion that the King of France has a wig.

We can now see also how to deny that there is such an object as the difference between A and B in the case when A and B do not differ. If A and B do differ, there is one and only one entity x such that "x is the difference between A and B" is a true proposition; if A and B do not differ, there is no such entity x. Thus according to the meaning of denotation lately explained, "the difference between A and B" has a denotation when A and B differ, but not otherwise. This difference applies to true and false propositions generally. If "a R b" stands for "a has the relation R to b," then when a R b is true, there is such an entity as the relation R between a and b; when a R b is false, there is no such entity. Thus out of any proposition we can make a denoting phrase, which denotes an entity if the proposition is true, but does not denote an entity if the proposition is false. E.g. it is true (at least we will suppose so) that the earth revolves round the sun, and false that the sun revolves round the earth; hence "the revolution of the earth round the sun" denotes an entity, while "the revolution of the sun round the earth" does not denote an entity.[13]

The whole realm of non-entities, such as "the round square," "the even prime other than 2," "Apollo," "Hamlet," etc., can now be satisfactorily dealt with. All these are denoting phrases which do not denote anything. A proposition about Apollo means what we get by substituting what the classical dictionary tells us is meant by Apollo, say "the sun-god." All propositions in which Apollo occurs are to be interpreted by the above rules for denoting phrases. If "Apollo" has a primary occurrence, the proposition containing the occurrence is false; if the occurrence is secondary, the proposition may be true. So again "the round square is round" means "there is one and only one entity x which is round and square, and that entity is round," which is a false proposition, not, as Meinong maintains, a true one. "The most perfect Being has all perfections; existence is a perfection; therefore the most perfect Being exists" becomes:

"There is one and only one entity x which is most perfect; that one has all perfections; existence is a perfection; therefore that one exists." As a proof, this fails for want of a proof of the premise "there is one and only one entity x which is most perfect."[14]

Mr. MacColl (*Mind*, n.s., Nos. 54, and again 55, p. 401) regards individuals as of two sorts, real and unreal; hence he defines the null-class as the class consisting of all unreal individuals. This assumes that such phrases as "the present King of France," which do not denote a real individual, do, nevertheless, denote an individual, but an unreal one. This is essentially Meinong's theory, which we have seen reason to reject because it conflicts with the law of contradiction. With our theory of denoting we are able to hold that there are no unreal individuals; so that the null-class is the class containing no members, not the class containing as members all unreal individuals.

It is important to observe the effect of our theory on the interpretation of definitions which proceed by means of denoting phrases. Most mathematical definitions are of this sort: for example, "$m - n$ means the number which, added to n, gives m." Thus $m - n$ is defined as meaning the same as a certain denoting phrase; but we agreed that denoting phrases have no meaning in isolation. Thus what the definition really ought to be is: "Any proposition containing $m - n$ is to mean the proposition which results from substituting for '$m - n$' 'the number which, added to n, gives m.'" The resulting proposition is interpreted according to the rules already given for interpreting propositions whose verbal expression contains a denoting phrase. In the case where m and n are such that there is one and only one number x which, added to n, gives m, there is a number x which can be substituted for $m - n$ in any proposition containing $m - n$ without altering the truth or falsehood of the proposition. But in other cases, all propositions in which "$m - n$" has a primary occurrence are false.

The usefulness of *identity* is explained by the above theory. No one outside a logic-book ever wishes to say "x is x," and yet assertions of identity are often made in such forms as "Scott was the author of *Waverley*" or "thou art the man." The meaning of such propositions cannot be stated without the notion of identity, although they are not simply statements that Scott is identical with another term, the author of *Waverley*, or that thou art identical with another term, the man. The shortest statement of "Scott is the author of *Waverley*" seems to be: "Scott wrote *Waverley*; and it is always true of y that if y wrote *Waverley*, y is identical with Scott." It is in this way that identity enters into "Scott is the author of *Waverley*"; and it is owing to such uses that identity is worth affirming.

One interesting result of the above theory of denoting is this: when there is anything with which we do not have immediate acquaintance, but only definition by denoting phrases, then the propositions in which this thing is introduced by means of a denoting phrase do not really contain this thing as a constituent, but contain instead the constituents expressed by the several words of the denoting phrase. Thus in every proposition that we can apprehend (i.e. not only in those whose truth or falsehood we can judge of, but in all that we can think about), all the constituents are really entities with which we have immediate acquaintance. Now such things as matter (in the sense in which matter occurs in physics) and the minds of other people are known to us only by denoting phrases, i.e. we are not *acquainted* with them, but we know them as what has such and such properties. Hence, although we can form propositional functions

$C(x)$, which must hold of such and such a material particle, or of So-and-so's mind, yet we are not acquainted with the propositions which affirm these things that we know must be true, because we cannot apprehend the actual entities concerned. What we know is "So-and-so has a mind which has such and such properties" but we do not know "A has such and such properties," where A *is* the mind in question. In such a case, we know the properties of a thing without having acquaintance with the thing itself, and without, consequently, knowing any single proposition of which the thing itself is a constituent.

Of the many other consequences of the view I have been advocating, I will say nothing. I will only beg the reader not to make up his mind against the view—as he might be tempted to do, on account of its apparently excessive complication—until he has attempted to construct a theory of his own on the subject of denotation. This attempt, I believe, will convince him that, whatever the true theory may be, it cannot have such a simplicity as one might have expected beforehand.

Notes

1. I have discussed this subject in *Principles of Mathematics*, ch. v, and para. 476. The theory there advocated is very nearly the same as Frege's, and is quite different from the theory to be advocated in what follows.

2. More exactly, a propositional function.

3. The second of these can be defined by means of the first, if we take it to mean, "It is not true that '$C(x)$ is false' is always true."

4. I shall sometimes use, instead of this complicated phrase, the phrase "$C(x)$ is not always false," or "$C(x)$ is sometimes true," supposed *defined* to mean the same as the complicated phrase.

5. As has been ably argued in Mr. Bradley's *Logic*, Book I, ch. ii.

6. Psychologically "C (a man)" has a suggestion of *only one*, and "C (some men)" has a suggestion of *more than one*; but we may neglect these suggestions in a preliminary sketch.

7. See *Untersuchungen zur Gegenstandstheorie und Psychologie* (Leipzig, 1904), the first three articles (by Meinong, Ameseder and Mally respectively).

8. See Frege, "On Sense and Meaning."

9. Frege distinguishes the two elements of meaning and denotation everywhere, and not only in complex denoting phrases. Thus it is the *meanings* of the constituents of a denoting complex that enter into its *meaning*, not their *denotation*. In the proposition "Mont Blanc is over 1,000 metres high," it is, according to him, the *meaning* of "Mont Blanc," not the actual mountain, that is a constituent of the *meaning* of the proposition.

10. In this theory, we shall say that the denoting phrase *expresses* a meaning; and we shall say both of the phrase and of the meaning that they *denote* a denotation. In the other theory, which I advocate, there is no *meaning*, and only sometimes a *denotation*.

11. I use these as synonyms.

12. This is the abbreviated, not the stricter, interpretation.

13. The propositions from which such entities are derived are not identical either with these entities or with the propositions that these entities have being.

14. The argument can be made to prove validly that all members of the class of most perfect Beings exist; it can also be proved formally that this class cannot have *more* than one member; but, taking the definition of perfection as possession of all positive predicates, it can be proved almost equally formally that the class does not have even one member.

Chapter 2

From *Principia Mathematica*   A. N. Whitehead and
Bertrand Russell

From Chapter I

Descriptions. By a "description" we mean a phrase of the form "*the* so-and-so" or of some equivalent form. For the present, we confine our attention to *the* in the singular. We shall use this word strictly, so as to imply uniqueness; *e.g.* we should not say "*A* is *the* son of *B*" if *B* had other sons besides *A*. Thus a description of the form "the so-and-so" will only have an application in the event of there being one so-and-so and no more. Hence a description requires some propositional function $\phi\hat{x}$ which is satisfied by one value of x and by no other values; then "the x which satisfies $\phi\hat{x}$" is a description which definitely describes a certain object, though we may not know what object it describes. For example, if y is a man, "x is the father of y" must be true for one, and only one, value of x. Hence "the father of y" is a description of a certain man, though we may not know *what* man it describes. A phrase containing "the" always presupposes some initial propositional function not containing "the"; thus instead of "x is the father of y" we ought to take as our initial function "x begot y"; then "the father of y" means the one value of x which satisfies this propositional function.

If $\phi\hat{x}$ is a propositional function, the symbol "$(\imath x)(\phi x)$" is used in our symbolism in such a way that it can always be read as "the x which satisfies $\phi\hat{x}$." But we do not define "$(\imath x)(\phi x)$" as standing for "the x which satisfies $\phi\hat{x}$," thus treating this last phrase as embodying a primitive idea. Every use of "$(\imath x)(\phi x)$," where it apparently occurs as a constituent of a

From A. N. Whitehead and Bertrand Russell, *Principia Mathematica*, Second Edition, pp. 30–32, 66–71, 173–175.

proposition in the place of an object, is defined in terms of the primitive ideas already on hand. An example of this definition in use is given by the proposition "E!$(\imath x)(\phi x)$" which is considered immediately. The whole subject is treated more fully in Chapter III [pp. 54–61, below].

The symbol should be compared and contrasted with "$\hat{x}(\phi x)$" which in use can always be read as "the x's which satisfy $\phi\hat{x}$." Both symbols are incomplete symbols defined only in use, and as such are discussed in Chapter III. The symbol "$\hat{x}(\phi x)$" always has an application, namely to the class determined by ϕx; but "$(\imath x)(\phi x)$" only has an application when $\phi\hat{x}$ is only satisfied by one value of x, neither more nor less. It should also be observed that the meaning given to the symbol by the definition, given immediately below, of E!$(\imath x)(\phi x)$ does not presuppose that we know the meaning of "one." This is also characteristic of the definition of any other use of $(\imath x)(\phi x)$.

We now proceed to define "E!$(\imath x)(\phi x)$" so that it can be read "the x satisfying ϕx exists." (It will be observed that this is a different meaning of existence from that which we express by "∃.") Its definition is

$$E!(\imath x)(\phi x) . = : (\exists c) : \phi x . \equiv_x . x = c \quad \text{Df,}$$

i.e. "the x satisfying $\phi\hat{x}$ exists" is to mean "there is an object c such that ϕx is true when x is c but not otherwise."

The following are equivalent forms:

$$\vdash :. E!(\imath x)(\phi x) . \equiv : (\exists c) : \phi c : \phi x . \supset_x . x = c,$$

$$\vdash :. E!(\imath x)(\phi x) . \equiv : (\exists c) . \phi c : \phi x . \phi y . \supset_{x,y} . x = y,$$

$$\vdash :. E!(\imath x)(\phi x) . \equiv : (\exists c) : \phi c : x \neq c . \supset_x . \sim \phi x.$$

The last of these states that "the x satisfying $\phi\hat{x}$ exists" is equivalent to "there is an object c satisfying $\phi\hat{x}$, and every object other than c does not satisfy $\phi\hat{x}$."

The kind of existence just defined covers a great many cases. Thus for example "the most perfect Being exists" will mean:

$$(\exists c) : x \text{ is most perfect} . \equiv_x . x = c,$$

which, taking the last of the above equivalences, is equivalent to

$$(\exists c) : c \text{ is most perfect} : x \neq c . \supset_x . x \text{ is not most perfect.}$$

A proposition such as "Apollo exists" is really of the same logical form, although it does not explicitly contain the word *the*. For "Apollo" means really "the object having such-and-such properties," say "the object having the properties enumerated in the Classical Dictionary."[1] If these properties make up the propositional function ϕx, then "Apollo" means "$(\imath x)(\phi x)$," and "Apollo exists" means "E!$(\imath x)(\phi x)$." To take another illustration, "the author of Waverley" means "the man who (or rather, the object which) wrote Waverley." Thus "Scott is the author of Waverley" is

Scott $= (\imath x)(x$ wrote Waverley$)$.

Here (as we observed before) the importance of *identity* in connection with descriptions plainly appears.

The notation "$(\imath x)(\phi x)$," which is long and inconvenient, is seldom used, being chiefly required to lead up to another notation, namely "$R'y$," meaning "the object having the relation R to y." That is, we put

$R'y = (\imath x)(xRy)$ Df.

The inverted comma may be read "of." Thus "$R'y$" is read "the R of y." Thus if R is the relation of father to son, "$R'y$" means "the father of y"; if R is the relation of son to father, "$R'y$" means "the son of y," which will only "exist" if y has one son and no more. $R'y$ is a function of y, but not a propositional function; we shall call it a *descriptive* function. All the ordinary functions of mathematics are of this kind, as will appear more fully in the sequel. Thus in our notation, "sin y" would be written "sin $'y$," and "sin" would stand for the relation which sin $'y$ has to y. Instead of a variable descriptive function fy, we put $R'y$, where the variable relation R takes the place of the variable function f. A descriptive function will in general exist while y belongs to a certain domain, but not outside that domain; thus if we are dealing with positive rationals, $\sqrt{y}$ will be significant if y is a perfect square, but not otherwise; if we are dealing with real numbers, and agree that "$\sqrt{y}$" is to mean the *positive* square root (or, is to mean the negative square root), $\sqrt{y}$ will be significant provided y is positive, but not otherwise; and so on. Thus every descriptive function has what we may call a "domain of definition" or a "domain of existence," which may be thus defined: If the function in question is $R'y$, its domain of definition or of existence will be the class of those arguments y for which we have E!$R'y$, *i.e.* for which E!$(\imath x)(xRy)$, *i.e.* for which there is one x, and no more, having the relation R to y.

. . .

From Chapter III

Incomplete Symbols

(1) Descriptions. By an "incomplete" symbol we mean a symbol which is not supposed to have any meaning in isolation, but is only defined in certain contexts. In ordinary mathematics, for example, d/dx and $\int_a^b$ are incomplete symbols: something has to be supplied before we have anything significant. Such symbols have what may be called a "definition in use." Thus if we put

$$\nabla^2 = \frac{\partial^2}{\partial x^2} + \frac{\partial^2}{\partial y^2} + \frac{\partial^2}{\partial z^2} \quad \text{Df},$$

we define the *use* of ∇^2, but ∇^2 by itself remains without meaning. This distinguishes such symbols from what (in a generalized sense) we may call *proper names*: "Socrates," for example, stands for a certain man, and therefore has a meaning by itself, without the need of any context. If we supply a context, as in "Socrates is mortal," these words express a fact of which Socrates himself is a constituent: there is a certain object, namely Socrates, which does have the property of mortality, and this object is a constituent of the complex fact which we assert when we say "Socrates is mortal." But in other cases, this simple analysis fails us. Suppose we say: "The round square does not exist." It seems plain that this is a true proposition, yet we cannot regard it as denying the existence of a certain object called "the round square." For if there were such an object, it would exist: we cannot first assume that there is a certain object, and then proceed to deny that there is such an object. Whenever the grammatical subject of a proposition can be supposed not to exist without rendering the proposition meaningless, it is plain that the grammatical subject is not a proper name, *i.e.* not a name directly representing some object. Thus in all such cases, the proposition must be capable of being so analysed that what was the grammatical subject shall have disappeared. Thus when we say "the round square does not exist," we may, as a first attempt at such analysis, substitute "it is false that there is an object x which is both round and square." Generally, when "the so-and-so" is said not to exist, we have a proposition of the form[2]

"$\sim E!(\imath x)(\phi x)$," *i.e.*

$\sim \{(\exists c) : \phi x . \equiv_x . x = c\},$

or some equivalent. Here the apparent grammatical subject $(\imath x)(\phi x)$ has completely disappeared; thus in " $\sim E!(\imath x)(\phi x)$," $(\imath x)(\phi x)$ is an *incomplete* symbol.

By an extension of the above argument, it can easily be shown that $(\imath x)(\phi x)$ is *always* an incomplete symbol. Take, for example, the following proposition: "Scott is the author of Waverley." [Here "the author of Waverley" is $(\imath x)$ $(x$ wrote Waverley).] This proposition expresses an identity; thus if "the author of Waverley" could be taken as a proper name, and supposed to stand for some object c, the proposition would be "Scott is c." But if c is any one except Scott, this proposition is false; while if c *is* Scott, the proposition is "Scott is Scott," which is trivial, and plainly different from "Scott is the author of Waverley." Generalizing, we see that the proposition

$$a = (\imath x)(\phi x)$$

is one which may be true or may be false, but is never merely trivial, like $a = a$; whereas, if $(\imath x)(\phi x)$ were a proper name, $a = (\imath x)(\phi x)$ would necessarily be either false or the same as the trivial proposition $a = a$. We may express this by saying that $a = (\imath x)(\phi x)$ is not a value of the propositional function $a = y$, from which it follows that $(\imath x)(\phi x)$ is not a value of y. But since y may be anything, it follows that $(\imath x)(\phi x)$ is nothing. Hence, since in use it has meaning, it must be an incomplete symbol.

It might be suggested that "Scott is the author of Waverley" asserts that "Scott" and "the author of Waverley" are two names for the same object. But a little reflection will show that this would be a mistake. For if that were the meaning of "Scott is the author of Waverley," what would be required for its truth would be that Scott should have been *called* the author of Waverley: if he had been so called, the proposition would be true, even if some one else had written Waverley; while if no one called him so, the proposition would be false, even if he had written Waverley. But in fact he was the author of Waverley at a time when no one called him so, and he would not have been the author if every one had called him so but some one else had written Waverley. Thus the proposition "Scott is the author of Waverley" is not a proposition about names, like "Napoleon is Bonaparte"; and this illustrates the sense in which "the author of Waverley" differs from a true proper name.

Thus all phrases (other than propositions) containing the word *the* (in the singular) are incomplete symbols: they have a meaning in use, but not in isolation. For "the author of Waverley" cannot mean the same as

"Scott," or "Scott is the author of Waverley" would mean the same as "Scott is Scott," which it plainly does not; nor can "the author of Waverley" mean anything other than "Scott," or "Scott is the author of Waverley" would be false. Hence "the author of Waverley" means nothing.

It follows from the above that we must not attempt to define "$(\imath x)(\phi x)$," but must define the *uses* of this symbol, *i.e.* the propositions in whose symbolic expression it occurs. Now in seeking to define the uses of this symbol, it is important to observe the import of propositions in which it occurs. Take as an illustration: "The author of Waverley was a poet." This implies (1) that Waverley was written, (2) that it was written by one man, and not in collaboration, (3) that the one man who wrote it was a poet. If any one of these fails, the proposition is false. Thus "the author of 'Slawkenburgius on Noses' was a poet" is false, because no such book was ever written; "the author of 'The Maid's Tragedy' was a poet" is false, because this play was written by Beaumont and Fletcher jointly. These two possibilities of falsehood do not arise if we say "Scott was a poet." Thus our interpretation of the uses of $(\imath x)(\phi x)$ must be such as to allow for them. Now taking ϕx to replace "x wrote Waverley," it is plain that any statement apparently about $(\imath x)(\phi x)$ requires (1) $(\exists x) . (\phi x)$ and (2) $\phi x . \phi y . \supset_{x,y} . x = y$; here (1) states that *at least* one object satisfies ϕx, while (2) states that *at most* one object satisfies ϕx. The two together are equivalent to

$$(\exists c) : \phi x . \equiv_x . x = c,$$

which we defined as

$$E!(\imath x)(\phi x).$$

Thus "$E!(\imath x)(\phi x)$" must be part of what is affirmed by any proposition about $(\imath x)(\phi x)$. If our proposition is $f\{(\imath x)(\phi x)\}$, what is further affirmed is fc, if $\phi x . \equiv_x . x = c$. Thus we have

$$f\{(\imath x)(\phi x)\} . = : (\exists c) : \phi x . \equiv_x . x = c : fc \quad \text{Df},$$

i.e. "the x satisfying ϕx satisfies fx" is to mean: "There is an object c such that ϕx is true when, and only when, x is c, and fc is true," or, more exactly: "There is a c such that 'ϕx' is always equivalent to 'x is c,' and fc." In this, "$(\imath x)(\phi x)$" has completely disappeared; thus "$(\imath x)(\phi x)$" is merely symbolic, and does not directly represent an object, as single small Latin letters are assumed to do.[3]

The proposition "$a = (\imath x)(\phi x)$" is easily shown to be equivalent to "$\phi x . \equiv_x . x = a$." For, by the definition, it is

$$(\exists c) : \phi x . \equiv_x . x = c : a = c,$$

i.e. "there is a c for which $\phi x . \equiv_x . x = c$, and this c is a," which is equivalent to "$\phi x . \equiv_x . x = a$." Thus "Scott is the author of Waverley" is equivalent to:

"'x wrote Waverley' is always equivalent to 'x is Scott,'"

i.e. "x wrote Waverley" is true when x is Scott and false when x is not Scott.

Thus although "$(\imath x)(\phi x)$" has no meaning by itself, it may be substituted for y in any propositional function fy, and we get a significant proposition, though not a value of fy.

When $f\{(\imath x)(\phi x)\}$, as above defined, forms part of some other proposition, we shall say that $(\imath x)(\phi x)$ has a *secondary* occurrence. When $(\imath x)(\phi x)$ has a secondary occurrence, a proposition in which it occurs may be true even when $(\imath x)(\phi x)$ does not exist. This applies, *e.g.* to the proposition: "There is no such person as the King of France." We may interpret this as

$$\sim \{E!(\imath x)(\phi x)\},$$

or as

$$\sim \{(\exists c) . c = (\imath x)(\phi x)\},$$

if "ϕx" stands for "x is King of France." In either case, what is asserted is that a proposition p in which $(\imath x)(\phi x)$ occurs is false, and this proposition p is thus part of a larger proposition. The same applies to such a proposition as the following: "If France were a monarchy, the King of France would be of the House of Orleans."

It should be observed that such a proposition as

$$\sim f\{(\imath x)(\phi x)\}$$

is ambiguous; it may deny $f\{(\imath x)(\phi x)\}$, in which case it will be true if $(\imath x)(\phi x)$ does not exist, or it may mean

$$(\exists c) : \phi x . \equiv_x . x = c : \sim fc,$$

in which case it can only be true if $(\imath x)(\phi x)$ exists. In ordinary language, the latter interpretation would usually be adopted. For example, the proposition "the King of France is not bald" would usually be rejected as false, being held to mean "the King of France exists and is not bald," rather than "it is false that the King of France exists and is bald." When $(\iota x)(\phi x)$ exists, the two interpretations of the ambiguity give equivalent results; but when $(\iota x)(\phi x)$ does not exist, one interpretation is true and one is false. It is necessary to be able to distinguish these in our notation; and generally, if we have such propositions as

$$\psi(\iota x)(\phi x) . \supset . p,$$

$$p . \supset . \psi(\iota x)(\phi x),$$

$$\psi(\iota x)(\phi x) . \supset . \chi(\iota x)(\phi x),$$

and so on, we must be able by our notation to distinguish whether the whole or only part of the proposition concerned is to be treated as the "$f(\iota x)(\phi x)$" of our definition. For this purpose, we will put "$[(\iota x)(\phi x)]$" followed by dots at the beginning of the part (or whole) which is to be taken as $f(\iota x)(\phi x)$, the dots being sufficiently numerous to bracket off the $f(\iota x)(\phi x)$; i.e. $f(\iota x)(\phi x)$ is to be everything following the dots until we reach an equal number of dots not signifying a logical product, or a greater number signifying a logical product, or the end of the sentence, or the end of a bracket enclosing "$[(\iota x)(\phi x)]$." Thus

$$[(\iota x)(\phi x)] . \psi(\iota x)(\phi x) . \supset . p$$

will mean

$$(\exists c) : \phi x . \equiv_x . x = c : \psi c : \supset . p,$$

but

$$[(\iota x)(\phi x)] : \psi(\iota x)(\phi x) . \supset . p$$

will mean

$$(\exists c) : \phi x . \equiv_x . x = c : \psi c . \supset . p.$$

It is important to distinguish these two, for if $(\iota x)(\phi x)$ does not exist, the first is true and the second false. Again

$$[(\iota x)(\phi x)] . \sim \psi(\iota x)(\phi x)$$

will mean

$$(\exists c) : \phi x . \equiv_x . x = c : \sim \psi c,$$

while

$$\sim \{[(\iota x)(\phi x)] . \psi(\iota x)(\phi x)\}$$

will mean

$$\sim\{(\exists c):\phi x.\equiv_x.x=c:\psi c\}.$$

Here again, when $(\imath x)(\phi x)$ does not exist, the first is false and the second true.

In order to avoid this ambiguity in propositions containing $(\imath x)(\phi x)$, we amend our definition, or rather our notation, putting

$$[(\imath x)(\phi x)].f(\imath x)(\phi x).=:(\exists c):\phi x.\equiv_x.x=c:fc \quad \text{Df}.$$

By means of this definition, we avoid any doubt as to the portion of our whole asserted proposition which is to be treated as the "$f(\imath x)(\phi x)$" of the definition. This portion will be called the *scope* of $(\imath x)(\phi x)$. Thus in

$$[(\imath x)(\phi x)].f(\imath x)(\phi x).\supset.p$$

the scope of $(\imath x)(\phi x)$ is $f(\imath x)(\phi x)$; but in

$$[(\imath x)(\phi x)]:f(\imath x)(\phi x).\supset.p$$

the scope is $f(\imath x)(\phi x).\supset.p$; in

$$\sim\{[(\imath x)(\phi x)].f(\imath x)(\phi x)\}$$

the scope is $f(\imath x)(\phi x)$; but in

$$[(\imath x)(\phi x)].\sim f(\imath x)(\phi x)$$

the scope is $\sim f(\imath x)(\phi x)$.

It will be seen that when $(\imath x)(\phi x)$ has the whole of the proposition concerned for its scope, the proposition concerned cannot be true unless $E!(\imath x)(\phi x)$; but when $(\imath x)(\phi x)$ has only part of the proposition concerned for its scope, it may often be true even when $(\imath x)(\phi x)$ does not exist. It will be seen further that when $E!(\imath x)(\phi x)$, we may enlarge or diminish the scope of $(\imath x)(\phi x)$ as much as we please without altering the truth-value of any proposition in which it occurs.

If a proposition contains two descriptions, say $(\imath x)(\phi x)$ and $(\imath x)(\psi x)$, we have to distinguish which of them has the larger scope, *i.e.* we have to distinguish

(1) $[(\imath x)(\phi x)]:[(\imath x)(\psi x)].f\{(\imath x)(\phi x),(\imath x)(\psi x)\}$,

(2) $[(\imath x)(\psi x)]:[(\imath x)(\phi x)].f\{(\imath x)(\phi x),(\imath x)(\psi x)\}$.

The first of these, eliminating $(\imath x)(\phi x)$, becomes

(3) $(\exists c):\phi x.\equiv_x.x=c:[(\imath x)(\psi x)].f\{c,(\imath x)(\psi x)\}$,

which, eliminating $(\imath x)(\psi x)$, becomes

(4) $(\exists c) :. \phi x . \equiv_x . x = c :. (\exists d) : \psi x . \equiv_x . x = c : f(c, d)$,

and the same proposition results if, in (1), we eliminate first $(\imath x)(\psi x)$ and then $(\imath x)(\phi x)$. Similarly (2) becomes, when $(\imath x)(\phi x)$ and $(\imath x)(\psi x)$ are eliminated,

(5) $(\exists d) :. \psi x . \equiv_x . x = d :. (\exists c) : \phi x . \equiv_x . x = c : f(c, d)$.

(4) and (5) are equivalent, so that the truth-value of a proposition containing two descriptions is independent of the question which has the larger scope.

It will be found that, in most cases in which descriptions occur, their scope is, in practice, the smallest proposition enclosed in dots or other brackets in which they are contained. Thus for example

$[(\imath x)(\phi x)] . \psi(\imath x)(\phi x) . \supset . [(\imath x)(\phi x)] . \chi(\imath x)(\phi x)$

will occur much more frequently than

$[(\imath x)(\phi x)] : \psi(\imath x)(\phi x) . \supset . \chi(\imath x)(\phi x)$.

For this reason it is convenient to decide that, when the scope of an occurrence of $(\imath x)(\phi x)$ is the smallest proposition, enclosed in dots or other brackets, in which the occurrence in question is contained, the scope need not be indicated by "$[(\imath x)(\phi x)]$." Thus *e.g.*

$p . \supset . a = (\imath x)(\phi x)$

will mean

$p . \supset . [(\imath x)(\phi x)] . a = (\imath x)(\phi x)$;

and

$p . \supset . (\exists a) . a = (\imath x)(\phi x)$

will mean

$p . \supset . (\exists a) . [(\imath x)(\phi x)] . a = (\imath x)(\phi x)$;

and

$p . \supset . a \neq (\imath x)(\phi x)$

will mean

$p . \supset . [(\imath x)(\phi x)] . \sim \{a = (\imath x)(\phi x)\}$;

but

$p . \supset . \sim \{a = (\imath x)(\phi x)\}$

will mean

$$p . \supset . \sim \{[(\imath x)(\phi x)] . a = (\imath x)(\phi x)\}.$$

This convention enables us, in the vast majority of cases that actually occur, to dispense with the explicit indication of the scope of a descriptive symbol; and it will be found that the convention agrees very closely with the tacit conventions of ordinary language on this subject. Thus for example, if "$(\imath x)(\phi x)$" is "the so-and-so," "$a \neq (\imath x)(\phi x)$" is to be read "$a$ is not the so-and-so," which would ordinarily be regarded as implying that "the so-and-so" exists; but "$\sim \{a = (\imath x)(\phi x)\}$" is to be read "it is not true that a is the so-and-so," which would generally be allowed to hold if "the so-and-so" does not exist. Ordinary language is, of course, rather loose and fluctuating in its implications on this matter; but subject to the requirement of definiteness, our convention seems to keep as near to ordinary language as possible.

In the case when the smallest proposition enclosed in dots or other brackets contains two or more descriptions, we shall assume, in the absence of any indication to the contrary, that one which typographically occurs earlier has a larger scope than one which typographically occurs later. Thus

$$(\imath x)(\phi x) = (\imath x)(\psi x)$$

will mean

$$(\exists c) : \phi x . \equiv_x . x = c : [(\imath x)(\psi x)] . c = (\imath x)(\psi x),$$

while

$$(\imath x)(\psi x) = (\imath x)(\phi x)$$

will mean

$$(\exists d) : \psi x . \equiv_x . x = d : [(\imath x)(\phi x)] . (\imath x)(\phi x) = d.$$

These two propositions are easily shown to be equivalent.

. . .

From *14.   Descriptions

Summary of *14
A *description* is a phrase of the form "the term which etc.," or, more explicitly, "the term x which satisfies $\phi \hat{x}$," where $\phi \hat{x}$ is some function satisfied by one and only one argument. For reasons explained in the

Introduction (Chapter III) [pp. 54–61, above], we do not define "the x which satisfies $\phi\hat{x}$," but we define any proposition in which this phrase occurs. Thus when we say: "The term x which satisfies $\phi\hat{x}$ satisfies $\psi\hat{x}$," we shall mean: "There is a term b such that ϕx is true when, and only when, x is b, and ψb is true." That is, writing "$(\imath x)(\phi x)$" for "the term x which satisfies ϕx," $\psi(\imath x)(\phi x)$ is to mean

$$(\exists b) : \phi x . \equiv_x . x = b : \psi b.$$

This, however, is not yet quite adequate as a definition, for when $(\imath x)(\phi x)$ occurs in a proposition which is part of a larger proposition, there is doubt whether the smaller or the larger proposition is to be taken as the "$\psi(\imath x)(\phi x)$." Take, for example, $\psi(\imath x)(\phi x) . \supset . p$. This may be either

$$(\exists b) : \phi x . \equiv_x . x = b : \psi b : \supset . p$$

or

$$(\exists b) :. \phi x . \equiv_x . x = b : \psi b . \supset . p.$$

If "$(\exists b) : \phi x . \equiv_x . x = b$" is false, the first of these must be true, while the second must be false. Thus it is very necessary to distinguish them.

The proposition which is to be treated as the "$\psi(\imath x)(\phi x)$" will be called the *scope* of $(\imath x)(\phi x)$. Thus in the first of the above two propositions, the scope of $(\imath x)(\phi x)$ is $\psi(\imath x)(\phi x)$, while in the second it is $\psi(\imath x)(\phi x) . \supset . p$. In order to avoid ambiguities as to scope, we shall indicate the scope by writing "$[(\imath x)(\phi x)]$" at the beginning of the scope, followed by enough dots to extend to the end of the scope. Thus of the above two propositions the first is

$$[(\imath x)(\phi x)] . \psi(\imath x)(\phi x) . \supset . p,$$

while the second is

$$[(\imath x)(\phi x)] : \psi(\imath x)(\phi x) . \supset . p.$$

Thus we arrive at the following definition:

$$[(\imath x)(\phi x)] . \psi(\imath x)(\phi x) . = : (\exists b) : \phi x . \equiv_x . x = b : \psi b \quad \text{Df} \qquad *14.01$$

It will be found in practice that the scope usually required is the smallest proposition enclosed in dots or brackets in which "$(\imath x)(\phi x)$" occurs. Hence when this scope is to be given to $(\imath x)(\phi x)$, we shall usually omit explicit mention of the scope. Thus *e.g.* we shall have

$$a \neq (\imath x)(\phi x) . = : \quad (\exists b) : \phi x . \equiv_x . x = b : a \neq b,$$

$$\sim\{a = (\imath x)(\phi x)\} . = . \sim\{(\exists b) : \phi x . \equiv_x . x = b : a = b\}.$$

Of these the first necessarily implies $(\exists b) : \phi x . \equiv_x . x = b$, while the second does not. We put

$$E!(\imath x)(\phi x) . = : (\exists b) : \phi x . \equiv_x . x = b \quad \text{Df} \qquad *14.02$$

This defines: "The x satisfying $\phi \hat{x}$ exists," which holds when, and only when, $\phi \hat{x}$ is satisfied by one value of x and by no other value.

When two or more descriptions occur in the same proposition, there is need of avoiding ambiguity as to which has the larger scope. For this purpose, we put

$$[(\imath x)(\phi x), (\imath x)(\psi x)] . f\{(\imath x)(\phi x), (\imath x)(\psi x)\} . = :$$
$$[(\imath x)(\phi x)] : [(\imath x)(\psi x)] . f\{(\imath x)(\phi x), (\imath x)(\psi x)\} \quad \text{Df} \qquad *14.03$$

It will be shown (*14.113) that the truth-value of a proposition containing two descriptions is unaffected by the question which has the larger scope. Hence we shall in general adopt the convention that the description occurring first typographically is to have the larger scope, unless the contrary is expressly indicated. Thus *e.g.*

$$(\imath x)(\phi x) = (\imath x)(\psi x)$$

will mean

$$(\exists b) : \phi x . \equiv_x . x = b : b = (\imath x)(\psi x),$$

i.e.

$$(\exists b) :. \phi x . \equiv_x . x = b :. (\exists c) : \psi x . \equiv_x . x = c : b = c.$$

By this convention we are able almost always to avoid explicit indication of the order of elimination of two or more descriptions. If, however, we require a larger scope for the later description, we put

$$[(\imath x)(\psi x)] . f\{(\imath x)(\phi x), (\imath x)(\psi x)\} . = .$$
$$[(\imath x)(\psi x), (\imath x)(\phi x)] . f\{(\imath x)(\phi x), (\imath x)(\psi x)\} \quad \text{Df} \qquad *14.04$$

Whenever we have $E!(\imath x)(\phi x)$, $(\imath x)(\phi x)$ behaves, formally, like an ordinary argument to any function in which it may occur. This fact is embodied in the following proposition:

$$\vdash :. E!(\imath x)(\phi x) . \supset : (x) . \psi x . \supset . \psi(\imath x)(\phi x) \qquad *14.18$$

That is to say, when $(\imath x)(\phi x)$ exists, it has any property which belongs to everything. This does not hold when $(\imath x)(\phi x)$ does not exist; for example, the present King of France does not have the property of being either bald or not bald.

If $(\imath x)(\phi x)$ has any property whatever, it must exist. This fact is stated in the proposition:

$$\vdash : \psi(\imath x)(\phi x) . \supset . \mathrm{E}!(\imath x)(\phi x) \qquad\qquad *14.21$$

This proposition is obvious, since "$\mathrm{E}!(\imath x)(\phi x)$" is, by the definitions, part of "$\psi(\imath x)(\phi x)$." When, in ordinary language or in philosophy, something is said to "exist," it is always something *described*, *i.e.* it is not something immediately presented, like a taste or a patch of colour, but something like "matter" or "mind" or "Homer" (meaning "the author of the Homeric poems"), which is known by description as "the so-and-so," and is thus of the form $(\imath x)(\phi x)$. Thus in all such cases, the existence of the (grammatical) subject $(\imath x)(\phi x)$ can be analytically inferred from any true proposition having this grammatical subject. It would seem that the word "existence" cannot be significantly applied to subjects immediately given; *i.e.* not only does our definition give no meaning to "$\mathrm{E}!x$," but there is no reason, in philosophy, to suppose that a meaning of existence could be found which would be applicable to immediately given subjects.

Besides the above, the following are among the more useful propositions of the present number.

$$\vdash :. \phi x . \equiv_x . x = b : \equiv : (\imath x)(\phi x) = b : \equiv : \phi x . \equiv_x . b = x : \equiv : b = (\imath x)(\phi x)$$
$$*14.202$$

From the first equivalence in the above, it follows that

$$\vdash : \mathrm{E}!(\imath x)(\phi x) . \equiv . (\exists b) . (\imath x)(\phi x) = b \qquad\qquad *14.204$$

I.e. $(\imath x)(\phi x)$ exists when there is something which $(\imath x)(\phi x)$ is.
We have

$$\vdash : \psi(\imath x)(\phi x) . \equiv . (\exists b) . b = (\imath x)(\phi x) . \psi b \qquad\qquad *14.205$$

I.e. $(\imath x)(\phi x)$ has the property ψ when there is something which is $(\imath x)(\phi x)$ and which has the property ψ.

We have to prove that such symbols as "$(\imath x)(\phi x)$" obey the same rules with regard to identity as symbols which directly represent objects. To this, however, there is one partial exception, for instead of having

$$(\imath x)(\phi x) = (\imath x)(\phi x),$$

we only have

$$\vdash : \mathrm{E}!(\imath x)(\phi x) . \equiv . (\imath x)(\phi x) = (\imath x)(\phi x) \qquad\qquad *14.28$$

I.e. "$(\imath x)(\phi x)$" only satisfies the reflexive property of identity if $(\imath x)(\phi x)$ exists.

The symmetrical property of identity holds for such symbols as $(\imath x)(\phi x)$, without the need of assuming existence, *i.e.* we have

$$\vdash : a = (\imath x)(\phi x) . \equiv . (\imath x)(\phi x) = a \qquad\qquad *14.13$$

$$\vdash : (\imath x)(\phi x) = (\imath x)(\psi x) . \equiv . (\imath x)(\psi x) = (\imath x)(\phi x) \qquad\qquad *14.131$$

Similarly the transitive property of identity holds without the need of assuming existence.

...

Notes

1. The same principle applies to many uses of the proper names of existent objects, *e.g.* to all uses of proper names for objects known to the speaker only by report, and not by personal acquaintance.

2. Cf. pp. 52, 53.

3. We shall generally write "$f(\imath x)(\phi x)$" rather than "$f\{(\imath x)(\phi x)\}$" in future.

Chapter 3

Descriptions   Bertrand Russell

We dealt in the preceding chapter with the words *all* and *some*; in this chapter we shall consider the word *the* in the singular, and in the next chapter we shall consider the word *the* in the plural. It may be thought excessive to devote two chapters to one word, but to the philosophical mathematician it is a word of very great importance: like Browning's Grammarian with the enclitic δε, I would give the doctrine of this word if I were "dead from the waist down" and not merely in a prison.

We have already had occasion to mention "descriptive functions," i.e. such expressions as "the father of x" or "the sine of x." These are to be defined by first defining "descriptions."

A "description" may be of two sorts, definite and indefinite (or ambiguous). An indefinite description is a phrase of the form "a so-and-so," and a definite description is a phrase of the form "the so-and-so" (in the singular). Let us begin with the former.

"Who did you meet?" "I met a man." "That is a very indefinite description." We are therefore not departing from usage in our terminology. Our question is: What do I really assert when I assert "I met a man"? Let us assume, for the moment, that my assertion is true, and that in fact I met Jones. It is clear that what I assert is *not* "I met Jones." I may say "I met a man, but it was not Jones"; in that case, though I lie, I do not contradict myself, as I should do if when I say I met a man I really mean that I met Jones. It is clear also that the person to whom I am speaking can understand what I say, even if he is a foreigner and has never heard of Jones.

From Bertrand Russell, *Introduction to Mathematical Philosophy* (London: George Allen and Unwin Ltd., 1919), pp. 167–180.

But we may go further: not only Jones, but no actual man, enters into my statement. This becomes obvious when the statement is false, since then there is no more reason why Jones should be supposed to enter into the proposition than why anyone else should. Indeed the statement would remain significant, though it could not possibly be true, even if there were no man at all. "I met a unicorn" or "I met a sea-serpent" is a perfectly significant assertion, if we know what it would be to be a unicorn or a sea-serpent, i.e. what is the definition of these fabulous monsters. Thus it is only what we may call the *concept* that enters into the proposition. In the case of "unicorn," for example, there is only the concept: there is not also, somewhere among the shades, something unreal which may be called "a unicorn." Therefore, since it is significant (though false) to say "I met a unicorn," it is clear that this proposition, rightly analyzed, does not contain a constituent "a unicorn," though it does contain the concept "unicorn."

The question of "unreality," which confronts us at this point, is a very important one. Misled by grammar, the great majority of those logicians who have dealt with this question have dealt with it on mistaken lines. They have regarded grammatical form as a surer guide in analysis than, in fact, it is. And they have not known what differences in grammatical form are important. "I met Jones" and "I met a man" would count traditionally as propositions of the same form, but in actual fact they are of quite different forms: the first names an actual person, Jones; while the second involves a propositional function, and becomes, when made explicit: "The function 'I met x and x is human' is sometimes true." (It will be remembered that we adopted the convention of using "sometimes" as not implying more than once.) This proposition is obviously not of the form "I met x," which accounts for the existence of the proposition "I met a unicorn" in spite of the fact that there is no such thing as "a unicorn."

For want of the apparatus of propositional functions, many logicians have been driven to the conclusion that there are unreal objects. It is argued, e.g. by Meinong,[1] that we can speak about "the golden mountain," "the round square," and so on; we can make true propositions of which these are the subjects; hence they must have some kind of logical being, since otherwise the propositions in which they occur would be meaningless. In such theories, it seems to me, there is a failure of that feeling for reality which ought to be preserved even in the most abstract studies. Logic, I should maintain, must no more admit a unicorn than zoology can; for logic is concerned with the real world just as truly as zoology, though with its more abstract and general features. To say that unicorns have an existence in heraldry, or in literature, or in imagination, is a most pitiful and paltry evasion. What exists in heraldry is not an animal, made of flesh and blood, moving and breathing of its own initiative. What exists is a picture, or a description in words. Similarly, to maintain that Hamlet, for example, exists in his own world, namely, in the world of Shakespeare's imagination, just as truly as (say) Napoleon existed in the ordinary world, is to say something deliberately confusing, or else confused to a degree which is scarcely credible. There is only one world, the "real" world: Shakespeare's imagination is part of it, and the thoughts that he had in writing Hamlet are real. So are the thoughts that we have in reading the play. But it is of the very essence of fiction that only the thoughts, feelings, etc., in Shakespeare and his readers are real, and that there is not, in addition to them, an objective Hamlet. When you have taken account of all the feelings roused by Napoleon in writers and readers of history, you have not touched the actual man; but in the case of Hamlet you have come to the end of him. If no one thought about Hamlet, there would be nothing left of him; if no one had thought about Napoleon, he would have soon seen to it that some one did. The sense of reality is vital in logic, and whoever juggles with it by pretending that Hamlet has another kind of reality is doing a disservice to thought. A robust sense of reality is very necessary in framing a correct analysis of propositions about unicorns, golden mountains, round squares, and other such pseudo-objects.

In obedience to the feeling of reality, we shall insist that, in the analysis of propositions, nothing "unreal" is to be admitted. But, after all, if there *is* nothing unreal, how, it may be asked, *could* we admit anything unreal? The reply is that, in dealing with propositions, we are dealing in the first instance with symbols, and if we attribute significance to groups of symbols which have no significance, we shall fall into the error of admitting unrealities, in the only sense in which this is possible, namely, as objects described. In the proposition "I met a unicorn," the whole four words together make a significant proposition, and the word "unicorn" by itself is significant, in just the same sense as the word "man." But the *two* words "a unicorn" do not form a subordinate group having a meaning of its own. Thus if we falsely attribute meaning to these two words, we find ourselves saddled with "a unicorn," and with the problem how there can be such a thing in a world where there are no unicorns. "A unicorn" is an indefinite description which describes nothing. It is not an indefinite description which describes something unreal. Such a proposition as "*x* is unreal" only has meaning when "*x*" is a description, definite or indefinite; in that case the proposition will be true if "*x*" is a description which describes nothing. But whether the description "*x*" describes something or describes nothing, it is in any case not a constituent of the proposition in which it occurs; like "a unicorn" just now, it is not a subordinate group having a meaning of its own. All this results from the fact that, when "*x*" is a description, "*x* is unreal" or "*x* does not exist" is not nonsense, but is always significant and sometimes true.

We may now proceed to define generally the meaning of propositions which contain ambiguous descriptions. Suppose we wish to make some statement about "a so-and-so," where "so-and-so's" are those objects that have a certain property ϕ, i.e. those objects *x* for which the propositional function ϕx is true. (E.g. if we take "a man" as our instance of "a so-and-so," ϕx will be "*x* is human.") Let us now wish to assert the property ψ of "a so-and-so," i.e. we wish to assert that "a so-and-so" has that property which *x* has when ψx is true. (E.g. in the case of "I met a man," ψx will be "I met *x*.") Now the proposition that "a so-and-so" has the property ψ is *not* a proposition of the form "ψx." If it were, "a so-and-so" would have to be identical with *x* for a suitable *x*; and although (in a sense) this may be true in some cases, it is certainly not true in such a case as "a unicorn." It is just this fact, that the statement that a so-and-so has the property ψ is not of the form ψx, which makes it possible for "a so-and-so" to be, in a certain clearly definable sense, "unreal." The definition is as follows:

The statement that "an object having the property ϕ has the property ψ"

means:

"The joint assertion of ϕx and ψx is not always false."

So far as logic goes, this is the same proposition as might be expressed by "some ϕs are ψs"; but rhetorically there is a difference, because in the one case there is a suggestion of singularity, and in the other case of plurality. This, however, is not the important point. The important point is that, when rightly analyzed, propositions verbally about "a so-and-so" are found to contain no constituent represented by this phrase. And that is why such propositions can be significant even when there is no such thing as a so-and-so.

The definition of *existence*, as applied to ambiguous descriptions, results from what was said at the end of the preceding chapter [chapter 15 of

Introduction to Mathematical Philosophy]. We say that "men exist" or "a man exists" if the propositional function "*x* is human" is sometimes true; and generally "a so-and-so" exists if "*x* is so-and-so" is sometimes true. We may put this in other language. The proposition "Socrates is a man" is no doubt *equivalent* to "Socrates is human," but it is not the very same proposition. The *is* of "Socrates is human" expresses the relation of subject and predicate; the *is* of "Socrates is a man" expresses identity. It is a disgrace to the human race that it has chosen to employ the same word "is" for these two entirely different ideas—a disgrace which a symbolic logical language of course remedies. The identity in "Socrates is a man" is identity between an object named (accepting "Socrates" as a name, subject to qualifications explained later) and an object ambiguously described. An object ambiguously described will "exist" when at least one such proposition is true, i.e. when there is at least one true proposition of the form "*x* is a so-and-so," where "*x*" is a name. It is characteristic of ambiguous (as opposed to definite) descriptions that there may be any number of true propositions of the above form—Socrates is a man, Plato is a man, etc. Thus "a man exists" follows from Socrates, or Plato, or anyone else. With definite descriptions, on the other hand, the corresponding form of proposition, namely, "*x* is the so-and-so" (where "*x*" is a name), can only be true for one value of *x* at most. This brings us to the subject of definite descriptions, which are to be defined in a way analogous to that employed for ambiguous descriptions, but rather more complicated.

We come now to the main subject of the present chapter, namely, the definition of the word *the* (in the singular). One very important point about the definition of "a so-and-so" applies equally to "the so-and-so"; the definition to be sought is a definition of propositions in which this phrase occurs, not a definition of the phrase itself in isolation. In the case of "a so-and-so," this is fairly obvious: no one could suppose that "a man" was a definite object, which could be defined by itself. Socrates is a man, Plato is a man, Aristotle is a man, but we cannot infer that "a man" means the same as "Socrates" means and also the same as "Plato" means and also the same as "Aristotle" means, since these three names have different meanings. Nevertheless, when we have enumerated all the men in the world, there is nothing left of which we can say, "This is a man, and not only so, but it is *the* 'a man,' the quintessential entity that is just an indefinite man without being anybody in particular." It is of course quite clear that whatever there is in the world is definite: if it is a man it is one definite man and not any other. Thus there cannot be such an entity as "a man" to be found in the world, as opposed to specific men. And accordingly it is natural that we do not define "a man" itself, but only the propositions in which it occurs.

In the case of "the so-and-so" this is equally true, though at first sight less obvious. We may demonstrate that this must be the case, by a consideration of the difference between a *name* and a *definite description*. Take the proposition, "Scott is the author of *Waverley*." We have here a name, "Scott," and a description, "the author of *Waverley*," which are asserted to apply to the same person. The distinction between a name and all other symbols may be explained as follows:

A name is a simple symbol whose meaning is something that can only occur as subject, i.e. something of the kind that we defined as an "individual" or a "particular." And a "simple" symbol is one which has no parts that are symbols. Thus "Scott" is a simple symbol, because, though it has parts (namely, separate letters), these parts are not symbols. On the other hand, "the author of *Waverley*" is not a simple symbol, because the separate words that compose the phrase are parts which are symbols. If, as may be the case, whatever *seems* to be an "individual" is really capable of further analysis, we shall have to content ourselves with what may be called "relative individuals," which will be terms that, throughout the context in question, are never analyzed and never occur otherwise than as subjects. And in that case we shall have correspondingly to content ourselves with "relative names." From the standpoint of our present problem, namely, the definition of descriptions, this problem, whether these are absolute names or only relative names, may be ignored, since it concerns different stages in the hierarchy of "types," whereas we have to compare such couples as "Scott" and "the author of *Waverley*," which both apply to the same object, and do not raise the problem of types. We may, therefore, for the moment, treat names as capable of being absolute; nothing that we shall have to say will depend upon this assumption, but the wording may be a little shortened by it.

We have, then, two things to compare: (1) a *name*, which is a simple symbol, directly designating an individual which is its meaning, and having this meaning in its own right, independently of the meanings of all other words; (2) a *description*, which consists of several words, whose meanings are already fixed, and from which results whatever is to be taken as the "meaning" of the description.

A proposition containing a description is not identical with what that proposition becomes when a name is substituted, even if the name names the same object as the description describes. "Scott is the author of *Waverley*" is obviously a different proposition from "Scott is Scott": the first is a fact in literary history, the second a trivial truism. And if we put anyone other than Scott in place of "the author of *Waverley*," our proposition would become false, and would therefore certainly no longer be the same proposition. But, it may be said, our proposition is essentially of the same form as (say) "Scott is Sir Walter," in which two names are said to apply to the same person. The reply is that, if "Scott is Sir Walter" really means "the person named 'Scott' is the person named 'Sir Walter,'" then the names are being used as descriptions: i.e. the individual, instead of being named, is being described as the person having that name. This is a way in which names are frequently used in practice, and there will, as a rule, be nothing in the phraseology to show whether they are being used in this way or *as* names. When a name is used directly, merely to indicate what we are speaking about, it is no part of the *fact* asserted, or of the falsehood if our assertion happens to be false: it is merely part of the symbolism by which we express our thought. What we want to express is something which might (for example) be translated into a foreign language; it is something for which the actual words are a vehicle, but of which they are no part. On the other hand, when we make a proposition about "the person called 'Scott,'" the actual name "Scott" enters into what we are asserting, and not merely into the language used in making the assertion. Our proposition will now be a different one if we substitute "the person called 'Sir Walter.'" But so long as we are using names *as* names, whether we say "Scott" or whether we say "Sir Walter" is as irrelevant to what we are asserting as whether we speak English or French. Thus so long as names are used *as* names, "Scott is Sir Walter" is the same trivial proposition as "Scott is Scott." This completes the proof that "Scott is the author of *Waverley*" is not the same proposition as results from substituting a name for "the author of *Waverley*," no matter what name may be substituted.

When we use a variable, and speak of a propositional function, ϕx say, the process of applying general statements about x to particular cases will consist in substituting a name for the letter "x," assuming that ϕ is a function which has individuals for its arguments. Suppose, for example, that ϕx is "always true"; let it be, say, the "law of identity," $x = x$. Then we may substitute for "x" any name we choose, and we shall obtain a true proposition. Assuming for the moment that "Socrates," "Plato," and "Aristotle" are names (a very rash assumption), we can infer from the law of identity that Socrates is Socrates, Plato is Plato, and Aristotle is Aristotle. But we shall commit a fallacy if we attempt to infer, without further premisses, that the author of *Waverley* is the author of *Waverley*. This results from what we have just proved, that, if we substitute a name for "the author of *Waverley*" in a proposition, the proposition we obtain is a different one. That is to say, applying the result to our present case: If "x" is a name, "$x = x$" is not the same proposition as "the author of *Waverley* is the author of *Waverley*," no matter what name "x" may be. Thus from the fact that all propositions of the form "$x = x$" are true we cannot infer, without more ado, that the author of *Waverley* is the author of *Waverley*. In fact, propositions of the form "the so-and-so is the so-and-so" are not always true: it is necessary that the so-and-so should *exist* (a term which will be explained shortly). It is false that the present King of France is the present King of France, or that the round square is the round square. When we substitute a description for a name, propositional functions which are "always true" may become false, if the description describes nothing. There is no mystery in this as soon as we realize (what was proved in the preceding paragraph) that when we substitute a description the result is not a value of the propositional function in question.

We are now in a position to define propositions in which a definite description occurs. The only thing that distinguishes "the so-and-so" from "a so-and-so" is the implication of uniqueness. We cannot speak of "*the* inhabitant of London," because inhabiting London is an attribute which is not unique. We cannot speak about "the present King of France," because there is none; but we can speak about "the present King of England." Thus propositions about "the so-and-so" always imply the corresponding propositions about "a so-and-so," with the addendum that there is not more than one so-and-so. Such a proposition as "Scott is the author of Waverley" could not be true if *Waverley* had never been written, or if several people had written it; and no more could any other proposition resulting from a propositional function x by the substitution of "the author of *Waverley*" for "x." We may say that "the author of *Waverley*" means "the value of x for which 'x wrote *Waverley*' is true." Thus the proposition "the author of *Waverley* was Scotch," for example, involves:

(1) "x wrote *Waverley*" is not always false

(2) "if x and y wrote *Waverley*, x and y are identical" is always true

(3) "if x wrote *Waverley*, x was Scotch" is always true

These three propositions, translated into ordinary language, state:

(1) at least one person wrote *Waverley*

(2) at most one person wrote *Waverley*

(3) whoever wrote *Waverley* was Scotch

All these three are implied by "the author of *Waverley* was Scotch." Conversely, the three together (but no two of them) imply that the author of *Waverley* was Scotch. Hence the three together may be taken as defining what is meant by the proposition "the author of *Waverley* was Scotch."

We may somewhat simplify these three propositions. The first and second together are equivalent to: "There is a term c such that 'x wrote *Waverley*' is true when x is c and is false when x is not c." In other words, "There is a term c such that 'x wrote *Waverley*' is always equivalent to 'x is c.'" (Two propositions are "equivalent" when both are true or both are false.) We have here, to begin with, two functions of x, "x wrote *Waverley*" and "x is c," and we form a function of c by considering the equivalence of these two functions of x for all values of x; we then proceed to assert that the resulting function of c is "sometimes true," i.e. that it is true for at least one value of c. (It obviously cannot be true for more than one value of c.) These two conditions together are defined as giving the meaning of "the author of *Waverley* exists."

We may now define "the term satisfying the function ϕx exists." This is the general form of which the above is a particular case. "The author of *Waverley*" is "the term satisfying the function 'x wrote *Waverley*.'" And "the so-and-so" will always involve reference to some propositional function, namely, that which defines the property that makes a thing a so-and-so. Our definition is as follows:

"The term satisfying the function ϕx exists" means: "There is a term c such that ϕx is always equivalent to 'x is c.'"

In order to define "the author of *Waverley* was Scotch," we have still to take account of the third of our three propositions, namely, "Whoever wrote *Waverley* was Scotch." This will be satisfied by merely adding that the c in question is to be Scotch. Thus "the author of *Waverley* was Scotch" is:

"There is a term c such that (1) 'x wrote *Waverley*' is always equivalent to 'x is c,' (2) c is Scotch."

And generally: "the term satisfying ϕx satisfies ψx" is defined as meaning:

"There is a term c such that (1) ϕx is always equivalent to 'x is c,' (2) ψx is true."

This is the definition of propositions in which descriptions occur.

It is possible to have much knowledge concerning a term described, i.e. to know many propositions concerning "the so-and-so," without actually knowing what the so-and-so is, i.e. without knowing any proposition of the form "x is the so-and-so," where "x" is a name. In a detective story propositions about "the man who did the deed" are accumulated, in the hope that ultimately they will suffice to demonstrate that it was A who did the deed. We may even go so far as to say that, in all such knowledge as can be expressed in words—with the exception of "this" and "that" and a few other words of which the meaning varies on different occasions—no names, in the strict sense, occur, but what seem like names are really descriptions. We may inquire significantly whether Homer existed, which we could not do if "Homer" were a name. The proposition "the so-and-so exists" is significant, whether true or false; but if a is the so-and-so (where "a" is a name), the words "a exists" are meaningless. It is only of descriptions—definite or indefinite—that existence can be significantly asserted; for, if "a" is a name, it *must* name something: what does not name anything is not a name, and therefore, if intended to be a name, is a symbol devoid of meaning, whereas a description, like "the present King of France," does not become incapable of occurring significantly merely on the ground that it describes nothing, the reason being that it is a *complex* symbol, of which the meaning is derived from that of its constituent symbols. And so, when we ask whether Homer existed, we are using the word "Homer" as an abbreviated description: we may replace it by (say) "the author of the *Iliad* and the *Odyssey*." The same considerations apply to almost all uses of what look like proper names.

When descriptions occur in propositions, it is necessary to distinguish what may be called "primary" and "secondary" occurrences. The abstract distinction is as follows. A description has a "primary" occurrence when the proposition in which it occurs results from substituting the description for "x" in some propositional function ϕx; a description has a "secondary" occurrence when the result of substituting the description for x in ϕx gives only *part* of the proposition concerned. An instance will make this clearer. Consider "the present King of France is bald." Here "the present King of France" has a primary occurrence, and the proposition is false. Every proposition in which a description which describes nothing has a primary occurrence is false. But now consider "the present King of France is not bald." This is ambiguous. If we are first to take "x is bald," then substitute "the present King of France" for "x," and then deny the result, the occurrence of "the present King of France" is secondary and our proposition is true; but if we are to take "x is not bald" and substitute "the present King of France" for "x," then "the present King of France" has a primary occurrence and the proposition is false. Confusion of primary and secondary occurrences is a ready source of fallacies where descriptions are concerned.

Descriptions occur in mathematics chiefly in the form of *descriptive functions*, i.e. "the term having the relation R to y," or "the R of y" as we may say, on the analogy of "the father of y" and similar phrases. To say "the father of y is rich," for example, is to say that the following propositional function of c: "'c is rich, and 'x begat y' is always equivalent to 'x is c,'" is "sometimes true," i.e. is true for at least one value of c. It obviously cannot be true for more than one value.

The theory of descriptions, briefly outlined in the present chapter, is of the utmost importance both in logic and in theory of knowledge. But for purposes of mathematics, the more philosophical parts of the theory are not essential, and have therefore been omitted in the above account, which has confined itself to the barest mathematical requisites.

Note

1. *Untersuchungen zur Gegenstandstheorie und Psychologie*, 1904.

Chapter 4

Grammatical Form, Logical Form, and Incomplete Symbols

Stephen Neale

1 Introduction

It is not uncommon to find philosophers appealing to Russell's Theory of Descriptions when attempting to shed light on the *logical forms* of certain statements, perhaps the premises or the conclusions of certain philosophical arguments. One philosopher might accuse another of committing a "substitution fallacy" by treating a particularly significant expression as a referring expression when really it is a description; or one philosopher might accuse another of committing a "scope fallacy" involving the interpretation of a description with respect to, say, a modal or temporal operator.

Curiously, it is less common for philosophers to construe Russell's theory as a component of a systematic and compositional semantics for natural language. Now I would have thought that it is only *because* the Theory of Descriptions can be construed as a component of a systematic semantical theory that philosophers are entitled to appeal to it in the ways they do. Consequently, I would maintain that there is an onus on anyone who wishes to appeal to the theory in explicating the logical forms of statements of English to be explicit about its rôle in a systematic semantics for English.

From a semantical perspective, the essence of the theory concerns *logical form* and *truth conditions*. Russell argued that descriptions are not genuine singular terms (genuine singular referring expressions). According

From A. D. Irvine and G. A. Wedeking (eds.), *Russell and Analytic Philosophy*. Toronto: University of Toronto Press, 1993, pp. 97–139. Reprinted by permission of The University of Toronto Press Incorporated and Stephen Neale. © 1993 University of Toronto Press Incorporated.

to Russell, sentences containing descriptions are *inherently quantificational*: they express *general* (rather than *singular*) propositions. Specifically, the truth conditions of (the proposition expressed by) an utterance of a simple sentence of the form ⌜the F is G⌝ are given by the familiar expansion (1):

(1) $(\exists x_1)((\forall x_2)(Fx_2 \equiv x_2 = x_1)$ & $Gx_1)$.

For the purposes of the present paper, I am going to assume that Russell's theory is at least truth-conditionally adequate (a view I defended at length in *Descriptions*). What I shall be concerned with here is the view that (1) gives the "logical form" of ⌜the F is G⌝ and the matter of the logical forms of sentences more generally. By drawing attention to a distinction between grammatical form and logical form, the Theory of Descriptions helps to raise some important questions about the rôle of logical form in semantical investigations. Furthermore, reflecting on Russell's theory as a contribution to semantics helps with the formulation of some very good answers. In my view, we are unlikely to progress much further in our understanding of the semantics of natural language without a well-worked out theory of logical form; and in view of the fundamental importance of natural language semantics to clear-headed philosophical inquiry, to my mind there is a pressing need for such a theory. As Russell stressed, much bad philosophy is the product of bad logical grammar.

Let me pose two questions straight away: (i) How should we understand the claim that the doubly quantified formula in (1) *gives the logical form* of ⌜the F is G⌝? and (ii) How is the claim that (1) gives the logical form of ⌜the F is G⌝ connected to Russell's conception of ⌜the F⌝ as an "incomplete symbol"? By addressing these questions I hope (a) to motivate a particular conception of logical form that borrows from philosophy and linguistics and promises to be of service to both, and (b) to help clarify the rôle of the Theory of Descriptions within a systematic semantical theory. (A related question is: (iii) How important is it that we view the implication relations between ⌜the F is G⌝ and (e.g.) ⌜an F is G⌝ and ⌜there is exactly one F⌝ as *formal*? Limitations of space prevent an adequate discussion of this question.)

2   Quantification and Logical Form

Often we say that a particular argument has such-and-such a *logical form*. For example, someone who infers from the truth of (2) and (3) to the truth of (4)

(2) Every farmer is happy

(3) Pierre is a farmer

(4) Pierre is happy

might be said to be endorsing an argument of the following logical form:

(5) $(\forall x_1)(Fx_1 \supset Hx_1)$,　　Fp/Hp.

My primary concern here is not with the logical form of *arguments* but with the prior notion of the logical forms of *sentences*. The philosophical logician might say that it is in virtue of being able to assign particular logical forms to the *sentences* (2), (3), and (4) that we are entitled to say that the *argument* from (2) and (3) to (4) has the logical form given in (5). And it is, perhaps, only a short step from here to the view that the logical forms of the sentences (2), (3), and (4) are given in the three formulae in (5), or rather by formulae very like these.

　　In some sense, then, the notion of the logical form of an argument is dependent upon a well-understood notion of the logical form of a sentence. Furthermore, to provide a theory of the logical forms of the sentences of a natural language L is (I maintain) to make an important contribution to the project of constructing a systematic semantical theory for L. To specify the logical form of a sentence S is to specify its structure in a way transparently related to its meaning, transparently related to the proposition S expresses in a given context, transparently related to the world.[1] Ultimately, I would like to espouse the view that the logical form of a sentence S belonging to a language L is the structure imposed upon S in the course of providing a systematic and principled mapping from sentences of L (as determined by the best syntactical theory for L) to the propositions (or perhaps proposition types) those sentences express. As a point of departure and with an important caveat, I propose to adopt a perspective one finds in the work of Davidson and many of those he has influenced:[2] the logical form of a sentence S belonging to a language L is the structure imposed upon S in the course of providing a systematic and principled truth definition for L. For present purposes it will have to be taken on trust that it is possible to provide a systematic and principled truth definition for a substantial fragment of English. My main efforts will be directed toward one way of cashing out the idea that there is a level of syntactical representation that satisfies this constraint on logical form and possesses other properties that philosophers have traditionally ascribed to logical form.[3] The first step in all this involves saying something about the nature of quantification in natural language.

When philosophers want to characterize the logical form of a quantified English sentence S, typically they will attempt to provide a sentence of some version of the first-order predicate calculus, a sentence that has the same truth conditions as S. From the perspective I am adopting here, reliance on the calculus brings up a variety of well-known logical puzzles involving such things as systematicity of translation, plurality-quantification, branching quantification, and donkey anaphora.[4] It is not necessary to venture very far in order to see that we need a more refined system than the standard calculus if we are to think of logical form as playing a serious rôle in a systematic semantics. In the calculus, in order to characterize the "logical forms" of sentences like (6) and (7):

(6) Some farmers are happy

(7) Every farmer is happy

we have to introduce sentential connectives as well as quantifiers, as in the translations (8) and (9):

(8) $(\exists x_1)(\text{farmers}(x_1) \ \& \ \text{happy}(x_1))$

(9) $(\forall x_1)(\text{farmer}(x_1) \supset \text{happy}(x_1))$.

And, if we buy into Russell's Theory of Descriptions, the logical form of (10) will be given by (11), which contains two quantifiers and two connectives, further obscuring the relationship between surface syntax and logical form:

(10) The farmer is happy

(11) $(\exists x_1)((\forall x_2)(\text{farmer}(x_2) \equiv x_2 = x_1) \ \& \ \text{happy}(x_1))$.

There is a worse problem however: there are syntactically simple, quantified sentences that cannot be handled within the calculus at all. (12) is such a sentence

(12) Most farmers are happy

because "most" is not definable in first-order logic, even if attention is restricted to finite domains.[5] (It should be stressed that this fact by itself does not undermine truth-theoretic semantics.)

A familiar way to solve all of these problems simultaneously is to view natural language quantification as *restricted*. A simple modification of the predicate calculus will serve our purposes. Call the resulting language RQ. In RQ, a determiner is an expression that combines with a formula to create a restricted quantifier.[6] For example, "some₁" combines with, say, "farmers x_1" to create the restricted quantifier given in (13)

(13) [some₁ farmers x_1]₁

This quantifier may combine with a second formula such as "happy x_1" to form a formula as in (14):

(14) [some₁ farmers x_1]₁ (happy x_1)

where the semantics of RQ (see below) ensures that (14) is equivalent to (8).

In order to provide a truth definition for RQ, we need first to specify its syntax clearly: to this end we can modify the formation rules of a standard first-order language. We replace the rules specifying that if α is a well-formed formula then so are $\ulcorner(\forall x_k)\alpha\urcorner$ and $\ulcorner(\exists x_k)\alpha\urcorner$ with the following (for any $k \geq 1$):

(Q1) If α is a well-formed formula and D is one of (e.g.) "every," "all," "each," "a," "no," "some," "most," then $\ulcorner[D_k\alpha]_k\urcorner$ is a well-formed restricted quantifier phrase.

(Q2) If β is a well-formed formula and $\ulcorner[D_k\alpha]_k\urcorner$ is a well-formed restricted quantifier phrase, then $\ulcorner[D_k\alpha]_k\beta\urcorner$ is a well-formed formula.

Second, we specify conditions on binding and scope in RQ. There are two types of variable-binding operator to worry about: determiners and restricted quantifiers. A determiner $\ulcorner D_k\urcorner$ is really an unrestricted quantifier that binds any free occurrences of $\ulcorner x_k\urcorner$ in the formula α with which it combines to form a restricted quantifier. And a restricted quantifier $\ulcorner[D_k\alpha]_k\urcorner$ binds any free occurrences of $\ulcorner x_k\urcorner$ in the formula β with which it combines to form a formula. The scope of a variable-binding operator (or any other expression) is just the expression (or expressions) with which it combines to form a well-formed expression, exactly as in the first-order predicate calculus.

Finally, we can supply a truth definition for RQ. For each proper name we provide an axiom similar to the following axiom for "Russell":

(i) Ref("Russell," s) = Russell.

This says that the referent of "Russell" with respect to an arbitrary sequence (or assignment) s is Russell (for simplicity, I shall suppress universal quantification over sequences, terms, and formulae throughout). For individual variables $\ulcorner x_k \urcorner$, we will have the following axiom schema:

(ii) $\text{Ref}(\ulcorner x_k \urcorner, s) = s_k$

which says that the referent of $\ulcorner x_k \urcorner$ with respect to a sequence s is the k-th element of s.

For each one- or two-place predicate there will be an axiom similar to one of the following

(iii) s satisfies $\ulcorner t \text{ snores} \urcorner$ iff $\text{Ref}(t, s)$ snores

(iv) s satisfies $\ulcorner t \text{ admires } u \urcorner$ iff $\text{Ref}(t, s)$ admires $\text{Ref}(u, s)$

where t and u are terms (i.e., names or variables).

The first recursive axioms, for connectives, are also no different from the analogous axioms in the predicate calculus. For example, for "&" we get the following:

(v) s satisfies $\ulcorner \alpha \text{ and } \beta \urcorner$ iff s satisfies α and s satisfies β.

We can replace the unrestricted quantifier axioms of a Tarski-style truth definition for a standard first-order language by axioms appropriate for restricted quantifiers:

(vi) s satisfies $\ulcorner [\text{every}_k \alpha]_k \beta \urcorner$ iff every sequence satisfying α and differing from s at most in the k-th place also satisfies β.

(vii) s satisfies $\ulcorner [\text{most}_k \alpha]_k \beta \urcorner$ iff most sequences satisfying α and differing from s at most in the k-th place also satisfy β.

As usual, a sentence is true iff it is satisfied by all sequences.

In a standard first-order language, no expressive power is obtained, of course, by introducing the existential quantifier as a primitive quantifier when the language already contains the universal quantifier and negation. Similarly, the expressive power of RQ is not increased by introducing a new determiner "some" along with the following axiom:

(viii) s satisfies $\ulcorner [\text{some}_k \alpha]_k \beta \urcorner$ iff at least one sequence satisfying α and differing from s at most in the k-th place also satisfies β.

But introducing (viii) makes it easier to translate sentences of English into RQ; let's add it, then, along with parallel axioms for "no," "each," and "a." And let's say (informally for now) that sentences of RQ "give the logical forms" of the English sentences with which they are paired. This will, of course, need to be justified because I am subscribing (as a first shot) to the view that the logical form of a sentence S of a language L is the structure imposed upon S in the course of providing a systematic and principled truth definition for L. An account is still needed of how, for example, (14) can be viewed as the structure imposed upon (6) in the course of discharging this obligation. Before addressing this matter, I need to say a few things about the expressive power of RQ and about Russell's account of definite descriptions.

The formal language RQ can be used in a systematic way to perspicuously and unambiguously capture the "logical forms" of sentences with more than one operator. For example, the negation sign "$\neg$" can be prefixed either to the entire sentence, as in (15), or to the open sentence that contains the predicate, as in (16):

(15) $\neg$[every$_1$ farmer x_1]$_1$ (happy x_1)

(16) [every$_1$ farmer x_1]$_1 \neg$ (happy x_1).

Quantifications on nonsubject positions and multiple quantifications can also be represented in RQ. For instance, the alleged scope ambiguity in

(17) Every farmer milked some cows

is captured as follows:

(17$_1$) [every$_1$ farmer x_1]$_1$ ([some$_2$ cows x_2]$_2$(x_1 milked x_2))

(17$_2$) [some$_2$ cows x_2]$_2$ ([every$_1$ farmer x_1]$_1$ (x_1 milked x_2)).[7]

In (17$_1$) and (17$_2$) a quantifier combines with an open sentence that is itself the product of combining a quantifier with an open sentence.

Before hooking all of this up with surface syntax, I want to bring definite descriptions back into the picture and also highlight some important points about Russell's conception of incomplete symbols more generally, especially in connection with the notion of logical form.

3 Formal Properties of the Theory of Descriptions

According to the Theory of Descriptions, the truth conditions of a simple sentence of the form ⌜the F is G⌝ are given by (18):

(18) $(\exists x_1)((\forall x_2)(Fx_2 \equiv x_2 = x_1) \ \& \ Gx_1)$.

As I said at the outset, I am not going to consider objections to the truth-conditional deliverances of the theory. Rather, I want to consider objections to, and issues raised by, what we might call its *formal* properties. For even among those who profess allegiance to the theory's truth-conditional content, there is sometimes resistance to (i) the idea that (18) reveals the logical form of ⌜the F is G⌝, (ii) the idea that descriptions may take various "scopes," and (iii) the idea that descriptions are "incomplete symbols." In my view, such resistance is based on either a failure to separate the essential from the inessential formal features of the theory or else a failure to grasp the nature of the connection between logical form and semantics.

In *Principia Mathematica*, a definite description ⌜the F⌝ is represented by a term of the form $(\iota x_1)(Fx_1)$, which might be read as "the unique x_1 satisfying (Fx_1)." On the face of it, then, the *iota*-operator is a variable-binding operator for creating terms from formulae: a simple one-place predicate symbol G may be prefixed to a description $(\iota x_1)(Fx_1)$ to form a formula $G(\iota x_1)(Fx_1)$. For Russell, descriptions were really just abbreviatory devices that enabled him to simplify his formulae and shorten his proofs: $G(\iota x_1)(Fx_1)$ is ultimately to be understood as (18) above.

On the face of it, complications seem to arise because of matters of scope. The formula (19)

(19) $\neg G(\iota x_1)(Fx_1)$

is ambiguous as there is not, on Russell's account, a unique formula for which it is an abbreviation:

(19₁) $\neg(\exists x_1)((\forall x_2)(Fx_2 \equiv x_2 = x_1)\ \&\ Gx_1)$

(19₂) $(\exists x_1)((\forall x_2)(Fx_2 \equiv x_2 = x_1)\ \&\ \neg Gx_1)$.

When working with the *iota* notation, Whitehead and Russell adopt an awkward device for representing what they call the "scope" of a description. In effect, the description is recopied within square brackets and placed immediately to the left of the formula that constitutes its scope. Thus (19₁) and (19₂) are represented as (19₃) and (19₄) respectively:

(19₃) $\neg[(\iota x_1)(Fx_1)]G(\iota x_1)(Fx_1)$

(19₄) $[(\iota x_1)(Fx_1)]\neg G(\iota x_1)(Fx_1)$.

In (19₄) the description has a "primary occurrence" by virtue of having scope over the negation; in (19₃) the description has a "secondary occurrence" by virtue of lying within the scope of the negation.

The main proposition of the Theory of Descriptions is *Principia Mathematica* *14.01:

$$[(\imath x_k)(Fx_k)]G(\imath x_k)(Fx_k) =_{df} (\exists x_i)((\forall x_k)(Fx_k \equiv x_k = x_i) \; \& \; Gx_i) \qquad *14.01$$

By successive applications of *14.01 and *14.02

$$E!(\imath x)(Fx_k) =_{df} (\exists x_i)((\forall x_k)(Fx_k \equiv x_k = x_i)) \qquad *14.02$$

any well-formed formula containing a definite description (regardless of the complexity of the predicate G) can be replaced by an equivalent formula that is description-free. It is clear then, that adding the definite description operator to an ordinary first-order language does not add to its expressive power.

I want now to state four claims about the formal properties of the Theory of Descriptions, each of which seems to me to do some sort of injustice to the theory as a whole, and each of which ought to be countered if we are to incorporate Russell's insights into a semantical theory that assigns a central rôle to logical form in the way I have suggested.

1. Russell's theory cannot play a rôle in a serious compositional semantics because the "logical forms" it delivers bear so little relation to surface syntax or to what we now know about syntactical structure in the light of developments in generative grammar.[8]

2. Attempts to provide theories that deliver improved "logical forms" in which descriptions are treated as "logical units" or "semantical units" must involve fundamental departures from Russell's theory, because on Russell's account descriptions are "incomplete symbols" that "disappear on analysis."[9]

3. Whitehead and Russell's notion of the *scope* of a description has no formal analogue in natural language; and besides, any theory of logical form that contains the resources necessary to represent descriptions as taking various scopes will have an *ad hoc* character.[10]

4. The existence of complex definite descriptions that contain as proper parts quantified noun phrases upon which subsequent pronouns are anaphoric (as in "the farmer who bought a brown cow vaccinated her") demonstrates conclusively that descriptions in natural language cannot be treated as logical or semantical units.[11]

By way of developing the account of logical form proposed in the previous section, I hope to show that each of these claims is fundamentally mistaken, and thereby demonstrate that there is no formal obstacle to incorporating Russell's insights into such a theory.

4 Logical Subjects and Incomplete Symbols

For Russell, a referring expression R may be combined with a predicate phrase to express a proposition that simply could not be entertained or expressed if the entity referred to by R did not exist. In places, Russell puts this point by saying that the referent of R is a *constituent* of such a proposition, but no substantive point will turn on this particular conception of a so-called *singular* (or *object-dependent*) proposition in what follows.

A sentence consisting of a definite description ⌜the F⌝ combined with a predicate phrase does not express a singular proposition; it expresses a *general* (or *object-independent*) proposition, a proposition that is not *about* a specific entity, in the sense that the existence of the proposition is not contingent upon the existence of the entity which in fact satisfies the predicate F (if anything does).

I am going to belabor this point because many people who appeal to (or at least claim to endorse) the Theory of Descriptions seem not to appreciate it. If one does not see that on Russell's account ⌜the F is G⌝ expresses a general proposition, that ⌜the F⌝ does not refer, one simply does not understand the theory.

Just as one can grasp the proposition expressed by (or the truth conditions of) an utterance of a sentence of the form ⌜every F is G⌝ or ⌜no F is G⌝ without knowing who or what satisfies the predicate F (if anything does), so one can perfectly well grasp the proposition expressed by an utterance of a sentence of the form ⌜the F is G⌝ without knowing who or what satisfies the predicate F (if anything does). That is, one can perfectly well understand or grasp the proposition expressed without knowing who or what answers to the description ⌜the F⌝, indeed independently of whether or not anything actually answers to ⌜the F⌝. And to this extent, it makes no sense to say that the existence of the proposition depends upon the identity of the "denotation" of ⌜the F⌝; so the proposition expressed is not singular, not object-dependent.

To say that the proposition expressed by a sentence S is singular is really just to say that the grammatical subject of S *stands for* an object and *contributes* that object to the proposition expressed by an utterance of S (or, if you prefer, contributes that object to a specification of the truth conditions of an utterance of S). To say that a sentence S expresses a *general* proposition is just to say that the grammatical subject of S is not the sort of expression that stands for an object and does not contribute an object to the proposition expressed by (or the truth conditions of) an utterance of S. This is the key to understanding Russell's position that phrases of the form ⌜every F⌝, ⌜some F⌝, and ⌜the F⌝ ("denoting phrases") are *incomplete* symbols. They are incomplete because they do not "stand for" or "directly represent" objects.[12] The proposition expressed by ⌜the F is G⌝ is the general proposition that there is one and only one F and everything that is F is also G. That is, the truth conditions of ⌜the F is G⌝ are given by the formula in (1), which contains quantifiers and predicates but no singular term corresponding to the grammatical subject of ⌜the F is G⌝. And this is what Russell means by saying that the *proposition* has no *logical subject*, even though the *sentence* has a *grammatical subject*; and what he means by saying that the sentence's *grammatical form* is not a good indication of its *logical form* (or the logical form of the proposition the sentence expresses). The proposition is not about an object at all; it is about the relationship between two properties, F-ness and G-ness: exactly one thing has F-ness, and nothing has F-ness while lacking G-ness. As we might put it, ⌜some F is G⌝ is true if and only if the SOME relation holds between F-ness and G-ness; and ⌜the F is G⌝ is true if and only if the THE relation holds between them.

Sometimes it is claimed that the Theory of Descriptions is too cumbersome and unfaithful to surface syntax to warrant a place in a serious compositional semantics. To represent the logical form of a sentence of the form "the king is happy" as

(20) $(\exists x_1)((\forall x_2)(Kx_2 \equiv x_2 = x_1) \ \& \ Hx_1)$.

is certainly to render obscure the relationship between surface syntax and "logical form." And of course the situation worsens when we turn to sentences containing more than one description. A sentence such as "The king married the countess" will come out as

(21) $(\exists x_1)(\exists x_3)((\forall x_2)(Kx_2 \equiv x_2 = x_1) \ \& \ (\forall x_4)(Cx_4 \equiv x_4 = x_3) \ \& \ Mx_1x_3)$.

But the formal language used in *Principia Mathematica* (or a notational variant thereof) plays no essential role in the Theory of Descriptions. If we wanted, we could translate (20) into RQ as (22):

(22) [some$_1$ Fx_1]$_1$ ([every$_2$ x_2]$_2$ $(x_2 = x_1 \ \& \ Gx_1)$).

To do this would *not* be to present an *alternative* to Russell's account of ⌜the F is G⌝; it would simply be to choose a different language in which to state it.

Clearly there is no need to use such an indirect method of implementing Russell's proposal. ⌜the F is G⌝ is true iff (i) all Fs are Gs and (ii) there is exactly one F. Since the word "the" is a one-place quantificational determiner just like "some," "every," "no," "most," etc., in RQ we can treat ⌜the$_k$⌝ as combining with a formula α to form a restricted quantifier ⌜[the$_k$ α]$_k$⌝.[13] On such an account, a sentence of the form ⌜the F is G⌝ will be represented as e.g.

(23) [the$_1$ Fx_1]$_1$ (Gx_1).

And Russell's insights are perfectly well captured by the following axiom for "the" (as it combines with singular complements):

(ix) s satisfies ⌜[the$_k$ α]$_k\beta$⌝ iff the sequence satisfying α and differing from s at most in the k-th position also satisfies β.

I have used a determiner "the" in the metalanguage so as to make (ix) congruent with the axioms for the other determiners. The right-hand side of (ix) is to be understood as equivalent to "there is exactly one sequence satisfying α and differing from s at most in the k-th position and every sequence satisfying α and differing from s at most in the k-th position also satisfies β."[14]

Plural descriptions are easily accommodated. Whereas ⌜the F is G⌝ is true iff every F is G and there is *exactly one F*, on its noncollective reading ⌜the Fs are Gs⌝ is true iff every F is G and there is *more than one F*.[15] We can therefore add the following axiom for "the" when it takes plural complements:

(x) s satisfies ⌜[the$_k$ α]$_k\beta$⌝ iff the sequences satisfying α and differing from s at most in the k-th position also satisfy β.

Again, I have used a determiner "the" in the metalanguage; the right-hand side of (x) is to be understood as equivalent to "there is more than one sequence satisfying α and differing from s at most in the k-th position, and every sequence satisfying α and differing from s at most in the k-th position also satisfies β."

It might be thought that by presenting a formal language in which descriptions are treated as restricted quantifiers, although I have succeeded in presenting an account of descriptions that might find a place within a general compositional semantics, I have achieved this only by presenting an account that is inconsistent with Russell's own account. For in RQ, definite descriptions are complete "logical units," but on Russell's account, as presented in *Principia Mathematica*, they are "incomplete symbols" that "disappear on analysis."

This is the position taken by Linsky in his review of *Descriptions*.[16] I do not think there is a legitimate complaint here. Before addressing the formal elements of Linsky's claim, I want to echo certain informal remarks I made in *Descriptions*. Although Russell did not have the resources of generalized quantifier theory at his disposal and although he had philosophical aims that went beyond semantics, it seems to me that the RQ account of descriptions is just Russell's theory stated in a way that allows us to see the relationship between surface syntax and logical form more clearly. By virtue of being Russellians about descriptions, we are not committed to the view that the only way to represent the logical form of a sentence S containing a description is to translate S into a formula of the language of *Principia Mathematica* (or a similar language). As far as explicating the logical structure of sentences containing descriptions is concerned, treating them as restricted quantifiers results not in a falling out with Russell but in an explanation of where the Theory of Descriptions fits into a more general theory of natural language quantification, a theory in which determiners like "every," "some," "all," "most," "a," "the," and so on, are treated as members of a unified syntactical and semantical category.

I turn now to the formal elements of Linsky's worry. Although Russell's theory is often put forward as the paradigm case of a theory that invokes a distinction between *grammatical form* and *logical form*, ironically there is a sense in which it preserves symmetry: the gap between grammatical form and logical form in the case of $\ulcorner$the F is $G\urcorner$ is no wider than it is in the case of $\ulcorner$every F is $G\urcorner$ or $\ulcorner$some F is $G\urcorner$ because "the" is of the same syntactical and semantical category as "every" and "some."[17] On this account, a description (or any other quantified noun phrase) is still an *incomplete* symbol: for Russell a *complete* symbol stands for some entity and contributes that entity to the propositions expressed by (or to specifications of the truth conditions of) utterances of sentences containing that symbol. And of course quantified noun phrases do not do this, *not even in RQ*. In fact, this is reflected in both the syntax and semantics of RQ. The formula β with which a description $\ulcorner$[the$_k$ α]$_k\urcorner$ combines to form a formula will contain a variable $\ulcorner x_k \urcorner$. Consider (24):

(24) [the$_1$ king x_1]$_1$ (x_1 likes Russell).

The variable "x_1" occupies the "subject position" of the formula "(x_1

likes Russell)" and, so to speak, marks the position upon which the quantifier operates, the position that, in effect, represents the spot the quantifier occupies in surface syntax. Since "Russell" stands for an object (the same object, whatever the sequence) it is a complete symbol:

(i) Ref("Russell," s) = Russell.

Now perhaps there is a sense in which the *variable* in (24) might be thought of as *complete-with-respect-to-a-sequence* by virtue of standing for an object in its own relativized way:

(ii) Ref($\ulcorner x_k \urcorner, s$) = s_k.

But however you look at it, the quantifier "[the$_1$ king x_1]$_1$" that binds the variable is an incomplete symbol. It doesn't even purport to stand for an object, not even when relativized to a sequence. There is no sense, then, in which the RQ account of descriptions conflicts with Russell's conception of descriptions as incomplete symbols.[18] It is the element of quantification in $\ulcorner$the F is $G\urcorner$, $\ulcorner$every F is $G\urcorner$, and $\ulcorner$some F is $G\urcorner$ that creates a gap between grammatical form and so-called logical form. The next step is to see how we can reduce, or at least systematize, even that gap.

5 Logical Form and Grammatical Form

We have now a formal language in which quantified noun phrases are treated as restricted quantifiers; but by the definition of logical form I took up earlier, we do not yet have a theory of the logical forms of sentences of English because we lack a mechanism capable of delivering formulae of RQ as the structures imposed on sentences of English in the course of providing a truth definition. We can make considerable headway here by appealing to Noam Chomsky's pioneering work on the syntax of natural language.[19] In the course of providing successively richer and more explanatory syntactical theories, Chomsky and others have explored the view that so-called "*wh*-phrases" like "which botanist," "whose party," and "who" are quasi-quantifiers that bind variables in the sentences in which they occur. Take (25):

(25) which country imprisoned Russell?

To anyone exposed to introductory logic, there is certainly an intuitive sense in which the "logical form" of (25) might be thought of as given by the quasi-English sentence (25$_1$):

(25_1) which country x is such that x imprisoned Russell?

On independent syntactical grounds that need not detain us here, Chomsky has argued that something very similar to the quantifier-variable structure in (25_1) is actually present in the syntactical structure of the English sentence (25). And out of this idea and detailed work on quantification and anaphora, there has emerged a level of syntactical representation called "LF" ("Logical Form") a level distinct from "surface structure" and "deep structure," but with some affinity to the conception of "deep structure" championed by Harman, Lakoff, McCawley, Ross and others in the late 1960s and early 1970s.[20]

LF is of interest to the theorist of logical form because it can be construed (and by some Chomskyans *is* construed) as the syntactical level at which scope assignments are made explicit and, consequently, the syntactical level relevant to semantical interpretation.[21] For concreteness, assume a three-tiered Chomskyan syntax comprising D(eep)-Structure, S(urface)-Structure, and LF, and take a sentence to be an ordered triple $\langle$DS, SS, LF$\rangle$ consisting of a D-Structure representation, an S-Structure representation, and an LF representation. A purported sentence is grammatical just in case it has a well-formed DS, SS, and LF. For the purposes of this paper, I shall be concerned only with the relationship between surface syntax and LF, so I will take the liberty of viewing a sentence as an ordered pair $\langle$SS, LF$\rangle$.[22]

A reasonable case can be made for the view that the distinction between S-Structure and LF provides an independently motivated way of capturing what Russell and Davidson are after when they appeal (in their own ways of course) to a distinction between *grammatical form* and *logical form*. Consider again (24), the RQ rendering of which is (24_1):

(24)   the king likes Russell

(24_1) [the$_1$ king x_1]$_1$ (x_1 likes Russell).

Something very close to (24_1) is the LF representation for (24).[23] S-Structure representations are mapped onto LF representations by an elementary syntactical operation sometimes known as "Quantifier Raising." With the aims of (a) focussing on the *phenomenon* rather than any rule of grammar, (b) avoiding any sort of commitment to particular implementations found in the literature, (c) allowing for the possibility of "lowering" as well as raising quantifiers, let us say that quantified NPs are *evacuated* rather than *raised* (they must be forced out of the matrix sentence at LF). The S-Structure (24_2) is mapped onto the LF representation (24_3) by the evacuation of 'the king':

(24_2) [s [NP the king]₁ [VP likes [NP Russell]₂]]

(24_3) [s [NP the king]₁ [s e_1 [VP likes [NP Russell]₂]]].

In tree notation:

(24_2)

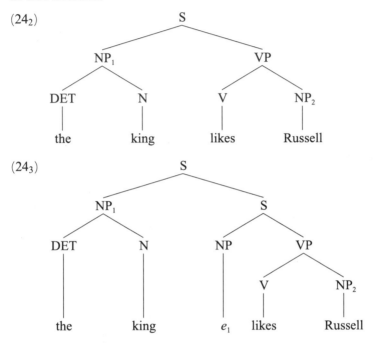

(24_3)

Here, the evacuation of the quantified NP creates an S node immediately dominating the original S node: at LF, the evacuated NP is an immediate constituent of the new S node and a sister to the original S node (to use some linguistics jargon, the quantified NP has been "Chomsky-adjoined" to the original S node). The trace "e_1" left by the evacuated quantifier functions as a variable bound by that quantifier. (In effect, then, quantified NP-evacuation might be viewed as the product of a "transformational" operation in the sense familiar from early generative grammar.[24])

How can the notion of LF in Chomsky's theory be of use to the philosopher or logician interested in logical form in the sense I advocated earlier? The answer to this question emerges if one reflects on the following points. (i) The semantic properties of a sentence are to some extent determined by its syntactical properties. (ii) If sentences have syntactical representations with the properties that LFs are supposed to possess, the vitally important semantical notion of the *scope* of an expression in natural language may well admit of a syntactical characterization: for the *scope* (in exactly the standard sense of Whitehead and Russell) of the evacuated quantifier can be identified with the S node to which it has been Chomsky-adjoined. (iii) The mapping from LF representations to sentences of RQ looks to be straightforward. (iv) RQ has many of the properties of a logically perfect language, and its truth definition is straightforward.

I suggest, then, that an independently motivated syntactical theory that delivers an S-Structure representation and an LF representation for each sentence of a fragment of a given language ought to be of considerable interest to philosophers and linguists who take the logical form of a sentence *S* belonging to a language *L* to be the structure imposed upon *S* in the course of providing a systematic and principled semantics for *L*. Arguably, we can make some serious progress by exploring the view that a fully worked out theory of LF will be a fully worked out theory of logical form.[25]

The relationship between (24_1) and (24_3) is transparent; and on the assumption that the objects of semantical interpretation are LFs rather than S-Structures, we can, in effect, use the truth definition for RQ as a truth definition for a quantified fragment of English. This idea becomes less offensive once more is said about scope and variable-binding. The scope of a quantified NP is just the S node to which it has been Chomsky-adjoined at LF; and this is really a consequence of a general characterization of scope that emerged from interactions in the late 1960s between linguists and philosophers interested in the relationship between "deep structure" and "logical form." In order to see this, we need to introduce a notion that has become a central component of syntactical theory through the work of (e.g.) Reinhart [1978]:

(A) An expression α c-commands an expression β if and only if the first branching node dominating α dominates β (and neither α nor β dominates the other).

Employing any of the usual sorts of formation rules and truth definitions, for the propositional calculus, the first-order predicate calculus, RQ, and standard modal extensions of each of these, we see straight away that an expression β is within the *scope* of an expression α iff α c-commands β. For example, The scope of a unary connective such as "¬" or "□" is just the wff it c-commands; the scope of a binary sentential connective such as "&" or "⊃" consists of the two wffs it c-commands; and the scope of a quantifier such as $\ulcorner(\forall x_k)\urcorner$, $\ulcorner[\text{the}_k \ \alpha]_k\urcorner$ or $\ulcorner[\text{some}_k \ \alpha]_k\urcorner$ is the wff it c-commands. This is a relatively trivial consequence of the way these languages are constructed and interpreted.

In the late 1960s and early 1970s, Bach, Harman, Lakoff, McCawley, and others suggested that the same is true of natural language; more precisely, they suggested that the scope of an expression in natural language is its c-command domain at the syntactical level relevant to semantical interpretation.[26] Thus we reach the following, which is in fact accepted by many linguists working within Chomsky's framework:

(B) The scope of an expression α is everything α c-commands at LF.

On the assumption that a trace $\ulcorner e_i \urcorner$ left by evacuation is understood as a variable and thereby falls under an instance of the axiom schema

(ii) $\text{Ref}(s, \ulcorner x_k \urcorner) = s_k$

we get exactly the right truth conditions for (24) as the occurrence of "e_1" in that sentence is bound by the evacuated description "$[\text{the}_1 \ \text{king}]_1$" by virtue of lying within its scope at LF.

For all intents and purposes, (24_1) and (24_3) can be viewed as notational variants. In a more developed theory, we would provide a truth definition for a fragment of English by modifying the axioms of the truth definition for RQ in such a way that it can be applied to LF representations directly. For today's purposes we can continue to use the truth definition for RQ, trading on the transparency of the relationship between an LF and the sentence of RQ with which it is associated. We have examined only one simple example, but in fact the aforementioned transparency is preserved even in considerably more complex cases. For our concerns, there is no harm, then, in using formulae of RQ to stand for LFs except where there is some specific syntactical reason for using LF representations.

The fact that certain pronouns anaphoric on quantified noun phrases appear to be understood as variables bound by those noun phrases, while others are not, is readily accommodated. For concreteness, let us say (provisionally) that

(C) An expression α is *anaphoric* on an expression β if and only if (i) the semantical value of α is determined, at least in part, by the semantical value of β, and (ii) β is not a constituent of α.

Where α is anaphoric on β, let's say (again, provisionally) that β is the *antecedent* of β.

Grammatical theory must provide an account of when a pronoun can be understood as anaphoric on some other NP (a name, a demonstrative, a restricted quantifier, another pronoun, or even a variable). In addition, for every sentence S containing a pronoun P that is understood as anaphoric on some other NP, semantical theory must provide an account of the contribution that P makes to the truth conditions of S. If the antecedent is a referring expression such as a name, it is plausible to suppose that the pronoun refers to the same thing as its antecedent and that this effectively answers any truth-conditional questions we might have about P.[27] The truth theory for RQ guarantees that a referring expression in a sentence S contributes just its bearer to a specification of the truth conditions of S. For example, the axiom

(i) Ref("Russell," s) = Russell

guarantees that "Russell" contributes Russell to a specification of the truth conditions of a sentence containing "Russell."[28] And it seems reasonable to suppose that a pronoun anaphoric on "Russell" should do likewise.

There are several ways one might proceed here and I pick one more or less at random. Consider (26) on the reading upon which "she" is understood as anaphoric on "Dora":[29]

(26) $Dora_2$ respects the man she_2 married.

As is customary, I have indicated the anaphoric connection by "coindexing" the NPs "Dora" and "she," i.e. by giving them matching numerical subscripts. Coindexing noun phrases in this way is more than just a way of indicating anaphoric connections to other linguists. Indices are ordinarily taken to be parts of syntax that are semantically relevant. If α is anaphoric on β then α is coindexed with β. But it would be wrong to equate "α is coindexed with β" and "α is anaphoric on β": (i) *being coindexed with* is a symmetric relation whereas *being anaphoric on* is an asymmetric relation; (ii) *being coindexed with* is syntactical relation whereas *being anaphoric on* is a semantical relation.

For concreteness, let us say (provisionally) that

(D) A pronoun $\ulcorner P_k \urcorner$ that is anaphoric on a referring expression $\ulcorner R_k \urcorner$ is understood as $\ulcorner R_k \urcorner$.

The net result of this is that the LF (26_1) will be understood as (26_2):

(26_1) [the man she_2 married]$_1$ [$_S$ $Dora_2$ respects e_1]

(26_2) [the$_1$ man x_1 & $Dora_2$ married x_1]$_1$ ($Dora_2$ respects x_1).

Probably something like this is tacitly assumed by many linguists (though there are, of course, other ways one might proceed that may ultimately turn out to be technically superior).

When it comes to pronouns anaphoric on quantified noun phrases, matters are more complex. Coindexing the pronoun with its antecedent so as to indicate an anaphoric connection is a start; but then we need to know which axiom of the truth definition to apply to the pronoun. Consider the following:[30]

(27) [some philosophers]$_2$ like [students who argue with them$_2$]$_3$

(28) [the president]$_1$ loves [the woman he$_1$ married]$_4$

(29) [most linguists]$_1$ admire [their$_1$ cousins]$_2$

It will not do to see the pronouns in these examples as subject to the same axioms as their antecedents. (For example, (27) simply does not have the same truth conditions as "some philosophers like students who argue with some philosophers.") As Geach and Quine have emphasized, the right truth conditions will be forthcoming for sentences such as (27) and (28) if the pronouns are understood as bound variables in the manner familiar from first-order logic. It is a simple matter to adapt this suggestion to suit the present discussion, and thereby provide the means of handling sentence (29) as well. For example, the truth conditions of (28) are given by the following sentence of RQ:

(28$_1$) [the$_2$ president x_2]$_2$ ([the$_1$ woman x_1 & x_2 married x_1]$_1$ (x_2 loves x_1)).

This suggests that we treat "he$_2$" exactly as we would treat an occurrence of a trace "e_2," i.e., as an occurrence of the variable "x_2." The pronoun will then be subject to an instance of axiom schema (ii).

In general, then, we might (provisionally) accept the following:

(E) When a pronoun $\ulcorner P_k \urcorner$ is anaphoric on a c-commanding quantifier $\ulcorner [D_k \ \alpha]_k \urcorner$, the axiom for $\ulcorner x_k \urcorner$ applies to $\ulcorner P_k \urcorner$.

The net result of all this is that such a pronoun will be understood as a bound variable.[31]

Given the usual assumptions of standard logics, it makes no sense of course to talk of a quantifier binding a variable that is not within its scope (its c-command domain). And on the assumption that the scope of an expression in natural language is to be characterized in exactly the same way as the scope of an expression in a standard logic, it will make no sense to talk of a quantified noun phrase binding a pronoun that it does not c-command (at LF). To say all this is not, of course, to deny that a pronoun *P* may be *anaphoric on* a quantifier *Q* that does not c-command it at LF; it is just to deny that in such a case *P* is *bound by Q*, and to maintain that some other account is needed of the semantics of *P*.

Before looking at a possible semantics for pronouns anaphoric on quantifiers that do not c-command them at LF, it is necessary to examine an important feature of natural language that the LF proposal seems to handle very effectively: the possibility of so-called ambiguities of scope. This will put us into position for a discussion of the fact that the members of a syntactically specifiable class of pronouns must be allowed to enter into scope interactions with quantifiers and other sentential operators, a fact that is itself explicable on the assumption (for which there is independent evidence) that the pronouns in question are understood as Russellian descriptions.

6 Truth Conditions and Scope Permutations

I turn now to a philosophically important feature of natural language that the LF proposal may help to illuminate: the matter of ambiguity involving quantifier scope. It is a commonplace of philosophy and linguistics that many sentences containing two or more quantifiers admit of distinct readings, i.e. readings with distinct truth conditions. Typically, the readings in question are captured in terms of relative scope; thus (30) is given the readings (30_1) and (30_2):

(30)   Every poet respects some sculptor

(30_1) [every$_1$ poet x_1]$_1$ ([some$_2$ sculptor x_2]$_2$ (x_1 respects x_2))

(30_2) [some$_2$ sculptor x_2]$_2$ ([every$_1$ poet x_1]$_1$ (x_1 respects x_2)).

By the truth definition for RQ, (30_1) and (30_2) are not equivalent; this suggests very strongly that if we want to pursue the idea that LF representations are representations of the logical forms of sentences in the sense given earlier, we need to associate two distinct LFs with the surface string (30), one corresponding to (30_1) the other to (30_2):

(30_3) [$_S$ [every poet]$_1$ [$_S$ [some sculptor]$_2$ [$_S$ e_1 respects e_2]]]

(30_4) [$_S$ [some sculptor]$_2$ [$_S$ [every poet]$_1$ [$_S$ e_1 respects e_2]]].

If the identity of a sentence is determined by an S-Structure representation and an LF representation (and also a D-Structure representation, irrelevant for immediate concerns), rather than saying that (30) is an ambiguous sentence, really we should say that (30) is the surface representation of two distinct sentences—viz. $\langle(30), (30_3)\rangle$ and $\langle(30), (30_4)\rangle$—that share an S-Structure representation and in fact look and sound alike (for convenience we might still want to say, loosely of course, that the "string" (30) is ambiguous).[32]

There are several ways one might structure the theory in order to obtain (30_3) and (30_4) as two distinct LF representations for the string (30). For reasons that will emerge, I suggest we view evacuation as the Chomsky-adjunction of any quantified NP in an argument position to any superior S-node. Evacuation is a phenomenon rather than a rule of grammar; it is the product of two very natural constraints on the well-formedness of representations at the syntactical level relevant to semantical interpretation, viz. LF: (i) only referential NPs (e.g., names, variables, and NPs anaphoric on referential NPs) may occupy argument positions; (ii) no variables may remain free. I will say more about these conditions later; for immediate purposes it will be enough to note that one consequence of such constraints is that every quantified NP will vacate its S-Structure position for a position that c-commands the "original" position at LF. On this account, we can derive (30_4) in one of two ways. (i) A first evacuation results in the adjunction of "every poet" to the S node of the original S-Structure representation to produce the "intermediate" representation (30_5):

(30_5) [s [every poet]₁ [s e_1 respects [some sculptor]₂]].

A second evacuation adjoins "some sculptor" to the higher S node of (30_5) to produce the LF representation (30_4). (ii) Alternatively, a first evacuation adjoins "some sculptor" to the S node of the original S-Structure representation to produce the intermediate representation (30_6):

(30_6) [s [some sculptor]₂ [s [every poet]₁ respects e_2]].

And a second evacuation results in the adjunction of "every poet" to the *lower* S node of the intermediate representation (30_6) to produce the LF representation (30_4).

A general point about redundancy should be taken up here. I am assuming that exactly one quantifier is evacuated at a time. For any sentence $\langle SS, LF \rangle$, let us say that the sentence has one or more *LF Histories*: an LF History is a sequence of representations $\langle R_1, \ldots, R_n \rangle$, where R_1 is

SS, R_n (for $n > 1$) is LF, and each R_k results from R_{k-1} after at most one evacuation. Let us now say that for any $k > 1$, a representation R_k in an LF History is a *candidate-LF* representation. Finally, let us say that if a candidate-LF representation satisfies the conditions on well-formedness for LF representations, it is an LF representation (we can now eliminate talk of "intermediate" representations).

The sentence $\langle(30),(30_4)\rangle$ has two distinct LF Histories: $\langle(30),(30_5),$ $(30_4)\rangle$ and $\langle(30),(30_6),(30_4)\rangle$. (Similarly, $\langle(30),(30_3)\rangle$ has two distinct LF Histories.) It might be thought that the theory ought to be tightened up so as to eliminate unnecessary redundancy. That is, it might be suggested that a sentence $\langle$SS, LF$\rangle$ should have *exactly one* LF History, and that a theory with this desirable consequence will result if evacuated quantified NPs adjoin only to the *topmost* S node of the relevant representation. Whatever the aesthetic merits of such a proposal, it is known to be empirically deficient. The following strings containing verbs of propositional attitude make the point very clearly:

(31) Bill thinks that someone downstairs is following him

(32) Bill thinks that the person upstairs is ignoring him.

Each of these strings is ambiguous between a *de re* and a *de dicto* reading. Following Russell, it is usual to account for this ambiguity in terms of the scopes of the quantified NPs ("someone upstairs" and "the person upstairs," respectively). Take (32). This is ambiguous between (32_1) and (32_2):

(32_1) Bill$_2$ thinks that [the$_1$ person upstairs x_1]$_1$ (x_1 is ignoring him$_2$))

(32_2) [the$_1$ person upstairs x_1]$_1$ (Bill$_2$ thinks that (x_1 is ignoring him$_2$)).[33]

While the LF associated with (32_2) can be derived from S-Structure by Chomsky-adjoining the quantifier to the higher S node, in order to derive the LF associated with (32_1) the quantifier adjoins to the *lower* S node. To my mind this demonstrates conclusively that if we are to follow Russell in capturing *de re–de dicto* ambiguities in terms of scope permutations (and I think we must), an adequate theory of LF, as currently understood, must allow evacuated quantified NPs to adjoin to S nodes other than the topmost S node. (There are also examples involving anaphora that demonstrate the same point (see below), but I do not want to rely on facts involving anaphora before saying something about the topic more generally).[34] For the present, then, I shall maintain that evacuated quantified NPs may adjoin to any superior S node.[35]

The original motivation in logic for wanting to allow quantifier per-mutation within a "sentence" was of course the desire to capture readings with distinct truth conditions. But as is well known, permuting quantifiers does not always result in a difference in truth conditions. For example, the truth conditions of

(33) Every poet respects every sculptor

(34) Some poet respects some sculptor.

Of course, the version of the LF theory I am advocating declares that each of (33) and (34) is the surface manifestation of two distinct but logi-cally equivalent sentences. This might strike some people as introducing yet another unnecessary redundancy; but again I think this is illusory. First, as theorists we should be striving after the most general and aes-thetically satisfying theory, and the fact that no truth-conditional differ-ences result from scope permutations in *some* simple sentences is of no great importance by itself. It should be noted that, contrary to what some people have claimed, in order to produce such examples, it is not neces-sary to use the same determiner twice. In effect, this was pointed out in *Principia Mathematica* by Whitehead and Russell when they emphasized that scope interactions involving definite descriptions and some other quantifiers are truth-conditionally inert. For example, (35) is the surface form of two distinct, but logically equivalent sentences, the LFs of which are (35_1) and (35_2):

(35) The king owns a bicycle

(35_1) [the$_1$ king x_1]$_1$ ([a$_2$ bicycle x_2]$_2$ (x_1 owns x_2))

(35_2) [a$_2$ bicycle x_2]$_2$ ([the$_1$ king x_1]$_1$ (x_1 owns x_2)).

Similarly for (36):

(36) Every knight talked to the king.

The moral that emerges, then, from reflecting on examples like (33)–(36) is that they reinforce the working assumption that a theory of logical form is rather more than a theory that associates a sentence of a well-behaved formal language with each sentence of a natural language. If the best syntax and semantics we have both say (or jointly entail) that there are two distinct logical forms associated with some particular string, then it would be absurd to claim that the string in question is not the surface form of two distinct sentences just because the two purported LFs are logically equivalent. My point here is not the familiar point that truth conditions are not fine-grained enough to serve as propositions or meanings. This matter is irrelevant to the point at hand—but notice that although, say, (35_1) and (35_2) are truth-conditionally equivalent, the axioms of the truth definition will apply in a different order, and to that extent there may still be room for the truth-conditional semanticist to say that the sentences differ *semantically*. My point is much simpler. We all accept that the string "Visiting professors can be a nuisance" is the surface manifestation of two distinct sentences with distinct truth conditions, and we don't mind saying this even though the two sentences are written and sound alike. Equally, we all accept that "Bill sold Mary a car" and "Mary bought a car from Bill" are the surface manifestations of two distinct sentences with the same truth conditions. So neither the "surface sameness" of two purported sentences nor the "truth-conditional sameness" of two purported sentences is sufficient to demonstrate that a single sentence is actually under scrutiny. And as far as I can see, there is no compelling reason to think that the combination of surface sameness and truth-conditional sameness demonstrates this either. So there is no compelling reason to reject the view that each of (33)–(36) is the surface manifestation of a pair of sentences. At times we must let the theory decide. If the best syntax and semantics we have say there are two distinct sentences corresponding to a single string, so be it.

In response to all this, it might be countered that the absence of a difference in truth conditions for (35_1) and (35_2) lends support to the view that descriptions are *not* ordinary quantified NPs that admit of various scope assignments.[36] However, there is plenty of evidence against this approach, much of which involves truth-conditionally active scope permutations. For example, as Russell observed, scope matters in (32) just as much as it does in (31). And as Russell also pointed out, even within the relative safety of extensional constructions, the scope of a description is important. Russell makes the point with the sentence "the king of France is not bald," which he claims has two readings according as the description or the negation has larger scope. Within the framework we have in place, we can bolster Russell's point by considering sentences containing a description together with a quantifier that is monotone decreasing:[37]

(37) Few women have met the king of France.

For present concerns, the importance of the various examples we have been considering is that they suggest very strongly that an adequate semantics for English must treat descriptions as quantified noun phrases with various scope possibilities, exactly as Russell claimed. (Russell's "The king of France is not bald" might also be taken to show that something very similar to evacuation results in the Chomsky-adjunction of "not" to an S node.[38] Indeed, if this were not the case, the LF theorist might have a hard time explaining the purported ambiguity.)

7 Pronouns and Incomplete Symbols

In order for a variable to be bound by a quantified noun phrase, the latter must c-command the former at LF.[39] So the following question naturally arises: can a pronoun be anaphoric on a quantified noun phrase that does not c-command it at LF, and if so how is such a pronoun understood? Russell's Theory of Descriptions is highly relevant to many of the issues raised by these questions. First, it seems to be the case that some pronouns are understood as descriptions; second, it is arguable that the pronouns in question are anaphoric on quantified noun phrases that do not c-command them at LF. Third, it has been claimed by Evans [1977, 1982] that the possibility of such anaphoric connections provides conclusive evidence for the view that definite descriptions are not "logical units."

Consider the following examples:

(38) Russell bought [some hens]$_1$ and Whitehead vaccinated them$_1$

(39) [Just one man]$_1$ drank rum and he$_1$ was ill afterward.

As pointed out by Evans [1977], the pronouns in these examples cannot be understood as variables bound by the quantifiers upon which they are anaphoric. If "them" in (38) were treated as a variable bound by "some hens," the quantifier would have to be understood as taking scope over the sentential connective "and," and so the truth conditions of (38) would be given by (38_1):

(38_1) [some$_1$ hens x_1]$_1$ (Russell bought x_1 and Whitehead vaccinated x_1).

But (38_1) captures the truth conditions of "Russell bought some hens that Whitehead vaccinated" not the truth conditions of (38). Suppose Russell bought twelve hens and Whitehead vaccinated only three of them. In such a situation, (38_1) is true but (38) is false.

Similarly, there would be trouble ahead if we attempted to treat the pronoun "he" in (39) as a variable bound by "just one man." We would have to understand the quantifier as taking scope over "and," and so the truth conditions of (39) would be given by (39_1):

(39_1) [just one$_1$ man x_1] (x_1 drank rum and x_1 was ill afterwards).

While (39_1) seems to capture the truth conditions of "Just one man drank rum and was ill afterward," it certainly does not capture the truth conditions of (39). Suppose two men drank rum and only one was ill afterward. In such a situation (39_1) is true but (39) is false.[40]

Interestingly, the most promising approach to such pronouns is Russellian in character: such pronouns are *quantificational* by virtue of being equivalent to definite descriptions.[41] The singular pronoun "he" in (39) seems to be understood as the singular description "the man who drank rum"; and the plural pronoun "them" in (38) seems to be understood as the plural description "the hens Russell bought." That is, (38) and (39) seem to be understood as meaning what is meant by (38_2) and (39_2) respectively:

(38_3) Russell bought some hens and Whitehead vaccinated the hens Russell bought

(39_3) Just one man drank rum and the man who drank rum was ill afterward.

These results appear to be forthcoming on the Evans-inspired theory I presented in *Descriptions*, according to which a pronoun P that is anaphoric on a quantifier Q that does not c-command P at LF is understood as a definite description typically recovered from Q and everything Q c-commands at LF. Adapting that idea to the present discussion, we get the following:

(F) If a pronoun $\ulcorner P_k \urcorner$ is anaphoric on but not within the scope β of a quantified NP of the form $\ulcorner [D_k \ \alpha]_k \urcorner$ then $\ulcorner P_k \urcorner$ is understood as $\ulcorner [\text{the}_k \ \alpha \ \& \ \beta]_k \urcorner$.[42]

An example will help fix ideas. The logical form of the first conjunct of (39) is

(39_4) [just one$_1$ man x_1]$_1$ (x_1 drank rum).

Since the pronoun "he$_1$" in the second conjunct is not c-commanded by "just one man" at LF, by (F), the pronoun will be understood as

(39_5) [the$_1$ man x_1 & x_1 drank rum]$_1$.

And so (39) as a whole will be understood as

(39_6) [just one$_1$ man x_1]$_1$ (x_1 drank rum) &
[the$_1$ man x_1 & x_1 drank rum]$_1$ (x_1 was ill afterward).

Analogously, (38) will be understood as

(38_4) [some$_1$ hens x_1]$_1$ (Russell bought x_1) &
[the$_1$ hens x_1 & Russell bought x_1]$_1$ (Whitehead vaccinated x_1).

And (40), in which the pronoun's antecedent is a *wh*-phrase (interrogative quantifier), will be understood as (40_1):

(40)   [which hen]$_1$ died and which philosopher vaccinated her$_1$?

(40_1) [which$_1$ hen x_1]$_1$ (x_1 died) & [which$_2$ philosopher x_2]$_2$
([the$_1$ hen x_1 & x_1 died]$_1$ (x_2 vaccinated x_1)).

Any pronoun that is understood as equivalent to a definite description we can call a *D-type* pronoun.[43]

The semanticist who endorses a D-type account of pronouns anaphoric on quantified NPs that do not c-command them at LF looks to be in a very attractive position. In conjunction with the axioms for the various determiners, the axiom schema for variables provides a plausible semantics for pronouns anaphoric on c-commanding quantifiers. And in conjunction with Principle (F), the axioms for "the" seem to provide a plausible semantics for pronouns anaphoric on non-c-commanding quantifiers.[44]

The range of a theory of unbound anaphora can be seen by returning to the matters of quantifier scope and incomplete symbols. On the assumption that (F) is a correct generalization, in addition to the pronouns in (38)–(40), the indexed pronouns in each of the following examples will be understood as definite descriptions:[45]

(41)   [A man]$_1$ has murdered Smith. The police have reason to think he$_1$ injured himself in the process

(42)   Next year [a man from Texas]$_1$ will be in charge of the economy and I'm sure he$_1$'ll help the oil business.[46]

If D-type pronouns are understood as descriptions, one might expect the clauses containing the pronouns in (41) and (42) to exhibit scope ambiguities of the sort found with overt descriptions; and indeed this seems to be the case. For example, there is a perfectly natural reading of (41) upon which both "a man" and "he (the man who murdered Smith)" are understood with large scope, and there is also a perfectly natural reading upon which they are both understood with small scope (mixed readings are much less natural, but not impossible). The main point is that there are pronouns for which matters of scope are important.

We are now in a position to remark on claims made by Gareth Evans about Russell's idea of descriptions as incomplete symbols and about the correct way to capture the anaphoric relations between pronouns and incomplete symbols. As is well-known, there is an alternative to the view that quantified noun phrases in natural language are restricted quantifiers. According to the alternative proposal, determiners are *binary quantifiers* (rather than unary quantifier-formers). That is, a determiner combines with a pair of formulae to form a formula (the quantifier is "binary" not in the sense that it simultaneously binds two distinct variables, but in the sense that it combines with two formulae).[47] On this account, the logical form of (43) might be given by (43_1), which corresponds to (43_2) in RQ:

(43)   The farmer bought Daisy

(43_1) [the]$_1$ (farmer x_1; x_1 bought Daisy)

(43_2) [the$_1$ farmer x_1]$_1$ (x_1 bought Daisy)

where the semi-colon in (43_1) is just a syntactical device for separating the two formulae with which the quantifier "[the]$_1$" combines. Again, it is a routine matter to specify a syntax, characterize variable-binding and scope, and provide the relevant axioms of a theory that defines truth in terms of satisfaction. Call the resulting system BQ. In place of principle (F), the BQ theorist will have something rather more complex—the "output" component will have to be stated in terms of the entire clause containing the pronoun—but still workable.[48]

As far as I can ascertain, RQ and BQ are equivalent in both expressive power and capacity to encode antecedent-anaphor relations. To begin with, sentences in which there is a description containing a restrictive relative clause can be represented in either system. Let us assume (counterfactually, but harmlessly for immediate concerns) that relative pronouns in restricted relative clauses are simple bound variables. Thus (44) can be represented as (44_1) in RQ or as (44_2) in BQ:

(44)   the farmer who bought Daisy is happy

(44_1) [the$_1$ farmer x_1 & x_1 bought Daisy]$_1$ (x_1 is happy)

(44_2) [the]$_1$ (farmer x_1 & x_1 bought Daisy; x_1 is happy).

Similarly, (45):

(45) the farmer whom Daisy kicked is unhappy

(45_1) [the$_1$ farmer x_1 & Daisy kicked x_1]$_1$ (x_1 is unhappy)

(45_2) [the]$_1$ (farmer x_1 & Daisy kicked x_1; x_1 is unhappy).[49]

However, according to Evans, there is a crucial difference between RQ and BQ. In (44_1) and (45_1), since the the descriptions are treated as restricted quantifiers they are treated, says Evans, as "logical units" whereas in the BQ renderings (44_2) and (45_2) they are not. Additionally, says Evans, once we take into account more complex sentences, we must abandon the view that descriptions are restricted quantifiers, indeed we will have to abandon RQ altogether in favor of BQ.

Evans appeals to cases of so-called donkey anaphora to make his point. Up to now, the examples of pronouns anaphoric on non-c-commanding quantified NPs we have examined have all been in structures of the form

[$_{S0}$ [$_{S1}$ ... Q ...] connective [$_{S2}$ ... P ...]]]

where the quantified NP Q is a constituent of S1 and the pronoun P is a constituent of S2. But, notoriously, there is at least one more type of structure in which it is possible to have a pronoun anaphoric on a non-c-commanding quantified NP.[50] Consider sentences like the following:

(46) [every farmer who bought [some cows]$_2$]$_1$ vaccinated them$_2$

(47) [most men who own [a car]$_2$]$_1$ wash it$_2$ on Sundays

(48) [the farmer who bought [a cow]$_2$]$_1$ vaccinated her$_2$

(49) [which farmer who bought [a donkey]$_2$]$_1$ paid cash for it$_2$?

The interesting fact about these sentences is that even if they admit of readings upon which the embedded quantified NPs ("some cows," "a car," "a cow," and "a donkey") have large scope, it is clear that they have perfectly natural readings upon which the NPs in question have small scope.[51] But upon such readings the pronouns cannot function as variables bound by their antecedents because they do not lie within their scopes (the pronouns are not c-commanded by the quantified NPs at LF). Take (46) and (48). If the pronouns "them" and "it" are construed as variables we would get the following logical forms:

(46_1) [every$_1$ farmer x_1 & [some$_2$ cows x_2]$_2$ (x_1 bought x_2)]$_1$ (x_1 vaccinated x_2)

(48_1) [the$_1$ farmer x_1 & [a$_2$ cow x_2]$_2$ (x_1 bought x_2)]$_1$ (x_1 vaccinated x_2).

But the final occurrences of "x_2" (corresponding to "them" in (46) and "her" in (48)) simply fail to be bound by their antecedents.

According to Evans, there is a problem here for RQ that is not shared by BQ, the upshot of which is that we will have to treat "every," "the," "which," "most" and other quantificational determiners as binary quantifiers in order to get the semantics to work out in any sentence exhibiting the sort of anaphoric connection exemplified in (46)–(49). Evans points out (correctly) that once we have distinguished clearly between bound and unbound/descriptive anaphora, we will see that the anaphoric pronouns in (46)–(49) are descriptive. But, in addition, he argues that it is not possible to evaluate (46)–(49) if the pronouns are treated descriptively and the subject NPs are treated as the sorts of "logical units" that RQ requires. And so, Evans concludes, quantified noun phrases are not restricted quantifiers.

With respect to (48), Evans sees his conclusion as supporting Russell's view that descriptions are incomplete symbols:

> For the language fragment Russell studied, there is in fact no need to regard "The" even as a binary quantifier. We can think of "The" as an expression which takes a simple or complex one-place concept-expression ("man who broke the bank at Monte Carlo") to yield a unary quantifier ("the man who broke the bank at Monte Carlo").... This would make Russell wrong in his claim that "the ϕ" does not form a logical unit in "the ϕ is F." However, once again Russell has ultimately turned out to have been right, but for the wrong reasons. [1982, p. 59]

Russell has turned out to be right, Evans claims, because in sentences such as (46)–(49) "... the quantifier expression and the main concept-expression ... cannot be independently constructed" (ibid.).

For the details of the argument Evans refers the reader to his technical work on pronouns.[52] Fortunately, it is not necessary to go into the details of the argument to see that it must contain a flaw. There are two points to take up, one conceptual, the other technical. First, as pointed out in section 4, it is simply a mistake to think that the RQ treatment of the determiner "the" as what Evans calls a "unary quantifier-former" conflicts with Russell's view that descriptions are incomplete symbols. In both RQ and BQ descriptions do not stand for objects and are not logical subjects. In RQ a description is replaced by a restricted quantifier and a variable that, so to speak, occupies the position the description occupies in surface syntax. The fact that the *syntax* of a binary quantifier analysis "breaks up" descriptions still further does not make the binary analysis *more* Russellian. Descriptions are no less incomplete symbols in RQ than they are in BQ. Evans and Linsky are making the same mistake.

More important than this point of interpretation is the fact that Evans is wrong when he claims that the semantics of the anaphoric connections in (46)–(49) cannot be captured in RQ. Given the way I presented principles (E) and (F), there is no formal problem for the RQ theorist. According to principle (E), a pronoun anaphoric on a quantified noun phrase is a bound variable only if it is c-commanded by its antecedent at LF. But on the readings in question, the embedded quantifiers have small scope and this corresponds to the fact that (on these readings) the quantifiers evacuate only as far as the embedded S node (relative clause). By Principle (F), the pronouns receive D-type interpretations. Take (46). The quantifier $\ulcorner[D_k \ \alpha]_k\urcorner$ upon which "it" is anaphoric is "[some$_2$ cows x_2]$_2$"; and its scope is "(x_1 bought x_2)." Thus k is "2," α is "cow x_2" and β is "(x_1 bought x_2)." Consequently the description $\ulcorner[\text{the}_k \ \alpha \ \& \ \beta]_k\urcorner$ that the pronoun "it" is understood as is

(50) [the$_2$ cows x_2 & (x_1 bought x_2)]$_2$

which contains a free occurrence of "x_1." Thus (46) ought to be interpretable as either (46$_2$) or (46$_3$), according as the subject quantifier or the D-type pronoun has larger scope:

(46$_2$) [every$_1$ farmer x_1 & [some$_2$ cows x_2]$_2$ (x_1 bought x_2)]$_1$
([the$_2$ cows x_2 & (x_1 bought x_2)]$_2$ (x_1 vaccinated x_2))

(46$_3$) [the$_2$ cows x_2 & (x_1 bought x_2)]$_2$
([every$_1$ farmer x_1 & [some$_2$ cows x_2]$_2$ (x_1 bought x_2)]$_1$
(x_1 vaccinated x_2)).

(46$_3$) is useless because it contains a free occurrence of "x_1." But (46$_2$) is fine: it also represents the English sentence "[every farmer who bought some cows]$_1$ vaccinated [the cows he$_1$ bought]$_2$" on the reading in which the pronoun "he" is understood as a variable bound by the subject NP "every farmer who bought some cows," which c-commands the pronoun as required.

Similarly, (48) will come out as (48$_2$):

(48$_2$) [the$_1$ farmer x_1 & [a$_2$ cow x_2]$_2$ (x_1 bought x_2)]$_1$
([the$_2$ cow x_2 & x_1 bought x_2]$_2$ (x_1 vaccinated x_2))

again, exactly as required.[53]

To the extent that it is possible to reconstruct Evans' argument against RQ, it appears to presuppose that the descriptions in terms of which unbound anaphors are understood may never take small scope. But as we saw earlier, there is ample evidence that this is false.[54] The following sentence reinforces the point and also highlights the fact that ontological problems analogous to those that can be eradicated by paying attention to the logic of descriptions can be eradicated by paying attention to the logic of anaphora:

(51) Hob_1 thinks that [a witch]$_2$ killed Trigger. He_1 also suspects that she_2 blighted Daisy.

Surely there is a reading of (51) that can be true even if there are no witches. Suppose Hob thinks there are witches and has been led to believe that a witch killed Trigger. Suppose he is then led to believe that a witch blighted Daisy and that *one* witch is responsible for both acts. When the pronoun "she" is understood as the small scope description "the witch who killed Trigger," (51) correctly describes this situation. In short, Russell's insights concerning overt descriptions carry over to pronouns interpreted as descriptions, and again we are assured a sensible interpretation of a sentence containing a non-denoting expression without ontological inflation.

There would appear to be no reason, then, to dispute the claim that RQ and BQ have precisely the same expressive power and exactly the same capacity for encoding antecedent-anaphor relations. I have used RQ because its formulae tend to be easier to parse and because it allows us to view quantified noun phrases as the sorts of *syntactical* units utilized in the best theory of syntax available. If the logical form of a sentence is the structure imposed upon it in the course of providing a systematic semantics based on a systematic syntax, at the present time RQ seems to be exactly what we need. Moreover, the general framework allows us to incorporate Russell's insights about the semantics of definite and indefinite descriptions at no cost, thereby vindicating Russell as far as technical and aesthetic objections motivated by syntactical and semantical considerations are concerned. Russell cannot be blamed for not having the resources of generalized quantifier theory and generative syntax at his disposal at the beginning of the century; but he can still be commended for a truly insightful theory, some of the merits of which are only now emerging.

Acknowledgment

Thanks to Saul Kripke, Richard Larson, Bernard Linsky, Peter Ludlow, Mark Sainsbury, and Scott Soames for valuable discussion. Some of the issues discussed here are taken up in more detail in my "Logical Form and LF." There is considerable overlap in sections 2, 5, and 6.

Notes

1. Some linguists see themselves as addressing semantical considerations simply by virtue of providing a theory of the relationship between representations of surface syntax and representations in some quasi-logical formalism, a view that appears to be based on the assumption that theories of "logical form," "psychological form," or "conceptual representation" completely obviate the need to explicate the relationship between language and the world (see (e.g.) Hornstein [1984]). I shall not dwell on the difficulties inherent in such views here.

2. Davidson [1967], Harman [1972, 1975], Platts [1979], Wiggins [1980].

3. Davidson [1967, 1975], Harman [1972, 1975], Higginbotham [1983, 1987], Lycan [1984], Platts [1979], Wiggins [1980], Russell [1905].

4. Barwise [1979]; Barwise and Cooper [1981]; Evans [1977]; Heim [1988]; Hintikka [1974]; McCawley [1981]; Montague, Kalish, and Mar [1980]; Neale [1990a]; Wiggins [1980].

5. Rescher [1962], Kaplan [1966], and Barwise and Cooper [1981].

6. Barwise and Cooper [1981]; Higginbotham and May [1981]; Higginbotham [1987]; McCawley [1981]; May [1987]; Neale [1990].

7. Sometimes it is suggested that (17) is unambiguous. The thought behind this suggestion seems to be that since (17_2) entails (17_1), the weaker reading can be viewed as giving the truth conditions of (17); however, in some contexts the speaker seeks to convey something stronger than this, a fact, so the suggestion continues, than can be explained pragmatically by invoking Gricean principles and a distinction between what a speaker literally *says* and what he or she *means*. Like Grice, I think it is fruitful to pursue pragmatic explanations of alleged ambiguities wherever possible; but in the present example the case for a genuine truth-conditional, structurally determined ambiguity is overwhelming.

8. Thomason [1969].

9. Evans [1982]; Linsky [1992].

10. Hintikka [1989]; Hintikka and Kulas [1985]; Hintikka and Sandu [1991].

11. Evans [1977, 1982].

12. There is also a purely formal way of understanding "incomplete symbol." On my account, it is a consequence of the characterization just given (see below).

13. Grice [1969]; Barwise and Cooper [1981]; Higginbotham and May [1981]; Neale [1990].

14. In fact, (ix) itself can be simplified. However, questions about the syntax, semantics, and systematicity of the axioms (and the metalanguage in which they are stated) as well as questions about the distinction between semantics and analysis have a considerable bearing on the proper form of any truth definition that is to play a serious rôle in a semantical theory for natural language and also on the characterization of that rôle itself.

15. Chomsky [1975]; Evans [1977].

16. Linsky [1992].

17. As Saul Kripke has pointed out to me, Russell himself seems to be aware of this in the opening paragraph of "On Denoting."

18. There are also a number of problems in Linsky's discussions of (a) quantified modal statements, (b) the relationship between logical form and truth conditions, and (c) the relationship between logical form and the formalisms of a representational system. I plan to comment in detail at some point as I am bemused by some of Linsky's remarks, particularly some of those that appear to be favorable.

19. Chomsky [1975, 1977, 1980, 1981, 1986].

20. See, e.g., Harman [1972, 1975], Lakoff [1971, 1972], McCawley [1968, 1970, 1972], and Ross [1974].

21. Chomsky [1977, 1981, 1986]; Higginbotham [1980, 1983, 1987]; Higginbotham and May [1981].

22. As a matter of fact, I am not convinced there is a need for D-Structure. My own inclination is to see LF as the most basic level with surface structure representations just projections of LF representations (for a preliminary discussion, see Neale [1992]). Although I use the label "S-Structure," Chomsky has pointed out to me that ultimately what I have in mind is arguably better thought of as PF ("Phonetic Form").

23. Chomsky [1977, 1981, 1986]; Higginbotham [1980, 1983]; Higginbotham and May [1981]; May [1987].

24. In current versions of the Chomsky's Extended Standard Theory, it can be viewed as an instance (along with, e.g., *wh*-movement ("*wh*-evacuation")) of the more general schema "move α." For detailed discussion, see Chomsky [1981, 1986]. Arguably, quantified NPs may be adjoined to categories other than S, for example NP or VP. For the concerns of the present paper, it will do no harm to assume that quantified NPs adjoin only to S nodes.

25. It is sometimes claimed that theories of LF or logical form cannot be contributions to *semantics* because they are theories about representations and inferential relations rather than about the relationship between language and the world. However, it should be perfectly clear that anyone who (a) views a fully worked out theory of LF as a fully worked out theory of logical form and (b) takes the logical form of a sentence to be the structure imposed upon it in the course of providing a truth definition cannot be accused of failing to hook up language and the world. By saying this, I hope it is clear that I am distancing myself from certain ways of viewing LF that have appeared in the literature. For

the record, I wish to explicitly distance myself from the LF theory proposed by Hornstein [1984] and the account of definite descriptions proposed therein. For important work on LF in the tradition to which I see the present paper as belonging, see Higginbotham [1980, 1983, 1987], Higginbotham and May [1981], and May [1987]. Criticisms of some conceptions of LF can be found in Hintikka [1989] and Hintikka and Sandu [1991].

26. Bach [1968], Harman [1972], Lakoff [1971, 1972], McCawley [1968, 1970, 1972]. This principle is stated explicitly in Harman's paper, though he does not use the *term* "c-command," which is due to Reinhart. For Harman *et al.*, the level of linguistic representation relevant to semantical interpretation was Deep Structure, but a Deep Structure with much more affinity to LF than current D-Structure. The relevance of c-command to the interpretation of certain anaphoric pronouns as variables bound by quantified NPs was noticed by, *inter alia*, Evans [1977] and Reinhart [1978]. With the benefit of hindsight, it is clear that the relevance of the notion of c-command to bound pronouns is a trivial consequence of the truth of the Bach-Harman-Lakoff-McCawley Thesis.

27. Soames [1990] suggests that this may be too simplistic a picture.

28. I am suppressing the difficulties raised by occurrences of names in the referentially opaque contexts created by verbs of propositional attitude. Contrary to what some people have thought, modal contexts are not referentially opaque (see Neale [1990] ch 4), so I am suppressing no difficulty raised by names in modal contexts.

29. According to Lasnik [1976] pronouns refer to salient objects; the referent of "Dora" is one such object, and since Lasnik's rule of noncoreference does not preclude "Dora" and "she" from being coreferential in (18), one possible way of understanding the sentence has "she" referring to Dora. So on Lasnik's account we do not get grammatically specified anaphora here. Lasnik's theory is criticized by Evans [1980].

30. "The reader is asked to ignore (until the next section) the fact that in each of (27)–(29) the VP contains a quantificational NP. I am concerned at this point only with the anaphoric pronoun within the VP.

31. Example (28) reinforces the Russellian point that the scope of a description matters even in an extensional context: if "the woman he married" contains a pronoun bound by "the president" then the first must have larger scope. The matter of quantifier-quantifier scope is addressed in the next section.

32. Higginbotham [1987]. In principle, we might also find two sentences that differ in respect of S-Structure representation but not in respect of LF representation. Examples might be (i) and (ii), where each is construed as the sentence on which "someone" has small scope:

(i) Someone is certain to win the lottery
(ii) It is certain someone will win the lottery.

33. I hope this point is clear despite the fact that I make no attempt to provide the additional axioms necessary to provide a truth definition for an extension of RQ

containing verbs of propositional attitude. As is well known, there are tremendous philosophical and technical problems involved in attempting to provide such axioms. Sufficie to say they will have to comport with the fact that (12) is the surface manifestation of (at least) two sentences that do not entail one another. (For interesting proposals, see Davidson [1968] and Larson and Ludlow [1992].)

As pointed out by Smullyan [1948], the same sort of ambiguity is found in constructions containing modal operators and descriptions:

(i) The first person to climb Kilimanjaro might have been American
(ii) The number of planets is necessarily odd.

By comparison with attitude verbs, modal adverbs do not create very much difficulty when it comes to formulating axioms that bring them within the purview of a truth definition (see Peacocke [1978] and Davies [1981]). As pointed out by Kripke [1977], the ambiguities of scope in attitude and modal constructions predicted by Russell's theory cannot be replaced by some sort of ambiguity in the definite article

34. Other ways have been suggested for capturing such ambiguities but they have not met with much success. For discussion, see Kripke [1977], Neale [1990], and Ludlow and Neale [1991].

35. A question that naturally arises at this point is whether evacuated quantified NPs can adjoin only to S nodes. There may well be reasons for holding that evacuees may adjoin to *any* superior node (or any superior node of specified types (e.g. maximal projections), or any node at all). This is not a matter for *a priori* stipulation, it is a question for empirical research. For discussion, see May [1985].

36. This appears to be the view of Hornstein [1984], who uses examples similar to (35) and (36) to motivate his non-Russellian account of descriptions according to which they are always interpreted as if they took wide interpretive scope, something he sees as explicable on the assumption that they are closer to ordinary referring expressions than quantifiers that undergo evacuation. This position is criticized by Soames [1987] and Neale [1990].

37. Following Barwise [1979] and Barwise and Cooper [1981], a determiner D is monotone decreasing just in case (i) is valid:

(i) $[D_k\alpha]_k \ \beta$
$[\text{every}_k\beta']_k\beta$

$\overline{[D_k\alpha]_k \ \beta'}$

Quick test: D is monotone decreasing just in case (ii) entails (iii):

(ii) D dog(s) were barking
(iii) D dog(s) were barking loudly.

Examples: "no," "few," "fewer than seven." (For convenience, if D is monotone decreasing, let's say that a quantifier $\ulcorner[D_k\alpha]_k\urcorner$ is also monotone decreasing, for any α.)

38. See e.g. Harman [1972], McCawley [1972].

39. It is not necessary for the quantified noun phrase to c-command the pronoun at S-Structure. Consider the following sort of example, due to May [1987]:

(i) [The father of [each girl]$_2$]$_1$ waved to her$_2$

(ii) [Some man from [every city]$_2$]$_1$ despises it$_2$.

In each of these sentences, the complex quantified NP in subject position contains, as a proper part, another quantified NP that (a) is understood with largest scope and (b) appears to bind a subsequent pronoun. Take (ii). Evacuating the subject quantifier to the top of the tree yields the intermediate representation (iii):

(iii) [$_S$ [some man from [every city]$_2$]$_1$ [$_S$ e_1 despises it$_2$]].

Evacuating "every city" to the top of the intermediate tree yields (iv):

(iv) [$_S$ [every city]$_2$ [$_S$ [some man from e_2]$_1$ [$_S$ e_1 despises it$_2$]]].

In RQ notation this is just (v)

(v) [every$_2$ city x_2]$_2$ ([some$_1$ man x_1 & x_1 is from x_2]$_1$ (x_1 despises x_2)).

which has exactly the right truth conditions. In the LF representation (iv) the pronoun "it" is within the scope of (i.e. c-commanded by) "every city," so it is legitimately understood as a variable bound by that quantified NP. From a truth-conditional perspective this turns out to be exactly right, witness the fidelity of (v). In short, the LF theorist has a very elegant account of the fact that (v) gives the truth conditions of (ii). Similarly with (i) and an indefinite number of similar examples. If we were to state a descriptive generalization, it would be the following: a pronoun P can be understood as a variable bound by a quantified NP Q only if Q c-commands P at LF. But of course this doesn't need to be stated anywhere in the theory: it is a consequence of the general theory.

40. Example like (38) and (39) raise a question that the LF theorist must confront at some point: If (i) LF is derived from S-Structure by a series of evacuations, and (ii) the S-Structure representation of a conjunction $\ulcorner\alpha$ and $\beta\urcorner$ contains two subsentences as in the structure [$_{S0}$ [$_{S1}$ α] and [$_{S2}$ β]], then some sort of constraint on evacuation appears to be required to prevent a QNP that is a constituent of S1 (or S2) in such a structure (whether or not S0 is a constituent of a larger S) from Chomsky-adjoining to S0. For without such a constraint the LFs (38$_2$) and (39$_2$) could be derived from the S-Structures for (38) and (39):

(38$_2$) [$_S$ [some hens]$_1$ [$_S$ [$_S$ [Russell bought e_1] and [$_S$ Whitehead vaccinated them$_1$]]]

(39$_2$) [$_S$ [just one man]$_1$ [$_S$ [$_S$ e_1 drank rum] and [$_S$ he$_1$ was ill this morning]]].

And in RQ notation (38$_2$) and (39$_2$) are just (38$_1$) and (39$_1$), which as we have already seen ascribe the wrong truth conditions to (38) and (39). For discussion, see Neale [1992].

41. Evans [1977, 1980]; Davies [1981]; Neale [1990].

42. There is no space here to discuss the question of the precise status of (F) vis-a-vis an adequate truth definition and its rôle within a theory of LF. For discussion, see Neale [1992].

43. This label (borrowed loosely from Sommers [1982]), is meant to conjure up both the similarities and differences between D-type pronouns and Evans' [1977, 1980] *E-type* pronouns. On the differences, see below.

44. I should stress that there is still considerable work to be done if the D-type theory of unbound anaphora is to form part of a general theory that appeals to LF as I am construing it. For a preliminary discussion, see Neale [1992].

45. Davies [1981]; Soames [1989].

46. It is important to see that the LF/D-type theory differs significantly from Evans' E-type theory. On Evans' account (i) a pronoun *P* anaphoric on a quantified NP *Q* is an *E-type* pronoun if and only if *P* is not c-commanded by *Q* at S-Structure, and (ii) E-type pronouns are referring expressions whose references are fixed rigidly by description (in the sense of Kripke [1972]). By contrast, Principle (F) of the LF/D-type theory is stated in terms of LF representations and the axioms for "the." This is a syntactically and semantically significant fact: (i) D-type pronouns are quantified NPs and hence undergo evacuation, and (ii) the axioms of the truth definition operate on LF representations. As Russell stressed, serious philosophical error may be the reward for confusing reference and quantification, so the philosophical grammarian must be sensitive to the distinction between E-type and D-type interpretations. And of course linguists who want to appeal to LF (as I have construed it) must also pay attention to the distinction.

Although the pronoun "he" in (39) is understood as "the man who drank rum," it certainly does not have its reference fixed by this description, and hence it would be a mistake to think of it is an E-type pronoun. If it had its reference fixed by description, it would refer to the man who actually drank rum—call him "Gideon"—and so what is expressed by (39) would be true at any circumstance of evaluation in which just one man drank rum and Gideon was ill this morning. But this is clearly wrong, so the occurrence of "he" in (39) does not receive an E-type interpretation (this type of argument against Evans' theory was first presented by Soames [1989]).

Although Evans says explicitly that E-type pronouns are rigid referring expressions, in his formalism they end up being treated as equivalent to Russellian descriptions that insist on large scope. But even this modified notion of an E-type interpretation will not do because of examples such as (41) and (42). In each case, it is clear that the description "he" can be understood with small scope (see above). It is clear, then, that at least some unbound anaphoric pronouns receive D-type rather than (modified) E-type interpretations.

In the absence of evidence for the existence of (modified) E-type interpretations, I suggested in *Descriptions* that natural languages are simply not the sorts of languages that contain E-type pronouns. To say this is not to say that the notion of an E-type pronoun is incoherent. On the contrary, it is a simple matter to construct an intelligible artificial language containing such expressions. My claim is an empirical one: such a language would indeed be *artificial*; natural languages are of such a nature that they do not contain E-type pronouns. The difference between E-type and D-type interpretations is, then, very marked. All the more so if there are, as maintained in Neale [1992], correlated syntactical, semantical and structural differences between referential and quantificational NPs.

47. Evans [1977]; Wiggins [1980]; Davies [1981].

48. See Davies [1981].

49. Following Quine [1960] and Evans [1977], it is usual to think of relative pronouns (as they occur in restrictive relative clauses) as devices of *predicate abstraction* rather than as variables. On such an account, the logical forms of (44) and (45) are given by (44_3) and (45_3), respectively:

(44_3) [the$_1$ farmer x_1 & [λx_2] (x_2 bought Daisy) x_1]$_1$ (x_1 is happy)
(45_3) [the$_1$ farmer x_1 & [λx_2] (Daisy kicked x_2) x_1]$_1$ (x_1 is unhappy).

However, for the sake of simplicity the relative pronouns in (44) and (45) are often thought of as variables bound by determiners since (44_1) and (45_1) are equivalent (by lambda-elimination) to (44_3) and (45_3). A good reason for preferring the semantical structures in (44_3) and (45_3) is that they fit well with the view that at LF (and in English at S-Structure) relative pronouns occupy nonargument positions and as such are naturally treated as variable-binding operators. For syntactical considerations that lend support for such a view, see Chomsky [1986], ch 2.

50. See (e.g.) Evans [1977], Kamp [1988], Heim [1981], Neale [1990a].

51. A large scope reading for the embedded quantifier comes through clearly in the following example:

(i) Every man who saw [a painting I bought last week]$_1$ wanted do buy it$_1$.

It is important not to confuse the idea that the indefinite description in (i) may take large scope with the idea that it admits of a semantically referential interpretation. See Kripke [1977] and Ludlow and Neale [1991].

52. Evans [1977], pp. 134–139.

53. The reading of (48) upon which the embedded quantifier has small scope is equivalent to the reading upon which it has large scope and binds "her." In essence, this is really a consequence of the fact that scope permutations involving definite descriptions and quantifiers that are not monotone decreasing are truth-conditionally inert; this has no bearing on the issue discussed in the text.

54. See also Davies [1981]; Wilson [1984]; McKinsey [1986]; Soames [1989]; Neale [1990].

References

Bach. E. [1968]. Nouns and Noun Phrases. In E. Bach and R. Harms (eds.), *Universals in Linguistic Theory*. New York: Holt, Reinhart, Winston, pp. 91–124.

Barwise, J. [1979]. Branching Quantifiers in English. *Journal of Philosophical Logic* 8, 47–80.

Barwise, J., and R. Cooper [1981]. Generalized Quantifiers and Natural Language. *Linguistics and Philosophy* 4, 159–219.

Chomsky, N. [1975]. *Reflections on Language*. New York: Pantheon.

——— [1977]. *Essays on Form and Interpretation*. New York: North Holland.

——— [1980]. *Rules and Representations*. Oxford: Blackwell.

―――― [1981]. *Lectures on Government and Binding*. Dordrecht: Foris.

―――― [1986]. *Knowledge of Language*. New York: Praeger.

Davidson, D. [1967]. Truth and Meaning. *Synthese* 17, 304–323.

―――― [1967a]. The Logical Form of Action Sentences. In N. Rescher (ed.), *The Logic of Decision and Action*. Pittsburgh: University of Pittsburgh Press, 81–95.

―――― [1968]. On Saying That. *Synthese*, 19, 130–146.

―――― [1973]. In Defense of Convention T. In H. Leblanc (ed.), *Truth, Syntax, and Modality*. Amsterdam: North Holland, pp. 65–75.

―――― [1975]. Semantics for Natural Languages. In D. Davidson and G. Harman (eds.), *The Logic of Grammar*. New York: Dickenson, pp. 18–24.

Davies, M. [1981]. *Meaning, Quantification, Necessity*. London: Routledge and Kegan Paul.

Evans, G. [1977]. "Pronouns, Quantifiers and Relative Clauses (I)," *Canadian Journal of Philosophy* 7, 467–536.

―――― [1977a]. Pronouns, Quantifiers and Relative Clauses (II), *Canadian Journal of Philosophy* 7, 777–797.

―――― [1980]. Pronouns. *Linguistic Inquiry* 11, 337–362.

―――― [1982]. *The Varieties of Reference*. Oxford: Clarendon Press.

Grice, H. P. [1969]. Vacuous Names. In D. Davidson and J. Hintikka (eds.), *Words and Objections*. Dordrecht: Reidel, pp. 118–145.

Harman, G. [1972]. Deep Structure as Logical Form. In D. Davidson and G. Harman (eds.), *Semantics of Natural Language*. Dordrecht: Reidel, pp. 25–47.

―――― [1975]. Logical Form. In D. Davidson and G. Harman (eds.) *The Logic of Grammar*. New York: Dickenson, pp. 289–307.

Heim, I. [1988]. *The Semantics of Definite and Indefinite Noun Phrases*, New York: Garland Press.

Higginbotham, J. [1980]. Pronouns and Bound Variables. *Linguistic Inquiry* 11, 679–708.

―――― [1983]. Logical Form, Binding, and Nominals. *Linguistic Inquiry* 14, 395–420.

―――― [1987]. On Semantics. In E. LePore (ed.) *New Directions in Semantics*. New York: Academic Press, pp. 1–54.

Higginbotham, J., and R. May [1981]. "Questions, Quantifiers, and Crossing," *Linguistic Review* 1, 41–80.

Hintikka, J. [1974]. Quantifiers and Quantification Theory. *Linguistic Inquiry* 5, 153–177.

―――― [1989]. Logical Form and Linguistic Theory. In A. George (ed.), *Reflections on Chomsky*, Oxford: Blackwell, pp. 41–57.

Hintikka, J., and J. Kulas [1985]. *Anaphora and Definite Descriptions*. Dordrecht: Reidel.

Hintikka, J., and G. Sandu [1991]. *The Methodology of Linguistics.* Oxford: Blackwell.

Hornstein, N. [1984]. *Logic as Grammar.* Cambridge, Mass.: MIT Press.

Kamp, H. [1981]. A Theory of Truth and Semantic Interpretation. In J. Groenendijk et al. (eds.), *Formal Methods in the Study of Natural Language.* Amsterdam: Amsterdam Centre, pp. 277–322.

Kaplan, D. [1966]. Rescher's Plurality-Quantification. *Journal of Symbolic Logic* 31, 153–154.

Kripke, S. A. [1972]. Naming and Necessity. In D. Davidson and G. Harman (eds.), *Semantics of Natural Language.* Dordrecht: Reidel, pp. 253–355, and 763–769.

——— [1977]. Speaker's Reference and Semantic Reference. In P. A. French, T. E. Uehling, Jr., and H. K. Wettstein, *Contemporary Perspectives in the Philosophy of Language.* Minneapolis: University of Minnesota Press, pp. 6–27.

Lakoff, G. [1971]. On Generative Semantics. In D. Steinberg and L. Jakobovits (eds.), *Semantics.* Cambridge: Cambridge University Press, pp. 232–296.

——— [1972]. Linguistics and Natural Logic. In D. Davidson and G. Harman (eds.), *Semantics of Natural Language.* Dordrecht: Reidel, pp. 545–665.

Larson, R., and P. Ludlow [1993]. Interpreted Logical Forms. *Synthese* 95, 305–355.

Lasnik, H. [1976]. Remarks on Coreference. *Linguistic Analysis* 2, 1–22.

Linsky, B. [1992]. The Logical Form of Descriptions. *Dialogue* 31, 677–683.

Ludlow, P., and S. Neale [1991]. Indefinite Descriptions: In Defense of Russell. *Linguistics and Philosophy* 14, 171–202.

Lycan, W. [1984]. *Logical Form in Natural Language.* Cambridge, Mass.: MIT Press.

McCawley, J. [1968]. The Role of Semantics in Grammar. In E. Bach and R. Harms (eds.), *Universals in Linguistic Theory.* New York: Holt, Reinhart, Winston, pp. 125–170.

——— [1970]. Where do Noun Phrases come from? In R. Jacobs and P. Rosenbaum (eds.), *Readings in English Transformational Grammar.* Waltham, Mass.: Ginnand Co., pp. 166–183.

——— [1972]. A Program for Logic. In D. Davidson and G. Harman (eds.), *Semantics of Natural Language.* Dordrecht: Reidel, pp. 498–544.

——— [1981]. *Everything that Linguists Have Always Wanted to Know About Logic.* Chicago: University of Chicago Press.

McKinsey, M. [1986]. Mental Anaphora. *Synthese* 66, 159–175.

May, R. [1985]. *Logical Form: its Structure and Derivation.* Cambridge, Mass.: MIT Press.

——— [1987]. Logical Form as a Level of Linguistic Representation. In E. LePore (ed.), *New Directions in Semantics.* New York: Academic Press, pp. 187–218.

Montague, R., D. Kalish, and G. Mar [1980]. *Logic: Techniques of Formal Reasoning*. New York: Harcourt, Brace, Jovanovich.

Neale, S. [1990]. *Descriptions*. Cambridge, Mass.: MIT Press.

——— [1990a]. Descriptive Pronouns and Donkey Anaphora. *Journal of Philosophy* 87, 113–150.

——— [1992]. Logical Form and LF. In C. Otero (ed.), *Noam Chomsky: Critical Assessments*. London: Routledge and Kegan Paul.

——— [forthcoming]. *The Language of Philosophy*. Oxford: Oxford University Press.

Peacocke, C. [1978]. Necessity and Truth Theories. *Journal of Philosophical Logic* 7, 473–500.

Platts, M. [1979]. *Ways of Meaning*. London: Routledge and Kegan Paul.

Quine, W. V. O. [1960]. *Word and Object*. Cambridge, Mass.: MIT Press.

Reinhart, T. [1978]. Syntactic Domains for Semantic Rules. In F. Guenthner and S. J. Schmidt (eds.), *Formal Semantics and Pragmatics for Natural Languages*. Dordrecht: Reidel, pp. 107–130.

Rescher, N. [1962]. Plurality-quantification. Abstract in *Journal of Symbolic Logic* 27, 373–374.

Ross, J. R. [1974]. Excerpts from *Constraints on Variables in Syntax*. In G. Harman (ed.), *On Noam Chomsky*. Amherst, Mass.: University of Massachusetts Press, 165–200.

Russell, B. [1905]. On Denoting, *Mind* 14, 479–493.

Russell, B., and A. N. Whitehead [1927]. *Principia Mathematica*, vol. I, 2nd ed. Cambridge: Cambridge University Press.

Smullyan, A. F. [1948]. Modality and Description. *Journal of Symbolic Logic* 13, 31–37.

Soames, S. [1987]. Review of Hornstein's *Logic as Grammar*. *Journal of Philosophy* 84, 447–455.

——— [1989]. Review of Gareth Evans' *The Collected Papers*. *Journal of Philosophy* 86, 141–156.

——— [1990]. Pronouns and Propositional Attitudes. *Proceedings of the Aristotelian Society* vol 40, 191–212.

Sommers, F. [1982]. *The Logic of Natural Language*. Oxford: Clarendon Press.

Thomason, R. [1969]. Modal Logic and Metaphysics. In K. Lambert (ed.), *The Logical Way of Doing Things*. New Haven: Yale University Press, pp. 119–146.

Wiggins, D. [1980]. "'Most' and 'All': Some Comments on a Familiar Programme, and on the Logical Form of Quantified Sentences," in M. Platts (ed.), *Reference, Truth, and Reality*. London: Routledge and Kegan Paul, pp. 318–346.

Wilson, G. [1984]. Pronouns and Pronominal Descriptions: A New Semantical Category. *Philosophical Studies* 45, 1–30.

Chapter 5

From *Meaning and Necessity*   Rudolf Carnap

5.1   Individual Descriptions

An individual description is an expression of the form "$(\imath x)(..x..)$"; it means "the one individual such that $..x..$". If there is one and only one individual such that $..x..$, we say that the description satisfies the uniqueness condition. In this case the *descriptum*, i.e., the entity to which the description refers, is that one individual. Logicians differ in their interpretations of descriptions in cases where the uniqueness condition is not satisfied. The methods of Hilbert and Bernays and of Russell are here discussed; that of Frege will be discussed in the next section.[1]

We use the term *individual* not for one particular kind of entity but, rather, relative to a language system S, for those entities which are taken as the elements of the universe of discourse in S, in other words, the entities of lowest level (we call it level zero) dealt with in S, no matter what these entities are. For one system the individuals may be physical things, for another space-time points, or numbers, or anything else. Consequently, we call the variables of level zero individual variables, the constants individual constants, and all expressions of this level, whether simple (variables and constants) or compound, *individual expressions*. The most important kinds of compound individual expressions are: (1) full expressions of functors (e.g., "$3 + 4$," where "$+$" is a functor and "3" and "4" are individual constants); within our systems, expressions of this kind occur only in S_3, not in S_1 and S_2;[2] (2) individual descriptions. We shall use here the term "description" mostly in the sense of "individual description." Descriptions of other types do not occur in our systems; a few remarks on them will be made at the end of 5.2.

Reprinted from Rudolf Carnap, *Meaning and Necessity*, pp. 32–42, by permission of The University of Chicago Press. © 1947 The University of Chicago.

A description in S_1 has the form "$(\imath x)(..x..)$"; it is interpreted as "the one individual such that $..x...$" "$(\imath x)$" is called an iota-operator; the scope "$..x..$" is a sentential matrix with "x" as a free variable. For example, "$(\imath x)(Px \bullet \sim Qx)$" means the same as "the one individual which is P and not Q."

The entity for which a description stands (if there is such an entity) will be called its descriptum; here, in the case of individual descriptions, the descriptum is an individual. With respect to a given description, there are two possible cases: either (1) there is exactly one individual which fulfils the condition expressed by the scope, or (2) this does not hold, that is, there are none or several such individuals. In the first case we shall say of the scope, and also of the whole description, that it satisfies the uniqueness condition.

5-1-1. DEFINITION. Let "$..x..$" be a (sentential) matrix (in S_1) with "x" as the only free variable. "$..x..$" (and "$(\imath x)(..x..)$") satisfies the *uniqueness condition* (in S_1) $=_{\text{Df}}$ "$(\exists z)(x)[..x.. \equiv (x \equiv z)]$" is true in S_1 ("$x \equiv z$" means "x is the same individual as z.")

In the case of a description satisfying the uniqueness condition, there is general agreement among logicians with respect to its interpretation; the one individual satisfying the scope is taken as descriptum. In the other case, however, there is, so far, no agreement. Various methods have been proposed. We shall outline three of them, those proposed by Hilbert and Bernays (I), Russell (II), and Frege (III). Then we shall adopt Frege's method for our systems. It should be noticed that the various conceptions now to be discussed are not to be understood as different opinions, so that at least one of them must be wrong, but rather as different proposals. The different interpretations of descriptions are not meant as assertions about the meaning of phrases of the form "the so-and-so" in English, but as proposals for an interpretation and, consequently, for deductive rules, concerning descriptions in symbolic systems. Therefore, there is no theoretical issue of right or wrong between the various conceptions, but only the practical question of the comparative convenience of different methods.

In order to make the following discussions more concrete, let us suppose that two (sentential) matrices are given, each with exactly one free variable; we indicate them here with the help of dots and dashes: "$..x..$" and "$- - y - -$" (e.g., "Axw" and "Hy"). We construct the description with the first as scope and substitute it for "y" in the second:

5-1-2. "$- - (\imath x)(..x..) - -.$" (*Example*: "$H(\imath x)(Axw).$")

Method I. Hilbert and Bernays,[3] in a system with natural numbers as individuals, permit the use of a description only if it satisfies the uniqueness condition. Since the system is constructed as a calculus, not as a semantical system, the formula of uniqueness is required to be C-true (provable) instead of true.[4] It seems that this method is quite convenient for practical work with a logico-arithmetical system; one uses a description only after he has proved the uniqueness. However, this method has a serious disadvantage, although of a chiefly theoretical nature: the rules of formation become indefinite, i.e., there is no general procedure for determining whether any given expression of the form 5-1-2 is a sentence of the system (no matter whether true or false, provable or not). For systems also containing factual sentences, the disadvantage would be still greater, because here the question of whether a given expression is a sentence or not would, in general, depend upon the contingency of facts.

Method II. Russell[5] takes the whole expression 5-1-2 in any case as a sentence. The uniqueness condition is here taken not as a precondition for the sentential character of the expression but rather as one of the conditions for its truth—in other words, as part of its content. Thus the translation of 5-1-2 into M [the metalanguage] is as follows:

5-1-3. "There is an individual y such that y is the only individual for which . . y . . holds, and - - y - -" (for example, "there is an individual y such that y is the only individual which is an author of Waverley, and y is human").

Hence, 1-2 is here interpreted as meaning the same as the following (with a certain restriction, see below):

5-1-4. "$(\exists y)[(x)(. . x . . \equiv (x \equiv y)) \bullet$ - - y - -]." (In the example, "$(\exists y)$ $[(x)(Axw \equiv (x \equiv y)) \bullet Hy]$.")

In order to incorporate this interpretation into his system, Russell lays down a contextual definition for descriptions; 5-1-2 is the definiendum, 5-1-4 the definiens. If we prefer to take the iota-operator as primitive instead of defining it, we can reach the same result by framing the semantical rules in such a way that any two sentences of the forms 5-1-2 and 5-1-4 become L-equivalent.

In comparison with Hilbert's method, Russell's has the advantage that an expression of the form 5-1-2 is always a sentence. In comparison with Frege's method, which will soon be explained, it has the disadvantage that the rules for descriptions are not so simple as those for other individual expressions, especially those for individual constants. In particular, the inferences of specification, leading from "$(y)(- - y - -)$" to "$- - a - -$," and of existential generalization, leading from "$- - a - -$" to "$(\exists y)(- - y - -)$," are, in general, not valid if a description takes the place of the individual constant "a"; here the uniqueness sentence for the description must be taken as an additional premise. A further disadvantage of Russell's method is the following: A sentence like "$\sim Q(\iota x)(Px)$" can be transformed in two ways. Either this whole sentence is taken as 5-1-2 and transformed into the corresponding sentence of the form 5-1-4; or the part "$Q(\iota x)(Px)$" is taken as 5-1-2, transformed into the corresponding sentence of the form 5-1-4, and then prefixed again with the sign of negation. The two resulting sentences are not L-equivalent (in distinction to Frege's method); hence Russell has to lay down an additional convention, which determines for each case what is to be taken as the context 5-1-2.[6]

5.2 Frege's Method for Descriptions

We adopt for our systems a method proposed by Frege for interpreting individual descriptions in cases of nonuniqueness. This method consists in choosing once for all an individual to be taken as descriptum for all such cases.

Method III. Frege[7] regards it as a defect in the logical structure of natural languages that in some cases an expression of the grammatical form "the so-and-so" is a name of one object while in other cases it is not; in our terminology: that some descriptions have a descriptum but others not. Therefore, he suggests that the rules of a language system should be constructed in such a way that every description has a descriptum. This requires certain conventions which are more or less arbitrary; but this disadvantage seems small in comparison with the gain in simplicity for the rules of the system. For instance, specification and existential generalization are here valid also for descriptions (at least in extensional contexts).

Frege's requirement can be fulfilled in various ways. The choice of a convenient procedure depends upon the particular features of the language system, especially upon the range of values of the variables in question. There are chiefly two methods which deserve consideration; we call them IIIa and IIIb. We shall explain them and then use IIIb for our systems.

Method IIIa. Frege[8] himself constructs a system without type difference between individuals and classes; that is to say, he counts both classes and their elements as objects, i.e., as values of the individual variables. To any of those descriptions which do not satisfy the condition of uniqueness he assigns as descriptum the class of those objects which fulfil the scope. Thus different descriptions of this kind may have different descripta.

Method IIIb. A simpler procedure consists in selecting, once for all, a certain entity from the range of values of the variables in question and assigning it as desciptum to all descriptions which do not satisfy the condition of uniqueness. This has been done in various ways.

(i) If the individuals of the system are numbers, the number 0 seems to be the most natural choice. Frege has already mentioned this possibility. . . .

(ii) For variables to whose values the null class Λ belongs, this class seems to be the most convenient choice. Such a choice has been made by Quine,[9] in whose system there is, as in Frege's, no type difference between individuals and classes.

(iii) How can Method IIIb be applied to a language system whose individuals are physical things or events? At first glance, it seems impossible to make here an even moderately natural choice of an individual as common descriptum for all individual descriptions which do not satisfy the condition of uniqueness. To select, say, Napoleon would be just as arbitrary as to select this dust particle on my paper. However, a natural solution offers itself if we construct the system in such a way that the spatiotemporal part-whole relation is one of its concepts.[10] Every individual in such a system, that is, every thing or event, corresponds to a class of space-time points in a system with space-time points as individuals. Therefore, it is possible, although not customary in the ordinary language, to count among the things also the *null thing*, which corresponds to the null class of space-time points. In the language system of things it is characterized as that thing which is part of every thing.[11] Let us take "a_0" as the name for the null thing; the other things may be called non-null things. If a system S includes a_0 among its individuals, then a_0 seems a natural and convenient choice as descriptum for those descriptions which do not satisfy the uniqueness condition. It is true that this procedure requires certain deviations from the ordinary language for the forms of sentences in S; but these deviations are smaller than we might expect at first glance. For most of the universal and existential sentences, the translation into S is straightforward, i.e., without change in structure;

in other cases "non-null" must be inserted. (Examples: The sentence "There is no thing which is identical with the king of France in 1905" is translated into a sentence of S of the form "There is no non-null thing . . . ." On the other hand, no such change in form is necessary for the sentence "All men are mortal" and not even for "There is no man who is identical with the king of France in 1905," because it follows from any suitably framed definition for "man" that every man is a non-null thing.)

In our further discussions we assume for our system S_1 that Frege's Method IIIb is applied and that the individual constant "a^*" is used for the common descriptum of all descriptions which do not satisfy the uniqueness condition. We leave it open which individual is meant by "a^*"; it may be the null thing a_0, if this belongs to the individuals in S_0; it may be 0, if numbers belong to the individuals (as, for instance, in S_3), but it may as well be any other individual. Consequently, a sentence containing a description is now interpreted in a way different from Russell's. The translation of 5-1-2 into M is now as follows (instead of 5-1-3):

5-2-1.   "Either there is an individual y such that y is the only individual for which . . y . . holds, and - - y - -; or there is no such individual, and - - a^* - -." (In the previous example: "Either there is an individual y such that y is the only author of Waverley, and y is human; or there is no such individual y [that is to say, there is either no author or several authors of Waverley], and a^* is human.")

Hence, the sentence 5-1-2 containing the description is L-equivalent in S_1 to the following (instead of to 5-1-4):

5-2-2.   "$(\exists y)[(x)(. . x . . \equiv (x \equiv y)) \bullet - - y - -] \vee [\sim (\exists y)(x)(. . x . . \equiv (x \equiv y)) \bullet - - a^* - -]$." (In the example: "$(\exists y) [(x)(Axw \equiv (x \equiv y)) \bullet Hy] \vee [\sim (\exists y)(x)(Axw \equiv (x \equiv y)) \bullet Ha^*]$.")

Here again, as in the case of Russell's method, we may set up either a contextual definition for 5-1-2 with 5-2-2 as definiens, or semantical rules for the iota-operator as a primitive sign such that 5-1-2 becomes L-equivalent to 5-2-2.

. . .

5.3   Extensions and Intensions of Individual Expressions

It is found to be in accord with our earlier conventions, to take as the extension of an individual expression the individual to which it refers. The intension of an individual expression is a concept of a new kind; it is called an *individual concept*.

Let us consider some examples of F-equivalence and L-equivalence of individual expressions.[12] We assume the following as a historical fact:

5-3-1. ASSUMPTION. There is one and only one individual which is an author of Waverley, and this individual is the same as Walter Scott. Then the descriptum of "$(\iota x)(Axw)$" is that individual which is author of Waverley and not a^* and "$(\iota x)(Axw) = s$" is, according to the rule 3-3 [from chap. 3 of *Meaning and Necessity*], true, but not L-true; hence it is F-true. This leads to the following result, according to the definition 3-5 [see Appendix for both rules]:

5-3-2. "$(\iota x)(Axw)$" is equivalent to "s", but not L-equivalent, hence F-equivalent.

On the other hand, let us compare the two descriptions "$(\iota x)(Hx \cdot Axw)$" and "$(\iota x)(RAx \cdot Axw)$." Let us see what we can find out about them if we make use of the rules of S_1, especially 1-2 [see Appendix], but not of any historical or other factual knowledge. If there is exactly one individual which is both human—or, which means the same, a rational animal—and an author of Waverley, then the descriptum of each of the two descriptions is this individual; otherwise the descriptum of each is a^*. Thus, in either case, the descriptum of the first description is the same individual as that of the second. Hence, according to rule 3-3, the sentence "$(\iota x)(Hx \cdot Axw) \equiv (\iota x)(RAx \cdot Axw)$" is true; it is, moreover, L-true because we have shown its truth by using merely the semantical rules. Therefore, the two descriptions are L-equivalent.

We found earlier that individual expressions are equivalent if and only if they are expressions for the same individual (3–12) [see Appendix]. Hence, according to the definition of identity of extensions (D-1) [see Appendix], individual expressions have the same extension if and only if they are expressions for the same individual. Therefore, it seems natural to regard as extensions of individual expressions the individuals themselves:

5-3-3. The *extension of an individual expression* is the individual to which it refers (hence the descriptum, if it is a description).

Since we adopted Frege's method, every description has exactly one descriptum. Hence, on the basis of the convention just made, there is no ambiguity with respect to the extension of an individual expression. For instance, the extension of "s" is the individual Walter Scott, and the same holds for each of the three descriptions discussed above as examples. If there were none or several authors of Waverley, then the extension of "$(\iota x)(Axw)$" would be the individual a^*.

Now let us look for entities which we might regard as intensions of individual expressions. According to our definition for the identity of intensions (D-2) [see Appendix], the intension must be something that L-equivalent individual expressions (for example, the two descriptions above containing "*H*" and "*RA*") have in common. We have earlier found entities which seemed suitable as intensions of designators of other types; for sentences, propositions; for predicators, properties or relations; for functors, functions. Thus, in these cases, the intensions are those entities which are sometimes regarded as the meanings of the expressions in question; and, in the case of predicators and functors, the intensions are concepts of certain types. Now it seems to me a natural procedure, in the case of individual expressions, likewise to speak of concepts, but of concepts of a particular type, namely, the individual type. Although it is not altogether customary to speak here of concepts in this sense, still it does not seem to deviate too much from ordinary usage. I propose to use the term *individual concept* for this type of concept. Thus we say:

5-3-4.   The *intension of an individual expression* is the individual concept expressed by it.

Examples:

5-3-5.   The intension of "*s*" is the individual concept Walter Scott.

5-3-6.   The intension of "$(\iota x)(Axw)$" is the individual concept The Author Of Waverley.

(Here, and further on, in translating descriptions into M, we omit for brevity the phrase "or a^*, if there is not exactly one such individual.") Instead of saying in the customary but ambiguous terminology that the two L-equivalent descriptions discussed above have the same meaning, we say now that they have the same intension and that their common intension is the individual concept The Human Author Of Waverley, which is the same as the individual concept The Rational Animal Author Of Waverley. On the other hand, the following are three different individual concepts: the one just mentioned, the individual concept Walter Scott, and the individual concept The Author Of Waverley. Here again the intensions of given expressions, and the identity or nonidentity of these intensions, can be determined on the basis of the semantical rules alone.

We have seen earlier how a sentence containing a predicator can be translated into M, that is, English, in different ways. Thus, for the sentence

"*Hs*," we had, in addition to the simple translation "Scott is human," two more explicit translations, one of which used the term "property" and the other the term "class" (see 4-2 and 4-3 [see Appendix]). In these two explicit translations, "*s*" was still simply translated by "Scott." Now, however, we have seen that, corresponding to the distinction between classes and properties, we have in the case of individual expressions the distinction between individuals and individual concepts. Hence, we may use in *M* instead of "Scott" the more explicit phrases "the individual Scott" and "the individual concept Scott." Since the distinction is perhaps clearer for a description than for an individual constant, let us take, instead of "*Hs*," the sentence "$H(\imath x)(Axw)$." In addition to the simple translation "the author of Waverley is human," we have here four more explicit translations in which both to "The Author Of Waverley" and to "Human" a characterizing word is added. Two of these translations are pure, two mixed. Of the two pure translations, the first contains two references to extensions, and the second two references to intensions; these translations are as follows:

"The individual The Author Of Waverley belongs to the class Human."

"The individual concept The Author Of Waverley is subsumable under the property Human."

Since it is not customary to speak about individual concepts, there is no word in customary usage for the relation between an individual concept and a property corresponding to the element-relation between an individual and a class; we have used here for this relation the word "subsumable" (in the sense of "truly subsumable"), but we shall not use it further on. Of the two mixed translations, which contain a reference to an extension and a reference to an intension, we shall give at least one, because it is not too far from customary usage:

"The individual The Author Of Waverley has the property Human."

Thus we find here a multiplicity of possible translations into *M*, some of them rather cumbersome and strange-looking. This multiplicity seems inevitable as long as we wish to distinguish explicitly between classes and properties and between individuals and individual expressions. The problem of whether and by which means this apparent multiplicity of entities and the corresponding multiplicity of formulations can be reduced will be discussed later. . . .

Appendix

The following propositions from *Meaning and Necessity* are referred to but not stated in the current selection:

3-3. RULE OF TRUTH. If $\mathfrak{U}i$ is an individual expression in S_1 for the individual x and $\mathfrak{U}j$ for y, then $\mathfrak{U}i \equiv \mathfrak{U}j$ is true if and only if x is the same individual as y.

3-5. DEFINITIONS. Let $\mathfrak{U}i$ and $\mathfrak{U}j$ be two designators of the same type [two expressions of the same syntactic category. Ed.] in S_1.

a. $\mathfrak{U}i$ is **equivalent** to $\mathfrak{U}j$ in (S_1) $=_{\mathrm{Df}}$ the sentence $\mathfrak{U}i \equiv \mathfrak{U}j$ is true (in S_1).
b. $\mathfrak{U}i$ is **L-equivalent** to $\mathfrak{U}j$ in (S_1) $=_{\mathrm{Df}}$ the sentence $\mathfrak{U}i \equiv \mathfrak{U}j$ is L-true (in S_1).
c. $\mathfrak{U}i$ is **F-equivalent** to $\mathfrak{U}j$ in (S_1) $=_{\mathrm{Df}}$ the sentence $\mathfrak{U}i \equiv \mathfrak{U}j$ is F-true (in S_1).

3-12. Individual expressions are equivalent if and only if they are expressions for the same individual.

4-2. Scott has the property Human.

4-3. Scott belongs to the class (is an element of) the class Human.

D-1. DEFINITION. Two designators *have the same extension* in (S_1) $=_{\mathrm{Df}}$ they are equivalent (in S_1).

D-2. DEFINITION. Two designators *have the same intension* in (S_1) $=_{\mathrm{Df}}$ they are L-equivalent (in S_1).

Notes

1. [Carnap employs dots and dashes rather than sentence letters to indicate the sentential context in which a variable or term occurs. Ed.]
2. [S_1 is the predicate calculus enriched with λ-abstraction, S_2 is an extension of S_1 containing modal operators. S_3 is an extension of S_1 containing number-theoretic expressions and relations. Ed.]
3. *Grundlagen der Mathematik*, vol. I, Berlin, 1934, p. 384.
4. [A *semantical system* contains, in addition to rules of formation, rules of designation and rules of truth; a *calculus*, as Carnap understands that term, contains, in addition to rules of formation, derivational rules, but lacks rules of designation and rules of truth. Ed.]
5. The reasons for this method are explained in detail by Russell in ["On Denoting," chapter 1 of this volume]; it has been applied by Russell and Whitehead in

the construction of the system of [*Principia Mathematica*], see I, 66 ff. and 173 ff. [chapter 3 of this volume, pp. 54 ff and 62 ff.].

6. [Two sentences X and Y of S_1 are L-equivalent just in case "$X \equiv Y$" is L-true, where a sentence of S_1 is L-true just in case it is true in all "state descriptions" (i.e., possible worlds). (See Appendix, 3–5.) Note that L-equivalence is a relation that may hold between any two expressions of the same syntactic category. Note also that, if X and Y are singular terms, the same criterion for L-equivalence applies: X and Y are L-equivalent just in case "$X \equiv Y$" is L-true. Ed.]

7. [Gottlob Frege, "On Sense and Meaning" (see *Origins* section of the bibliography). Frege had written that a logically perfect language would contain no nondenoting singular terms. This required a "special stipulation" for descriptions whose matrices fail to pick out exactly one object. Each such description "shall count as referring to 0 when the concept applies to no object or to more than one" (p. 71). Ed.]

8. Gottlob Frege, *The Basic Laws of Arithmetic, Vol. I*. [See *Origins* section of the bibliography. Ed.]

9. *Mathematical Logic* (Cambridge, Mass.: Harvard University Press, 1940), p. 147.

10. This is, for instance, the case with the following systems: a system for certain biological concepts by J. H. Woodger (*The Axiomatic Method in Biology* [1937]; *The Technique of Theory Construction* ["International Encyclopedia of Unified Science," Vol. II, No. 5 (1939)]); a calculus of individuals by H. S. Leonard and N. Goodman ("The Calculus of Individuals and Its Uses," *Journal of Symbolic Logic*, V [1940], 45–55) and a general system of logic recently constructed by R. M. Martin ("A Homogeneous System for Formal Logic," *Journal of Symbolic Logic*, VIII [1943], 1–23), where the customary symbol of inclusion and the term "inclusion" apparently refer to the part-whole relation among things.

11. In the system by Martin mentioned in the preceding footnote the null thing is indeed introduced (op. cit., p. 3, and D7, p. 9), while in the paper by Leonard and Goodman there is an explicit "refusal to postulate a null element" (op. cit., p. 46).

12. [Two individual expressions (singular terms) X and Y are F-equivalent (for "factually equivalent") just in case "$X \equiv Y$" is F-true, where a sentence is F-true just in case it is true but not L-true (i.e., true, but not necessarily true). Ed.]

Chapter 6

On Referring   P. F. Strawson

I

We very commonly use expressions of certain kinds to mention or refer to some individual person or single object or particular event or place or process, in the course of doing what we should normally describe as making a statement about that person, object, place, event, or process. I shall call this way of using expressions the "uniquely referring use." The classes of expressions which are most commonly used in this way are: singular demonstrative pronouns ("this" and "that"); proper names e.g. "Venice," "Napoleon," "John"); singular personal and impersonal pronouns ("he," "she," "I," "you," "it"); and phrases beginning with the definite article followed by a noun, qualified or unqualified, in the singular (e.g. "the table," "the old man," "the king of France"). Any expression of any of these classes can occur as the subject of what would traditionally be regarded as a singular subject-predicate sentence; and would, so occurring, exemplify the use I wish to discuss.

I do not want to say that expressions belonging to these classes never have any other use than the one I want to discuss. On the contrary, it is obvious that they do. It is obvious that anyone who uttered the sentence, "The whale is a mammal," would be using the expressions "the whale" in a way quite different from the way it would be used by anyone who had occasion seriously to utter the sentence, "The whale struck the ship." In the first sentence one is obviously *not* mentioning, and in the second sentence one obviously *is* mentioning, a particular whale. Again if I said, "Napoleon was the greatest French soldier," I should be using the word

Reprinted from *Mind* 59 (1950), pp. 320–344, by permission of P. F. Strawson and Oxford University Press. © 1950 Oxford University Press.

"Napoleon" to mention a certain individual, but I should not be using the phrase, "the greatest French soldier," to mention an individual, but to say something about an individual I had already mentioned. It would be natural to say that in using this sentence I was talking *about* Napoleon and that what I was *saying* about him was that he was the greatest French soldier. But of course I *could* use the expression, "the greatest French soldier," to mention an individual; for example, by saying: "The greatest French soldier died in exile." So it is obvious that at least some expressions belonging to the classes I mentioned *can* have uses other than the use I am anxious to discuss. Another thing I do not want to say is that in any given sentence there is never more than one expression used in the way I propose to discuss. On the contrary, it is obvious that there may be more than one. For example, it would be natural to say that, in seriously using the sentence, "The whale struck the ship," I was saying something about both a certain whale and a certain ship, that I was using each of the expressions "the whale" and "the ship" to mention a particular object; or, in other words, that I was using each of these expressions in the uniquely referring way. In general, however, I shall confine my attention to cases where an expression used in this way occurs as the grammatical subject of a sentence.

I think it is true to say that Russell's theory of descriptions, which is concerned with the last of the four classes of expressions I mentioned above (i.e. with expressions of the form "the so-and-so"), is still widely accepted among logicians as giving a correct account of the use of such expressions in ordinary language. I want to show in the first place, that this theory, so regarded, embodies some fundamental mistakes.

What question or questions about phrases of the form "the so-and-so" was the theory of descriptions designed to answer? I think that at least one of the questions may be illustrated as follows. Suppose someone were now to utter the sentence, "The king of France is wise." No one would say that the sentence which had been uttered was meaningless. Everyone would agree that it was significant. But everyone knows that there is not at present a king of France. One of the questions the theory of descriptions was designed to answer was the question: How can such a sentence as "The king of France is wise" be significant even when there is nothing which answers to the description it contains, i.e., in this case, nothing which answers to the description "The king of France"? And one of the reasons why Russell thought it important to give a correct answer to this question was that he thought it important to show that another answer which might be given was wrong. The answer that he thought was wrong, and to which he was anxious to supply an alternative, might be exhibited as the conclusion of either of the following two fallacious arguments. Let us call the sentence "The king of France is wise" the sentence *S*. Then the first argument is as follows:

(1) The phrase, "the king of France," is the subject of the sentence *S*.

Therefore (2) if *S* is a significant sentence, *S* is a sentence *about* the king of France.

But (3) if there in no sense exists a king of France, the sentence is not about anything, and hence not about the king of France.

Therefore (4) since *S* is significant, there must in some sense (in some world) exist (or subsist) the king of France.

And the second argument is as follows:

(1) If *S* is significant, it is either true or false.
(2) *S* is true if the king of France is wise and false if the king of France is not wise.
(3) But the statement that the king of France is wise and the statement that the king of France is not wise are alike true only if there is (in some sense, in some world) something which is the king of France.

Hence (4) since *S* is significant, there follows the same conclusion as before.

These are fairly obviously bad arguments, and, as we should expect, Russell rejects them. The postulation of a world of strange entities, to which the king of France belongs, offends, he says, against "that feeling for reality which ought to be preserved even in the most abstract studies." The fact that Russell rejects these arguments is, however, less interesting than the extent to which, in rejecting their conclusion, he concedes the more important of their principles. Let me refer to the phrase, "the king of France," as the phrase *D*. Then I think Russell's reasons for rejecting these two arguments can be summarized as follows. The mistake arises, he says, from thinking that *D*, which is certainly the *grammatical* subject of *S*, is also the *logical* subject of *S*. But *D* is not the logical subject of *S*. In fact *S*, although grammatically it has a singular subject and a predicate, is not logically a subject-predicate sentence at all. The proposition it expresses is a complex kind of *existential* proposition, part of which might be described as a "uniquely existential" proposition. To exhibit the logical form of the proposition, we should rewrite the sentence in a logically appropriate grammatical form, in such a way that the deceptive similarity of S to a sentence expressing a subject-predicate proposition would disappear, and we should be safeguarded against arguments such as the bad ones I outlined above. Before recalling the details of Russell's analysis of S, let us notice what his answer, as I have so far given it, seems to imply. His answer seems to imply that in the case of a sentence which is similar to S in that (1) it is grammatically of the subject-predicate form and (2) its grammatical subject does not refer to anything, then the only alternative to its being meaningless is that is should not really (i.e. logically) be of the subject-predicate form at all, but of some quite different form. And this in its turn seems to imply that if there are any sentences which are genuinely of the subject-predicate form, then the very fact of their being significant, having a meaning, guarantees that there *is* something referred to by the logical (and grammatical) subject. Moreover, Russell's answer seems to imply that there are such sentences. For if it is true that one may be misled by the grammatical similarity of S to other sentences into thinking that it is logically of the subject-predicate form, then surely there must be other sentences grammatically similar to S, which *are* of the subject-predicate form. To show not only that Russell's answer seems to imply these conclusions, but that he accepted at least the first two of them, it is enough to consider what he says about a class of expressions which he calls "logically proper names" and contrasts with expressions, like D, which he calls "definite descriptions." Of logically proper names Russell says or implies the following things:

1. That they and they alone can occur as subjects of sentences which are genuinely of the subject-predicate form.
2. That an expression intended to be a logically proper name is *meaningless* unless there is some single object for which it stands: for the *meaning* of such an expression just is the individual object which the expression designates. To be a name at all, therefore, it *must* designate something.

It is easy to see that if anyone believes these two propositions, then the only way for him to save the significance of the sentence S is to deny that it is a logically subject-predicate sentence. Generally, we may say that Russell recognizes only two ways in which sentences which seem, from their grammatical structure, to be about some particular person or individual object or event, can be significant:

1. The first is that their grammatical form should be misleading as to their logical form, and that they should be analyzable, like S, as a special kind of existential sentence.

2. The second is that their grammatical subject should be a logically proper name, of which the meaning is the individual thing it designates.

I think that Russell is unquestionably wrong in this, and that sentences which are significant, and which begin with an expression used in the uniquely referring way, fall into neither of these two classes. Expressions used in the uniquely referring way are never either logically proper names or descriptions, if what is meant by calling them "descriptions" is that they are to be analyzed in accordance with the model provided by Russell's theory of descriptions.

There are no logically proper names and there are no descriptions (in this sense).

Let us now consider the details of Russell's analysis. According to Russell, anyone who asserted *S* would be asserting that:

(1) There is a king of France

(2) There is not more than one king of France

(3) There is nothing which is king of France and is not wise

It is easy to see both how Russell arrived at this analysis, and how it enables him to answer the question with which we began, viz. the question: How can the sentence *S* be significant when there is no king of France? The way in which he arrived at the analysis was clearly by asking himself what would be the circumstances in which we would say that anyone who uttered the sentence *S* had made a true assertion. And it does seem pretty clear, and I have no wish to dispute, that the sentences (1)–(3) above do describe circumstances which are at least *necessary* conditions of anyone making a true assertion by uttering the sentence *S*. But, as I hope to show, to say this is not at all the same thing as to say that Russell has given a correct account of the use of the sentence *S* or even that he has given an account which, though incomplete, is correct as far as it goes; and is certainly not at all the same thing as to say that the model translation provided is a correct model for all (or for any) singular sentences beginning with a phrase of the form "the so-and-so."

It is also easy to see how this analysis enables Russell to answer the question of how the sentence *S* can be significant, even when there is no king of France. For, if this analysis is correct, anyone who utters the sentence *S* today would be jointly asserting three propositions, one of which (viz. that there is a king of France) would be false; and since the conjunction of three propositions, of which one is false, is itself false, the

assertion as a whole would be significant, but false. So neither of the bad
arguments for subsistent entities would apply to such an assertion.

II

As a step towards showing that Russell's solution of his problem is mistaken, and towards providing the correct solution, I want now to draw
certain distinctions. For this purpose I shall, for the remainder of this
section, refer to an expression which has a uniquely referring use as "an
expression" for short; and to a sentence beginning with such an expression as "a sentence" for short. The distinctions I shall draw are rather
rough and ready, and, no doubt, difficult cases could be produced which
would call for their refinement. But I think they will serve my purpose.
The distinctions are between:

(A1) a sentence

(A2) a use of a sentence

(A3) an utterance of a sentence

and, correspondingly, between:

(B1) an expression

(B2) a use of an expression

(B3) an utterance of an expression

   Consider again the sentence, "The king of France is wise." It is easy
to imagine that this sentence was uttered at various times from, say, the
beginning of the seventeenth century onwards, during the reigns of each
successive French monarch; and easy to imagine that it was also uttered
during the subsequent periods in which France was not a monarchy.
Notice that it was natural for me to speak of "the sentence" or "this
sentence" being uttered at various times during this period; or, in other
words, that it would be natural and correct to speak of *one and the same*
sentence being uttered on all these various occasions. It is in the sense in
which it would be correct to speak of one and the same sentence being
uttered on all these various occasions that I want to use the expression (A1) "a sentence." There are, however, obvious differences between
different *occasions of the use* of this sentence. For instance, if one man
uttered it in the reign of Louis XIV and another man uttered it in the
reign of Louis XV, it would be natural to say (to assume) that they were

respectively talking about different people; and it might be held that the first man, in using the sentence, made a true assertion, while the second man, in using the same sentence, made a false assertion. If on the other hand two different men simultaneously uttered the sentence (e.g. if one wrote it and the other spoke it) during the reign of Louis XIV, it would be natural to say (assume) that they were both talking about the same person, and, in that case, in using the sentence, they *must* either both have made a true assertion or both have made a false assertion. And this illustrates what I mean by *a use* of a sentence. The two men who uttered the sentence, one in the reign of Louis XV and one in the reign of Louis XIV, each made a different use of the same sentence; whereas the two men who uttered the sentence simultaneously in the reign of Louis XIV, made the same use[1] of the same sentence. Obviously in the case of this sentence, and equally obviously in the case of many others, we cannot talk of *the sentence* being true or false, but only of its being used to make a true or false assertion or (if this is preferred) to express a true or a false proposition. And equally obviously we cannot talk of *the sentence* being *about* a particular person, for the same sentence may be used at different times to talk about quite different particular persons, but only of *a use* of the sentence to talk about a particular person. Finally it will make sufficiently clear what I mean by an utterance of a sentence if I say that the two men who simultaneously uttered the sentence in the reign of Louis XIV made two different utterances of the same sentence, though they made the same *use* of the sentence.

If we now consider not the whole sentence, "The king of France is wise," but that part of it which is the expression, "the king of France," it is obvious that we can make analogous, though not identical distinctions between (1) the expression, (2) a use of the expression, and (3) an utterance of the expression. The distinctions will not be identical; we obviously cannot correctly talk of the expression "the king of France" being used to express a true or false proposition, since in general only sentences can be used truly or falsely; and similarly it is only by using a sentence and not by using an expression alone, that you can talk about a particular person. Instead, we shall say in this case that you *use* the expression to *mention* or *refer to* a particular person in the course of using the sentence to talk about him. But obviously in this case, and a great many others, the *expression* (B1) cannot be said to mention, or refer to, anything, any more than the *sentence* can be said to be true or false. The same expression can have different mentioning-uses, as the same sentence can be used to make statements with different truth-values. "Mentioning," or "referring," is not something an expression does; it is something that someone can use an expression to do. Mentioning, or referring to, something is a characteristic of *a use* of an expression, just as "being about" something, and truth-or-falsity, are characteristics of *a use* of a sentence.

A very different example may help to make these distinctions clearer. Consider another case of an expression which has a uniquely referring use, viz. the expression "I"; and consider the sentence, "I am hot." Countless people may use this same sentence; but it is logically impossible for two different people to make *the same use* of this sentence: or, if this is preferred, to use it to express the same proposition. The expression "I" may correctly be used by (and only by) any one of innumerable people to refer to himself. To say this is to say something about the expression "I": it is, in a sense, to give its meaning. This is the sort of thing that can be said about *expressions*. But it makes no sense to say of the *expression* "I" that it refers to a particular person. This is the sort of thing that can be said only of a particular use of the expression.

Let me use "type" as an abbreviation for "sentence or expression." Then I am not saying that there are sentences and expressions (types), *and* uses of them, *and* utterances of them, as there are ships *and* shoes *and* sealing-wax. I am saying that we cannot say *the same things* about types, uses of types, and utterances of types. And the fact is that we do talk about types; and that confusion is apt to result from the failure to notice the differences between what we can say about these and what we can say only about the *uses* of types. We are apt to fancy we are talking about sentences and expressions when we are talking about the uses of sentences and expressions.

This is what Russell does. Generally, as against Russell, I shall say this. Meaning (in at least one important sense) is a function of the sentence or expression; mentioning and referring and truth or falsity, are functions of the use of the sentence or expression. To give the meaning of an expression (in the sense in which I am using the word) is to give *general directions* for its use to refer to or mention particular objects or persons; to give the meaning of a sentence is to give *general directions* for its use in making true or false assertions. It is not to talk about any particular occasion of the use of the sentence or expression. The meaning of an expression cannot be identified with the object it is used, on a particular occasion, to refer to. The meaning of a sentence cannot be identified with the assertion it is used, on a particular occasion, to make. For to talk about the meaning of an expression or sentence is not to talk about its use on a particular occasion, but about the rules, habits, conventions governing its correct use, on all occasions, to refer or to assert. So the question of whether a sentence or expression *is significant or not* has nothing whatever to do with the question of whether the sentence, *uttered on a particular occasion*, is, on that occasion, being used to make a true-or-false assertion or not, or of whether the expression is, on that occasion, being used to refer to, or mention, anything at all.

The source of Russell's mistake was that he thought that referring or mentioning, if it occurred at all, must be meaning. He did not distinguish (B1) from (B2); he confused expressions with their use in a particular context; and so confused meaning with mentioning, with referring. If I talk about my handkerchief, I can, perhaps, produce the object I am referring to out of my pocket. I cannot produce the meaning of the expression, "my handkerchief," out of my pocket. Because Russell confused meaning with mentioning, he thought that if there were any expressions having a uniquely referring use, which were what they seemed (i.e. logical subjects) and not something else in disguise, their meaning must *be* the particular object which they were used to refer to. Hence the troublesome mythology of the logically proper name. But if someone asks me the meaning of the expression "this"—once Russell's favorite candidate for this status—I do not hand him the object I have just used the expression to refer to, adding at the same time that the meaning of the word changes every time it is used. Nor do I hand him all the objects it ever has been, or might be, used to refer to. I explain and illustrate the conventions governing the use of the expression. This *is* giving the meaning of the expression. It is quite different from giving (in any sense of giving) the object to which it refers; for the expression itself does not refer to anything; though it can be used, on different occasion, to refer innumerable things. Now as a matter of fact there is, in English, a sense of the word "mean" in which this word does approximate to "indicate, mention or refer to"; e.g. when somebody (unpleasantly) says, "I mean you"; or when I point and say, "That's the one I mean." But *the one I meant* is quite different from *the meaning of the expression* I used to talk of it. In this special sense of "mean," it is people who mean, not expressions. People use expressions to refer to particular things. But the meaning of an expression is not the set of things or the single thing it may correctly be used to refer to: the meaning is the set of rules, habits, conventions for its use in referring.

It is the same with sentences: even more obviously so. Everyone knows that the sentence, "The table is covered with books," is significant, and everyone knows what it means. But if I ask, "What object is that sentence about?" I am asking an absurd question—a question which cannot be asked about the sentence, but only about some use of the sentence: and in this case the sentence has not been used to talk about something, it has only been taken as an example. In knowing what it means, you are knowing how it could correctly be used to talk about things: so knowing the meaning has nothing to do with knowing about any particular use of the sentence to talk about anything. Similarly, if I ask: "Is the sentence true or false?" I am asking an absurd question, which becomes no less absurd if I add, "It must be one or the other since it is significant." The question is absurd, because the *sentence* is neither true nor false any more than it is *about* some object. Of course the fact that it is significant is the same as the fact that it *can* correctly be used to talk about something and that, in so using it, someone will be making a true or false assertion. And I will add that it will be used to make a true or false assertion *only* if the person using it *is* talking about something. If, when he utters it, he is not talking about anything, then his use is not a genuine one, but a spurious or pseudo-use: he is not making either a true or a false assertion, though he may think he is. And this points the way to the correct answer to the puzzle to which the theory of descriptions gives a fatally incorrect answer. The important point is that the question of whether the sentence is significant or not is quite independent of the question that can be raised about a particular use of it, viz. the question whether it is a genuine or a spurious use, whether it is being used to talk about something, or in make-believe, or as an example in philosophy. The question whether the sentence is significant or not is the question whether there exist such language habits, conventions or rules that the sentence logically could be used to talk about something; and is hence quite independent of the question whether it is being so used on a particular occasion.

III

Consider again the sentence, "The king of France is wise," and the true and false things Russell says about it.

There are at least two true things which Russell would say about the sentence:

1. The first is that it is significant; that if anyone were now to utter it, he would be uttering a significant sentence.

2. The second is that anyone now uttering the sentence would be making a true assertion only if there in fact at present existed one and only one king of France, and if he were wise.

What are the false things which Russell would say about the sentence? They are:

1. That anyone now uttering it would be making a true assertion or a false assertion.

2. That part of what he would be asserting would be that there at present existed one and only one king of France.

I have already given some reasons for thinking that these two statements are incorrect. Now suppose someone were in fact to say to you with a perfectly serious air: "The king of France is wise." Would you say, "That's untrue"? I think it is quite certain that you would not. But suppose he went on to *ask* you whether you thought that what he had just said was true, or was false; whether you agreed or disagreed with what he had just said. I think you would be inclined, with some hesitation, to say that you did not do either; that the question of whether his statement was true or false simply *did not arise*, because there was no such person as the king of France. You might, if he were obviously serious (had a dazed astray-in-the-centuries look), say something like: "I'm afraid you must be under a misapprehension. France is not a monarchy. There is no king of France." And this brings out the point that if a man seriously uttered the sentence, his uttering it would in some sense be *evidence* that he *believed* that there was a king of France. It would not be evidence for his believing this simply in the way in which a man's reaching for his raincoat is evidence for his believing that it is raining. But nor would it be evidence for his believing this in the way in which a man's saying, "It's raining," is evidence for his believing that it is raining. We might put it as follows. To say "The king of France is wise" is, in some sense of "imply," to *imply* that there is a king of France. But this is a very special and odd sense of "imply." "Implies" in this sense is certainly not equivalent to "entails" (or "logically implies"). And this comes out from the fact that when, in response to his statement, we say (as we should) "There is no king of France," we should certainly *not* say we were *contradicting* the statement that the king of France is wise. We are certainly not saying that it is false.

We are, rather, giving a reason for saying that the question of whether it is true or false simply does not arise.

And this is where the distinction I drew earlier can help us. The sentence, "The king of France is wise," is certainly significant; but this does not mean that any particular use of it is true or false. We use it truly or falsely when we use it to talk about someone; when, in using the expression, "The king of France," we are in fact mentioning someone. The fact that the sentence and the expression, respectively, are significant just is the fact that the sentence *could* be used, in certain circumstances, to say something true or false, that the expression *could* be used, in certain circumstances, to mention a particular person; and to know their meaning is to know what sort of circumstances these are. So when we utter the sentence without in fact mentioning anybody by the use of the phrase, "The king of France," the sentence does not cease to be significant: We simply *fail* to say anything true or false because we simply fail to mention anybody by this particular use of that perfectly significant phrase. It is, if you like, a spurious use of the sentence, and a spurious use of the expression; though we may (or may not) mistakenly think it a genuine use.

And such spurious[2] uses are very familiar. Sophisticated romancing, sophisticated fiction,[3] depend upon them. If I began, "The king of France is wise," and went on, "and he lives in a golden castle and has a hundred wives," and so on, a hearer would understand me perfectly well, without supposing *either* that I was talking about a particular person, *or* that I was making a false statement to the effect that there existed such a person as my words described. (It is worth adding that where the use of sentences and expressions is overtly fictional, the sense of the word "about" may change. As Moore said, it is perfectly natural and correct to say that some of the statements in *Pickwick Papers* are *about* Mr. Pickwick. But where the use of sentences and expressions is not overtly fictional, this use of "about" seems less correct; i.e. it would not *in general* be correct to say that a statement was about Mr. X or the so-and-so, unless there were such a person or thing. So it is where the romancing is in danger of being taken seriously that we might answer the question, "Who is he talking about?" with "He's not talking about anybody"; but, in saying this, we are not saying that what he is saying is either false or nonsense.)

Overtly fictional uses apart, however, I said just now that to use such an expression as "The king of France" at the beginning of a sentence was, in some sense of "imply," to imply that there was a king of France. When a man uses such an expression, he does not *assert*, nor does what he says *entail*, a uniquely existential proposition. But one of the conventional functions of the definite article is to act as a *signal* that a unique reference is being made—a signal, not a disguised assertion. When we begin a sentence with "the such-and-such" the use of "the" shows, but does not state, that we are, or intended to be, referring to one particular individual of the species "such-and-such." *Which* particular individual is a matter to be determined from context, time, place, and any other features of the situation of utterance. Now, whenever a man uses any expression, the presumption is that he thinks he is using it correctly: so when he uses the expression, "the such-and-such," in a uniquely referring way, the presumption is that he thinks both that there is *some* individual of that species, and that the context of use will sufficiently determine which one he has in mind. To use the word "the" in this way is then to imply (in the relevant sense of "imply") that the existential conditions described by Russell are fulfilled. But to use "the" in this way is not to *state* that those conditions are fulfilled. If I begin a sentence with an expression of the form, "the so-and-so," and then am prevented from saying more, I have made no statement of any kind; but I may have succeeded in mentioning someone or something.

The uniquely existential assertion supposed by Russell to be part of any assertion in which a uniquely referring use is made of an expression of the form "the so-and-so" is, he observes, a compound of two assertions. To say that there is a ϕ is to say something compatible with there being several ϕs; to say there is not more than one ϕ is to say something compatible with there being none. To say there is one ϕ and one only is to compound these two assertions. I have so far been concerned mostly with the alleged assertion of existence and less with the alleged assertion of uniqueness. An example which throws the emphasis on the latter will serve to bring out more clearly the sense of "implied" in which a uniquely existential assertion is implied, but not entailed, by the use of expressions in the uniquely referring way. Consider the sentence, "The table is covered with books." It is quite certain that in any normal use of this sentence, the expression "the table" would be used to make a unique reference, i.e. to refer to some one table. It is a quite strict use of the definite article, in the sense in which Russell talks on p. 30 of *Principia Mathematica* [p. 51, above], of using the article "*strictly*, so as to imply uniqueness." On the same page Russell says that a phrase of the form "the so-and-so," used strictly, "will only have an application in the event of there being one so-and-so and no more." Now it is obviously quite false that the phrase "the table" in the sentence "the table is covered with books," used normally, will "only have an application in the event of there being one table and no more." It is indeed tautologically true that, in such a use, the phrase will have an application only in the event of there being one table and no more *which is being referred to*, and that it will be understood to have an application only in the event of there being one table and no more which it is understood as being used to refer to. To use the sentence is not to assert, but it is (in the special sense discussed) to imply, that there is only one thing which is *both* of the kind specified (i.e. a table) *and is being referred to* by the speaker. It is obviously not to assert this. To refer is not to say you are referring. To say there is *some table or other* to which you are referring is not the same as referring to a particular table. We should have no use for such phrases as "the individual I referred to" unless there were something which counted as referring. (It would make no sense to say you had pointed if there were nothing which counted as pointing.) So once more I draw the conclusion that referring to or mentioning a particular thing cannot be dissolved into any kind of assertion. To refer is not to assert, though you refer in order to go on to assert.

Let me now take an example of the uniquely referring use of an expression not of the form, "the so-and-so." Suppose I advance my hands, cautiously cupped, towards someone, saying, as I do so, "This is a fine red one." He, looking into my hands and seeing nothing there, may say: "What is? What are you talking about?" Or perhaps, "But there's nothing in your hands." Of course it would be absurd to say that, in saying "But you've got nothing in your hands," he was *denying* or *contradicting* what I said. So "this" is not a disguised description in Russell's sense. Nor is it a logically proper name. For one must know what the sentence means in order to react in that way to the utterance of it. It is precisely because the significance of the word "this" is independent of any particular reference it may be used to make, though not independent of the way it may be used to refer, that I can, as in this example, use it to *pretend* to be referring to something.

The general moral of all this is that communication is much less a matter of explicit or disguised assertion than logicians used to suppose. The particular application of this general moral in which I am interested is its application to the case of making a unique reference. It is a part of the significance of expressions of the kind I am discussing that they can be used, in an immense variety of contexts, to make unique references. It is no part of their significance to assert that they are being so used or that the conditions of their being so used are fulfilled. So the wholly important distinction we are required to draw is between

(1) using an expression to make a unique reference; and

(2) asserting that there is one and only one individual which has certain characteristics (e.g. is of a certain kind, or stands in a certain relation to the speaker, or both).

This is, in other words, the distinction between

(1) sentences containing an expression used to indicate or mention or refer to a particular person or thing; and

(2) uniquely existential sentences.

What Russell does is progressively to assimilate more and more sentences of class (1) to sentences of class (2), and consequently to involve himself in insuperable difficulties about logical subjects, and about values for individual variables generally: difficulties which have led him finally to the logically disastrous theory of names developed in the *Enquiry into Meaning and Truth* and in *Human Knowledge*. That view of the meaning of logical-subject-expressions which provides the whole incentive to the Theory of Descriptions at the same time precludes the possibility of Russell's ever finding any satisfactory substitutes for those expressions which, beginning with substantival phrases, he progressively degrades from the status of logical subjects.[4] It is not simply, as is sometimes said, the fascination of the relation between a name and its bearer, that is the root of the trouble. Not even names come up to the impossible standard set. It is rather the combination of two more radical misconceptions: first, the failure to grasp the importance of the distinction (section II above) between what may be said of an expression and what may be said of a particular use of it; second, a failure to recognize the uniquely referring use of expressions for the harmless, necessary thing it is, distinct from, but complementary to, the predicative or ascriptive use of expressions. The expressions which can in fact occur as singular logical subjects are expressions of the class I listed at the outset (demonstratives, substantival phrases, proper names, pronouns): to say this is to say that these expressions, together with context (in the widest sense), are what one uses to make unique references. The point of the conventions governing the uses of such expressions is, along with the situation of utterance, to secure uniqueness of reference. But to do this, enough is enough. We do not, and we cannot, while referring, attain the point of complete explicitness at which the referring function is no longer performed. The actual unique reference made, if any, is a matter of the particular use in the particular context; the significance of the expression used is the set of rules or conventions which permit such references to be made. Hence we can, using significant expressions, pretend to refer, in make-believe or in fiction, or mistakenly think we are referring when we are not referring to anything.[5]

This shows the need for distinguishing two kinds (among many others) of linguistic conventions or rules: rules for referring, and rules for attributing and ascribing; and for an investigation of the former. If we recognize this distinction of use for what it is, we are on the way to solving a number of ancient logical and metaphysical puzzles.

My last two sections are concerned, but only in the barest outline, with these questions.

IV

One of the main purposes for which we use language is the purpose of stating facts about things and persons and events. If we want to fulfill this purpose we must have some way of forestalling the question, "What (who, which one) are you talking about?" as well as the question, "What are you saying about it (him, her)?" The task of forestalling the first question is the referring (or identifying) task. The task of forestalling the second is the attributive (or descriptive or classificatory or ascriptive) task. In the conventional English sentence which is used to state, or to claim to state, a fact about an individual thing or person or event, the performance of these two tasks can be roughly and approximately assigned to separable expressions.[6] And in such a sentence, this assigning of expressions to their separate rôles corresponds to the conventional grammatical classification of subject and predicate. There is nothing sacrosanct about the employment of separable expressions for these two tasks. Other methods could be, and are, employed. There is, for instance, the method of uttering a single word or attributive phrase in the conspicuous presence of the object referred to; or that analogous method exemplified by, e.g., the painting of the words "unsafe for lorries" on a bridge, or the tying of a label reading "first prize" on a vegetable marrow. Or one can imagine an elaborate game in which one never used an expression in the uniquely referring way at all, but uttered only uniquely existential sentences, trying to enable the hearer to identify what was being talked of by means of an accumulation of relative clauses. (This description of the purposes of the game shows in what sense it would be a game: this is not the normal use we make of existential sentences.) Two points require emphasis. The first is that the necessity of performing these two tasks in order to state particular facts requires no transcendental explanation: To call attention to it is partly to elucidate the meaning of the phrase, "stating a fact." The second is that even this elucidation is made in terms derivative from the grammar of the conventional singular sentence; that even the overly functional, linguistic distinction between the identifying and attributive rôles that words may play in language is prompted by the fact that ordinary speech offers us separable expressions to which the different functions may be plausibly and approximately assigned. And this functional distinction has cast long philosophical shadows. The distinctions between particular and universal, between substance and quality, are such pseudo-material shadows, cast by the grammar of the conventional sentence, in which separable expressions play distinguishable roles.[7]

To use a separate expression to perform the first of these tasks is to use an expression in the uniquely referring way. I want now to say something in general about the conventions of use for expressions used in this way, and to contrast them with conventions of ascriptive use. I then proceed to the brief illustration of these general remarks and to some further applications of them.

What in general is required for making a unique reference is, obviously, some device, or devices, for showing both *that* a unique reference is intended and *what* unique reference it is; some device requiring and enabling the hearer or reader to identify what is being talked about. In securing this result, the context of utterance is of an importance which it is almost impossible to exaggerate; and by "context" I mean, at least, the time, the place, the situation, the identity of the speaker, the subjects which form the immediate focus of interest, and the personal histories of both the speaker and those he is addressing. Besides context, there is, of course, convention—linguistic convention. But, except in the case of genuine proper names, of which I shall have more to say later, the fulfillment of more or less precisely stateable contextual conditions is *conventionally* (or, in a wide sense of the word, *logically*) required for the correct referring use of expressions in a sense in which this is not true of correct ascriptive uses. The requirement for the correct application of an expression in its ascriptive use to a certain thing is simply that the thing should be of a certain kind, have certain characteristics. The requirement for the correct application of an expression in its referring use to a certain thing is something over and above any requirement derived from such ascriptive meaning as the expression may have; it is, namely, the requirement that the thing should be in a certain relation to the speaker and to the context of utterance. Let me call this the contextual requirement. Thus, for example, in the limiting case of the word "I" the contextual requirement is that the thing should be identical with the speaker; but in the case of most expressions which have a referring use this requirement cannot be so precisely specified. A further, and perfectly general, difference between conventions for referring and conventions for describing is one we have already encountered, viz. that the fulfillment of the conditions for a correct ascriptive use of an expression is a part of what is stated by such a use; but the fulfillment of the conditions for a correct referring use of an expression is never part of what is stated, though it is (in the relevant sense of "implied") implied by such a use.

Conventions for referring have been neglected or misinterpreted by logicians. The reasons for this neglect are not hard to see, though they are hard to state briefly. Two of them are, roughly: (1) the preoccupation of most logicians with definitions; (2) the preoccupation of some logicians with formal systems.

(1) A definition, in the most familiar sense, is a specification of the conditions of the correct ascriptive or classificatory use of an expression. Definitions take no account of contextual requirements. So that in so far as the search for the meaning or the search for the analysis of an expression is conceived as the search for a definition, the neglect or misinterpretation of conventions other than ascriptive is inevitable. Perhaps it would be better to say (for I do not wish to legislate about "meaning" or "analysis") that logicians have failed to notice that problems of use are wider than problems of analysis and meaning.

(2) The influence of the preoccupation with mathematics and formal logic is most clearly seen (to take no more recent examples) in the cases of Leibniz and Russell. The constructor of calculuses, not concerned or required to make factual statements, approaches applied logic with a prejudice. It is natural that he should assume that the types of convention with whose adequacy in one field he is familiar should be really adequate, if only one could see how, in a quite different field—that of statements of fact. Thus we have Leibniz striving desperately to make the uniqueness of

unique references a matter of logic in the narrow sense, and Russell striving desperately to do the same thing, in a different way, both for the implication of uniqueness and for that of existence.

It should be clear that the distinction I am trying to draw is primarily one between different roles or parts that expressions may play in language, and not primarily one between different groups of expressions; for some expressions may appear in either role. Some of the kinds of words I shall speak of have predominantly, if not exclusively, a referring role. This is most obviously true of pronouns and ordinary proper names. Some can occur as wholes or parts of expressions which have a predominantly referring use, and as wholes or parts of expressions which have a predominantly ascriptive or classificatory use. The obvious cases are common nouns; or common nouns preceded by adjectives, including participial adjectives; or, less obviously, adjectives or participial adjectives alone. Expressions capable of having a referring use also differ from one another in at least the three following, not mutually independent, ways.

(1) They differ in the extent to which the reference they are used to make is dependent on the context of their utterance. Words like "I" and "it" stand at one end of this scale—the end of maximum dependence—and phrases like "the author of *Waverley*" and "the eighteenth king of France" at the other.

(2) They differ in the degree of "descriptive meaning" they possess: by "descriptive meaning" I intend "conventional limitation, in application, to things of a certain general kind, or possessing certain general characteristics." At one end of this scale stand the proper names we most commonly use in ordinary discourse; men, dogs, and motor-bicycles may be called "Horace." The pure name has no descriptive meaning (except such as it may acquire *as a result of* some one of its uses as a name). A word like "he" has minimal descriptive meaning, but has some. Substantival phrases like "the round table" have the maximum descriptive meaning. An interesting intermediate position is occupied by "impure" proper names like "The Round Table"—substantival phrases which have grown capital letters.

(3) Finally, they may be divided into the following two classes: (i) those of which the correct referring use is regulated by some *general* referring-cum-ascriptive conventions; (ii) those of which the correct referring use is regulated by no general conventions, either of the contextual or the ascriptive kind, but by conventions which are ad hoc for each particular use (though not for each particular utterance). To the first class belong

both pronouns (which have the least descriptive meaning) and substantival phrases (which have the most). To the second class belong, roughly speaking, the most familiar kind of proper names. Ignorance of a man's name is not ignorance of the language. This is why we do not speak of the meaning of proper names. (But it won't do to say they are meaningless.) Again an intermediate position is occupied by such phrases as "The Old Pretender." Only an old pretender may be so referred to; but to know which old pretender is not to know a general, but an ad hoc, convention.

   In the case of phrases of the form "the so-and-so" used referringly, the use of "the" together with the position of the phrase in the sentence (i.e. at the beginning, or following a transitive verb or preposition) acts as a signal *that* a unique reference is being made; and the following noun, or noun and adjective, together with the context of utterance, shows *what* unique reference is being made. In general the functional difference between common nouns and adjectives is that the former are naturally and commonly used referringly, while the latter are not commonly, or so naturally, used in this way, except as qualifying nouns; though they can be, and are, so used alone. And of course this functional difference is not independent of the descriptive force peculiar to each word. In general we should expect the descriptive force of nouns to be such that they are more efficient tools for the job of showing what unique reference is intended when such a reference is signalized; and we should also expect the descriptive force of the words we naturally and commonly use to make unique references to mirror our interest in the salient, relatively permanent and behavioral characteristics of things. These two expectations are not independent of one another; and, if we look at the differences between the commoner sort of common nouns and the commoner sort of adjectives, we find them both fulfilled. These are differences of the kind that Locke quaintly reports, when he speaks of our ideas of substances being *collections* of simple ideas; when he say that "powers make up a great part of our ideas of substances"; and when he goes on to contrast the identity of real and nominal essence in the case of simple ideas with their lack of identity and the shiftingness of the nominal essence in the case of substances. "Substance" itself is the troublesome tribute Locke pays to his dim awareness of the difference in predominant linguistic function that lingered even when the noun had been expanded into a more or less indefinite string of adjectives. Russell repeats Locke's mistake with a difference when, admitting the inference from syntax to reality to the extent of feeling that he can get rid of this metaphysical unknown only if he can purify language of the referring function altogether, he draws up his program for "abolishing particulars"; a programme, in fact, for abolishing the distinction of logical use which I am here at pains to emphasize.

The contextual requirement for the referring use of pronouns may be stated with the greatest precision in some cases (e.g. "I" and "you") and only with the greatest vagueness in others ("it" and "this"). I propose to say nothing further about pronouns, except to point to an additional symptom of the failure to recognize the uniquely referring use for what it is; the fact, namely, that certain logicians have actually sought to elucidate the nature of a variable by offering such *sentences* as "he is sick," "it is green," as examples of something in ordinary speech like a *sentential function*. Now of course it is true that the word "he" may be used on different occasions to refer to different people or different animals: so may the word "John" and the phrase "the cat." What deters such logicians from treating these two expressions as quasi-variables is, in the first case, the lingering superstition that a name is logically tied to a single individual, and, in the second case, the descriptive meaning of the word "cat." But "he," which has a wide range of applications and minimal descriptive force, only acquires a use as a referring word. It is this fact, together with the failure to accord to expressions, used referringly, the place in logic which belongs to them (the place held open for the mythical logically proper name), that accounts for the misleading attempt to elucidate the nature of the variable by reference to such words as "he," "she," "it."

Of ordinary proper names it is sometimes said that they are essentially words each of which is used to refer to just one individual. This is obviously false. Many ordinary personal names—names *par excellence*—are correctly used to refer to numbers of people. An ordinary personal name is, roughly, a word, used referringly, of which the use is *not* dictated by any descriptive meaning the word may have, and is *not* prescribed by any such general rule for use as a referring expression (or a part of a referring expression) as we find in the case of such words as "I," "this" and "the," but is governed by ad hoc conventions for each particular set of applications of the word to a given person. The important point is that the correctness of such applications does not follow from any *general* rule or convention for the use of the word as such. (The limit of absurdity and obvious circularity is reached in the attempt to treat names as disguised descriptions in Russell's sense; for what is in the special sense implied, but not entailed, by my now referring to someone by name is simply the existence of someone, *now being referred to*, who is *conventionally referred to* by that name) Even this feature of names, however, is only a symptom of the purpose for which they are employed. At present our choice of names is partly arbitrary, partly dependent on legal and social observances. It would be perfectly possible to have a thorough-going *system* of names, based e.g. on dates of birth, or on a minute classification of physiological and anatomical differences. But the success of any such system would depend entirely on the convenience of the resulting name-allotments for the purpose of making unique references; and this would depend on the multiplicity of the classifications used and the degree to which they cut haphazardly across normal social groupings. Given a sufficient degree of both, the selectivity supplied by context would do the rest; just as in the case with our present naming habits. Had we such a system, we could use name-words descriptively (as we do at present, to a limited extent and in a different way, with some famous names) as well as referringly. But it is by criteria derived from consideration of the requirements of the referring task that we should assess the adequacy of any system of naming. From the naming point of view, no kind of classification would be better or worse than any other simply because of the kind of classification—natal or anatomical—that it was.

I have already mentioned the class of quasi-names, of substantival phrases which grow capital letters, and of which such phrases as "the Glorious Revolution," "the Great War," "the Annunciation," "the Round Table" are examples. While the descriptive meaning of the words which follow the definite article is still relevant to their referring role, the capital letters are a sign of that extralogical selectivity in their referring use, which is characteristic of pure names. Such phrases are found in print or in writing when one member of some class of events or things is of quite outstanding interest in a certain society. These phrases are embryonic names. A phrase may, for obvious reasons, pass into, and out of, this class (e.g. "the Great War").

V

I want to conclude by considering, all too briefly, three further problems about referring uses.

1 *Indefinite references* Not all referring uses of singular expressions forestall the question "What (who, which one) are you talking about?" There are some which either invite this question, or disclaim the intention or ability to answer it. Examples are such sentence-beginnings as "A man told me that ... ," "Someone told me that ..." The orthodox (Russellian) doctrine is that such sentences are existential, but not uniquely existential. This seems wrong in several ways. It is ludicrous to suggest that part of what is asserted is that the class of men or persons is not empty. Certainly this is *implied* in the by now familiar sense of implication; but the implication is also as much an implication of the *uniqueness* of the particular object of reference as when I begin a sentence with such a phrase as "the table." The difference between the use of the definite and indefinite articles is, very roughly, as follows. We use "the" either when a previous reference has been made, and when "the" signalizes that the same reference is being made; or when, in the absence of a previous indefinite reference, the context (including the hearer's assumed knowledge) is expected to enable the hearer to tell *what* reference is being made. We use "a" either when these conditions are not fulfilled, or when, although a definite reference *could* be made, we wish to keep dark the identity of the individual to whom, or to which, we are referring. This is the *arch* use of such a phrase as "a certain person" or "someone"; where it could be expanded, not into "someone, but you wouldn't (or I don't) know who" but into "someone, but I'm not telling you who."

2 *Identification statements* By this label I intend statements like the following:

(ia) That is the man who swam the channel twice on one day.

(iia) Napoleon was the man who ordered the execution of the Duc d'Enghien.

The puzzle about these statements is that their grammatical predicates do not seem to be used in a straightforwardly ascriptive way as are the grammatical predicates of the statements:

(ib) That man swam the channel twice in one day.

(iib) Napoleon ordered the execution of the Duc d'Enghien.

But if, in order to avoid blurring the difference between (ia) and (ib) and (iia) and (iib), one says that the phrases which form the grammatical complements of (ia) and (iia) are being used referringly, one becomes puzzled about what is being said in these sentences. We seem then to be referring to the same person twice over and either saying nothing about

him and thus making no statement, or identifying him with himself and
thus producing a trivial identity.

The bogy of triviality can be dismissed. This only arises for those who
think of the object referred to by the use of an expression as its meaning,
and thus think of the subject and complement of these sentences as
meaning the same because they could be used to refer to the same person.

I think the differences between sentences in the (a) group and sentences
in the (b) group can best be understood by considering the differences
between the circumstances in which you would say (ia) and the circumstances in which you would say (ib). You would say (ia) instead of (ib) if
you knew or believed that your hearer knew or believed that *someone* had
swum the channel twice in one day. You say (ia) when you take your
hearer to be in the position of one who can ask: "Who swam the channel
twice in one day?" (And in asking this, he is not saying that anyone did,
though his asking it implies—in the relevant sense—that someone did.)
Such sentences are like answers to such questions. They are better called
"identification-statements" than "identities." Sentence (ia) does not assert
more or less than sentence (ib). It is just that you say (ia) to a man whom
you take to know certain things that you take to be unknown to the man
to whom you say (ib).

This is, in the barest essentials, the solution to Russell's puzzle about
"denoting phrases" joined by "is"; one of the puzzles which he claims for
the theory of descriptions the merit of solving.

3 *The logic of subjects and predicates* Much of what I have said of the
uniquely referring use of expressions can be extended, with suitable modifications, to the nonuniquely referring use of expressions; i.e. to some
uses of expressions consisting of "the," "all the," "all," "some," "some
of the," etc. followed by a noun, qualified or unqualified, in the *plural*;
to some uses of "they," "them," "those," "these"; and to conjunctions
of names. Expressions of the first kind have a special interest. Roughly
speaking, orthodox modern criticism, inspired by mathematical logic, of
such traditional doctrines as that of the Square of Opposition and of some
of the forms of the syllogism traditionally recognized as valid, rests on the
familiar failure to recognize the special sense in which existential assertions may be implied by the referring use of expressions. The universal
propositions of the fourfold schedule, it is said, must *either* be given a
negatively existential interpretation (e.g. for A, "there are no Xs which

are not Ys") *or* they must be interpreted as conjunctions of negatively and positively existential statements of, e.g., the form (for A) "there are no Xs which are not Ys, and there are Xs." The I and O forms are normally given a positively existential interpretation. It is then seen that, whichever of the above alternatives is selected, some of the traditional laws have to be abandoned. The dilemma, however, is a bogus one. If we interpret the propositions of the schedule as neither positively, nor negatively, nor positively *and* negatively, existential, but as sentences such that *the question of whether they are being used to make true or false assertions does not arise except when the existential condition is fulfilled for the subject term*, then all the traditional laws hold good together. And this interpretation is far closer to the most common uses of expressions beginning with "all" and "some" than is any Russellian alternative. For these expressions are most commonly used in the referring way. A literal-minded and childless man asked whether all his children are asleep will certainly not answer "Yes" on the ground that he has none; but nor will he answer "No" on this ground. Since he has no children, the question does not arise. To say this is not to say that I may not use the sentence, "All my children are asleep," with the intention of letting someone know that I have children, or of deceiving him into thinking that I have. Nor is it any weakening of my thesis to concede that singular phrases of the form "the so-and-so" may sometimes be used with a similar purpose. Neither Aristotelian nor Russellian rules give the exact logic of any expression of ordinary language; for ordinary language has no exact logic.

Notes

1. This usage of "use" is, of course, different from (a) the current usage in which "use" (of a particular word, phrase, sentence) = (roughly) "rules for using" = (roughly) "meaning"; and from (b) my own usage in the phrase "uniquely referring use of expressions" in which "use" = (roughly) "way of using."

2. The choice of the word "spurious" now seems to me unfortunate, at least for some nonstandard uses. I should now prefer to call some of these "secondary" uses.

3. The unsophisticated kind begins: "Once upon time there was ..."

4. And this in spite of the danger-signal of that phrase, "*misleading* grammatical form."

5. This sentence now seems to me objectionable in a number of ways, notably because of an unexplicitly restrictive use of the word "refer." It could be more exactly phrased as follows: "Hence we can, using significant expressions, refer in

secondary ways, as in make-believe or in fiction, or mistakenly think we are re-ferring to something in the primary way when we are not, in that way, referring to anything."

6. I neglect relational sentences; for these require, not a modification in the principle of what I say, but a complication of the detail.

7. What is said or implied in the last two sentences of this paragraph no longer seems to me true, unless considerably qualified.

Chapter 7

A Theory of Definite Descriptions

Karel Lambert

I

For the purpose of explaining ordinary singular inference it is desirable to
have a logic that is free of existence assumptions with respect to its argument constants.[1] In this kind of logic *any* singular term purporting to
refer to an existent, whether it actually succeeds in so referring or not, can
replace the free argument variables (parameters) $x, y, z, \ldots$ in the logical
formulas of the system. The key step in securing what I have called elsewhere a *free logic*[2] is to replace the rule of universal instantiation (or the
law of specification) in an otherwise "standard" first-order predicate calculus by a rule (or a law) that makes the tacit existence assumption in the
associated reasoning (or declaration) explicit. For example, a free logic
can be obtained from *Principia* by replacing

(1) $(x)(\phi x) \supset \phi y$

by

(2) $((x)(\phi x) \ \& \ E! \, y) \supset \phi y$

A theory of definite descriptions based on free logic demands certain
changes in Russell's theory of descriptions. For example, from Russell's
definition of "$\psi(\imath x)\phi x$" in *Principia* *14.01, the theorem

(3a) $\psi(\imath x)\phi x \supset (\exists x)(\phi x)$

is derivable. In effect, (3a) says that any sentence containing a description
containing "ϕ" logically implies the sentence that there are ϕs. From (3),

Reprinted from Karel Lambert (ed.) *Philosophical Applications of Free Logic*,
pp. 17–27, by permission of Karel Lambert, Kluwer Academic Publishers, and
Oxford University Press. © 1962 and 1964 Kluwer Academic Publishers, and
1991 Oxford University Press.

letting "ψ" be "$(\lambda y)(y = (\imath x)\phi x)$," with the help of the axiom of self-identity, one can obtain

(3a$_1$) $(\exists x)(\phi x)$

that is, any predicate "ϕ" is exemplified. But (3a$_1$) is not always true as is shown by letting "ϕ" be "is a headless horseman." Another consequence of *14.01 is the theorem

(3b) $\psi(\imath x)\phi x \supset (\exists y)((x)(\phi x \supset x = y))$

In effect, (3b) says that any sentence containing a description containing "ϕ" logically implies the sentence that there is at most one thing that is ϕ. (3b) is also defective. The theorem

(3b$_1$) $(\exists y)((x)(\phi x \supset x = y))$

can be deduced from (3b) in precisely the same way that (3a$_1$) was deduced from (3a). Theorem (3b$_1$) is not always true as is shown by letting "ϕ" be "is a writer." Rejection of (3a) and (3b), first, demands rejection of, or at least a change in, Russell's definition in *Principia* *14.01 and, second, supports the intuition of some ordinary language philosophers (e.g., Strawson) that, in general, descriptional statements logically imply neither existence nor uniqueness.

Moreover, free description theory can at least entertain the unconditional acceptance of certain "natural" theorems that, in *Principia*, are assertable only under restriction. Cases in point are the propositions that the such and such is (a) such and such, that is, in symbols,

(4) $\phi(\imath x)\phi x$

and

(4$_1$) $(\imath x)\phi x = (\imath x)\phi x$

In *Principia*, (4) and (4$_1$) are not independently assertable; they are assertable if and only if the descriptum exists. That is, for instance,

(5) $E!(\imath x)\phi x \equiv \phi(\imath x)\phi x$[3]

In Hintikka's[4] recent revision of description theory (4) is unconditionally assertable. It is a direct consequence of the axiom

(6) $y = (\imath x)\phi x \equiv (x)(\phi x \supset x = y \;\&\; \phi y)$

The proof sketch is as follows:

(a) From (6), $y = (\imath x)\phi x \supset (x)(\phi x \supset x = y \;\&\; \phi y)$: by Definition of "$\equiv$" and Simplification.

(b) From (a), $y = (\imath x)\phi x \supset \phi y$: by Distribution and Simplification.

(c) From (b), $\phi(\imath x)\phi x$: by Substitution $(\imath x)\phi x/y$ and Self-identity.

However, Henry Leonard[5] has noted that if (4), and Russell's definition in *Principia* *14.02, that is,

(7) $E!(\imath x)\phi x = \mathrm{Df}(\exists y)((x)(\phi x \equiv x = y))$

are accepted, the following difficulty arises. From (4), one can obtain by substitution,

(8) $(\exists y)(y = (\imath x)(\exists y)(y = x))$

Given the biconditional (acceptable both to Leonard and to Hintikka)

(9) $E!x \equiv (\exists y)(y = x)$

from (8), one gets

(10) $E!(\imath x)E!x$

Performing like operations on the biconditional licensed by Russell's definition in (7) one can obtain

(11) $E!(\imath x)E!x \equiv (\exists y)((x)(E!x \equiv x = y))$

Propositions (10) and (11) yield

(12) $(\exists y)((x)(E!x \equiv x = y))$,

a proposition that says there is exactly one existent!

In his own free modal theory of descriptions, Leonard avoids (12) by putting a restriction on (4), namely,[6]

(13) $\sim(x)(\sim\Diamond \sim\phi x \supset E!x) \supset \phi(\imath x)\phi x$

Proposition (13) does not allow deduction of the bothersome $E!(\imath x)E!x$.

The problem posed by (12) arises in free description theory, whether it be modal in character as is Leonard's theory, or nonmodal in character as is preferred by both Hintikka and myself, on the assumption of the essential correctness of "$\phi(\imath x)\phi x$." But "$\phi(\imath x)\phi x$" is defective in other ways that are more important than merely replacement of "ϕ" by "$E!$"

1 The Description Paradox

On the face of it, nothing could be more natural than the truth of "The such and such is (a) such and such." In symbols, again, this is

(14) $\phi(\imath x)\phi x$

But naturalness is not always a good measure of truth; witness the difficulties that ensue from an unwary acceptance of the natural method of
identifying classes specified in an unrestricted version of the principle of
class abstraction, that is, in

(15) $(x)(x \in \hat{y}(\phi y) \equiv \phi x))$

Substitution of "$\sim (x \in x)$" into "ϕ" in (15) produces a straightforward
contradiction, the famous paradox of classes, as Russell saw. Similarly
with (14), let us replace "ϕ" by the predicate "$(\lambda x)(\phi x \ \& \ \sim \phi x)$" in that
formula. By concretion one concludes from (14), under this interpretation
of "ϕ," that

(16) $\phi(\imath x)(\phi x \ \& \ \sim \phi x). \ \sim \phi(\imath x)(\phi x \ \& \ \sim \phi x),$

which is a contradiction. It follows that Hintikka's nonmodal theory of
descriptions is inconsistent. Leonard's modal theory, as the reader can
verify by a consideration of (13), avoids this result.

    One of the virtues of Russell's theory of descriptions, then, lies in the
fact that the description paradox is not derivable there. The most that can
be deduced in Russell's theory is

(17) $\sim E!(\imath x)(\phi x \ \& \ \sim \phi x)$

    The blemish, of course, must also be removed from the otherwise more
plausible free description theory. Accordingly,

(18) $\phi(\imath x)\phi x$

and, hence,

(19) $y = (\imath x)\phi x \supset \phi y$

and, hence, the axiom (6) in Hintikka's theory must be rejected. We are now
free to entertain Russell's definition of "$E!(\imath x)\phi x$" (in the more usable form),

(20) $E!(\imath x)\phi x = \mathrm{Df}(\exists y)((x)(\phi x \supset x = y) \ \& \ \phi y)$

Some important problems now are these: Can "$\phi(\imath x)\phi x$" be asserted under
some restriction without leading (1) to contradiction or (2) to the problem
posed by (12)? How much, if any, of Hintikka's key biconditional in (6)
can we accept? What conditions, if any, are necessary so that descriptional expressions in general can be eliminated in favor of the materials of
quantification theory with identity?

    Let us take these problems in the reverse order. In Hintikka's theory,
the biconditional[7]

(21) $(E!(\imath x)\phi x \ \& \ \psi(\imath x)\phi x) \equiv (\exists y)((x)(\phi x \supset x = y) \ \& \ \phi y \ \& \ \psi y)$

is acceptable. In fact, (21) is deducible with the help of (6). Proposition (21) seems quite reasonable. It allows us to eliminate a description in favor of quantificational materials only under the condition that the descriptum exists. Notice that the unwarranted (3a) and (3b) are not derivable from (21); the most that can be obtained are

(22) $(E!(\imath x)\phi x \ \& \ \psi(\imath x)\phi x) \supset (\exists x)(\phi x)$

and

(23) $(E!(\imath x)\phi x \ \& \ \psi(\imath x)\phi x) \supset (\exists y)((x)(\phi x \supset x = y))$

which appear entirely reasonable. Of additional importance is the fact that there can be deduced from (21),

(24) $E!(\imath x)\phi x \equiv (\exists y)((x)(\phi x \supset x = y) \ \& \ \phi y)$

a proposition that justifies acceptance of the definition in (20).

Let us now turn to the second question posed at the end of the preceding section.

It has already been established that (4) follows from the now rejected axiom in (6). Specifically, it follows from the already rejected part [see (19)] of the half of (6) that reads

(25) $y = (\imath x)\phi x \supset (x)(\phi x \supset x = y \ \& \ \phi y)$

But how is it with the other part of (25), the part that reads

(26) $y = (\imath x)\phi x \supset (x)(\phi x \supset x = y)$?

Taking our cue from the fallacious (3b), we ought at least to be suspicious of (26). Indeed, this attitude is justified; (26) is, in fact, defective. Substituting "$(\imath x)\phi x$" into "y" in (26), and with the help of the axiom of self-identity, one gets

(27) $(x)(\phi x \supset x = (\imath x)\phi x)$

Proposition (27), in turn, yields, with the help of (2),

(28) $(E!y \ \& \ \phi y) \supset y = (\imath x)\phi x$

But (28) is not always true as is shown by letting "y" be "Russell" and "ϕ" be "is a man who is a writer." So (26), and hence, all of (25), must be rejected in their present form.

Consider the other half of the axiom in (6), which reads:

(29) $(x)((\phi x \supset x = y) \ \& \ \phi y) \supset y = (\imath x)\phi x$

Is (29) acceptable? The answer is, "Almost!" But from (29), it follows that

(30) $\sim (\exists x)(\phi x \ \& \ \phi y) \supset y = (\imath x)\phi x$

But (30) can be false as is shown by letting "ϕ" be "is a flying horse" and "y" be "the flying horse captured by Bellerophon." It appears then that none of the rather direct consequences of (6) are unconditionally assertable.

Notice that (30) would not fail on the assumption that y exists. The same would hold for (29). I believe the same condition applies to the other half of (6) [see (25)]. Accordingly, let us adopt the following revision of Hintikka's axiom:

(31) $E!y \supset (y = (\imath x)\phi x \equiv (x)(\phi x \supset x = y \ \& \ \phi y)$

In effect (31) says that y is $(\imath x)\phi x$ if and only if y is uniquely characterized by ϕ, provided that y exists.

In free logic, with the help of universal generalization, the identity theorem, "$(x)(\exists y)(x = y)$" and the biconditional "$E! x \equiv (\exists y)(y = x)$," one can obtain from "$E!y \supset \phi y$," "$(y)\phi y$." Further, with revised specification [see (2)], one can obtain from "$(y)\phi y$," "$E!y \supset \phi y$." Accordingly, (31) may be rewritten as[8]

A_1 $(y)(y = (\imath x)\phi x \equiv ((x)(\phi x \supset x = y) \ \& \ \phi y)))$[9]

Adoption of this axiom has the following desirable consequences. First, the two important biconditionals in Hintikka's system described here in (21) and (24) are deducible from Axiom 1. Second, as suggested earlier, we can no longer deduce the faulty "$y = (\imath x)\phi x \supset \phi y$" or the faulty "$y = (\imath x)\phi x \supset (x)(\phi x \supset x = y)$" but only the reasonable

(32) $(E!y \ \& \ y = (\imath x)\phi x) \supset \phi y$

and

(33) $(E!y \ \& \ y = (\imath x)\phi x) \supset (x)(\phi x \supset x = y)$

Third, from (32) and (33) we can deduce the legitimate

(34) $E!(\imath x)\phi x \supset (\exists x)\phi x$

and

(35) $E!(\imath x)\phi x \supset (\exists y)((x)(\phi x \supset x = y))$

but not the defective

(36) $\psi(\imath x)\phi x \supset (\exists x)\phi x$

or

(37) $\psi(\iota x)\phi x \supset (\exists y)((x)(\phi x \supset x = y))$

Propositions (34) and (35) suggest that the descriptional context "$E!(\iota x)\phi x$" does logically imply both existence and uniqueness. This analysis also provides the answer to the first question posed at the end of the last section.

From (32) we can deduce, with the help of the axiom of self-identity,

(38) $E!(\iota x)\phi x \supset \phi(\iota x)\phi x$

That is, the such and such is (a) such and such, provided that the such and such exists. Proposition (38) neatly avoids the too-weak "$\phi(\iota x)\phi x$" and the too-strong "$E!(\iota x)\phi x \equiv \phi(\iota x)\phi x$" of Russell; the half of the Russell biconditional that reads

$\phi(\iota x)\phi x \supset E!(\iota x)\phi x$

is sometimes false, as is shown by letting "ϕ" be "is identical with the headless horseman." On the other hand, (38) is strong enough to preclude the description paradox while yet avoiding the bothersome "$E!(\iota x)E!x$." Concerning the former point, the present theory has the Russellian virtue that

(39) $\sim E!(\iota x)(\phi x \,\&\, \sim \phi x)$

Let me close this part with a recommendation. An important theorem in traditional description theory (which, also, is deducible in Hintikka's theory) is

(40) $y = (\iota x)(x = y)$

In the present version of free description theory, (40) is not deducible without restriction. But (40) appears to be unconditionally assertable. Therefore, let us add, as our second axiom in free description theory,

A_2 $y = (\iota x)(x = y)$

II

In the previous part, a free description theory based on the axioms

A_1 $(y)(y = (\iota x)\phi x \equiv ((x)(\phi x \supset x = y) \,\&\, \phi y)))$

and

A_2 $y = (\imath x)(x = y)$

was presented.

An unnoticed result of the theory is that, when appended to identity theory, the identity principle

(41) $x = x$

gets reduced to the status of a derived principle. Replace A_2 by the variant

A_2 $(\imath x)(y = x) = y$

Replace "x" by "$(\imath x)(y = x)$" and "ϕ" by "$(\lambda x)(x = y)$" in

(42) $x = y \supset (\phi x \supset \phi y)$

and (41) follows with the help of A_2.[10]

Is it possible to reduce the present version of free description theory without risk of the untoward results mentioned in the previous part? Yes; such a theory can be formulated with a single axiom. Further, variants of A_1 and A_2 are rather direct consequences of this theory. The result is a very elegant free quantification theory with identity. For example, Hintikka has shown that his version of free quantification theory with identity is simpler by one principle than the traditional version.[11] If the present suggestion for treating descriptional contexts of the form "$y = (\imath x)\phi x$" is appended to Hintikka's theory, his theory is reducible by two principles, viz. (in his notation) the principles

(4a) $f \rightarrow x = x$, where f contains a free occurrence of x

and

(4b) $f \rightarrow a = a$, where a occurs in f

are reducible to the status of derivable principles.

Assume the following variant of A_1:

A_1 $(y)((\imath x)\phi x = y \equiv (\phi y \ \& \ (x)(\phi x \supset y = x)))$

In free identity theory we have the theorem

(43) $(\imath x)\phi x = z \supset (y)(z = y \equiv (\imath x)\phi x = y)$

A_1 and (43), by quantification theory, yield

(44) $(\imath x)\phi x = z \supset (y)(z = y \equiv (\phi y \ \& \ (x)(\phi x \supset y = x)))$

The suggestion of the present paper is that the converse of (44) is also plausible, for example,

(45) $(y)(z = y \equiv (\phi y \ \& \ (x)(\phi x \supset y = x))) \supset (\imath x)\phi x = z$

If the converse of (43) were deducible in free quantification theory with identity, (45) would also be deducible. But in free quantification theory with identity, the converse of (43) is deducible only under the condition that $E!x$ [i.e., $(\exists z)(x = z)$]. This shows that neutrality of free quantification theory with identity on the question of the truthvalue to be assigned to identity contexts containing nonreferential singular terms. Note especially that it follows from the converse of (43) that

(46) $(\sim (\exists y)(y = z) \ \& \ \sim (\exists y)(\imath x)\phi x = y) \supset (\imath x)\phi x = z$

that is, if the substitution instances of "z" and "$(\imath x)\phi x$" have no designata any statement of the form "$(\imath x)\phi x = z$" is true. Such cases of what Quine calls "don't cares" can be decided arbitrarily in a way consistent with the rest of the theory.[12] For example, in the present theory no principle can be condoned that allows "$(\imath x)\phi x = (\imath x)\phi x$" to turn out false where "$(\imath x)\phi x$" is nonreferential. For the truth of "$(\imath x)\phi x = (\imath x)\phi x$," even where "$(\imath x)\phi x$" is nonreferential, follows from the unexceptionable identity principle "$x = x$."[13] Accordingly, I shall adopt (45), noticing particularly that where "$\sim (\exists y)(y = z)$" and "$\sim (\exists x)\phi x$," "$(\imath x)\phi x = z$" is deducible, and that (44) and (45) yield the biconditional justifying the axiom

A_3 $(\imath x)\phi x = z \equiv (y)(z = y \equiv (\phi y \ \& \ (x)(\phi x \supset y = x)))$

The common sense of A_3 is explicit in its verbal rendition. For what A_3 says is this: "The so and so is z just in case everything is z if and only if it and it only is so and so."

It remains to be proved that A_3 yields (41) (and, hence, A_1 and A_2) when appended to free quantification theory with identity where the only identity axiom is (42). A consequence of A_3 is

(47) $(\imath x)(z = x) = z \equiv (y)(z = y \equiv (z = y \ \& \ (x)(z = x \supset y = x)))$

Now, as the reader may verify, the right-hand side of (47) requires only (42) for its proof. Hence, we obtain

(48) $(\imath x)(z = x) = z$

But it has been pointed out earlier that (48) and (42) yield

(49) $x = x$

An instance of (49) is

(50) $(\imath x)\phi x = (\imath x)\phi x$

A_3 and (50) yield A_1. And this completes the task, for A_1 and A_2 easily follows.

The proof that "$x = x$" can be removed from among the basic assumptions of identity theory offers some additional support for free quantification theory with identity, via-à-vis simplicity.[14] For in traditional identity theory, "$x = x$" is not derivable without additional assumptions.

Notes

1. The definitive papers are by Henry S. Leonard, "The logic of existence," *Philosophical Studies*, vol. 4 (June 1956) pp. 49–64; Hugues Leblanc and Theodore Hailperin,"Non-designating singular terms," *Philosophical Review* (April 1959) pp. 239–244; and by Jaakko Hintikka, "Existential presuppositions and existential commitments," *Journal of Philosophy*, vol. 3 (Jan. 1959) pp. 125–137.

2. See the abstract of my address "The definition of E(xistence)! in free logic" in *Abstracts: The International Congress for Logic, Methodology and Philosophy of Science*, Stanford University Press (1960).

3. Another example is the faultless "$(\iota x)\phi x = (\iota x)\phi x$," which, in *Principia*, is not unconditionally assertable.

4. K. J. J. Hintikka, "Towards a theory of definite descriptions," *Analysis*, vol. 19 (1959) pp. 79–85.

5. "The logic of existence," p. 62.

6. Ibid.

7. The symbolic language in the present paper departs from that of Hintikka's and is similar to Leonard's. But this difference is not essential to my arguments.

8. The relationship between Axiom 1 and (31) is one of the key points of difference between free and classical predicate logic. In the latter, given "ϕx" one can always obtain "$(x)\phi x$," and vice versa. Among the consequences of this difference between the two logics is that a completeness proof for free logic based on the universal closures of the formulas of free logic will no longer work. In free logic, it is not true that to every wff ϕ containing free argument variables there corresponds a wff ϕ^c containing no free argument variables (= the closure of ϕ) such that ϕ is a theorem if and only if ϕ^c is a theorem, and such that ϕ is valid if and only if ϕ^c is valid. For example, "$(y)((x)(\phi x) \supset \phi y)$" is an example in free logic that violates the requisite condition.

9. [Among free logicians, A_1 is known as "Lambert's Law." Ed.]

10. In general, given a formula of the form "$x = y$," where "x" and "y" are distinct and "y" is a variable, (41) is deducible with the help of (42).

11. Jaakko Hintikka, "Existential presuppositions and existential commitments," *Journal of Philosophy*, vol. 56 (no. 3) (1959) pp. 126–127. Hintikka's system is truly one without existential presuppositions, both in the sense that the system does not require that its argument constants have bearers and in the sense that its principles hold in every domain including the empty one (i.e., in *all* possible worlds!).

12. W. V. Quine, *Word and Object*, Wiley, New York (1960) p. 259.

13. This is the case because, in free logic, nonreferential terms are admitted to the position of the argument variables.

14. The usefulness of free logic in ontological questions is shown by Hintikka (cf. note 3). He shows that an intuitive object language counterpart of Quine's thesis "To be is to be the value of a variable" is provable is free logic. It is not possible to do so in traditional symbolic logic, since the thesis has no suitable equivalents in that logic. Further, as I hope to show in the near future, free logic has important implications for the theory of classes; for example, "$(x)(x \in \hat{y}(\phi) \equiv \phi x)$," a proposition not assertable without restriction in class theories based on traditional symbolic logic, is assertable in free logic.

Historical Note. The theory of definite descriptions outlined in this essay, later called FD_2, was the first sound and complete free theory of definite descriptions ever devised. This was known by me in the early 1960s based on a semantics which later was to be called "outer domain semantics" (and independently discovered by Nuel Belnap). In that semantics a model structure intuitively was a triple consisting of an outer domain of nonexistents, an inner domain of existents and an interpretation function which assigned all individual constants to members in the union of the inner and outer domains, all n-adic predicates to sets of n-tuples of members in the union of those two domains, the individual in the inner domain of which the basis of a definite description is uniquely true to that definite description and an arbitrary member of the outer domain to all definite descriptions that did not meet the previous condition. Truth in a model was absolutely conventional except for the quantifiers which were defined only on the inner domain to give them their requisite existential force. This outer domain semantical approach, which I elaborated in logic classes in the late 1950s and early 1960s, did not then appeal to me because of its Meinong-like cast. Indeed it was this concern which helped to motivate Bas van Fraassen, who, as an undergraduate, did logic with me, to develop his own later anti-Meinongian supervaluational approach to free logic.

Chapter 8

Reference and Definite Descriptions
Keith Donnellan

I

Definite descriptions, I shall argue, have two possible functions. They are used to refer to what a speaker wishes to talk about, but they are also used quite differently. Moreover, a definite description occurring in one and the same sentence may, on different occasions of its use, function in either way. The failure to deal with this duality of function obscures the genuine referring use of definite descriptions. The best-known theories of definite descriptions, those of Russell and Strawson, I shall suggest, are both guilty of this. Before discussing this distinction in use, I will mention some features of these theories to which it is especially relevant.

On Russell's view a definite description may denote an entity: "if '*C*' is a denoting phrase [as definite descriptions are by definition], it may happen that there is one entity *x* (there cannot be more than one) for which the proposition '*x* is identical with *C*' is true.... We may then say that the entity *x* is the denotation of the phrase '*C*.'"[1] In using a definite description, then, a speaker may use an expression which denotes some entity, but this is the only relationship between that entity and the use of the definite description recognized by Russell. I shall argue, however, that there are two uses of definite descriptions. The definition of denotation given by Russell is applicable to both, but in one of these the definite description serves to do something more. I shall say that in this use the speaker uses the definite description to *refer* to something, and call this use the "referential use" of a definite description. Thus, if I am right, referring is not

Reprinted from *Philosophical Review* 75 (1966), pp. 281–304, by permission of the publisher. © 1966 Cornell University.

the same as denoting and the referential use of definite descriptions is not recognized on Russell's view.

Furthermore, on Russell's view the type of expression that comes closest to performing the function of the referential use of definite descriptions turns out, as one might suspect, to be a proper name (in "the narrow logical sense"). Many of the things said about proper names by Russell can, I think, be said about the referential use of definite descriptions without straining senses unduly. Thus the gulf Russell thought he saw between names and definite descriptions is narrower than he thought.

Strawson, on the other hand, certainly does recognize a referential use of definite definitions. But what I think he did not see is that a definite description may have a quite different role—may be used nonreferentially, even as it occurs in one and the same sentence. Strawson, it is true, points out nonreferential uses of definite descriptions,[2] but which use a definite description has seems to be for him a function of the kind of sentence in which it occurs; whereas, if I am right, there can be two possible uses of a definite description in the same sentence. Thus, in "On Referring," he says, speaking of expressions used to refer, "Any expression of any of these classes [one being that of definite descriptions] can occur as the subject of what would traditionally be regarded as a singular subject-predicate sentence; and would, so occurring, exemplify the use I wish to discuss."[3] So the definite description in, say, the sentence "The Republican candidate for president in 1968 will be a conservative" presumably exemplifies the referential use. But if I am right, we could not say this of the sentence in isolation from some particular occasion on which it is used to state something; and then it might or might not turn out that the definite description has a referential use.

Strawson and Russell seem to me to make a common assumption here about the question of how definite descriptions function: that we can ask how a definite description functions in some sentence independently of a particular occasion upon which it is used. This assumption is not really rejected in Strawson's arguments against Russell. Although he can sum up his position by saying, "'Mentioning' or 'referring' is not something an expression does; it is something that someone can use an expression to do,"[4] he means by this to deny the radical view that a "genuine" referring expression *has* a referent, functions to refer, independent of the context of some use of the expression. The denial of this view, however, does not entail that definite descriptions cannot be identified as referring expressions in a sentence unless the sentence is being used. Just as we can speak of a function of a tool that is not at the moment performing its function, Strawson's view, I believe, allows us to speak of the referential function of a definite description in a sentence even when it is not being used. This, I hope to show, is a mistake.

A second assumption shared by Russell's and Strawson's account of definite descriptions is this. In many cases a person who uses a definite description can be said (in some sense) to presuppose or imply that something fits the description.[5] If I state that the king is on his throne, I presuppose or imply that there is a king. (At any rate, this would be a natural thing to say for anyone who doubted that there is a king.) Both Russell and Strawson assume that where the presupposition or implication is false, the truth value of what the speaker says is affected. For Russell the statement made is false; for Strawson it has no truth value. Now if there are two uses of definite descriptions, it may be that the truth value is affected differently in each case by the falsity of the presupposition or implication. This is what I shall in fact argue. It will turn out, I believe, that one or the other of the two views, Russell's or Strawson's, may be correct about the nonreferential use of definite descriptions, but neither fits the referential use. This is not so surprising about Russell's view, since he did not recognize this use in any case, but it is surprising about Strawson's since the referential use is what he tries to explain and defend. Furthermore, on Strawson's account, the result of there being nothing which fits the description is a failure of reference.[6] This too, I believe, turns out not to be true about the referential use of definite descriptions.

II

There are some uses of definite descriptions which carry neither any hint of a referential use nor any presupposition or implication that something fits the description. In general, it seems, these are recognizable from the sentence frame in which the description occurs. These uses will not interest us, but it is necessary to point them out if only to set them aside.

An obvious example would be the sentence "The present King of France does not exist," used, say, to correct someone's mistaken impression that de Gaulle is the King of France.

A more interesting example is this. Suppose someone were to ask, "Is de Gaulle the King of France?" This is the natural form of words for a person to use who is in doubt as to whether de Gaulle is King or President of France. Given this background to the question, there seems to be no presupposition or implication that someone is the King of France. Nor is the person attempting to refer to someone by using the definite description. On the other hand, reverse the name and description in the question and the speaker probably would be thought to presuppose or imply this. "Is the King of France de Gaulle?" is the natural question for one to ask who wonders whether it is de Gaulle rather than someone else who occupies the throne of France.[7]

Many times, however, the use of a definite description does carry a presupposition or implication that something fits the description. If definite descriptions do have a referring role, it will be here. But it is a mistake, I think, to try, as I believe both Russell and Strawson do, to settle this matter without further ado. What is needed, I believe, is the distinction I will now discuss.

III

I will call the two uses of definite descriptions I have in mind the attributive use and the referential use. A speaker who uses a definite description attributively in an assertion states something about whoever or whatever is the so-and-so. A speaker who uses a definite description referentially in an assertion, on the other hand, uses the description to enable his audience to pick out whom or what he is talking about and states something about that person or thing. In the first case the definite description might be said to occur essentially, for the speaker wishes to assert something about whatever or whoever fits that description; but in the referential use the definite description is merely one tool for doing a certain job—calling attention to a person or thing—and in general any other device for doing the same job, another description or a name, would do as well. In the attributive use, the attribute of being the so-and-so is all important, while it is not in the referential use.

To illustrate this distinction, in the case of a single sentence, consider the sentence, "Smith's murderer is insane." Suppose first that we come upon poor Smith foully murdered. From the brutal manner of the killing and the fact that Smith was the most lovable person in the world, we might exclaim, "Smith's murderer is insane." I will assume, to make it a simpler case, that in a quite ordinary sense we do not know who murdered Smith (though this is not in the end essential to the case). This, I shall say, is an attributive use of the definite description.

The contrast with such a use of the sentence is one of those situations in which we expect and intend our audience to realize whom we have in mind when we speak of Smith's murder and, most importantly, to know that it is this person about whom we are going to say something.

For example, suppose that Jones has been charged with Smith's murder and has been placed on trial. Imagine that there is a discussion of Jones's odd behavior at his trial. We might sum up our impression of his behavior by saying, "Smith's murderer is insane." If someone asks to whom we are referring, by using this description, the answer here is "Jones." This, I shall say, is a referential use of the definite description.

That these two uses of the definite description in the same sentence are really quite different can perhaps best be brought out by considering the consequences of the assumption that Smith had no murderer (for example, he in fact committed suicide). In both situations, in using the definite description "Smith's murderer," the speaker in some sense presupposes or implies that there is a murderer. But when we hypothesize that the presupposition or implication is false, there are different results for the two uses. In both cases we have used the predicate "is insane," but in the first case, if there is no murderer, there is no person of whom it could be correctly said that we attributed insanity to him. Such a person could be identified (correctly) only in case someone fitted the description used. But in the second case, where the definite description is simply a means of identifying the person we want to talk about, it is quite possible for the correct identification to be made even though no one fits the description we used.[8] We were speaking about Jones even though he is not in fact Smith's murderer and, in the circumstances imagined, it was his behavior we were commenting upon. Jones might, for example, accuse us of saying false things of him in calling him insane and it would be no defense, I should think, that our description, "the murderer of Smith," failed to fit him.

It is, moreover, perfectly possible for our audience to know to whom we refer, in the second situation, even though they do not share our presupposition. A person hearing our comment in the context imagined might know we are talking about Jones even though he does not think Jones guilty.

Generalizing from this case, we can say, I think, that there are two uses of sentences of the form, "The ϕ is ψ." In the first, if nothing is the ϕ then nothing has been said to be ψ. In the second, the fact that nothing is the ϕ does not have this consequence.

With suitable changes the same difference in use can be formulated for uses of language other than assertions. Suppose one is at a party and, seeing an interesting-looking person holding a martini glass, one asks, "Who is the man drinking a martini?" If it should turn out that there is only water in the glass, one has nevertheless asked a question about a particular person, a question that it is possible for someone to answer. Contrast this with the use of the same question by the chairman of the local Teetotalers Union. He has just been informed that a man is drinking a martini at their annual party. He responds by asking his informant, "Who is the man drinking a martini?" In asking the question the chairman does not have some particular person in mind about whom he asks the question; if no one is drinking a martini, if the information is wrong, no person can be singled out as the person about whom the question was asked. Unlike the first case, the attribute of being the man drinking a martini is all-important, because if it is the attribute of no one, the chairman's question has no straight-forward answer.

This illustrates also another difference between the referential and the attributive use of definite descriptions. In the one case we have asked a question about a particular person or thing even though nothing fits the description we used; in the other this is not so. But also in the one case our question can be answered; in the other it cannot be. In the referential use of a definite description we may succeed in picking out a person or thing to ask a question about even though he or it does not really fit the description; but in the attributive use if nothing fits the description, no straightforward answer to the question can be given.

This further difference is also illustrated by commands or orders containing definite descriptions. Consider the order, "Bring me the book on the table." If "the book on the table" is being used referentially, it is possible to fulfill the order even though there is no book on the table. If, for example, there is a book *beside* the table, though there is none *on* it, one might bring that book back and ask the issuer of the order whether this is "the book you meant." And it may be. But imagine we are told that someone has laid a book on our prize antique table, where nothing should be put. The order, "Bring me the book on the table" cannot now be obeyed unless there is a book that has been placed on the table. There is no possibility of bringing back a book which was never on the table and having it be the one that was meant, because there is no book that in that sense was "meant." In the one case the definite description was a device for getting the other person to pick the right book; if he is able to pick the

right book even though it does not satisfy the description, one still succeeds in his purpose. In the other case, there is, antecedently, no "right
book" except one which fits the description; the attribute of being the
book on the table is essential. Not only is there no book about which an
order was issued, if there is no book on the table, but the order itself
cannot be obeyed. When a definite description is used attributively in a
command or question and nothing fits the description, the command
cannot be obeyed and the question cannot be answered. This suggests
some analogous consequences for assertions containing definite descriptions used attributively. Perhaps the analogous result is that the assertion
is neither true nor false: this is Strawson's view of what happens when the
presupposition of the use of a definite description is false. But if so,
Strawson's view works not for definite descriptions used referentially, but
for the quite different use, which I have called the attributive use.

I have tried to bring out the two uses of definite descriptions by pointing out the different consequences of supposing that nothing fits the description used. There are still other differences. One is this: when a definite
description is used referentially, not only is there in some sense a presupposition or implication that someone or something fits the description,
as there is also in the attributive use, but there is a quite different presupposition; the speaker presupposes of some *particular* someone or
something that he or it fits the description. In asking, for example, "Who
is the man drinking a martini?" where we mean to ask a question about
that man over there, we are presupposing that that man over there is
drinking a martini—not just that *someone* is a man drinking a martini.
When we say, in a context where it is clear we are referring to Jones,
"Smith's murderer is insane," we are presupposing that Jones is Smith's
murderer. No such presupposition is present in the attributive use of definite descriptions. There is, of course, the presupposition that someone *or
other* did the murder, but the speaker does not presuppose of someone in
particular—Jones or Robinson, say—that he did it. What I mean by this
second kind of presupposition that someone or something in particular
fits the description—which is present in a referential use but not in an
attributive use—can perhaps be seen more clearly by considering a
member of the speaker's audience who believes that Smith was not murdered at all. Now in the case of the referential use of the description,
"Smith's murderer," he could accuse the speaker of mistakenly presupposing both that someone or other is the murderer and that also Jones
is the murderer, for even though he believes Jones not to have done the

deed, he knows that the speaker was referring to Jones. But in the case of the attributive use, he can accuse the speaker of having only the first, less specific presupposition; he cannot pick out some person and claim that the speaker is presupposing that that person is Smith's murderer. Now the more particular presuppositions that we find present in referential uses are clearly not ones we can assign to a definite description in some particular sentence in isolation from a context of use. In order to know that a person presupposes that Jones is Smith's murderer in using the sentence "Smith's murderer is insane," we have to know that he is using the description referentially and also to whom he is referring. The sentence by itself does not tell us any of this.

IV

From the way in which I set up each of the previous examples it might be supposed that the important difference between the referential and the attributive use lies in the beliefs of the speaker. Does he believe of some particular person or thing that he or it fits the description used? In the Smith murder example, for instance, there was in the one case no belief as to who did the deed, whereas in the contrasting case it was believed that Jones did it. But this is, in fact, not an essential difference. It is possible for a definite description to be used attributively even though the speaker (and his audience) believes that a certain person or thing fits the description. And it is possible for a definite description to be used referentially where the speaker believes that nothing fits the description. It is true—and this is why, for simplicity, I set up the examples the way I did—that if a speaker does not believe that anything fits the description or does not believe that he is in a position to pick out what does fit the description, it is likely that he is not using it referentially. It is also true that if he and his audience would pick out some particular thing or person as fitting the description, then a use of the definite description is very likely referential. But these are only presumptions and not entailments.

To use the Smith murder case again, suppose that Jones is on trial for the murder and I and everyone else believe him guilty. Suppose that I comment that the murderer of Smith is insane, but instead of backing this up, as in the example previously used, by citing Jones's behavior in the dock, I go on to outline reasons for thinking that *anyone* who murdered poor Smith in that particularly horrible way must be insane. If now it turns out that Jones was not the murderer after all, but someone else was,

I think I can claim to have been right if the true murderer is after all insane. Here, I think, I would be using the definite description attributively, even though I believe that a particular person fits the description.

It is also possible to think of cases in which the speaker does not believe that what he means to refer to by using the definite description fits the description, or to imagine cases in which the definite description is used referentially even though the speaker believes *nothing* fits the description. Admittedly, these cases may be parasitic on a more normal use; nevertheless, they are sufficient to show that such beliefs of the speaker are not decisive as to which use is made of a definite description.

Suppose the throne is occupied by a man I firmly believe to be not the king, but a usurper. Imagine also that his followers as firmly believe that he is the king. Suppose I wish to see this man. I might say to his minions, "Is the king in his countinghouse?" I succeed in referring to the man I wish to refer to without myself believing that he fits the description. It is not even necessary, moreover, to suppose that his followers believe him to be the king. If they are cynical about the whole thing, know he is not the king, I may still succeed in referring to the man I wish to refer to. Similarly, neither I nor the people I speak to may suppose that *anyone* is the king and, finally, each party may know that the other does not so suppose and yet the reference may go through.

V

Both the attributive and the referential use of definite descriptions seem to carry a presupposition or implication that there is something which fits the description. But the reasons for the existence of the presupposition or implication are different in the two cases.

There is a presumption that a person who uses a definite description referentially believes that what he wishes to refer to fits the description. Because the purpose of using the description is to get the audience to pick out or think of the right thing or person, one would normally choose a description that he believes the thing or person fits. Normally a misdescription of that to which one wants to refer would mislead the audience. Hence, there is a presumption that the speaker believes *something* fits the description—namely, that to which he refers.

When a definite description is used attributively, however, there is not the same possibility of misdescription. In the example of "Smith's murderer" used attributively, there was not the possibility of misdescribing

Jones or anyone else; we were not referring to Jones nor to anyone else by using the description. The presumption that the speaker believes *someone* is Smith's murder does not arise here from a more specific presumption that he believes Jones or Robinson or someone else whom he can name or identify is Smith's murderer.

The presupposition or implication is borne by a definite description used attributively because if nothing fits the description the linguistic purpose of the speech act will be thwarted. That is, the speaker will not succeed in saying something true, if he makes an assertion; he will not succeed in asking a question that can be answered, if he has asked a question; he will not succeed in issuing an order that can be obeyed, if he has issued an order. If one states that Smith's murderer is insane, when Smith has no murderer, and uses the definite description nonreferentially, then one fails to say anything *true*. If one issues the order "Bring me Smith's murderer" under similar circumstances, the order cannot be obeyed; nothing would count as obeying it.

When the definite description is used referentially, on the other hand, the presupposition or implication stems simply from the fact that normally a person tries to describe correctly what he wants to refer to because normally this is the best way to get his audience to recognize what he is referring to. As we have seen, it is possible for the linguistic purpose of the speech act to be accomplished in such a case even though nothing fits the description; it is possible to say something true or to ask a question that gets answered or to issue a command that gets obeyed. For when the definite description is used referentially, one's audience may succeed in seeing to what one refers even though neither it nor anything else fits the description.

VI

The result of the last section shows something to be wrong with the theories of both Russell and Strawson; for though they give differing accounts of the implication or presupposition involved, each gives only one. Yet, as I have argued, the presupposition or implication is present for a quite different reason, depending upon whether the definite description is used attributively or referentially, and exactly what presuppositions or implications are involved is also different. Moreover, neither theory seems a correct characterization of the referential use. On Russell's there is a logical entailment: "The ϕ is ψ" entails "There exists one and only one

ϕ." Whether or not this is so for the attributive use, it does not seem true of the referential use of the definite description. The "implication" that something is the ϕ, as I have argued, does not amount to an entailment; it is more like a presumption based on what is *usually* true of the use of a definite description to refer. In any case, of course, Russell's theory does not show—what is true of the referential use—that the implication that *something* is the ϕ comes from the more specific implication that *what is being referred to* is the ϕ. Hence, as a theory of definite descriptions. Russell's view seems to apply, if at all, to the attributive use only.

Russell's definition of denoting (a definite description denotes an entity if that entity fits the description uniquely) is clearly applicable to either use of definite descriptions. Thus whether or not a definite description is used referentially or attributively, it may have a denotation. Hence, denoting and referring, as I have explicated the latter notion, are distinct and Russell's view recognizes only the former. It seems to me, moreover, that this is a welcome result, that denoting and referring should not be confused. If one tried to maintain that they are the same notion, one result would be that a speaker might be referring to something without knowing it. If someone said, for example, in 1960 before he had any idea that Mr. Goldwater would be the Republican nominee in 1964, "The Republican candidate for president in 1964 will be a conservative" (perhaps on the basis of an analysis of the views of party leaders) the definite description here would *denote* Mr. Goldwater. But would we wish to say that the speaker had referred to, mentioned, or talked about Mr. Goldwater? I feel these terms would be out of place. Yet if we identify referring and denoting, it ought to be possible for it to turn out (after the Republican Convention) that the speaker had, unknown to himself, referred in 1960 to Mr. Goldwater. On my view, however, while the definite description used did *denote* Mr. Goldwater (using Russell's definition), the speaker used it *attributively* and did not *refer* to Mr. Goldwater.

Turning to Strawson's theory, it was supposed to demonstrate how definite descriptions are referential. But it goes too far in this direction. For there are nonreferential uses of definite descriptions also, even as they occur in one and the same sentence. I believe that Strawson's theory involves the following propositions:

(1) If someone asserts that the ϕ is ψ he has not made a true or false statement if there is no ϕ.[9]

(2) If there is no ϕ then the speaker has failed to refer to anything.[10]

(3) The reason he has said nothing true or false is that he has failed to refer.

Each of these propositions is either false or, at best, applies to only one of the two uses of definite descriptions.

Proposition (1) is possibly true of the attributive use. In the example in which "Smith's murderer is insane" was said when Smith's body was first discovered, an attributive use of the definite description, there was no person to whom the speaker referred. If Smith had no murderer, nothing true was said. It is quite tempting to conclude, following Strawson, that nothing true *or* false was said. But where the definite description is used referentially, something true may well have been said. It is possible that something true was said of the person or thing referred to.[11]

Proposition (2) is, as we have seen, simply false. Where a definite description is used referentially it is perfectly possible to refer to something though nothing fits the description used.

The situation with proposition (3) is a bit more complicated. It ties together, on Strawson's view, the two strands given in (1) and (2). As an account of why, when the presupposition is false, nothing true or false has been stated, it clearly cannot work for the attributive use of definite descriptions, for the reason it supplies is that reference has failed. It does not then give the reason why, if indeed this is so, a speaker using a definite description attributively fails to say anything true or false if nothing fits the description. It does, however, raise a question about the referential use. Can reference fail when a definite description is used referentially?

I do not fail to refer merely because my audience does not correctly pick out what I am referring to. I can be referring to a particular man when I use the description "the man drinking a martini," even though the people to whom I speak fail to pick out the right person or any person at all. Nor, as we have stressed, do I fail to refer when nothing fits the description. But perhaps I fail to refer in some extreme circumstances, when there is nothing that *I* am willing to pick out as that to which I referred.

Suppose that I think I see at some distance a man walking and ask, "Is the man carrying a walking stick the professor of history?" We should perhaps distinguish four cases at this point. (a) There is a man carrying a walking stick; I have then referred to a person and asked a question about him that can be answered if my audience has the information. (b) The man over there is not carrying a walking stick, but an umbrella; I have still referred to someone and asked a question that can be answered, though if my audience sees that it is an umbrella and not a walking stick, they may also correct my apparently mistaken impression. (c) It is not a man at all, but a rock that looks like one; in this case, I think I still have referred to something, to the thing over there that happens to be a rock but that I took to be a man. But in this case it is not clear that my question can be answered correctly. This, I think, is not because I have failed to refer, but rather because, given the true nature of what I referred to, my question is not appropriate. A simple "No, that is not the professor of history" is at least a bit misleading if said by someone who realizes that I mistook a rock for a person. It may, therefore, be plausible to conclude that in such a case I have not asked a question to which there is a straightforwardly correct answer. But if this is true, it is not because nothing fits the description I used, but rather because what I referred to is a rock and my question has no correct answer when asked of a rock. (d) There is finally the case in which there is nothing at all where I thought there was a man with a walking stick; and perhaps here we have a genuine failure to refer at all, even though the description was used for the purpose of referring. There is no rock, nor anything else, to which I meant to refer; it was, perhaps, a trick of light that made me think there was a man there. I cannot say of anything, "That is what I was referring to, though I now see that it's not a man carrying a walking stick." This failure of reference, however, requires circumstances much more radical than the mere nonexistence of anything fitting the description used. It requires that there be nothing of which it can be said, "That is what he was referring to." Now perhaps also in such cases, if the speaker has asserted something, he fails to state anything true or false if there is nothing that can be identified as that to which he referred. But if so, the failure of reference and truth value does not come about merely because nothing fits the description he used. So (3) may be true of some cases of the referential use of definite descriptions; it may be true that a failure of reference results in a lack of truth value. But these cases are of a much more extreme sort than Strawson's theory implies.

I conclude, then, that neither Russell's nor Strawson's theory represents a correct account of the use of definite descriptions—Russell's because it ignores altogether the referential use, Strawson's because it fails to make the distinction between the referential and the attributive and mixes together truths about each (together with some things that are false).

VII

It does not seem possible to say categorically of a definite description in a particular sentence that it is a referring expression (of course, one could say this if he meant that it *might* be used to refer). In general, whether or not a definite description is used referentially or attributively is a function of the speaker's intentions in a particular case. "The murderer of Smith" may be used either way in the sentence "The murderer of Smith is insane." It does not appear plausible to account for this, either, as an ambiguity in the sentence. The grammatical structure of the sentence seems to me to be the same whether the description is used referentially or attributively: that is, it is not syntactically ambiguous. Nor does it seem at all attractive to suppose an ambiguity in the meaning of the words; it does not appear to be semantically ambiguous. (Perhaps we could say that the sentence is pragmatically ambiguous: the distinction between roles that the description plays is a function of the speaker's intentions.) These, of course, are intuitions; I do not have an argument for these conclusions. Nevertheless, the burden of proof is surely on the other side.

This, I think, means that the view, for example, that sentences can be divided up into predicates, logical operators, and referring expressions is not generally true. In the case of definite descriptions one cannot always assign the referential function in isolation from a particular occasion on which it is used.

There may be sentences in which a definite description can be used only attributively or only referentially. A sentence in which it seems that the definite description could be used only attributively would be "Point out the man who is drinking my martini." I am not so certain that any can be found in which the definite description can be used only referentially. Even if there are such sentences, it does not spoil the point that there are many sentences, apparently not ambiguous either syntactically or semantically, containing definite descriptions that can be used either way.

If it could be shown that the dual use of definite descriptions can be accounted for by the presence of an ambiguity, there is still a point to be made against the theories of Strawson and Russell. For neither, so far as I can see, has anything to say about the possibility of such an ambiguity and, in fact neither seems compatible with such a possibility. Russell's does not recognize the possibility of the referring use, and Strawson's, as I have tried to show in the last section, combines elements from each use into one unitary account. Thus the view that there is an ambiguity in such sentences does not seem any more attractive to these positions.

VIII

Using a definite description referentially, a speaker may say something true even though the description correctly applies to nothing. The sense in which he may say something true is the sense in which he may say something true about someone or something. This sense is, I think, an interesting one that needs investigation. Isolating it is one of the byproducts of the distinction between the attributive and referential uses of definite descriptions.

For one thing, it raises questions about the notion of a statement. This is brought out by considering a passage in a paper by Leonard Linsky in which he rightly makes the point that one can refer to someone although the definite description used does not correctly describe the person:

... said of a spinster that "Her husband is kind to her" is neither true nor false. But a speaker might very well be referring to someone using these words, for he may think that someone is the husband of the lady (who in fact is a spinster). Still, the statement is neither true nor false, for it presupposes that the lady has a husband, which she has not. This last refutes Strawson's thesis that if the presupposition of existence is not satisfied, the speaker has failed to refer.[12]

There is much that is right in this passage. But because Linsky does not make the distinction between the referential and the attributive uses of definite descriptions, it does not represent a wholly adequate account of the situation. A perhaps minor point about this passage is that Linsky apparently thinks it sufficient to establish that the speaker in his example is referring to someone by using the definite description "her husband," that he *believe* that someone is her husband. This will only approximate the truth provided that the "someone" in the description of the belief means "someone in particular" and is not merely the existential quantifier, "there is someone or other." For in both the attributive and the referential use the belief that someone *or other* is the husband of the lady is very likely to be present. If, for example, the speaker has just met the lady and, noticing her cheerfulness and radiant good health, makes his remark from his conviction that these attributes are always the result of having good husbands, he would be using the definite description attributively. Since she has no husband, there is no one to pick out as the person to whom he was referring. Nevertheless, the speaker believed that *someone or other* was her husband. On the other hand, if the use of "her husband" was simply a way of referring to a man the speaker has just met whom he assumed to be the lady's husband, he would have referred to that man even though neither he nor anyone else fits the description. I think it is likely that in this passage Linsky did mean by "someone," in his description of the belief, "someone in particular." But even then, as we have seen, we have neither a sufficient nor a necessary condition for a referential use of the definite description. A definite description can be used attributively even when the speaker believes that some particular thing or person fits the description, and it can be used referentially in the absence of this belief.

My main point, here, however, has to do with Linsky's view that because the presupposition is not satisfied, the *statement* is neither true nor false. This seems to me possibly correct *if* the definite description is thought of as being used attributively (depending upon whether we go with Strawson or Russell). But when we consider it as used referentially, this categorical assertion is no longer clearly correct. For the man the speaker referred to may indeed be kind to the spinster; the speaker may have said something true about that man. Now the difficulty is in the notion of "the statement." Suppose that we know that the lady is a spinster, but nevertheless know that the man referred to by the speaker is kind to her. It seems to me that we shall, on the one hand, want to hold that the speaker said something true, but be reluctant to express this by "It is true that her husband is kind to her."

This shows, I think, a difficulty in speaking simply about "the statement" when definite descriptions are used referentially. For the speaker stated something, in this example, about a particular person, and his statement, we may suppose, was true. Nevertheless, we should not like to agree with his statement by using the sentence he used; we should not like to identify the true statement via the speaker's words. The reason for this is not so hard to find. If we say, in this example, "It is true that her husband is kind to her," *we* are now using the definite description either attributively or referentially. But we should not be subscribing to what the original speaker truly said if we use the description attributively, for it was only in its function as referring to a particular person that the definite description yields the possibility of saying something true (since the lady had no husband). Our reluctance, however, to endorse the original speaker's statement by using the definite description referentially to refer to the same person stems from quite a different consideration. For if we too were laboring under the mistaken belief that this man was the lady's husband, we could agree with the original speaker using his exact words. (Moreover, it is possible, as we have seen, deliberately to use a definite description to refer to someone we believe not to fit the description.) Hence, our reluctance to use the original speaker's words does not arise from the fact that if we did we should not succeed in stating anything true or false. It rather stems from the fact that when a definite description is used referentially there is a presumption that the speaker believes that what he refers to fits the description. Since we, who know the lady to be a spinster, would not normally want to give the impression that we believe otherwise, we would not like to use the original speaker's way of referring to the man in question.

How then would we express agreement with the original speaker without involving ourselves in unwanted impressions about our beliefs? The answer shows another difference between the referential and attributive uses of definite descriptions and brings out an important point about genuine referring.

When a speaker says, "The ϕ is ψ," where "the ϕ" is used attributively, if there is no ϕ, we cannot correctly report the speaker as having said *of* this or that person or thing that it is ψ. But if the definite description is used referentially we can report the speaker as having attributed ψ to something. And *we* may refer to what the speaker referred to, using whatever description or name suits our purpose. Thus, if a speaker says, "Her husband is kind to her," referring to the man he was just talking to, and if that man is Jones, we may report him as having said *of Jones* that he is kind to her. If Jones is also the president of the college, we may report the speaker as having said *of the president of the college* that he is kind to her. And finally, if we are talking to Jones, we may say, referring to the original speaker, "He said of you that *you* are kind to her." It does not matter here whether or not the woman has a husband or whether, if she does, Jones is her husband. If the original speaker referred to Jones, he said of him that he is kind to her. Thus where the definite description is used referentially, but does not fit what was referred to, we can report what a speaker said and agree with him by using a description or name which does fit. In doing so we need not, it is important to note, choose a description or name which the original speaker would agree fits what he was referring to. That is, we can report the speaker in the above case to have said truly of Jones that he is kind to her even if the original speaker did not know that the man he was referring to is named Jones or even if he thinks he is not named Jones.

Returning to what Linsky said in the passage quoted, he claimed that, were someone to say "Her husband is kind to her," when she has no husband, *the statement* would be neither true nor false. As I have said, this is a likely view to hold if the definite description is being used attributively. But if it is being used referentially it is not clear what is meant by "the statement." If we think about what the speaker said about the person he referred to, then there is no reason to suppose he has not said something true or false about him, even though he is not the lady's husband. And Linsky's claim would be wrong. On the other hand, if we do not identify the statement in this way, what is the statement that the speaker made? To say that the statement he made was that her husband is kind to her lands us in difficulties. For we have to decide whether in using the definite description here in the identification of the statement, we are using it attributively or referentially. If the former, then we misrepresent the linguistic performance of the speaker; if the latter, then we are ourselves referring to someone and reporting the speaker to have said something of that person, in which case we are back to the possibility that he did say something true or false of that person.

I am thus drawn to the conclusion that when a speaker uses a definite description referentially he may have stated something true or false even if nothing fits the description, and that there is not a clear sense in which he has made a statement which is neither true nor false.

IX

I want to end by a brief examination of a picture of what a genuine referring expression is that one might derive from Russell's views. I want to suggest that this picture is not so far wrong as one might suppose and that strange as this may seem, some of the things we have said about the referential use of definite descriptions are not foreign to this picture.

Genuine proper names, in Russell's sense, would refer to something without ascribing any properties to it. They would, one might say, refer to the thing itself, not simply the thing in so far as it falls under a certain description.[13] Now this would seem to Russell something a definite description could not do, for he assumed that if definite descriptions were capable of referring at all, they would refer to something only in so far as that thing satisfied the description. Not only have we seen this assumption to be false, however, but in the last section we saw something more. We saw that when a definite description is used referentially, a speaker can be reported as having said something *of* something. And in reporting what it was of which he said something we are not restricted to the description he used, or synonyms of it; we may ourselves refer to it using any descriptions, names and so forth, that will do the job. Now this seems to give a sense in which we are concerned with the thing itself and not just the thing under a certain description, when we report the linguistic act of a speaker using a definite description referentially. That is, such a definite description comes closer to performing the function of Russell's proper names than certainly he supposed.

Second, Russell thought, I believe, that whenever we use descriptions, as opposed to proper names, we introduce an element of generality which ought to be absent if what we are doing is referring to some particular thing. This is clear from his analysis of sentences containing definite descriptions. One of the conclusions we are supposed to draw from that analysis is that such sentences express what are in reality completely general propositions: there is a ϕ and only one such and any ϕ is ψ. We might put this in a slightly different way. If there is anything which might be identified as reference here, it is reference in a very weak sense—namely, reference to *whatever* is the one and only one ϕ, if there is any such. Now this is something we might well say about the attributive use of definite descriptions, as should be evident from the previous discussion. But this lack of particularity is absent from the referential use of definite descriptions precisely because the description is here merely a device for getting one's audience to pick out or think of the thing to be spoken about, a device which may serve its function even if the description is incorrect. More importantly perhaps, in the referential use as opposed to the attributive, there is a *right* thing to be picked out by the audience and its being the right thing is not simply a function of its fitting the description.

Acknowledgements

I should like to think my colleagues, John Canfield, Sydney Shoemaker, and Timothy Smiley, who read an earlier draft and gave me helpful suggestions. I also had the benefit of the valuable and detailed comments of the referee for the paper, to whom I wish to express my gratitude.

Notes

1. "On Denoting," reprinted in *Logic and Knowledge*, ed. Robert C. Marsh (London: 1956), p. 51 (this volume, p. 44).

2. "On Referring," reprinted in *Philosophy and Ordinary Language*, ed. Charles
C. Caton (Urbana: 1963), pp. 162–163 (this volume, p. 135).

3. *Ibid.*, p. 162.

4. *Ibid.*, p. 170.

5. Here and elsewhere I use the disjunction "presuppose or imply" to avoid taking
a stand that would side me with Russell or Strawson on the issue of what the relationship involved is. To take a stand here would be beside my main point as well
as being misleading, since later on I shall argue that the presupposition or implication arises in a different way depending upon the use to which the definite
description is put. This last also accounts for my use of the vagueness indicator,
"in some sense."

6. In a footnote added to the original version of "On Referring" (this volume,
p. 159) Strawson seems to imply that where the presupposition is false, we still
succeed in referring in a "secondary" way, which seems to mean "as we could
be said to refer to fictional or make-believe things." But his view is still that we
cannot refer in such a case in the "primary" way. This is, I believe, wrong. For
a discussion of this modification of Strawson's view see Charles E. Caton,
"Strawson on Referring," *Mind*, LXVIII (1959), 539–544.

7. This is an adaptation of an exampole (used for a somewhat different purpose)
given by Leonard Linsky in "Reference and Referents," in *Philosophy and Ordinary Language*, p. 80.

8. In "Reference and Referents" (pp. 74–75, 80), Linsky correctly points out that
one does not fail to refer simply because the description used does not in fact fit
anything (or fits more than one thing). Thus he pinpoints one of the difficulties in
Strawson's view. Here, however, I use this fact about referring to make a distinction I believe he does not draw, between two uses of definite descriptions. I later
discuss the second passage from Linsky's paper.

9. In "A Reply to Mr. Sellars," *Philosophical Review*, LXIII (1954), 216–231,
Strawson admits that we do not always refuse to ascribe truth to what a person
says when the definite description he uses fails to fit anything (or fits more than
one thing). To cite one of his examples, a person who said, "The United States
Chamber of Deputies contains representatives of two major parties," would be
allowed to have said something true even though he had used the wrong title.
Strawson thinks this does not constitute a genuine problem for his view. He thinks
that what we do in such cases, "where the speaker's intended reference is pretty
clear, is simply to amend his statement in accordance with his guessed intentions
and assess the amended statement for truth or falsity: we are not awarding a truth
value at all to the original statement" (p. 230).

The notion of an "amended statement," however, will not do. We may note,
first of all, that the sort of case Strawson has in mind could arise only when a
definite description is used referentially. For the "amendment" is made by seeing
the speaker's intended reference. But this could happen only if the speaker had
an intended reference, a particular person or thing in mind, independent of the
description he used. The cases Strawson has in mind are presumably not cases of

slips of the tongue or the like; presumably they are cases in which a definite description is used because the speaker believes, though he is mistaken, that he is describing correctly what he wants to refer to. We supposedly amend the statement by knowing to what he intends to refer. But what description is to be used in the amended statement? In the example, perhaps, we could use "the United States Congress." But this description might be one the speaker would not even accept as correctly describing what he wants to refer to, because he is misinformed about the correct title. Hence, this is not a case of deciding what the speaker meant to say as opposed to what he in fact said, for the speaker did not mean to say "the United States Congress." If this is so, then there is no bar to the "amended" statement containing any description that does correctly pick out what the speaker intended to refer to. It could be, e.g., "The lower house of the United States Congress." But this means that there is no one unique "amended" statement to be assessed for truth value. And, in fact, it should now be clear that the notion of the amended statement really plays no role anyway. For if we can arrive at the amended statement only by first knowing to what the speaker intended to refer, we can assess the truth of what he said simply by deciding whether what he intended to refer to has the properties he ascribed to it.

10. As noted earlier (note 6), Strawson may allow that one has possibly referred in a "secondary" way, but, if I am right, the fact that there is no ϕ does not preclude one from having referred in the same way one does if there is a ϕ.

11. For a further discussion of the notion of saying something true *of* someone or something, see section VIII.

12. "Reference and Referents," p. 80. It should be clear that I agree with Linsky in holding that a speaker may refer even though the "presupposition of existence" is not satisfied. And I agree in thinking this an objection to Strawson's view. I think, however, that this point, among others, can be used to define two distinct uses of definite descriptions which, in turn, yields a more general criticism of Strawson. So, while I develop here a point of difference, which grows out of the distinction I want to make, I find myself in agreement with much of Linsky's article.

13. Cf. "The Philosophy of Logical Atomism," reprinted in *Logic and Knowledge*, p. 200.

Chapter 9

From "Vacuous Names"   H. P. Grice

9.1 Names and Descriptions

It might be objected that, in setting up Q^1 in such a way as to allow for the representation of vacuous names, I have ensured the abandonment, at least in spirit, of one of the desiderata which I have had in mind; for (it might be suggested) if Q is extended so as to include a Theory of Descriptions, its individual constants will be seen to be indistinguishable, both syntactically and semantically, from unanalysed definite descriptions; they will be related to representations of descriptions in very much the same way as propositional letters are related to formulae, having lost the feature which is needed to distinguish them from representations of descriptions, namely that of being interpretable only by the assignment of a designatum.

I do not propose to prolong this paper by including the actual presentation of an extension of Q which includes the representation of descriptions, but I hope to be able to say enough about how I envisage such an extension to make it clear that there will be a formal difference between the individual constants of Q and definite descriptions. It is a familiar fact that there are at least two ways in which a notation for representing definite descriptions may be developed within a classical system; one may represent "The haberdasher of Mr. Spurgeon is bald" either by (1) $G(\imath x . Fx)$ or by (2) $(\imath x . Fx)Gx$; one may, that is, treat "$\imath x . Fx$" either as a term or as being analogous to a (restricted) quantifier. The first method does not allow for the representation of scope-differences, so a general

Reprinted from "Vacuous Names," in D. Davidson and J. Hintikka (eds.) *Words and Objections*, pp. 138–144, by permission of Kluwer Academic Publishers. © 1969 Kluwer Academic Publishers.

decision will have to be taken with regard to the scope of definite descriptions, for example that they are to have maximal scope. The second method does provide for scope-distinctions; there will be a distinction between, for example, $(\imath x . Fx) \sim Gx$ and $\sim (\imath x . Fx)Gx$. The apparatus of Q, however, will allow us, if we wish, to combine the first method, that of representing definite descriptions by terms, with the representation of differences of scope; we can, if we like, distinguish between e.g., $\sim_2 G_1 \imath x_3 F_1 x_2$ and $\sim_4 G_1 \imath x_3 F_1 x_2$, and ensure that from the first formula we may, and from the second we may not, derive $E!_1 \imath x_3 F_1 x_2$. We might, alternatively, treat descriptions as syntactically analogous to restricted quantifiers, if we so desire. Let us assume (arbitrarily) that the first method is adopted, the scope-boundaries of a descriptive term being, in each direction, the first operator with a higher subscript than that borne by the iota-operator or the first sentential boundary, whichever is nearer. Let us further assume (perhaps no less arbitrarily) that the iota-operator is introduced as a defined expression, so that such a formula as $G_1 \imath x_3 F_1 x_2 \leftrightarrow_8 \exists x_7 F_1 x_6 \;\&_2\; G_1 x_6 \;\&_5\; \forall y_4 F_1 y_2 \leftrightarrow_3 y_2 =_1 x_2$ is provable by definitional substitution for the right-hand side of the formula $G_1 \imath x_3 F_1 x_2 \leftrightarrow_4 G_1 \imath x_3 F_1 x_2$, together with applications of the rules for subscript-adjustment.

Now, as I envisage the appropriate extension of Q, the formal difference between individual constants and descriptive terms will lie in there being a legitimate step (by E. G.) from a formula containing a non-dominant individual constant to the related "weak" existential form, e.g., from $\sim_3 F_1 a_2$ to $\exists x_4 \sim_3 F_1 x_2$, while there will, for example, be no analogous step from $\sim_4 G_1 \imath x_3 F_1 x_2$ to $\exists x_4 \sim_3 G_1 x_2$. Such a distinction between individual constants and descriptive terms seems to me to have, at least *prima facie*, a basis in intuition; I have at least some inclination to say that, if Mr. Spurgeon has no haberdasher, then it would be true (though no doubt conversationally odd) to say "It is not the case that Mr. Spurgeon's haberdasher is bald" (S), even though no one has even suggested or imagined that Mr. Spurgeon has a haberdasher; even though, that is, there is no answer to the question who Mr. Spurgeon's haberdasher is or has been supposed to be, or to the question whom the speaker means by the phrase "Mr. Spurgeon's haberdasher." If that inclination is admissible, then it will naturally be accompanied by a reluctance to allow a step from S to "Someone is not bald" (S_1) even when S_1 is given its "weak" interpretation. I have, however, already suggested that an utterance of the sentence "It is not the case that Mr. Spurgeon is bald" (S') is not assessable for truth or falsity unless something can be said about who Mr.

Spurgeon is or is supposed to be; in which case the step from S' to S_1 (weakly interpreted) seems less unjustifiable.

I can, nevertheless, conceive of this argument's failing to produce conviction. The following reply might be made: "If one is given the truth of S, on the basis of there being no one who is haberdasher to Mr. Spurgeon, all one has to do is first to introduce a name, say "Bill," laying down that "Bill" is to designate whoever is haberdasher to Mr. Spurgeon, then to state (truly) that it is not the case that Bill is bald (since there is no such person), and finally to draw the conclusion (now legitimate) that someone is not bald (on the "weak" reading of that sentence). If only a stroke of the pen, so to speak, is required to legitimize the step from S to S_1 (weakly interpreted), why not legitimize the step directly, in which case the formal distinction ... between individual constants and descriptive terms must either disappear or else become wholly arbitrary?"

A full treatment of this reply would, I suspect, be possible only within the framework of a discussion of reference too elaborate for the present occasion; I can hope only to give an indication of *one* of the directions in which I should have some inclination to proceed. It has been observed[2] that a distinction may be drawn between at least two ways in which descriptive phrases may be employed.

(1) A group of men is discussing the situation arising from the death of a business acquaintance, of whose private life they know nothing, except that (as they think) he lived extravagantly, with a household staff which included a butler. One of them says "Well, Jones' butler will be seeking a new position."

(2) Earlier, another group has just attended a party at Jones' house, at which their hats and coats were looked after by a dignified individual in dark clothes and a wing-collar, a portly man with protruding ears, whom they heard Jones addressing as "Old Boy," and who at one point was discussing with an old lady the cultivation of vegetable marrows. One of the group says "Jones' butler got the hats and coats mixed up."

(i) The speaker in example (1) could, without impropriety, have inserted after the descriptive phrase "Jones' butler" the clause "whoever he may be." It would require special circumstances to make a corresponding insertion appropriate in the case of example (2). On the other hand we may say, with respect to example (2), that some particular individual has been "described as," "referred to as," or "called" Jones' butler by the speaker; furthermore, any one who was in a position to point out that Jones has no butler, and that the man with the protruding ears was Jones' gardener, or someone hired for the occasion, would also be in a position to claim that the speaker had *mis*described that individual as Jones' butler. No such comments are in place with respect to example (1).

(ii) A schematic generalized account of the difference of type between examples (1) and (2) might proceed along the following lines. Let us say that X has a dossier for a definite description δ if there is a set of definite descriptions which includes δ, all the members of which X supposes (in one or other of the possible senses of "suppose") to be satisfied by one and the same item. In a type (2) case, unlike a type (1) case, the speaker intends the hearer to think (*via* the recognition that he is so intended) (a) that the speaker has a dossier for the definite description δ which he has used, and (b) that the speaker has selected δ from this dossier at least partly in the hope that the hearer has a dossier for δ which "overlaps" the speaker's dossier for δ (that is, shares a substantial, or in some way specially favoured, subset with the speaker's dossier). In so far as the speaker expects the hearer to recognize this intention, he must expect the hearer to think that in certain circumstances the speaker will be prepared to replace the remark which he has made (which contains δ) by a further remark in which some element in the speaker's dossier for δ is substituted for δ. The standard circumstances in which it is to be supposed that the speaker would make such a replacement will be (a) if the speaker comes to think that the hearer either has no dossier for δ, or has one which does not overlap the speaker's dossier for δ (i.e., if the hearer appears not to have identified the item which the speaker means or is talking about), (b) if the speaker comes to think that δ is a misfit in the speaker's dossier for δ, i.e., that δ is not, after all, satisfied by the same item as that which satisfies the majority of, or each member of a specially favoured subset of, the descriptions in the dossier. In example (2) the speaker might come to think that Jones has no butler, or that though he has, it is not the butler who is the portly man with the protruding ears, etc., and whom the speaker thinks to have mixed up the hats and coats.

(iii) If in a type (2) case the speaker has used a descriptive phrase (e.g., "Jones' butler") which in fact has no application, then what the speaker has *said* will, strictly speaking, be false; the truth-conditions for a type (2) statement, no less than for a type (1) statement, can be thought of as being given by a Russellian account of definite descriptions (with suitable provision for unexpressed restrictions, to cover cases in which, for example, someone uses the phrase "the table" meaning thereby "the table in this room"). But though what, in such a case, a speaker has *said* may be false, what he *meant* may be true (for example, that a certain particular individual [who is in fact Jones' gardener] mixed up the hats and coats).

Let us introduce two auxiliary devices, italics and small capital letters, to indicate to which of the two specified modes of employment a reported use of a descriptive phrase is to be assigned. If I write "*S* said '*The F is G*,'" I shall indicate that *S* was using "the *F*" in a type (1), non-identificatory way, whereas if I write "*S* said 'THE F is *G*,'" I shall indicate that *S* was using "the *F*" in a type (2), identificatory way. It is important to bear in mind that I am *not* suggesting that the difference between these devices represents a difference in the *meaning* or *sense* which a descriptive phrase may have on different occasions; on the contrary, I am suggesting that descriptive phrases have no relevant systematic duplicity of meaning; their meaning is given by a Russellian account.

We may now turn to names. In my type (1) example, it might be that in view of the prospect of repeated conversational occurrences of the expression "Jones' butler," one of the group would find it convenient to say "Let us call Jones' butler 'Bill.'" Using the proposed supplementation, I can represent him as having remarked "Let us call *Jones' butler* 'Bill.'" Any subsequent remark containing "Bill" will have the same truth-value as would have a corresponding remark in which "Jones' butler" replaces "Bill." If Jones has no butler, and if in consequence it is false that Jones' butler will be seeking a new position, then it will be false that Bill will be seeking a new position.

In the type (2) example, also, one of the group might have found it convenient to say "Let us call Jones' butler 'Bill,'" and his intentions might have been such as to make it a correct representation of his remark for me to write that he said "Let us call JONES' BUTLER 'Bill.'" If his remark is correctly thus represented, then it will *not* be true that, in all conceivable circumstances, a subsequent remark containing "Bill" will have the same truth-value as would have a corresponding remark in which "Bill" is replaced by "Jones's butler." For the person whom the speaker proposes to call "Bill" will be the person whom he *meant* when he said "Let us call JONES' BUTLER 'Bill,'" viz., the person who looked after the hats and coats, who was addressed by Jones as "Old Boy," and so on; and if this person turns out to have been Jones's gardener and not Jones's butler, then it may be *true* that Bill mixed up the hats and coats and *false* that Jones's butler mixed up the hats and coats. Remarks of the form "Bill is such-and-such" will be inflexibly tied, as regards truth-value, not to possible remarks of the form "Jones's butler is such-and-such," but to possible remarks of the form "The person whom *X* meant when he said 'Let us call Jones's butler "Bill"'" is such-and-such."

It is important to note that, for a definite description used in the explanation of a name to be employed in an identificatory way, it is not required that the item which the explainer means (is referring to) when he uses the description should actually exist. A person may establish or explain a use for a name α by saying "Let us call THE F α" or "THE F is called α" even though every definite description in his dossier for "the F" is vacuous; he may mistakenly think, or merely deceitfully intend his hearer to think, that the elements in the dossier are non-vacuous and are satisfied by a single item; and in secondary or "parasitic" types of case, as in the narration of or commentary upon fiction, that this is so may be something which the speaker non-deceitfully pretends or "feigns." So names introduced or explained in this way may be vacuous.

I may now propound the following argument in answer to the objection that any distinction in Q between individual constants and descriptive terms will be arbitrary.

(1) For a given definite description δ, the difference between a type (1) and type (2) employment is not to be construed as the employment of δ in one rather than another of two systematically different senses of δ.

(2) A name α may be introduced *either* so as to be inflexibly tied, as regards the truth-value of utterances containing it, to a given definite description δ, *or* so as to be not so tied (δ being univocally employed); so the difference between the two ways of introducing α may reasonably be regarded as involving a difference of sense or meaning for α; a sense in which α may be said to be equivalent to a definite description and a sense in which it may not.

(3) It is, then, not arbitrary so to design Q that its individual constants are to be regarded as representing, among other linguistic items, names used with *one* of their possible kinds of meaning, namely that in which a name is not equivalent to a definite description.

. . .

Notes

1. [Q is a version of first order logic according to which individual constants posses scope. In Q, the scope-precedence of a connective or quantifier is indicated by the level of its subscript ("the higher the subscript, the larger the scope"). This convention allows the scope of a name to be represented, enabling one to distinguish (e.g.) between two readings of "Pegasus does not fly." Ed.]

2. E.g. by Keith Donnellan, "Reference and Definite Descriptions," *Philosophical Review* 75 (1966) 281–304; as may perhaps be seen from what follows, I am not sure that I am wholly sympathetic towards the conclusions which he draws from the existence of the distinction.

Chapter 10

Proper Names, Reference, and Rigid Designation

Christopher Peacocke

Dissatisfied as we may now be with "disguised description" treatments of ordinary proper names, theories thus based at least purported to give an account of each of the following:

(a) the contribution made by a name to the truth-conditions of the sentences in which it occurs

(b) the requirements for mastery of a name in a language

(c) the alleged puzzles over names in existential and identity statements

(d) what is constitutive of a name in a community being a name of a given object

(e) what is constitutive of a speaker's denoting an object on a particular occasion of use of a name.

Any alternative view of names must speak to these issues, and my immediate concern in this paper is with the first of them, (a), together with the relation between the contribution made to truth-conditions by names and that made by other singular terms.

My starting point is the concept of a *rigid designator* introduced by Kripke in "Naming and Necessity" (Kripke [1972]); for my first claim is that we can restate Kripke's thesis that proper names are rigid designators in a way free of the apparatus in terms of which it was made, a way that provides a plausible answer to issue (a).

Reprinted from S. Blackburn (ed.) *Meaning, Reference, Necessity*, pp. 109–132, with the permission of Cambridge University Press and Christopher Peacocke. © Cambridge University Press 1975.

I

Kripke says "Let's call something a *rigid designator* if in any possible world it designates the same object" (Kripke [1972] p. 269). The "in" in the definition could with increase of perspicuity be replaced by "with respect to." To ask whether an expression α is a rigid designator is not to ask a question about α *as used in* another possible world. Rather, we specify counterfactually a certain possible situation and then ask what α, used as an expression of *our* actual language, denotes with respect to that possible state of affairs. (On the mistaken interpretation, it would be absurd to suppose that *any* expression is a rigid designator.)

Kripke's definition quantifies over possible worlds and appeals to transworld identity; our task is to avoid this, or at least provide an alternative. To avoid unnecessary complexity at this stage, we will offer a criterion for

t is a rigid designator in language L

only for the case in which $t(s, u, \ldots)$ ranges over singular terms and L over languages free of both ambiguity and indexicals. We will drop the last restriction later. Then we may say

t is a rigid designator in L iff there is an object x such that for any sentence $G(t)$ in which t occurs, the truth (falsity) condition for $G(t)$ is that $\langle x \rangle$ satisfy (respectively, fail to satisfy) $G(\ )$.

If we omit "there is an object x such that" from the right-hand side we obtain a definition for

t is a rigid designator of x in L.

We may say, metaphorically, that we are here basing rigid designation on the idea of a certain object entering the truth-conditions of all the sentences of the language in which t occurs. What a rigid designator designates is just the object that so enters the truth-conditions.

Definite descriptions, in the use of them with which Kripke was concerned when he denied that they are rigid designators, are not rigid designators on this criterion either. There is no object such that the truth-condition for $G(\text{the } F)$ is that *that object* (or its unit sequence) satisfy $G(\ )$. The truth-condition for $G(\text{the } F)$ is certainly not that the object y that is in fact the F satisfy $G(\ )$; that is not sufficient, for the truth-condition requires y also to be the F. And it is not necessary, since $G(\text{the}$

F) would be true if any object other than y were the F and also satisfied G( ). This point, granted the notion of a truth-condition, can be made without appeal to the possible worlds apparatus; and it can be seen as an explicit formulation of one of the ideas in Russell [1905].

This criterion of rigid designation can be seen too as merely a more explicit formulation of an idea variously expressed as that of a term's "serving ... simply to refer to its object" (Quine [1953]), "tagging" an individual (Marcus [1961]), or in general of an expression's being "used to enable ... individuals to be made subjects of discourse" (Mill [1843]); and the view that proper names are rigid designators in our sense seems a natural elucidation of Miss Anscombe's remark that the proper name contributes "to the meaning of the sentence precisely by standing for its bearer" (Anscombe [1958]).

There is a consequence of the view that proper names are rigid designators in our sense. If it is true, we can predict a point remarked by Geach (Geach [1972] pp. 117, 140, 144), that genuine proper names "gives us no scope trouble"; guinine proper names are "essentially scopeless." The point is that there is no difference in respect of truth-conditions between (for example)

Concerning Heath: he might not have been prime minister

and

It might have been the case that: Heath is not prime minister;

whereas there is actually a difference in truth-*value* between

Concerning the prime minister: he might not have been prime minister

and

It might have been the case that: the prime minister is not prime minister.[1]

If "Heath" is a rigid designator, then by our criterion, there is an object x such that the truth-condition for "concerning Heath: he might not have been prime minister" is that: concerning it (x), it might not have been prime minister. Similarly, the truth-condition for "it might have been the case that: Heath is not prime minister" is that the same object x satisfies the condition: it might have been that ( ) is not prime minister. But of course, these are one and the same condition; there is no difference between being such that concerning it, it might not have been prime minister, and being such that it might have been that *it* is not prime minister. In this argument, the existential-universal ($\exists\forall$) form of our criterion is crucial; without it, we could not conclude that it is the same object that the truth-conditions of the two sentences both concern. One might say that proper names always have maximum scope, but of course one might equally say they always have minimum scope on the basis of *these* facts; rather, as Geach says, they are scopeless.

Kripke's definition of a rigid designator, no doubt because of the problems to which he was concerned to apply the notion, used specifically modal concepts. Ours uses none, and in virtue of this we have a bonus: any expression that is a rigid designator on our criterion is, as it were, a rigid designator with respect to *every* operator, modal or non-modal. An argument strictly parallel to that of the previous paragraph will yield the conclusion that the truth-conditions of

Concerning Heath: in the past, he edited *The Church Times*

and

In the past: Heath edited *The Church Times*

do not differ, as indeed they do not. We could, if we wished, set up a syntactical device which marked a distinction of scope for proper names as well as for definite descriptions; but it would be a distinction without a semantic difference.

Dummett holds that, for the sorts of cases so far considered, distinctions of scope with respect to operators apply to proper names as much as to definite descriptions (Dummett [1973], especially pp. 113–117). There is, he holds, a "clear sense in which we may rightly say, St. Anne cannot but have been a parent,'" and we should give the same account of this as we give of the truth-conditions of the true sentence "The mother of Mary cannot but have been a parent," rather than invoke the *a priori*/necessary distinction. But there is an argument independent of the present issue against Dummett's position. On his view, there ought to be a true reading of almost any sentence of the form

α might not have been α

where α is a proper name, viz. that reading on which the first occurrence of α has wider scope than the modal operator, and the second narrower scope. For in the typical case, the object that is in fact α might not have satisfied our criterion (being the F, say) for recognising an object as the referent of α. Yet there seems to be no such reading of the sentence for genuine proper names.[2] Worse; in many cases, something other than the thing that is in fact α might be the F, and so on Dummett's view it ought (on one reading of the sentence) to be true to say

Something other than the thing that is α might have been α.

In general, we must distinguish between the true metalinguistic statement (i) and statement (ii):

(i) necessarily, if our criterion for recognising an object as the referent of α is that it be the F, the referent of α cannot be anything but the F

This is compatible with the falsity of the non-metalinguistic statement (on any reading),

(ii) α is necessarily F.

Kripke puts the relevant distinction here in terms of "fixing the referent" as opposed to "giving the meaning" (Kripke [1972] pp. 273–277). Our criterion suggests another way of expressing it. One who holds both that a proper name α should be assigned a sense that is not uniquely determined by its referent and further holds that this sense "gives the meaning" of α will deny that there is an object x such that what is (strictly and literally) said in an utterance of $G(α)$ is that x satisfies condition $G(\ )$; one who holds that the sense serves only to "fix the referent" will not deny it. Frege (with an exception noted below) did in effect deny it; in his theory, what is said could only be the "thought" expressed by the sentence, and it is the sense, not the referent, of a singular term occurring in the sentence that contributes to the determination of this.

The existence of a distinction between fixing a referent and giving the meaning shows that it is consistent to hold both that proper names are rigid designators on our criterion, and that no full account of the role of a proper name in the language of a community can be given without assigning it a sense not determined by its referent. But the claim that proper names are rigid designators must, if anything, help the case of those who deny, for one reason or another, there is a need to assign proper names a sense not fixed by their referent; for, if true, it shows that, at least in point of getting the truth conditions right, no such assignment is needed.

Someone may object, "Since we are not obliged to accept the possible worlds semantics for necessity, why do we need your criterion? Suppose we follow the convention that "$\underline{αβ}$" is to abbreviate "the concatenation of expression type α with expression type $β$" and that object language expressions are used as names of themselves when they occur in expressions thus underlined. Then can we not simply say: t is a rigid designator in L iff it is true in L that nothing else might have been t, or, more carefully, iff $T(\exists x(x = t \;\&\; \sim \Diamond \exists y(y = t \;\&\; y \neq x)), L)$?" But this criterion is not necessary, for it presumes that the object language is capable of defining a possibility operator, which is not, intuitively, required for a language to contain rigid designators. It is not sufficient either; for if t is, intuitively, a rigid designator, then so, by this criterion, is $(\iota x)(x = t \;\&\; p)$, for any true sentence replacing p. The most we can say is that this criterion is necessary in the case in which L does contain a possibility operator. But that it is so follows from our adopted criterion. By that criterion, for any rigid designator t of L, there is an object z such that the truth condition for the sentence mentioned in the alternative criterion is that

$\langle z \rangle$ satisfy $\underline{\exists x(x = \xi_1 \;\&\; \sim \Diamond \exists y(y = \xi_1 \;\&\; y \neq x))}$

and it is sufficient for this that

$\langle z, z \rangle$ satisfy $\underline{\xi_2 = \xi_1 \;\&\; \sim \Diamond \exists y(y = \xi_1 \;\&\; y \neq \xi_2)}$

But this last condition *is* so satisfied; for $z = z$, and it is *not* possible that there is an object both identical with z and not identical with z. (No particular semantics for "$\Diamond$" are assumed here, but only the results that any coherent semantics will deliver.)

Our criterion of rigid designation, and much of the talk of this section, reifies *conditions*; it is our next task to try to avoid such reification.

II

A natural way to try to eliminate talk of conditions, in a way that prevents the notion of a truth-condition of a sentence from collapsing into that of a material equivalent of it, is to *mention* the Tarski–Davidson truth theory for the language L in question. We label this theory T_L. The idea is more easily stated than implemented, and not until after the discussion of demonstratives in the next section can we have a plausible basis for a criterion.

Let "T" be the truth predicate for any given language, and let "$\vdash_{T_L}$" abbreviate "it is a theorem of T_L that." One's very first thought in writing out "t is a rigid designator in L" in terms of T_L is to produce this piece of nonsense:

$\exists x(\text{for all sentences } G(t) \text{ of L}, \vdash_{T_L} (T(\underline{G(t)}) \equiv \langle x \rangle \text{ sats } \underline{G(\xi_1)}))$.

This is nonsense for the same reason that

$\exists x$(John said "I am going to x")

is nonsense; the context governed by "$\vdash_{T_L}$" is of course quoted and not used.

One's second thought may be to move the existential quantifier inside "$\vdash_{T_L}$":

for all sentences $\underline{G(t)}$ of L, $\vdash_{T_L} \exists x(T(\underline{G(t)}) \equiv \langle x \rangle$ sats $\underline{G(\xi_1)})$.

The difficulty with this formulation is that the objector can protest that, for classical formulations of the truth theory, the only reason that (for the case of first order extensional languages) proper names meet it and definite descriptions do not is that proper names that denote can be proved to denote in the truth theory, but "denoting" definite descriptions cannot. If we made the same assumptions about descriptions as we make about names in classical theory, then for such languages, definite descriptions meet the criterion in the case of such simple languages. A simple example brings home the general point. Suppose all descriptions were expanded out in Russell's fashion, so that for sentences in which the description had maximal scope, we had theorems of the form

$T(G(\iota x)Fx) \equiv \exists x(\forall z(Fz \equiv z = x) \ \& \ Gx)$

Then it is easily checked that if T_L contains classical first-order logic,

$\exists x(\forall z(Fz \equiv z = x)) \vdash_{T_L} \exists x(\forall z(Fz \equiv z = x) \ \& \ T(\underline{G(\iota x)Fx}) \equiv Gx)$

So, granted the premiss $\exists x \forall z(Fz \equiv z = x)$, the analogue of which for proper names is a theorem of classical truth theories, definite descriptions even when handled in Russell's way would meet the criterion. There may of course be good reasons why the truth theory should exhibit the asymmetry that would legitimise this criterion; but if these reasons in any way tacitly appeal to the notion of rigid designation, we cannot appeal to them at *this* point.

We can coherently quantify into the context governed by "$\vdash_{T_L}$" if the quantifiers range over expressions. So, letting α be a variable over expressions, we might offer as a third attempt

$\exists \alpha$(for all sentences $\underline{G(t)}$ of L, $\vdash_{T_L} T(\underline{G(t)}) \equiv \langle \alpha \rangle$ sats $\underline{G(\xi_1)})$.

The problems with this are at least twofold. Provided T_L is cast in a free logic, it is possible to write out a truth theory for a first-order extensional language that evaluates definite descriptions directly (as *terms*), and which contains as theorems sentences of form

$$T(\underline{G(\imath x)Fx}) \equiv \langle (\imath x)Fx \rangle \text{ sats } \underline{G(\xi_1)}.$$

(Cf. in particular Grandy [1972], Scott [1967], and for discussion of some (but not all) philosophical issues surrounding direct evaluation of descriptions, Lambert and van Fraassen [1972].) The appropriateness of such truth theories in this particular area can be rejected only on some substantive grounds. The second problem concerns the natural way of writing out T_L which would make this criterion plausible; that is, of applying Russell's theory of descriptions everywhere, so that definite descriptions simply do not occupy singular term position in the metalanguage of the truth theory, and so certainly will not feature as values of "α" in the criterion in a fashion that would count definite descriptions as rigid designators. The trouble is that, even if we presume underspecification in the description adequately accommodated, Russell's theory seems to be unsatisfactory as an account of the *truth conditions* of sentences containing definite descriptions in some of their uses; for definite descriptions on some occasions of their use seem to function quite legitimately in the language as rigid designators. The matter is worth some discussion, *inter alia* simply because one's stand on it affects one's final criterion and one's attitude to direct evaluation in this field.

There is a relatively clear criterion for picking out historic uses of definite descriptions that are, as then used, rigid designators; if, in an utterance of "the F is G," what is strictly and literally said would equally and appropriately be said by an utterance of "*that F* is G," then "the F" functioned as a rigid designator. I shall label this an *entity-invoking* use of the description. The criterion is unsurprising; for when "that F is G" is appropriately uttered, there is an answer to the question "Which object is the one of which the speaker is saying that *it* is G?" The criterion, unlike some other accounts, is not stated in terms of factors that can bear at most upon the issue of what the speaker *meant* by uttering a sentence, as opposed to what he said; and the fact that there are such uses seems to be one way of making Strawson's original point against Russell's theory of descriptions.

Underspecification—the fact that in an utterance of "the F is G" there is not strictly just one object in the universe that is F, even relative to a fixing of the referents of demonstratives—is not sufficient and not necessary for entity-invoking uses of descriptions. If you and I visited the Casino at Monte Carlo yesterday, and saw a man break the bank, and on the same day saw a man break the bank at Nice, and it is common knowledge between us that this is so, then the description

"The man who broke the bank at Monte Carlo yesterday"

as it occurs in a particular utterance *today* of

"The man who broke the bank at Monte Carlo yesterday had holes in his shoes"

may well be satisfied by just one object in the universe; but it is here entity-invoking both intuitively and by our criterion. That underspecification is not sufficient is shown by the case of two school inspectors visiting an institution for the first time: one may say to the other, on the basis of the activities around him, "The headmaster doesn't have much control over the pupils." Here there is no object such that the inspector said of it that it doesn't have much control over its pupils. One cannot say the headmaster is such an object, since what this inspector (*actually*) said would be true even if someone else were headmaster. Moreover, the features that, as Strawson has taught us (Strawson [1964]), are important *in concreto* in entity-invoking uses are absent from this example; the speaker does not invoke stretches of his audience's *identifying* knowledge.

The whole topic bristles with complexities we can only ignore here; but we have enough before us to conclude that any criterion of rigid designation stated in terms of truth theories must embrace whatever expressions in the input to the truth theory are taken as representing entity-invoking uses of definite descriptions. The close tie between such uses of "the F" and that of "that F" supplies a hint of how to do this.

III

It is not hard to expand our intuitive criterion of rigid designation to cover demonstratives, the paradigm rigid designators. Suppose person p utters a complete sentence A at time t. We form an expression A # thus: we omit all demonstratives, syntactically identified (I, that, this, that F, you, here, ...) from A, replacing the ith by the ith placeholder ξi until all are replaced. So

(that man stole the money from me) #

is the expression

ξ_1 stole the money from ξ_2.

Let $d(p, t)$ be that sequence of objects whose ith member is the object *demonstrated*[3] by p at the ith occurrence of a demonstrative in the sentence p uttered at t if the demonstrative is non-complex; let it be the demonstrated F if the demonstrative is "this F" or "that F." (This is only rough.) So, if you say "that man stole the money from me" at noon today, then d (you, noon today) is the sequence consisting of the man you demonstrate and you, in that order. Now, that demonstratives are rigid designators in a sense not very distant from that of our original criterion is brought out by this fact: we can say that if $d(p, t) = s$ then *whatever* sentence A p in fact uttered at t, the truth-condition of his utterance is that the sequence s (of *objects*) satisfy A $\#$. Whereas previously, our criterion started: there is an object x such that for all sentences ..., it now starts (in effect): for any given historic occasion of utterance, there are objects (there is a sequence of objects) such that for any sentence.... Thus the two crucial and related features of the old criterion, its existential-universal character and the idea that the truth-conditions for the (uttered) sentence concern certain objects directly, are retained.

By arguments essentially parallel to those given earlier, we would not expect demonstratives to interact with modal and other operators to produce scope distinctions; and this does indeed seem to be the case. The truth-conditions for an utterance of

It might have been the case that: that man is not bald.

are one and the same as those for

Concerning that man: he might not have been bald.

provided that the same man is demonstrated and the same time indicated. The same applies to the following pairs:

In the past: I lived in Russia.
I am such that I: lived in Russia in the past.

It is possible that: it rained yesterday.
Yesterday is a day such that: it is possible that it rained on that day.

Demonstratives, like other genuinely referential singular terms, are essentially scopeless. It is interesting that even Frege conceded that (certain) demonstratives are rigid designators in the sense of the intuitive criterion; in "Der Gedanke" he remarks that the very same *thought* can be expressed by uttering on Wednesday a sentence containing "today" as by uttering a certain sentence on Thursday containing the word "yesterday" (Frege

[1968]). Here a particular *day*, a certain Wednesday, directly enters the truth-conditions of the uttered sentence.

It is illuminating, and important for our later development of a criterion of rigid designation or genuine reference, to see how a truth theory for a language containing demonstratives might be written out. Let us consider a simple extensional first-order language containing the demonstratives "I," "here," "now," and "that." The following theory is meant to cover only those historic uses of "that" unsupplemented by a substantival expression that can be said to be used as rigid designators of an object on their occasion of utterance. Not all unsupplemented uses of "that" are such uses, but some are: if we are to give the most plausible explanation of the soundness of the argument (on a particular occasion of utterance)

That is the Radcliffe Camera
The Radcliffe Camera was built in 1737
∴ That was built in 1737

the first premiss must be taken as an identity statement, and "that" as then used as referential. "$L(p, t, c)$" is to be read in the sequel as "c is the location of p at time t" and "$D(n, p, t, x)$" as "x is an object demonstrated by p at the nth occurrence of a demonstrative in the sentence uttered by p at t."[4] "τ_1," "τ_2," ... are variables over terms of the given language. We suppose given a finite stock of atomic predicates and relation-letters and some standard axioms about sequences of objects and about expressions. "$s_i(k)$" denotes the kth element of sequence s_i, and "$s_i \underset{k}{\approx} s_j$" is an abbreviation for the formula that states that sequences s_i and s_j differ in at most the kth place. "var(i)" denotes the ith variable; there are also placeholders $\xi_1, \xi_2, \ldots$ A # is defined as we defined it earlier, except that now we do not replace occurrences of "I," "now," and "here" by placeholders. For simplicity, we consider the case in which translation is homophonic.

We define the evaluation function (of terms with respect to sequences) thus:

$$(D_1) \quad \kappa(s_1, s_2, s_3, \tau_1) = \begin{cases} s_1(i) \text{ if } \tau_1 \text{ is the } i\text{th variable} \\ s_2(i) \text{ if } \tau_1 \text{ is the } i\text{th placeholder} \\ s_3(1) \text{ if } \tau_1 \text{ is } \underline{I} \\ s_3(2) \text{ if } \tau_1 \text{ is } \underline{now} \\ s_3(3) \text{ if } \tau_1 \text{ is } \underline{here}^5 \end{cases}$$

(The motivation for this will be given by the definition of "A is true as (potentially) uttered by p at t.") Finally we can give the satisfaction axioms:

$$\mathrm{sats}(s_1, s_2, s_3, \underline{P^n_j \tau_1 \cdots \tau_n}) \equiv P^n_j \kappa(s_1, s_2, s_3, \tau_1) \cdots \kappa(s_1, s_2, s_3, \tau_n),$$

$$\text{for each atomic predicate } P^n_j;$$

$$\mathrm{sats}(s_1, s_2, s_3, \underline{(A\mathrm{v}B)}) \equiv . \, \mathrm{sats}(s_1, s_1, s_3, A) \text{ v } \mathrm{sats}(s_1, s_2, s_3, B)$$

$$\mathrm{sats}(s_1, s_2, s_3, \underline{(\sim A)}) \equiv . \sim \mathrm{sats}(s_1, s_2, s_3, A)$$

$$\mathrm{sats}(s_1, s_2, s_3, \underline{\exists \, \mathrm{var}(i)(A)}) \equiv . \, \exists s_4 (s_4 \underset{i}{\approx} s_1 \text{ \& } \mathrm{sats}(s_4, s_2, s_3, A))$$

"A is true as (potentially) uttered by p at t," "$T(A, p, t)$," is given by the following definitional schema, for the case in which A contains n occurrences ($n > 0$) of "that":

(D_2) $T(A, p, t) =_{df} .$

$$\exists x_{i_1} \cdots x_{i_{n+1}} \left[\bigwedge_{j=1}^{n} \forall z(D(j, p, t, z) \equiv z = x_{i_j}) \text{ \& } L(p, t, x_{i_{n+1}}) \right.$$

$$\left. \text{ \& } \forall s_1 (\mathrm{sats}(s_1, \langle x_{i_1}, \ldots, x_{i_n} \rangle, \langle p, t, x_{i_{n+1}} \rangle, A \#)) \right]$$

In the case in which A contains no indexicals at all, we set

$$T(A, p, t) =_{df} . \, \forall s_1 (\mathrm{sats}(s_1, \langle - \rangle, \langle - \rangle, A))$$

in classical fashion; and the case in which A contains no occurrences of "that" but some of "I," "here," or "now" is equally straightforward.

It is an illusion to think that we could accommodate singular terms of the form "that F' (where $\underline{(\text{that } x) \cdots x \cdots}$ is a singular term forming operator on one-place predicables) by simply altering the relevant occurrences of "$\forall z(D(j, p, t, z) \equiv z = x_{i_j})$" in this definition of truth to a formula having the force of: x_{i_j} is the unique thing that is both demonstrated and satisfies $F(\xi_1)$. For this involves that suspect view that "is the demonstrated F" splits up logically into "is uniquely both demonstrated and an F." Whatever the correct analysis of the notion of demonstration, there is every reason to think that the role of F in "that F" in fixing the demonstrated object is more intimate than that of just adding an extra condition which picks out one of a number of demonstrated objects. In the general case of utterances of sentences of the form $\underline{G(\text{that } F)}$, there is no such "first-stage" initial fixing of a *number* of objects.

The given truth theory largely implements our naïve exposition of the truth-conditions of sentences containing indexicals. A simple example shows its operation. Suppose a person p_0 located at c_0 at time t_0 then utters this sentence of the language for which the truth definition is given:

$$\exists z(Bz \ \& \ N(I, z, \text{now}) \ \& \ W(z, \text{that}, \text{now}))$$

or, as we would say, "I am now north of some building which is west of that"; and suppose the object p_0 demonstrates while uttering "that" at this time is z. Given as hypothesis that these are the circumstances of the utterance, we can conclude in the truth theory from definition (D_2) that the utterance is true iff

$$\forall s_1 (\text{sats}(s_1, \langle z \rangle, \langle p_0, t_0, c_0 \rangle), \underline{\exists z(Bz \ \& \ N(I, z, \text{now}) \ \& \ W(z, \xi_1, \text{now}))})$$

Working through the clauses of the truth definition in the usual way, we conclude that the last displayed sentence is equivalent to

$$\forall s_1 \exists s_2 (s_2 \underset{3}{\approx} s_1 \ \& \ Bs_2(3) \ \& \ N(p_0, s_2(3), t_0) \ \& \ W(s_2(3), t_0))$$

and with the help of the theory of sequences this in turn reduces to

$$\exists x(Bx \ \& \ N(p_0, x, t_0) \ \& \ W(x, z, t_0))$$

This is of course just the desired truth-condition.

With such a treatment of demonstratives in the truth theory, it seems appropriate to suggest that entity-invoking (historic) uses of "the F" be treated at the level of the input to the theory of truth as occurrences of "that F," the truth of utterances so employing "the F" requiring the existence of a unique demonstrated F (with respect to that occurrence of "the F"); while, modulo the problems of underspecification, those historic uses that are not entity-invoking be treated by Russell's theory of descriptions. I shall presume, in the development of a criterion of rigid designation, that some such divided treatment is correct.

Pursuing this policy leaves no role for direct evaluation of definite descriptions, even in relation to the entity-invoking uses. But there seems to be the following argument against so using it, in any case.

It is a constraint on any truth theory that, if α is the term that is used to represent entity-invoking uses of "the F," it should be provable in the truth theory (without additional hypotheses) that

$$T(\underline{G(\alpha)}, p, t) \supset T(\underline{\exists y G(y)}, p, t)$$

for some variable y not occurring in $G(\ )$. Pretheoretically, the reason for the constraint is clear: if "the F" is used entity-invokingly, then if the utterance is true, there is an object x such that the truth-condition for that utterance is that x meet condition $G(\ )$; and so if it *is* true, x will meet condition $G(\ )$. Thus $\exists y G(y)$ will be true.

The simple truth theory given above meets this constraint with respect to demonstratives. It follows in fact from (D_2) plus the satisfaction axioms that

$$T(\underline{G(that)}, p, t) \supset T(\underline{\exists y G(y)}, p, t)$$

for arbitrary one-place predicables G and F.

Let us consider, in the homophonic case, what would result if this constraint were fulfilled in a theory that evaluated entity-invoking uses of definite descriptions directly, as terms. To give such a theory a run for its money, we must suppose it employs a free logic in the metalanguage. For if it did not, we would have as a theorem

$$T(\underline{G(\imath x)Fx}, p, t) \equiv G(\imath x)Fx$$

where F and G are one-place predicables free of indexicals; hence we would also have as a theorem

$$\exists y (T(\underline{G(\imath x)Fx}, p, t) \equiv G(y))$$

But this last "theorem" is not even *true*; a quick way to see this is to observe that if everything is G and nothing is F, it would follow that a (putatively) entity-invoking utterance of "the F is G" is true. So let us grant the use of free logic.

Such a theory will contain as theorems

$$T(\underline{G(\imath x)Fx}, p, t) \equiv G(\imath x)Fx$$

and

$$T(\underline{\exists x G x}, p, t) \equiv \exists x G x$$

Thus if we fulfilled our constraint by having as a theorem

$$T(\underline{G(\imath x)Fx}, p, t) \supset T(\exists x G x, p, t)$$

we would also have as a theorem

$$G(\imath x)Fx \supset \exists x G x$$

given only that the theory contained the weaker parts of the sentential calculus. But this effectively reinstates existential generalisation; even if there is no such rule of inference in the theory, we can secure the effect of any given application by using other theorems and modus ponens. By the observations of the preceding paragraph, we find ourselves again with the unacceptable theorem

$$\exists y(T(G(\imath x)Fx, p, t) \equiv Gy).[6]$$

This objection is not answered by having as theorems sentences of the form

$$\exists y(y = (\imath x)Fx) \supset (T(\underline{G(\imath x)Fx}, p, t) \equiv G(\imath x)Fx)$$

for again from this would follow in the truth theory

$$\exists z [\exists y(y = z) \supset (T(\underline{G(\imath x)Fx}, p, t) \equiv Gz)]$$

and since it is a theorem of classical and free logic that

$$\exists z [\exists y(y = z) \supset A(z)] \equiv \exists z A(z)$$

the last but one displayed sentence implies in the truth theory the already rejected

$$\exists z(T(\underline{G(\imath x)Fx}, p, t) \equiv Gz).$$

This argument might be rejected on the ground that we had shown only that "$G\imath x(Fx) \supset \exists x Gx$" is a theorem of such theories for predicables not containing semantical vocabulary used to implicitly define truth for the object language. But other questions crowd in if the argument is blocked this way. Since we are concerned with the homophonic case, terms of the form $(\imath x)Fx$ are as much entity-invoking in the metalanguage as the object language; how then can "$\exists x Gx$" fail to follow from "$G(\imath x)Fx$" for an *arbitrary* predicable G? And how can the truth theory fail to include some theorems that are, at very least, not true, viz. any theorem of the form $G(\imath x)Fx$, where nothing is in fact F? If the theory is adequate only if we restrict the range of predicables for which

$$G(\imath x)Fx \supset \exists x Gx$$

is provable in the theory, why does this not provide an objection to that treatment if no non-circular reason can be given for the restriction?

I conclude, though tentatively—for there may be technically ingenious ways of fulfilling these constraints—that any direct-evaluation treatment of entity-invoking uses of descriptions is less satisfactory than their partial assimilation to demonstratives proposed above. This being so, the way is now open to a rather different ontologically acceptable criterion of rigid designation based on the theory of truth. We again abstract from ambiguity, but not now from indexicality:

Truth theory T treats expression α of language L as a rigid designator iff for any sentence $G(\alpha)$ of L containing α, given as premisses specifications of the objects demonstrated by person p at time t, then: in any maximally short derivation in T from those premisses of a target biconditional of the form

$$T(\underline{G(\alpha)}, p, t) \equiv A,$$

where A does not contain *sats*, the evaluation function of T is applied to some expression e (e.g. α itself or a placeholder) which occupies the place of this occurrence of α via the application of the satisfaction axiom for the atomic predicate in which the given occurrence of α features as argument in the original sentence $G(\alpha)$; where the evaluation is such that *either* given p,t, and the fixing of the indexical referents, there is a sequence of objects s_0 such that evaluation of e only with respect to s_0 occurs in maximally short derivations, *or* e is such that the result of evaluating it with respect to *any* sequence of objects is always the same.

(Variables fail the hurdles in the last two clauses of this rough criterion.) Proper names, demonstratives, and correspondingly entity-invoking uses of definite descriptions will all be treated as rigid designators by any adequate truth theory for their language: such has been our argument so far. What a rigid designator t is a rigid designator of, relative to adequate truth theory T, will be further relative to an occasion of utterance, but we have the resources for defining the notion: for it will be the object which is the result of the evaluation of any expression functioning in relation to t as e does to α in the above criterion, this evaluation occurring in a maximally short derivation in T of a target biconditional giving the truth-conditions of the uttered sentence, from premisses specifying the demon-strated objects on that occasion of utterance.

I should note two points. First, the intended account of a truth theory T treating an expression as a rigid designator makes use of denotation rela-tions for singular terms of the *metalanguage* of T: for the only sort of "evaluation" that literally takes place in a truth theory is that of writing function *symbols* next to other symbols. Second, the plausibility of the whole account rests upon a certain conception of singular term position; for I would say about genuine singular terms what Quine so clearly states about names:

What distinguishes a name is that it can stand coherently in the place of a variable, in predication, and will yield true results when used to instantiate true universal quantifications. (Quine [1970])

It is in a clear sense true to say that our final criterion, though demarcating the right class of expressions, and for the right reasons, presupposes that the argument over whether any *particular* expression is a rigid designator will come over how we are to treat it in the regimented language that we feed into an adequate truth theory. But it seems to me that this is, or should be, the actual situation.

IV

It may be objected that if proper names were rigid designators on even our intuitive criterion of rigid designation, non-relational readings of sentences in which a proper name falls within the scope of a propositional attitude verb would be impossible. For if proper names are rigid designators on that criterion, then the truth-condition for

John believes that Cicero was bald

is that

$\langle$Cicero$\rangle$ satisfies "John believes ξ_1 was bald";

and that simply *is* the relational reading of that sentence.

My response is to insist that our criterion be applied not to surface structure sentences, but to those that are the input to the theory of truth for a language; and then to follow Davidson (Davidson [1968]) in holding that "John believes that Cicero was bald" is to be regimented as two sentences, the first, on an occasion of utterance, containing a demonstrative reference ("that") to an utterance of the second. Our problem now dissolves; "Cicero" occurs only in the sentence

Cicero was bald.

We are committed to saying that the truth-condition for *this* sentence is that Cicero satisfy ξ_1 was bald, but that is fine.

We may feel reassured that this is somewhere near the truth by the observation that if n and m are proper names, for the non-relational reading it is a *sufficient* condition for the move from "John believes that $G(n)$" and "$n = m$" to "John believes that $G(m)$" be to a *non sequitur* that n and m be distinct *expressions*. But matters are slightly more complex than this happy confirmation suggests.

The problem is that if the semantic contribution of a proper name n to the truth-conditions of $G(n)$ is simply to fix an object x such that the truth-condition for $G(n)$ is that $\langle x \rangle$ satisfy $G(\xi_1)$, then if proper names

m and n denote the same object, $G(n)$ and $G(m)$ have identical truth-conditions; how then can a pair of such sentences fail to *samesay*? But since fuller analysis of the "believes" that occurs in

John believes that. Cicero was bald

must make reference to the samesaying relations of the demonstrated utterance (and perhaps make reference *only* to that aspect of the utterance), and since an utterance of "Tully is bald" will samesay with an utterance of "Cicero is bald," the objection arises that on this account it is hard to see how "John believes that Cicero was bald" could be true without "John believes that Tully was bald" also being true.

It is important that this objection should have no tendency to incline one to assign senses, modes of presentation, or anything else to names to explain the phenomenon it adduces: for it remains, as noted, a sufficient condition for *non sequitur* that the *names* used in the report of the propositional attitude be distinct.

A pragmatic explanation may be in order. If we are to follow the conversational policy of being maximally informative on relevant matters, when reporting the beliefs (desires, hopes, . . .) of a being who speaks the language we ourselves speak, we should actually use in our report of the belief a name the believer might use in expressing it; so we cannot expect what is conversationally implicated to be preserved under substitution of a co-denoting proper name, and this might be held to explain the appearance of *non sequitur*. It might seem to support this explanation that we are able to imagine nothing that would make it appropriate to report in English a native, with whom we share no language nor even proper names with a common history, as believing that $G(n)$ but not $G(m)$, where n and m are distinct co-denoting proper names; but of course this fact, if it is a fact, is also explained on a view which makes the putative believer's relation to the *name* "Cicero" feature in the truth-conditions of

John believes that Cicero was bald

read non-relationally. Moreover, in a sense the pragmatic explanation does not explain but explains away the original datum; for according to it, strictly speaking, in the matter of what is *said* as opposed to what is conversationally implicated, there are no such non-relational propositional attitude sentences containing proper names after all.

We need not choose here between the pragmatic account and some different story altogether which brings "Cicero" rather than Cicero into the truth-conditions of the problem sentences. For in the case of any latter such theory, which will of course deny that if utterances x and y samesay, $\langle x \rangle$ satisfies the Davidsonian predicate <u>John believes ξ</u> iff $\langle y \rangle$ does, "Cicero" will be mentioned and not, as a *component* of the relevant sentence, used in the regimented sentences that are the input to the truth theory. In saying this I have in mind a theory of quotation endorsed by Davidson (in his third John Locke lecture at Oxford in 1970) according to which quotation marks themselves have a demonstrative force akin to that of:

the expression with the shape here pictured.

On this theory, one may say that the occurrence of "slowly" within quotation marks in the sentence

"slowly" is an English adverb

contributes to what is strictly and literally said in an utterance of that sentence; but it does so by being the referent of a demonstrative, not by occurring as a truth-significant part of the corresponding regimented sentence. So again we have no counter-example to the thesis that proper names are rigid designators.

We have in this reply an instance of a general strategy that it is natural for the defender of the view that names are rigid designators to adopt; that is, of explaining any apparent difference in truth-conditions of surface structure sentences differing only in the occurrences of distinct proper names α and β, where α and β denote the same object, by the difference between the *expressions* α and β themselves.

V

There are, among others, three issues each worthy of extended separate treatment that are closely connected with the question of whether proper names are rigid designators in our sense; I will briefly comment on positions on them that support or enlarge the claims so far made.

(i)   There is the question of positive and negative existentials containing proper names. It is important to see that what has been claimed *already* implies that a general uniformity of treatment of both denoting and non-denoting names in both existentials and other contexts is impossible. For while the truth-condition of

Uranus has a satellite

is that a certain object have a satellite, there is no object, actual or possible, such that one can reasonably claim that the truth-condition of

Vulcan does not exist

is that that object satisfy "ξ does not exist." Yet "Vulcan does not exist" is a *true* sentence. The impossibility of uniformity is especially clear when we ask how to treat negative existentials containing denoting names. If we treat

Uranus does not exist

along the lines of "Vulcan does not exist" we make the contribution of the denoting name "Uranus" differ with the context in which it occurs; but if on the other hand we assimilate it to contexts like "ξ has a satellite," we have to say that the truth-conditions of

α does not exist

vary with whether α is a denoting name or not. So, if we accept the earlier arguments, uniformity is a chimaera, and non-uniformity is no objection to a theory of these contexts.

If we accept that the name "Uranus" is used and not mentioned in a regimented version of "Uranus does not exist," then it follows from our criterion and the assumption that "Uranus" is a rigid designator that the truth-condition for this negative existential is that a certain object not exist; and correspondingly for "Uranus exists." It is sometimes thought that this makes all such assertions of existence pleonastic, and such denials self-contradictory. Now it is certainly true that if, as it is, "Uranus" is a genuine singular term, on which existential generalisation is valid, we can prove in first-order classical logic that Uranus exists, and also that the literally self-contradictory

there exists an object such that it does not exist,

i.e. $\exists x \sim \exists y (y = x)$, follows from "Uranus does not exist." But this does not show an utterance of "Uranus exists" to be pleonastic in the sense that one who utters or hears it *knows* that the utterer is repeating himself (or, more carefully, saying something that, properly regimented, is derivable in first order logic); all we have is that *if* a man knows the logical form of the sentence, then he knows that it is true (or false in the negative case). But in situations where existentials are of interest to us, the antecedent of this conditional is untrue. Why should we not say that there are some sentences such that only when we know whether the names in them denote do we know their logical form? (One has, however, to agree that these considerations do show that the rule of Necessitation, if ⊢A then ⊢□A, needs restriction in any system we use for regimenting these existentials; for it would take us to the false $\Box \exists x \ (x = \text{Uranus})$ as a theorem from $\vdash \exists x \ (x = \text{Uranus})$.)

This argument against an argument is essentially permissive; it *allows* us to say that in "Uranus exists" we have a first level predication of an object, but we need further reasons actually to take that step. Some strong reasons can be found in terms of the occurrence of existentials, positive and negative, inside other operators. In

$$\Diamond \sim (\text{E!}(\text{Uranus}))$$

or

$$(\lambda x . \Diamond \sim \text{E!}x)\text{Uranus}$$

i.e. "Uranus might not have existed," we seem to have a statement that says of an object that it is possible that *it* does not exist; existential generalisation holds; and the context is transparent when substitution is properly carried out: if Hesperus might not have existed, and Phosphorus is the very same object as Hesperus, Phosphorus might not have existed. For the case of the positive existential, similar arguments can be applied to

$$\sim \Box (\text{E!}(\text{Uranus})).$$

There is no commitment here to any particular account of negative or positive existentials containing *non*-denoting names; on these I shall make only the remark that every adequately precise account of the matter I have seen or constructed has been open to more or less obvious objections.

(ii) The objects which the truth-conditions of sentences containing ordinary proper names concern are genuine continuant particulars; they are objects of which it is true to say that they can have a property at one time and, remaining one and the same object, lack it at another. Now Dummett, among others, has claimed that "any verbal specification [of the sense of a proper name] ... must ... include a stipulation of the criterion of identity for the object which is the referent of the name." (Dummett

[1973] p. 545.) Will this thought, if correct, prompt us to assign something else besides an object to a name in giving its semantic role in a language?

Here we must distinguish sharply between these two claims:

(a) for every object, there is an associated criterion of identity

(b) when specifying the referent of a proper name, we must actually specify a criterion of identity (perhaps in the form of a sortal predicate) for the referent of the name.

(a) seems undeniable; to say it is to say that for every object, there is some biconditional of the form

$$x = y \text{ iff } \phi(x, y)$$

whose variables range over that object, that does not contain the identity sign on its right-hand side, that is a necessary (which is not to say *a priori*) truth, and that guarantees that whatever is true of x is so of y (and conversely).[7] But (a) does not commit us to (b); on the contrary. The thought that is commonly offered in support of (b) is that if we fix the referent of the name α by some complex description "the F," one will not thereby have specified what object one refers to in using α in a sentence with a time reference other than that to which the description F relates. This is a confusion. Either the predicable $F(\xi_1)$ is satisfied by only one object, or it is not. If it is, the instruction "trace *that object* through space and time" is perfectly intelligible, even if "the concept under which" it is to be traced (as David Wiggins would say) can only be discovered by investigating the world to discover what kind of object it is that uniquely satisfies $F(\xi_1)$. If $F(\xi_1)$ is not uniquely satisfied, then the referent-fixing procedure in this case was *already* inadequate, and the absence of a specification of a criterion of identity is not to the point.

(iii)   We are naturally driven to enquire whether there is any close connexion between the utility we derive from having proper names in our language and the fact that proper names are rigid designators. The conditions under which we may expect to find that a proper name for a spatio-temporal particular has useful currency in a group have been investigated by Strawson;[8] he reaches the conclusion that these conditions are that that group has frequent need to refer to that particular, in virtue of its being that particular (as opposed to a need based on the fact that it always happened to satisfy a description of interest), and finally that the group has no short description of the particular always available or natural to all the members of the group. The name will be useful, approximately, just because it preserves the same "referential force" through its referent's changes of relations to other things and because it has the same referential force for speakers who encounter the referent in different connections.

It is hardly to be conceived that any expression that meets these needs fails to be a rigid designator on our intuitive criterion; for any departure from the paradigm that criterion represents is a departure from the idea that the truth (fulfilment, ...) conditions for a sentence $F(\alpha)$ containing the name α require a certain object to be $F(\ )$. In so far as there is a departure, the needs are not being fulfilled in the best possible way, for a departure involves the truth-conditions for some sentence $G(\alpha)$ not simply being a matter of the object which the need concerns being $G(\ )$. But we can say more than this.

Could any other sort of rigid designator, of the kinds we currently possess, fulfil these needs? Demonstratives are no help if the object cannot be relied upon to be literally present, or if the speaker cannot rely upon his audience to have the sort of knowledge enabling him to work out the speaker's referent in a less direct use of "that F," for some F; similar remarks apply to entity-invoking uses of "the F," and Strawson's plausible conditions seem designed to ensure that speakers in a group where there is such a need cannot rely on such factors. I conclude that only rigid designators in our sense can meet the needs Strawson's conditions express, and that among rigid designators, only proper names can meet them in a way that allows us to do what we wish to with language with maximum efficiency.

Acknowledgment

I have benefited from discussions on these matters with Richard Grandy, John McDowell, Dana Scott, and David Wiggins; and I am especially indebted to Gareth Evans for incisive remarks made in reply to an ancestor of the present paper.

Notes

1. In this example, the first occurrence of "the prime minister" is intended to have large scope with respect to "not."
2. The "St." in "St. Anne" may make one suspicious of whether this expression is such a genuine proper name.

3. Some important remarks on the relevant notion of demonstration are contained in Appendix VIII of Kaplan [1973].

4. For full generality, this relation should have a sentential, and perhaps even a (token) event, argument; on the relevant notion of utterance, a man may utter two sentences at once. They might even be utterances of the same sentence type.

5. With a little loss of perspicuity, the evaluation function could be compressed so as to have the usual two arguments; and similarly for the satisfaction relation.

6. Reservations about this step will be given later.

7. For examples of such criteria, see for the case of material objects, Wiggins [1968], and for one account for the case of events, Davidson [1969].

8. In a seminar in Oxford in 1978.

References

Anscombe, G. E. M. (1958). *An Introduction to Wittgenstein's Tractatus.* Hutchinson.

Davidson, Donald. (1969). "The Individuation of Events." In N. Rescher (ed.) *Essays in Honor of Carl Hempel.* Reidel.

Dummett, Michael. (1973). *Frege: Philosophy of Language.* Duckworth.

Frege, Gottlob. (1968). "The Thought: A Logical Inquiry." In E. D. Klemke (ed.) *Essays on Frege.* University of Illinois Press.

Geach, Peter. (1972). *Logic Matters.* Berkeley: University of California Press.

Grandy, Richard. (1972). "A Definition of Truth for Sentences Containing Intensional Definite Description Operators." *Journal of Philosophical Logic* 1.

Kaplan, David. (1973). "Bob and Carol and Ted and Alice." In J. Hintikka et al. (eds.) *Approaches to Natural Language.* Reidel.

Kripke, Saul. (1972). Naming and Necessity. In Donald Davidson and Gilbert Harman (eds.) *Semantics of Natural Language.* Reidel, 253–355, 763–769.

Lambert, Karel and Bas van Fraassen. (1972). *Derivation and Counterexample.* Dickenson.

Marcus, Ruth Barcan. (1961). Modalities and Intensional Languages. *Synthese.*

Mill, J. S. (1843). A System of Logic. Longmans, 1872.

Quine, Willard Van Orman. (1953). Three Grades of Modal Involvement. *Proceedings of the XIth International Congress of Philosophy* 14, 65–81; reprinted in *The Ways of Paradox*, 2nd Ed. Cambridge, Mass.: Harvard University Press, 1976.

———. (1970). *Philosophy of Logic.* Prentice-Hall.

Scott, Dana, (1967). Existence and Description in Formal Logic. In Ralph Schoenman (ed.) *Bertrand Russell, Philosopher of the Century.* Allen & Unwin.

Strawson, P. F. (1964). "Identifying Reference and Truth Values." *Theoria* 30, 96–118.

Wiggins, David. (1968). On Being in the Same Place at the Same Time. *Philosophical Review.*

Chapter 11

Speaker's Reference and Semantic Reference   Saul Kripke

I am going to discuss some issues inspired by a well-known paper of Keith Donnellan, "Reference and Definite Descriptions,"[1,2] but the interest—to me—of the contrast mentioned in my title goes beyond Donnellan's paper: I think it is of considerable constructive as well as critical importance to the philosophy of language. These applications, however and even everything I might want to say relative to Donnellan's paper, cannot be discussed in full here because of problems of length.

Moreover, although I have a considerable interest in the substantive issues raised by Donnellan's paper, and by related literature, my own conclusions will be methodological, not substantive. I can put the matter this way: Donnellan's paper claims to give decisive objections both to Russell's theory of definite descriptions (taken as a theory about English) and to Strawson's. My concern is *not* primarily with the question: is Donnellan right, or is Russell (or Strawson)? Rather, it is with the question: do the considerations *in Donnellan's paper* refute Russell's theory (or Strawson's)? For definiteness, I will concentrate on Donnellan versus Russell, leaving Strawson aside. And about this issue I will draw a definite conclusion, one which I think will illuminate a few methodological maxims about language. Namely, I will conclude that the considerations in Donnellan's paper, *by themselves*, do *not* refute Russell's theory.

Any conclusions about Russell's views *per se*, or Donnellan's, must be tentative. If I were to be asked for a tentative stab about Russell, I would say that although his theory does a far better job of handling ordinary discourse than many have thought, and although many popular

Reprinted from P. A. French, et al. (eds.), *Contemporary Perspectives in the Philosophy of Language*, pp. 6–27, by permission of Saul Kripke. © 1979 Saul Kripke.

arguments against it are inconclusive, probably it ultimately fails. The considerations I have in mind have to do with the existence of "improper" definite descriptions, such as "the table," where uniquely specifying conditions are not contained in the description itself. Contrary to the Russellian picture, I doubt that such descriptions can always be regarded as elliptical with some uniquely specifying conditions added. And it may even be the case that a true picture will resemble various aspects of Donnellan's in important respects. But such questions will largely be left aside here.

I will state my preference for one substantive conclusion (although I do not fell completely confident of it either): that unitary theories, like Russell's, are preferable to theories that postulate an ambiguity. And much, though not all, of Donnellan's paper seems to postulate a (semantic) ambiguity between his "referential" and "attributive" uses. But—as we shall see—Donnellan is not entirely consistent on this point, and I therefore am not sure whether I am expressing disagreement with him even here.[3]

1 Preliminary Considerations

Donnellan claims that a certain linguistic phenomenon argues against Russell's theory. According to Russell, if someone says, "The x such that $\phi(x)\psi$s," he mans that there is an χ which uniquely satisfies "$\phi(x)$" and that any such χ satisfies "$\psi(x)$." [I.e., $(\exists\chi)(\phi!(x) \wedge \psi(x))$, where "$\phi!(x)$" abbreviates "$\phi(x) \wedge (y)(\phi(y) \supset y = x$."] Donnellan argues that some phenomenon of the following kind tells against Russell: Suppose someone at a gathering, glancing in a certain direction, says to his companion,

(1) "The man over there drinking champagne is happy tonight."

Suppose both the speaker and hearer are under a false impression, and that the man to whom they refer is a teetotaler, drinking sparkling water. He may, nevertheless, be happy. Now, if there is no champagne drinker over there, Russell would regard (1) as false, and Frege and Strawson would give it a truth-value gap. Nevertheless, as Donnellan emphasizes, we have a substantial intuition that the speaker said something true of the man to whom he referred in spite of his misimpression.

Since no one is really drinking champagne, the case involves a definite description that is empty, or vacuous, according to both Russell and Frege. So as to avoid any unnecessary and irrelevant entanglements of the present question with the issues that arise when definite descriptions are vacuous, I shall modify this case (and all other cases where, in Donnellan's paper, the description was vacuous).[4] Suppose that "over there," exactly one man *is* drinking champagne, although his glass is not visible to the speaker (nor to his hearer). Suppose that he, unlike the teetotaler to whom the speaker refers, has been driven to drink precisely by his misery. Then *all* the classical theories (both Russellian and Fregean) would regard (1) as false (since exactly one man over there is drinking champagne, and he is *not* happy tonight). Now the speaker has spoken *truly* of the man to whom he refers (the teetotaler), yet this dimension is left out in all the classical analyses, which would assign falsehood to his assertion solely on the basis of the misery of *someone else* whom *no one* was talking about (the champagne drinker). Previously Linsky had given a similar example. He gave it as an empty case; once again I modify it to make the description nonvacuous. Someone sees a woman with a man. Taking the man to be her husband, and observing his attitude towards her, he says, "Her husband is kind to her," and someone else may nod. "Yes, he seems to be." Suppose the man in question is not her husband. Suppose he is her lover, to whom she has been driven precisely by her husband's cruelty. Once again both the Russellian analysis and the Fregean analysis would assess the statement as false, and both would do so one the basis of the cruelty of a man neither participant in the dialogues was talking about.

Again, an example suggested to me by a remark of L. Crocker: suppose a religious narrative (similar, say, to the Gospels) consistently refers to its main protagonist as "The Messiah." Suppose a historian wishes to assess the work for *historical accuracy*—that is, he wishes to determine whether it gives an accurate account of the life of its hero (whose identity we assume to be established). Does it matter to this question whether the hero really was the Messiah, as long as the author took him to be so, and addressed his work to a religious community that shared this belief? Surely not. And note that it is no mere "principle of charity" that is operating here. On the contrary, if someone other than the person intended were really the Messiah, and if, by a bizarre and unintended coincidence, the narrative gave a fairly true account of *his* life, we would not for that reason call it "historically true." On the contrary, we would regard the work as historically *false* if the events mentioned were false of its intended protagonist. Whether the story happened to fit the true Messiah—who may have been totally unknown to the author and even have lived after the time the work was composed—would be irrelevant. Once again, this fact seems inconsistent with the positions both of Frege and of Russell.

On the basis of such examples, Donnellan distinguishes two uses of definite descriptions. In the "attributive" use, a speaker "states something about whoever or whatever is the so-and-so." In the "referential" use, a speaker "uses the description to enable his audience to pick out whom or what he is talking about and states something about that person or thing. In the first [attributive] case, the definite description might be said to occur essentially, for the speaker wishes to assert something about whatever or whoever fits that description; but in the referential use the definite description is merely one tool for ... calling attention to a person or thing ... and ... any other device for doing the same job, another description or name, would do as well."[5] For example, suppose I come upon Smith foully murdered. The condition of Smith's body moves me to say, "Smith's murderer is (must be) insane." Then we have an *attributive* use: we speak of the murderer, whoever he may be. On the other hand, suppose that Jones is on trial for Smith's murder and that I am among the spectators in the courtroom. Observing the wild behavior of the defendant at the dock, I may say, "Smith's murderer is insane." (I forgot the defendant's name, but am firmly convinced of his guilt.) Then my use is referential: whether or not Jones was the real murderer, and even if someone else was, if Jones accused me of libel, his failure to fit my description would give me no defense. All of the previous cases, (the teetotaling "champagne" drinker, the lover taken for a husband, the false Messiah), are all referential in Donnellan's sense.

An intuitive mark of the attributive use is the legitimacy of the parenthetical comment, "whoever he is." In the first case, we may say "Smith's murderer, whoever he is, is insane," but not in the second. But we should not be misled: a definite description may be used attributively even if the speaker believes that a certain person, say, Jones, fits it, provided that he is talking about *whoever* fits, and his belief that Jones in fact fits is not relevant. In the case where I deduce the murderer's insanity from the condition of Smith's body, I use the description attributively even if I suspect, or even am firmly convinced, that Jones is the culprit.

I have no doubt that the distinction Donnellan brings out exists and is of fundamental importance, though I do not regard it as exclusive or exhaustive. But Donnellan also believes that Russell's theory applies, if at all, only to attributive uses, and that referential uses of definite descriptions are close to proper names, even to Russell's "logically proper" names. And he appears to believe that the examples of the referential uses mentioned above are inexplicable on Russell's theory. It is these views that I wish to examine.

2 Some Alleged Applications of the Distinction

Some alleged applications of Donnellan's distinction have entered the oral tradition, and even to an extent, the written tradition, that are not in Donnellan's paper. I will mention some that I find questionable. Unfortunately I will have to discuss these applications more briefly than the issues in question really deserve, since they are ancillary to the main theme.

2a De Dicto–De Re

Many able people, in and out of print, have implied that Donnellan's distinction has something to do with, can be identified with, or can replace, the *de dicto–de re* distinction, or the small scope–large scope distinction in modal or intensional contexts.

"The number of planets is necessarily odd" can mean two things, depending on whether it is interpreted *de dicto* or *de re*. If it is interpreted *de dicto*, it asserts that the proposition that the number of planets is odd is a necessary truth—something I take to be false (there might have been eight planets). If it is interpreted *de re*, it asserts that the actual number of planets (nine) has the property of necessary oddness (essentialists like me take this to be true). Similarly, if we say, "Jones believes that the richest debutante in Dubuque will marry him," we may mean that Jones's belief has a certain content, viz., that the richest debutante in Dubuque will marry him; or we may mean that he believes, *of* a girl who is (in fact) the richest in Dubuque, that she will marry him. The view in question suggests that the *de dicto* case is to be identified with Donnellan's *attributive* use, the *de re* with the *referential*.

Any such assimilation, in my opinion, is confused. (I don't think Donnellan makes it.) There are many objections; I will mention a few. First, the *de dicto* use of the definite description cannot be identified with either the *referential* or the *attributive* use. Here the basic point was already noticed by Frege. If a description is embedded in a (*de dicto*) intensional context, we cannot be said to be talking *about* the thing described, either *qua* its satisfaction of the description or *qua* anything else. Taken *de dicto*, "Jones believes that the richest debutante in Dubuque will marry him," can be asserted by someone who thinks (let us suppose, wrongly) that there are *no* debutantes in Dubuque; certainly then, he is in no way talking about the richest debutante, even "attributively." Similarly, "It is possible that (France should have a monarchy in 1976, and that) the King of France in 1976 should have been bald" is true, if read *de dicto*; yet we are not using "the King of France in 1976" attributively to speak of the King of France in 1976, for there is none. Frege concluded that "the King of France in 1976" refers, in these contexts, to its ordinary sense; at any rate, if we wish to speak of "reference" here, it cannot be to the nonexistent king. Even if there were such a king, the quoted assertion would say nothing about *him*, if read *de dicto*: to say that *he* might have been bald, would be *de re* (indeed, this *is* the distinction in question).

Second, and even more relevantly, Donnellan's referential use cannot be identified with the *de re* use. (I think Donnellan would agree.) Suppose I have no idea how many planets there are, but (for some reason) astronomical theory dictates that that number must be odd. If I say, "The number of planets (whatever it may be) is odd," my description is used attributively. If I am an essentialist, I will also say, "The number of planets (whatever it may be) is necessarily odd," on the grounds that all odd numbers are necessarily odd; and my usage is just as attributive as in the first case. In "Smith's murderer, whoever he may be, is known to the police, but they're not saying," or, more explicitly, "The police know concerning Smith's murderer, whoever he is, that he committed the murder; but they're not saying who he is," "Smith's murderer" is used attributively, but is *de re*.

Finally: Russell wished to handle the *de dicto–de re* distinction by his notion of the *scope* of a description. Some have suggested that Donnellan's referential–attributive distinction can replace Russell's distinction of scope. But *no* twofold distinction can do this job. Consider:

(2) The number of planets might have been necessarily even.

In a natural use, (2) can be interpreted as true; for example, there might have been exactly eight planets, in which case the number of planets would have been even, and hence necessarily even. (2), interpreted as true, is neither *de re* nor *de dicto*; that is, the definite description neither has the largest nor the smallest possible scope. Consider:

(2a) $\Diamond \Box (\exists x)$ (There are exactly x planets and x is even)

(2b) $(\exists x)$ (There are exactly x planets and $\Diamond \Box (x$ is even)).

(2c) $\Diamond (\exists x)$ (There are exactly x planets and $\Box (x$ is even)).

(2a)–(2c) give three alternative Russellian analyses of (2). (2a) gives the description the smallest possible scope (*de dicto*); it says, presumably falsely, that it might have been necessary that there was an even number of planets. (2b) gives the description the largest possible scope (*de re*); it says, still falsely, of the actual number of planets (viz., nine) that it might have been necessarily even. (2c) is the interpretation which makes (2) true. When intensional operators are iterated, intermediate scopes are possible. Three analogous interpretations are possible, say, for "Jones doubts that Holmes believes that Smith's murderer is insane"; or (using an indefinite description) for "Hoover charged that the Berrigans plotted to kidnap a high American official." (I actually read something like this last in a newspaper and wondered what was meant.)[6] This may mean: (a) there is a particular high official such that Hoover charged that the Berrigans plotted to kidnap him (largest scope, *de re*, this was the interpretation intended); or (b) Hoover charged that the Berrigans plotted as follows: let's kidnap a high official (smallest scope, *de dicto*); or (c) Hoover charged that there was a high official (whose identity may have been unknown to Hoover) whom the Berrigans planned to kidnap (intermediate scope).

As intensional (or other) constructions are iterated, there are more and more possible scopes for a definite description. No *twofold* distinction can replace Russell's notion of scope.[7] In particular, neither the *de dicto–de re* distinction nor the referential–attributive distinction can do so.

2b Rigid Definite Descriptions

If definite descriptions $\imath x\phi(x)$, are taken as primitive and assigned reference, then the conventional nonrigid assignment assigns to such a description, with respect to each possible world, the unique object, if any, which would have ϕd in that world. (Forget the vacuous case, which requries a further convention.) For example, "the number of planets" denotes eight, speaking of a counterfactual situation where there would have been eight planets (and "the number of planets is even" is true of such a situation). Another type of definite description, $\imath x\phi x$, a "rigid" definite description, could be introduced semantically by the following stipulation: let $\imath x\phi x$ denote, with respect to all possible worlds, the unique object that (actually) ϕs (then "the number of planets is odd," as interpreted, expresses a necessary truth). Both kinds of definite descriptions can obviously be introduced, theoretically, into a single formal language, perhaps by the notations just given. Some have suggested that definite descriptions, in English, are *ambiguous* between the two readings. It has further been suggested that the two types of definite descriptions, the nonrigid and the rigid, are the source of the *de dicto–de re* distinction and should replace Russell's notion of scope for the purpose. Further, it has been suggested that they amount to the same thing as Donnellan's attributive–referential distinction.[8]

My comments will be brief, so as to avoid too much excursus. Although I have an open mind on the subject, I am not yet convinced that there is any clear evidence for such an ambiguity. Being a twofold distinction, the ambiguity alleged cannot replace Russell's notion of scope, for the reasons given above. Once Russell's notion is available, it can be used to handle the *de dicto–de re* distinction; a further ambiguity seems unnecessary. More relevant to the present context, the "rigid" sense of a definite description, if it exists, cannot be identified with Donnellan's "referential" use. I take it that the identification of the referential use with the rigid definite description was inspired by some line of reasoning like this: Donnellan holds that referential descriptions are those close to proper names, even to Russell's "logically proper names." But surely proper names, or at least, Russellian "logically proper names," are rigid. Hence Donnellan's referential descriptions are just the rigid definite descriptions.

If we assume that Donnellan thinks of names as rigid, as I think of them, his referential definite descriptions *would* most plausibly be taken to refer rigidly to their referents. But it is not clear that he does agree with me on the rigidity of such reference.[9] More important, a rigid definite description, as defined above, still determines its referent via its unique satisfaction of the associated property—and this fact separates the notion of such a description from that of a referential description, as Donnellan defines it. David Kaplan has suggested that a demonstrative "that" can be used, in English, to make any definite description rigid. "That bastard —the man who killed Smith, whoever he may be—is surely insane!" The subject term rigidly designates Smith's murderer, but it is still attributive in Donnellan's sense.[10]

2c Referential Descriptions

In "Naming and Necessity,"[11] one argument I presented against the description (or cluster-of-descriptions) theory of proper names concerned cases where the referent of a name, the person named by the name, did not satisfy the descriptions usually associated with it, and someone else did. For example, the name "Gödel" might be taken to mean "the man who proved the incompleteness of arithmetic"; but even if Gödel had been a fraud, who had proved nothing at all and had misappropriated his work from an unknown named "Schmidt," our term "Gödel" would refer to the fraud, not to the man who really satisfied the definite description. Against this it has been said that although the argument does succeed in its main purpose of refuting the description theory as a theory of reference (that is, it shows that the descriptive properties cited do not determine the referent), it does nothing to show that names are not abbreviated definite descriptions, because we could take the descriptions in question to be referential in Donnellan's sense. Referential descriptions can easily refer to things that fail to satisfy the descriptions; nothing in my argument shows that names are not synonymous with such descriptions.[12]

My reaction to such an argument may become clearer later. For the moment, (too) briefly: In the case of "Her husband is kind to her," and similar cases, "her husband" can refer to her lover, as long as we are under the misapprehension that the man to whom we refer (the lover) *is* her husband. Once we are apprised of the true facts, we will no longer so refer to him. Similarly, someone can use "the man who proved the incompleteness of arithmetic," as a referential definite description, to refer to Gödel; it might be so used, for example, by someone who had forgotten his name. If the hypothetical fraud were discovered, however, the description is no longer usable as a device to refer to Gödel; henceforth it can be used only to refer to Schmidt. We would withdraw any previous assertions using the description to refer to Gödel (unless they also were true of Schmidt). We would *not* similarly withdraw the *name* "Gödel," even after the fraud was discovered; "Gödel," would still be used to name Gödel, not Schmidt. The name and the description, therefore, are not synonymous. (See also note 27 below).

3   The Main Problem

3a   A Disagreement with Russell?
Do Donnellan's observations provide an argument against Russell's theory? Do his *views* contradict Russell's? One might think that if Donnellan is right, Russell must be wrong, since Donnellan's truth conditions for statements containing referential definite descriptions differ from Russell's. Unfortunately, this is not so clear. Consider the case of "her husband is kind to her," mistakenly said of the lover. If Donnellan had roundly asserted that the quoted statement is true if and only if the *lover* is

kind to her, regardless of the kindness of the husband, the issue between him and Russell would be clearly joined. But Donnellan doesn't say this: rather he says that the speaker has referred to a certain person, the lover, and said *of him* that he is kind to her. But if we ask, "Yes, but was the statement he made true?" Donnellan would hedge. For if *we* are not under the misimpression that the man the speaker referred to was her husband, *we* would not express the same assertion by "Her husband is kind to her." "If it ['her husband'] is being used referentially, it is not clear what is meant by 'the statement.' ... To say that the statement he made was that her husband is kind to her lands us in difficulties. For we [in so reporting what the speaker said must use the definite description] either attributively or referentially. If the former, then we misrepresent the linguistic performance of the speaker; if the latter, then we ourselves are referring to someone," and ordinarily we can refer to someone as "her husband" only if we take him to be her husband.[13]

Since Donnellan does not clearly assert that the statement "her husband is kind to her" ever has non-Russellian truth conditions, he has *not*, so far, clearly contradicted Russell's theory. His argument, as he presents it, that there is a problem in reporting "the statement" is questionable, in two ways.

First, it uses the premise that if we say, "Jones said that her husband is kind to her," we ourselves must use the description attributively or referentially; but, as we saw, a definite description in indirect discourse is *neither* referential nor attributive.[14]

Second, there is an important problem about the nature of the referential–attributive distinction. Donnellan says that his distinction is neither syntactic nor semantic:

The grammatical structure of the sentence seems to me to be the same whether the description is used referentially or attributively: that is, it is not syntactically ambiguous. Nor does it seem at all attractive to suppose an ambiguity in the meaning of the words; it does not appear to be semantically ambiguous. (Perhaps we could say that the sentence is pragmatically ambiguous: the distinction between roles that the description plays is a function of the speaker's intentions.) These, of course, are intuitions; I do not have an argument for these conclusions. Nevertheless, the burden of proof is surely on the other side.[15]

Suppose for the moment that this is so. Then if the referential–attributive distinction is pragmatic, rather than syntactic or semantic, it is presumably a distinction about speech acts. There is no reason to suppose that in making an indirect discourse report on what someone else has said I myself must have similar intentions, or be engaged in the same kind of speech act; in fact, it is clear that I am not. If I say "Jones said the police were around the corner," Jones may have said it as a warning, but *I* need not say it as a warning. If the referential–attributive distinction is neither syntactic nor semantic, there is no reason, without further argument, to suppose that my usage, in indirect discourse, should match the man on whom I report, as referential or attributive. The case is quite different for a genuine semantic ambiguity. If Jones says, "I have never been at a bank," and I report this, saying, "Jones denied that he was ever at a bank," the sense I give to "bank" must match Jones's if my report is to be accurate.

Indeed, the passage seems inconsistent with the whole trend of Donnellan's paper. Donnellan suggests that there is no syntactic or semantic ambiguity in the statement, "Her husband is kind to her." He also suggests that Russell may well give a correct analysis of the attributive use but not of the referential use. Surely this is not coherent. It is not "uses," in some pragmatic sense, but *senses* of a sentence which can be analyzed. If the sentence is *not* (syntactically or) semantically ambiguous, it has only *one* analysis; to say that it has two distinct analyses is to attribute a syntactic or semantic ambiguity to it.

Donnellan's arguments for his refusal to give a truth value to the speaker's assertion, "Her husband is kind to her," seem to be fallacious. My own suggested account of the matter below—in terms of a theory of speech acts—creates no problem about "the statement"; it is simply the statement that her husband is kind to her. But Donnellan's cautious refusal to say, under the circumstances mentioned, that "Her husband is kind to her" is true, seems nevertheless to be intuitively correct. The man to whom the speaker refers is—let us suppose—kind to her. But it seems hard for us to say that when he uttered, "Her husband is kind to her," it expressed a truth, if *we* believe that her husband is unkind to her.

Now Donnellan thinks that he has refuted Russell. But all he has clearly claimed, let alone established, is that a speaker can refer to the lover and say, of him, that he is kind to her by saying "Her husband is kind to her." So, first, we can ask: *If* this claim is correct, does it conflict with Russell's views?

Second, since Donnellan's denial that he advocates a semantic ambiguity in definite descriptions seems inconsistent with much of his paper, we can try ignoring the denial, and take his paper to be arguing for such an ambiguity. Then we may ask: has Donnellan established a (semantic) ambiguity inconsistent with Russell's theory?

3b General Remarks: Apparatus

We need a general apparatus to discuss these questions. Some of the apparatus is well known, but I review it for its intrinsic importance and interest. First, let us distinguish, following Grice,[16] between what *the speaker's words meant*, on a given occasion, and what *he meant*, in saying these words, on that occasion. For example, one burglar says to another, "The cops are around the corner." What *the words meant* is clear: the police were around the corner. But *the speaker may well have meant*, "We can't wait around collecting any more loot: Let's split!" That is not *the meaning of the words*, even on that occasion, though that is *what he meant in saying those words, on that occasion*. Suppose he had said, "The cops are inside the bank." Then on that occasion, "bank" meant a commercial bank, not a river bank, and this is relevant to what the *words* meant, on that occasion. (On other occasions, the same words might mean that the police were at a river bank.) But, if the speaker *meant* "Let's split," this is no part of the *meaning of his words*, even on that occasion.

Again (inspired by an example of Grice):[17] A magician makes a hand-kerchief change color. Someone says, recalling the trick, "Then he put the red handkerchief on the side of the table"; and someone else interjects, cautiously, "It *looked* red." The words meant, on that occasion, that the object referred to (the handkerchief) looked red. What we speak of when we speak of the meaning of his words, on that occasion, includes a dis-ambiguation of the utterance. (Perhaps, on some occasions, where "it" refers to a book, a phonetically identical utterance might mean, "it looked read," well-thumbed and well-perused.) But the speaker meant, on this occasion, to suggest that perhaps the handkerchief wasn't really red, that perhaps the trick relied on some kind of illusion. (Note that, on this occasion, not only do the *words* "it looked red" mean what they mean, but also the *speaker* means that it looked red, as well as that it may not have been red. On the other hand, the speaker has no intention of pro-ducing a belief in the hearer that the handkerchief looked red, or a belief in the hearer that he (the speaker) believed it looked red. Both facts are common knowledge. The same *could* hold for "The cops are around the corner."[18] Do these examples contradict Grice's analysis of "meaning"? Grice's theory has become very complex and I am not quite sure.)

The notion of what words can mean, in the language, is semantical: it is given by the conventions of our language. What they mean, on a given occasion, is determined, on a given occasion, by these conventions, together with the intentions of the speaker and various contextual features. Finally what the speaker meant, on a given occasion, in saying certain words, derives from various further special intentions of the speaker, together with various general principles, applicable to all human languages regardless of their special conventions. (Cf. Grice's "conversational maxims.") For example, "It looks red" replaced a categorical affirmation of redness. A plausible general principle of human discourse would have it that if a second speaker insists that a stronger assertion should be replaced by a weaker one, he thereby wishes to cast doubt on the stronger assertion; whence, knowing the semantics of English, and the meaning of the speaker's words on this occasion, we can deduce what was meant (the Gricean "coversational implicature").[19]

Let us now speak of speaker's reference and semantic reference: these notions are special cases of the Gricean notions discussed above. If a speaker has a designator in his idiolect, certain conventions of his idiolect[20] (given various facts about the world) determine the referent in the idiolect: that I call the *semantic referent* of the designator. (If the designator is ambiguous, or contains indexicals, demonstratives, or the like, we must speak of the semantic referent on a given occasion. The referent will be determined by the conventions of the language plus the speaker's intentions and various contextual features.)

Speaker's reference is a more difficult notion. Consider, for example, the following case, which I have mentioned elsewhere.[21] Two people see Smith in the distance and mistake him for Jones. They have a brief colloquy: "What is Jones doing?" "Raking the leaves." "Jones," in the common language of both, is a name of Jones; it *never* names Smith. Yet, in some sense, on this occasion, clearly both participants in the dialogue have referred to Smith, and the second participant has said something true about the man he referred to if and only if Smith was raking the leaves (whether or not Jones was). How can we account for this? Suppose a speaker takes it that a certain object a fulfills the conditions for being the semantic referent of a designator, "d." Then, wishing to say something about a, he uses "d" to speak about a; say, he says "$\phi(d)$." Then, he said, for a, on that occasion, that it ϕd in the appropriate Gricean sense (explicated above), he *meant* that a ϕd. This is true even if a is not really the semantic referent of "d." If it is not, then *that a ϕs* is included in what he meant (on that occasion), but not in the meaning of his words (on that occasion).

So, we may tentatively define the speaker's referent of a designator to be that object which the speaker wishes to talk about, on a given occasion, and believes fulfills the conditions for being the semantic referent of the designator. He uses the designator with the intention of making an assertion about the object in question (which may not really be the semantic referent, if the speaker's belief that it fulfills the appropriate semantic conditions is in error). The speaker's referent is the thing the speaker referred to by the designator, though it may not be the referent of the designator, in his idiolect. In the example above, Jones, the man named by the name, is the semantic referent. Smith is the speaker's referent, the correct answer to the question, "To whom were you referring?"[22]

Below, the notion of speaker's reference will be extended to include more cases where existential quantification rather than designation is involved.

In a given idiolect, the semantic referent of a designator (without indexicals) is given by a *general* intention of the speaker to refer to a certain object whenever the designator is used. The speaker's referent is given by a *specific* intention, on a given occasion, to refer to a certain object. If the speaker believes that the object he wants to talk about, on a given occasion, fulfills the conditions for being the semantic referent, then he believes that there is no clash between his general intentions and his specific intentions. My hypotheses is that Donnellan's referential–attributive distinction should be generalized in this light. For the speaker, on a given occasion, may believe that his specific intention coincides with his general intention for one of two reasons. In one case (the "simple" case), his specific intention is simply to refer to the semantic referent: that is, his specific intention *is* simply his general semantic intention. (For example, he uses "Jones" as a name of Jones—elaborate this according to your favorite theory of proper names—and, on this occasion, simply wishes to use "Jones" to refer to Jones.) Alternatively—the "complex" case—he has a specific intention, which is distinct from his general intention, but which he believes, as a matter of fact, to determine the same object as the one determined by his general intention. (For example, he wishes to refer to the man "over there" but believes that he *is* Jones.) In the "simple" case, the speaker's referent is, *by definition*, the semantic referent. In the "complex" case, they may coincide, if the speaker's belief is correct, but they need not. (The man "over there" may be Smith and not Jones.) To anticipate, my hypothesis will be that Donnellan's "attributive" use is nothing but the "simple" case, specialized to definite descriptions, and that the "referential" use is, similarly, the "complex" case. If such a conjecture is correct, it would be wrong to take Donnellan's "referential" use, as he does, to be a use of a description as if it were a proper name. For the distinction of simple and complex cases will apply to proper names just as much as to definite descriptions.

3c Donnellan's Argument against Russell: Methodological and Substantive Considerations

In the light of the notions just developed, consider the argument Donnellan adduces against Russell. Donnellan points to a phenomenon which he alleges to be inexplicable on a Russellian account of English definite descriptions. He accounts for it by positing an ambiguity. Alternatively, we wish to account for the phenomenon on pragmatic grounds, encapsulated in the distinction between speaker's reference and semantic reference. How can we see whether Donnellan's phenomenon conflicts with a Russellian account?

I propose the following test for any alleged counterexample to a linguistic proposal: If someone alleges that a certain linguistic phenomenon in English is a counterexample to a given analysis, consider a hypothetical language which (as much as possible) is like English except that the analysis is *stipulated* to be correct. Imagine such a hypothetical language introduced into a community and spoken by it. *If the phenomenon in question would still arise in a community that spoke such a hypothetical language (which may not be English), then the fact that it arises in English cannot disprove the hypothesis that the analysis is correct for English.* An example removed from the present discussion: Some have alleged that identity cannot be the relation that holds between, and only between, each thing and itself, for if so, the nontriviality of identity statements would be inexplicable. If it is conceded, however, that such a relation makes sense, and if it can be shown that a hypothetical language involving such a relation would generate the same problems, it will follow that the existence of these problems does not refute the hypothesis that "identical to" stands for this same relation in English.[23]

By "the weak Russell language," I will mean a language similar to English except that the truth conditions of sentences with definite descriptions are *stipulated* to coincide with Russell's: for example, "The present King of France is bald" is to be true iff exactly one person is King of France, and that person is bald. On the weak Russell language, this effect can be achieved by assigning semantic reference to definite descriptions: the semantic referent of a definite description is the unique object that satisfies the description, if any; otherwise there is no semantic referent. A sentence of the simple subject-predicate form will be true if the predicate is true of the (semantic) referent of its subject; false, if either the subject has no semantic referent or the predicate is not true of the semantic referent of the subject.

Since the weak Russell language takes definite descriptions to be primitive designators, it is not fully Russellian. By "the intermediate Russell language," I mean a language in which sentences containing definite descriptions are taken to be abbreviations or paraphrases of their Russellian analyses: for example, "The present King of France is bald" *means* (or has a "deep structure" like) "Exactly one person is at present King of France, and he is bald," or the like. Descriptions are not terms, and are not assigned reference or meaning in isolation. The "strong Russell language" goes further: definite descriptions are actually *banned* from the language and Russellian paraphrases are used in their place. Instead of saying "Her husband is kind to her," a speaker of this language must say "Exactly one man is married to her, and he is kind to her," or even (better), "There is a unique man who is married to her, and every man who is married to her is kind to her," or the like. If Russell is right, longwindedness is the only defect of these versions.

Would the phenomenon Donnellan adduces arise in communities that spoke these languages? Surely speakers of these languages are no more infallible than we. They too will find themselves at a party and mistakenly think someone is drinking champagne even though he is actually drinking sparkling water. If they are speakers of the weak or intermediate Russell languages, they will say, "The man in the corner drinking champagne is happy tonight." They will say this precisely because *they think, though erroneously, that the Russellian truth conditions are satisfied.* Wouldn't we say of these speakers that they are referring to the teetotaler, under the misimpression that he is drinking champagne? And, if he is happy, are they not saying of him, *truly*, that he is happy? Both answers seem obviously affirmative.

In the case of the weak Russell language, the general apparatus previously developed seems fully adequate to account for the phenomenon. The semantic referent of a definite description is given by the conditions laid down above: it is a matter of the specific conventions of the (weak)

Russell language, in this case that the referent is the unique object satisfying the descriptive conditions. The speaker's referent, on the other hand, is determined by a general theory of speech acts, applicable to all languages: it is the object to which the speaker wishes to refer, and which he believes fulfills the Russellian conditions for being the semantic referent. Again, in asserting the sentence he does, the speaker means that the speaker's referent (the teetotaler) satisfied the predicate (is happy). Thus the rough theoretical apparatus above accounts fully for our intuitions about this case.

What about the other Russellian languages? Even in the strong Russell language, where explicit descriptions are outlawed, the same phenomena can occur. In fact, they occur in English in "arch" uses of existential quantification: "Exactly *one person* (or: *some* person or other) is drinking champagne in that corner, and I hear he is romantically linked with Jane Smith." The circumlocution, in English, expresses the delicacy of the topic, but the speaker's reference (in quite an ordinary sense) may well be clear, even if he in fact is drinking sparkling water. In English such circumlocutions are common only when the speaker wishes to achieve a rather arch and prissy effect, but in the strong Russell language (which of course isn't English), they would be made more common because the definite article is prohibited.

This example leads to an extension of the notion of speaker's reference. When a speaker asserts an existential quantification, $(\exists x)(\phi x \wedge \psi x)$, it may be clear which thing he has in mind as satisfying "ϕx," and he may wish to convey to his hearers that that thing satisfies "ψx." In this case, the thing in question (which may or may not actually satisfy "ϕx") is called the "speaker's referent" when he makes the existential assertion. In English, as I have mentioned, such cases ("arch" uses) are rather rare; but they can be carried off even if the existential quantification is expressed in a highly roundabout and apparently nonreferring fashion. "Not *everyone* in this room is abstaining from champagne, and any such nonabstainer...."[24]

If the notion of speaker's reference applies to the strong Russell language, it can apply to the intermediate Russell language as well, since the speaker's referent of "$\psi((\imath x \phi)(x))$" is then the thing he has in mind as uniquely instantiating "$\phi(x)$" and about which he wishes to convey that it ψs.

Since the phenomenon Donnellan cites *would* arise in all the Russell languages, if they *were* spoken, the fact that they *do* arise in English, as *actually* spoken, can be no argument that English is not a Russell language.

We may contrast the Russell languages with what may be called the D-languages. In the D-languages the apparent ambiguity between referential and attributive definite descriptions is explicitly built into the semantics of the language and affects truth conditions. (The D-languages are meant to suggest "Donnellan," but are not called the "Donnellan languages," since Donnellan, as we have seen, is "ambiguous" as to whether he posits a semantic ambiguity.) The *unambiguous D-language* contains two distinct words, "the" and "ze" (rhymes with "the"). A statement of the form ". . . the F . . ." is true if the predicate represented by the dots is true of the unique object fulfilling F (we need not specify what happens if there is no such thing; if we wish to follow Russell, take it to be false). A statement of the form ". . . ze F . . ." is to be true iff the predicate represented by the dots is true of the unique thing the speaker thinks F is true of. (Once again, we leave free what happens if there is no such thing.) *The ambiguous D-language* is like the unambiguous D-language except that "the," ambiguously, can be interpreted according to the semantics either of "the" *or* of "ze." The general impression conveyed by Donnellan's paper, in spite of his statement at one point to the contrary, is that English is the ambiguous D-language; only on such a hypothesis could we say that the "referential use" (really referential *sense*) diverges from Russell's theory. The truth-conditions of statements containing "ze," and therefore of one sense of "the" in the ambiguous D-language, *are* incompatible with Russell's theory.[25]

We have two hypotheses: one says that English is a Russell language, while the other says that English is the ambiguous D-language. Which hypothesis is preferable? Since, as we have argued, the phenomena Donnellan adduces would arise in a hypothetical society that spoke any of the Russell languages, the existence in English of such phenomena provides no argument against the hypothesis that English is a Russell language. If Donnellan had possessed a clear intuition that "Her husband is kind to her," uttered in reference to the kind lover of a woman married to a cruel husband, expressed the literal truth, then he *would* have adduced a phenomenon that conforms to the ambiguous D-language but is incompatible with any Russell language. But Donnellan makes no such assertion: he cautiously, and correctly, confines himself to the weaker claim that the speaker spoke truly of the man to whom he referred. This weaker claim, we have seen, *would* hold for a speaker of a Russell language.

So Donnellan's examples provide, in themselves, no evidence that English is the ambiguous D-language rather than a Russell language. Granting that this is so, we can ask whether there is any reason to favor the Russell language hypothesis over the D-language hypothesis. I think there are several general methodological considerations that are relevant.

The Russell language theory, or any other unitary account (that is, any account that postulates no semantic ambiguity), accounts for Donnellan's referential-attributive phenomenon by a general pragmatic theory of speech acts, applicable to a very wide range of languages; the D-language hypothesis accounts for these same phenomena by positing a semantic ambiguity. The unitary account appeals to a general apparatus that applies to cases, such as the "Smith-Jones" case, where it is completely implausible that a semantic ambiguity exists. According to the unitary account, far from the referential use constituting a special namelike use of definite descriptions, the referential–attributive distinction is simply a special case of a general distinction, applicable to proper names as well as to definite descriptions, and illustrated in practice by the (leaf-raking) Smith-Jones case. And anyone who compares the Smith-Jones case, where presumably no one is tempted to posit a special semantic ambiguity, with Donnellan's cases of definite descriptions, must surely be impressed by the similarity of the phenomena.[26]

Under these circumstances, surely general methodological principles favor the existing account. The apparatus of speaker's reference and semantic reference, and of simple and complex uses of designators, is needed *anyway*, to explain the Smith-Jones case; it is applicable to all languages.[27] Why posit a semantic ambiguity when it is both insufficient in general and superfluous for the special case it seeks to explain?[28] And why are the phenomena regarding proper names so similar to those for definite descriptions, if the one case involves no semantic ambiguity while the other does?

It is very much the lazy man's approach in philosophy to posit ambiguities when in trouble. If we face a putative counterexample to our favorite philosophical thesis, it is always open to us to protest that some key term is being used in a special sense, different from its use in the thesis. We may be right, but the ease of the move should counsel a policy of caution: Do not posit an ambiguity unless you are really forced to, unless there are really compelling theoretical or intuitive grounds to suppose that an ambiguity really is present.

Let me say a bit more in defense of this. Many philosophers, for example, have advocated a "strong" account of knowledge according to which it is very hard to know anything; stiff requirements must be satisfied. When such philosophers have been confronted with intuitive counter-examples to such strong requirements for knowledge they either have condemned them as popular and loose usages or they have asserted that "know" is being used in a different "weak" sense. The latter move—distinguishing two or more "strong" and "weak" senses of "know"—strikes me as implausible. There *are* different sense of "know," distinguished in German as "kennen" and "wissen," and in French as "connaître" and "savoir"; a person is usually known in the one sense, a fact in the other. It is no surprise that other languages use distinct words for these various senses of "know"; there is no reason for the ambiguity to be preserved in languages unrelated to our own. But what about the uses of "know" that characteristically are followed by that-clauses, knowing that *p*? Are these ambiguous? I would be very surprised to be told that the Eskimos have two separate words, one for (say) Hintikka's "strong" sense of "know," another for his "weak" sense. Perhaps this indicates that we think of knowledge as a unitary concept, unlikely to be "disambiguated" by two separate words in any language.

We thus have two methodological considerations that can be used to test any alleged ambiguity. "Bank" is ambiguous; we would expect the ambiguity to be disambiguated by separate and unrelated words in some other languages. Why should the two separate senses be reproduced in languages unrelated to English? First, then, we can consult our linguistic intuitions, independently of any empirical investigation. Would we be surprised to find languages that used two separate words for the two alleged senses of a given word? If so, then, to that extent our linguistic intuitions are really intuitions of a unitary concept, rather than of a word that expresses two distinct and unrelated senses. Second, we can ask empirically whether languages are in fact found that contain distinct words expressing the allegedly distinct senses. If no such language is found, once again this is evidence that a unitary account of the word or phrase in question should be sought.

As far as our main question is concerned, the first of these two tests, that of our intuitive expectation, seems to me overwhelmingly to favor a unitary account of descriptions, as opposed to the ambiguity postulated in the ambiguous D-language. If English really is the ambiguous D-language, we should expect to find other languages where the referential and attributive uses are expressed by two separate words, as in the *unambiguous* D-language. I at least would find it quite surprising to learn that say, the Eskimo, used two separate words "the" and "ze," for the attributive and referential uses. To the extent that I have this intuition, to that extent I think of "the" as a unitary concept. I should have liked to be able to report that I have reinforced this guess by an actual empirical examination of other languages—the second test—but as of now I haven't done so.[29]

Several general methodological considerations favor the Russell language (or some other unitary account) against the ambiguous D-language as a model for English. First, the unitary account conforms to considerations of economy in that it does not "multiply senses beyond necessity." Second, the metalinguistic apparatus invoked by the unitary account to explain the referential–attributive distinction is an apparatus that is needed in *any case* for other cases, such as proper names. The separate referential sense of descriptions postulated by the D-language hypothesis, is an idle wheel that does no work: if it were absent, we would be able to express everything we wished to express, in the same way. Further, the resemblance between the case of descriptions and that of proper names (where presumably no one would be tempted to postulate an ambiguity) is so close that any attempt to explain the cases differently is automatically suspect. Finally, we would not expect the alleged ambiguity to be disambiguated in other languages, and this means we probably regard ourselves as possessing a unitary concept.

Aside from methodological considerations, is there any direct evidence that would favor one of our two rival accounts? As I remarked above, if we had a direct intuition that "Her husband is kind to her" could be true even when her actual husband is cruel, then we would have decisive evidence for the D-language model; but Donnellan rightly disclaims any such intuition. On the other hand, I myself feel that such a sentence expresses a falsehood, even when "her husband" is used referentially to refer to a kind man; but the popularity of Donnellan's view has made me uncertain that this intuition should be pressed very far. In the absence of such direct intuitions that would settle the matter conclusively, it would seem that the actual practice of English speakers is compatible with either model, and that only general methodological considerations favor one hypothesis rather than another. Such a situation leaves me uneasy. If there really is no direct evidence to distinguish the two hypotheses, how are they different hypotheses? If two communities, one of whom spoke the ambiguous D-language and the other of whom spoke the (weak) Russell language, would be able to intermingle freely without detecting any linguistic difference, do they really speak two different languages? If so, wherein is the difference?

Two hypothetical communities, one of which was explicitly taught the ambiguous D-language and the other of which was taught the (weak) Russell language (say, in school), would have direct and differing intuitions about the truth-value of "Her husband was kind to her," but it is uncertain whether English speakers have any such intutions. If they have none, is this a respect in which English differs from both the Russell languages and the D-languages, and thus differentiates it from both? Or, on the contrary, is there a pragmatic consideration, deriving no doubt from the fact that the relevant rules of language are not explicitly taught, that will explain why we lack such intuitions (if we do) without showing that neither the D-language nor the Russell language is English?

Some commentators on the dispute between Russell and Frege and Strawson over sentences containing vacuous definite descriptions have held that no direct linguistic phenomena conclusively decide between the two views: we should therefore choose the most economical and theoretically satisfying model. But if this is so, are there really two views, and if there are, shouldn't we perhaps say that neither is correct? A hypothetical community that was explicitly taught Russellian or Frege-Strawsonian truth-conditions for sentences containing vacuous definite descriptions would have no difficulty producing direct intuitions that decide the Russell-Strawson dispute. If the commentators in question are correct, speakers of English have no such intuitions. Surely this fact, too, would be a significant fact about English, for which linguistic theory should give an account. Perhaps pragmatic considerations suffice for such an account; or, perhaps, the alleged lack of any such intuition must be accounted for by a feature built into the semantics of English itself. In the latter case, neither the Russellian nor the Frege-Strawsonian truth-conditions would be appropriate for English. Similar considerations would apply to the issue between Donnellan and Russell.[30]

I am uncertain about these questions. Certainly it would be best if there were directly observable phenomena that differentiated between the two hypotheses. Actually I can think of one rather special and localized phenomenon that may indeed favor the Russellian hypothesis, or some other unitary hypothesis. Consider the following two dialogues:

DIALOGUE I:

A: "Her husband is kind to her."

B: "No, he isn't. The man you're referring to isn't her husband."

DIALOGUE II:

A: "Her husband is kind to her."

B: "He is kind to her, but he isn't her husband."

In the first dialogue the respondent (B) uses "he" to refer to the semantic referent of "her husband" as used by the first speaker (A); in the second dialogue the respondent uses "he" to refer to the speaker's referent. My tendency is to think that both dialogues are proper. The unitary account can explain this fact, by saying that pronominalization can pick up *either* a previous semantic reference or a previous speaker's references.[31,32] In the case of the two contrasting dialogues, these diverge.

If English were the ambiguous D-language, the second dialogue would be easy to explain. "He" refers to the object that is both the semantic referent and the speaker's referent of "her husband." (Recall that the notions of spaker's reference and semantic reference are general notions applicable to all languages, even to the D-languages.[33]) The first dialogue, however, would be much more difficult, perhaps impossible, to explain. When A said "her husband," according to the D-language hypothesis he was using "her husband" in the referential sense. Both the speaker's referent and the semantic referent would be the kind lover; only if B had misunderstood A's use as attributive could he have used "he" to refer to the husband, but such a misunderstanding is excluded by the second part of B's utterance. If the first dialogue is proper, it seems hard to fit it into the D-language model.[34]

4 Conclusion

I said at the beginning that the main concern of this paper was methodological rather than substantive. I do think that the considerations in this paper make it overwhelmingly probable that an ultimate account of the phenomena behind Donnellan's distinction will make use of the pragmatic ambiguity between "simple" and "complex" uses, as I defined them above, rather than postulating an ambiguity of the D-language type. But any ultimate substantive conclusion on the issue requires a more extensive and thorough treatment than has been given here. First, I have not here examined theories that attempt to explain Donnellan's distinction as a *syntactic* ambiguity, either of scope or of restrictive and nonrestrictive clauses in deep structure.[35] Both these views, like the line suggested in the present paper, are compatible with a unitary hypothesis such as the hypothesis that English is a Russell language. Although I am not inclined to accept either of these views, some others have found them plausible and unless they are rebutted, they too indicate that Donnellan's observations cannot be taken as providing a conclusive argument against Russell without further discussion.

Second, and most important, no treatment of definite descriptions can be complete unless it examines the complete range of uses of the definite article and related linguistic phenomena. Such a treatment should attempt, as I have argued above, to make it clear why the same construction with a definite article is used for a wide range of cases. It would be wrong for me not to mention the phenomena most favorable to Donnellan's intuitions. In a demonstrative use such as "that table," it seems plausible, as I have mentioned above,[36] that the term rigidly designates its referent. It also seems plausible that the reference of such a demonstrative construction can be an object to which the descriptive adjectives in the construction do not apply (for example, "that scoundrel" may be used to refer to someone who is not, in fact, a scoundrel) and it is not clear that the distinction between speaker's reference and semantic reference should be invoked to account for this. As I also said above, it seems to me to be likely that "indefinite" definite descriptions[37] such as "the table" present difficulties for a Russellian analysis. It is somewhat tempting to assimilate such descriptions to the corresponding demonstratives (for example, "that table") and to the extent that such a temptation turns out to be plausible, there may be new arguments in such cases for the intuitions of those who have advocated a rigid vs. nonrigid ambiguity in definite descriptions, or for Donnellan's intuitions concerning the referential case, or for both.[38]

Because I have not yet worked out a complete account that satisfies me, and because I think it would be wrong to make any definitive claim on the basis of the restricted class of phenomena considered here, I regard the primary lessons of this paper as methodological. They illustrate some general methodological considerations and apparatus that I think should be applied to the problems discussed here and to other linguistic problems. They show in the present case that the argument Donnellan actually presents in his original paper shows nothing against a Russellian or other unitary account, and they make it highly probable to me that the problems Donnellan handles by semantic ambiguity should instead be treated by a general theory of speech acts. But at this time nothing more definitive can be said. I think that the distinction between semantic reference and speaker's reference will be of importance not only (as in the present paper) as a critical tool to block postulation of unwarranted ambiguities, but also will be of considerable constructive importance for a theory of language. In particular, I find it plausible that a diachronic account of the evolution of language is likely to suggest that what was originally a mere speaker's reference may, if it becomes habitual in a community, evolve into a semantic reference. And this consideration may be *one* of the factors neded to clear up some puzzles in the theory of reference.[39,40]

Acknowledgments

I should like to thank Margaret Gilbert and Howard Wettstein for their assistance in the preparation of this paper.

Notes

1. Versions of this paper—not read from the present manuscript—were given from 1971 onward to colloquia at New York University, M.I.T., the University of California (Los Angeles), and elsewhere. The present version was written on the basis of a transcript of the M.I.T. version prepared by P. A. French, T. E. Uehling, Jr., and H. K. Wettstein. Donnellan himself heard the talk at U.C.L.A., and his "Speaker Reference, Descriptions, and Anaphora," to a large extent appears to be a comment on considerations of the type mentioned here. (He does not, however, specifically refer to the present paper.) I decided *not* to alter the paper I gave in talks to take Donnellan's later views into account: largely I think the earlier version stands on its own, and the issues Donnellan raises in the later paper can be discussed elsewhere. Something should be said here, however, about the pronominalization phenomena. In his paper, Donnellan seems to think that these phenomena are incompatible with the suggestion that speaker's reference is a pragmatic notion. On the contrary, at the end of the present paper (and of the talk Donnellan heard), I emphasize these very phenomena and argue that they support this suggestion. See also note 31 below.

2. [Reprinted in this volume, chapter 8.] See also Keith S. Donnellan, "Putting Humpty Dumpty Together Again," *The Philosophical Review*, 77 (1968): 203–215.

3. In his later paper mentioned above in note 1, Donnellan seems more clearly to advocate a semantic ambiguity; but he hedges a bit even in the later paper.

4. I will also avoid cases of "improper" descriptions, where the uniqueness condition fails. Such descriptions may or may not be important for an ultimate evaluation of Donnellan's position, but none of the arguments in his paper rest on them.

5. "Reference and Definite Descriptions" [this volume, p. 176]. My discussion in this paragraph and the next is based on Donnellan's paper [this volume, pp. 176, 181–185].

6. At the time, it had not yet been revealed that Kissinger was the official in question.

7. In fact, no *n*-fold distinction can do so, for any fixed *n*. Independently of the present writer, L. Karttunen has argued similarly that no dual or *n*-fold distinction can replace scope distinctions. I discussed the matter briefly in "Identity and Necessity," *Identity and Individuation*, ed. M. Munitz (New York: 1972), p. 149, n. 10.

8. See the papers of Stalnaker and Partee in *The Semantics of Natural Language*, eds. D. Davidson and G. Harman (Dordrecht: 1971) for such suggestions and also for some of the views mentioned in the previous section. I should emphasize that most of the stimulating discussion in these papers can be made independent of any of the identifications of Donnellan's distinction with others which are rejected here.

9. See his paper "The Contingent *A Priori* and Rigid Designators" [in which] Donnellan asks whether I think proper names (in natural language) are *always* rigid: obviously, he thinks, proper names *could* be introduced to abbreviate nonrigid definite descriptions. My view is that proper names (except perhaps, for some quirky and derivative uses, that are not used as *names*) *are* always rigid. In particular this applies to "Neptune." It would be logically possible to have single words that abbreviated nonrigid definite descriptions, but these would not be *names*. The point is not merely terminological: I mean that such abbreviated nonrigid definite descriptions would differ in an important semantical feature from (what we call) typical proper names in our actual speech. I merely state my position and do not argue it; nor can I digress to comment on the other points raised in Donnellan's paper.

10. See Kaplan's paper "Dthat." In that paper, however, he also has some tendency to confuse rigidity with Donnellan's referentiality. [In P. Cole (ed.), *Syntax and Semantics*. Vol. 9: *Pragmatics* (New York: 1978), pp. 221–253].

11. Kripke, S. "Naming and Necessity." In D. Davidson and G. Harman (eds.), *Semantics of Natural Language*, 253–355.

12. For this view, see Jerrold J. Katz, "Logic and Language: An Examination of Recent Criticisms of Intensionalism," in *Minnesota Studies in the Philosophy of Science*, vol. VII (Minneapolis: 1975), pp. 36–130. See especially sections 5.1 and 5.2. As far as proper names are concerned, Katz thinks that *other* arguments tell against the description theory even as a theory of meaning.

13. See Donnellan, "Reference and Definite Descriptions" [this volume, p. 190].

14. So I argued in the talks, and rightly, if Donnellan is taken literally. See note 25 below, however, for a more charitable reading, which probably corresponds to Donnellan's intent. We must, however, take descriptions to be *semantically* ambiguous if we are to maintain the reading in question: see the point raised immediately after this one.

15. "Reference and Definite Descriptions" [this volume, p. 186].

16. For Grice, see the following papers, which I follow loosely in a good deal of the discussion at the beginning of this section: "The Causal Theory of Perception," *Proceedings of the Aristotelian Society*, supplementary vol. 35 (1961); "Meaning;" *Philosophical Review* 66 (1957): 337–388; "Utterer's Meaning, Sentence-Meaning and Word-Meaning," *Foundations of Language* 4 (1968): 225–242, "Utterer's Meaning and Intentions," *Philosophial Review* 78 (1969): 147–177; "Logic and Conversation," in *Studies in the Way of Words* (Cambridge, Mass.: Harvard University Press, 1989).

17. In "The Causal Theory of Perception."

18. Suppose the second burglar is well aware of the proximity of the police, but procrastinates in his greed for more loot. Then the first burglar imparts no *information* by saying what he does, but simply urges the second burglar to "split."

19. Although conversational principles are applicable to *all languages*, they may apply differently to *different societies*. In a society where blunt statement was considered rude, where "it looks red" replaced "it is red" just because of such a custom, "it looks red" might carry different conversational implicatures from our own. This might be the case even though the members of the society spoke *English*, just as we do. Conversational principles are matters for the psychology, sociology, and anthropology of linguistic communities; they are applicable to these communities no matter what language they may speak, though the applicable principles may vary somewhat with the communities (and may even, to some extent, be conditioned by the fact that they speak languages with certain structures.) Often, of course, we can state widely applicable, "cross-cultural," general conversational principles. Semantic and syntactic principles, on the other hand, are matters of the conventions of a language, in whatever cultural matrix it may be spoken. *Perhaps* sometimes it is difficult to draw the line, but it exists in general nonetheless.

20. If the views about proper names I have advocated in "Naming and Necessity" are correct (Donnellan, in fact, holds similar views), the conventions regarding names in an idiolect usually involve the fact that the idiolect is no mere idiolect, but part of a common language, in which reference may be passed from link to link.

As the present paper attests, my views on proper names in "Naming and Necessity" have no special connection with the referential–attributive distinction.

21. "Naming and Necessity," p. 343, n. 3.

22. Donnellan shows in his paper that there are "referential" uses, of a somewhat exceptional kind, where the speaker, or even both the speaker and the hearer, are aware that the description used does not apply to the thing they are talking about. For example, they use "the King," knowing him to be a usurper, but fearing the secret police. Analogous cases can be given for proper names: if Smith is a lunatic who thinks he is Napoleon, they may humor him. Largely for the sake of simplicity of exposition, I have excluded such both from the notion of speaker's reference and from Donnellan's "referential" use (and the "D-languages" below). I do not think that the situation would be materially altered if both notions were

revised so as to admit these cases, in a more refined analysis. In particular, it would probably *weaken* the case for a semantic ambiguity if these cases were allowed: for they shade into ironical and "inverted commas" cases. "He is a 'fine friend,'" may be ironical (whether or not inverted commas are used in the transcription). "'The King' is still in power"; "'Napoleon' has gone to bed" are similar, whether or not explicit inverted commas are used. It is fairly clear that "fine friend," "brilliant scholar," etc., do not have ironical and inverted commas *senses*: irony is a certain form of speech act, to be accounted for by pragmatic considerations. The case for a semantic ambiguity in definite descriptions is similarly *weakened* if we include such cases as referential uses.

In ordinary discourse, we say that the speaker was referring to someone under a wide variety of circumstances, including linguistic errors, verbal slips, and deliberate misuses of language. (If Mrs. Malaprop says, "The geography teacher said that equilateral triangles are equiangular," she *refers* to the geometry teacher.) The more such phenomena one includes in the notion of speaker's reference, the further one gets from any connection of the notion with semantical matters.

23. See the discussion of "schmidentity" in "Naming and Necessity."

24. Or, using variables explicitly, "there is a person x such that ..." Notice that in an utterance of "$(\exists x)(\phi x \wedge \psi x)$," as long as it is clear *which* thing allegedly satisfying "ϕx" the speaker has in mind, there can be a speaker's referent, even if both the speaker and the hearer are aware that many things satisfy "ϕx."

25. This description of the D-languages specifies nothing about semantical features more "intensional" than truth conditions. It is plausible to assume that "ze F" is a *rigid* designator of the thing believed to be uniquely F, but this is not explicitly included in the extensional truth conditions. Nor has anything been said about the behavior of "ze F" in belief and indirect discourse contexts. *If* we stipulate that "ze F," even in such contexts, designates the thing the speaker believes uniquely Fs, then indeed "Jones said that ze man she married is kind to her," will not be a proper way of reporting Jones's utterance "Ze man she married is kind to her" (even if Jones and the speaker happen to have the same belief as to who her husband is; the difficulty is more obvious if they do not.) No doubt it is this fact that lies behind Donnellan's view that, in the referential case, it is hard to speak of "the statement," even though his exposition of the matter seems to be defective. Such implications, which are not present in the Russell language, lend only further implausibility to the supposition that English is the ambiguous D-language.

To repeat note 22, actually there are many other ways, other than taking something uniquely to satisfy "F," that might be included under referential uses of "the F." The best short way to specify the semantics of "ze F" would seem to be this: "ze F" refers, in the unambiguous D-language, to what would have been the speaker's referent of "the F" in the weak Russell language (under the same circumstances)! But this formulation makes it very implausible that the ambiguous D-language is anything but a chimerical model for English.

26. There is one significant difference between the case of proper names and that of definite descriptions. If someone uses "Jones" to refer to Smith, he has *mis-*

identified Smith as Jones, taken Smith for someone else. To some extent I *did* think that *Jones* was raking the leaves. (I assume that "Jones" is already in this idiolect as a name of Jones. If I am introduced to an impostor and am told, "This man is none other than Albert Einstein," if I am fooled I will have *taken* him, falsely, to be Einstein. Someone else, who has never heard of Einstein before, may merely be mistaken as to the impostor's name.) On the other hand, if I think that someone is "her husband" and so refer to him, I need not at all have confused two people. I merely think that one person possesses a property—that of being married to her— that in fact he lacks. The real husband is irrelevant.

27. In terms of this apparatus, I can sharpen the reply to Katz, note 12 above. If Schmidt had discovered the incompleteness of arithmetic but I had thought it was Gödel who did so, a complex ("referential") use of the description has a semantic reference to Schmidt but a speaker's reference to Gödel. Once I am apprised of the true facts, speaker's reference and semantic reference will coincide thereafter and I will no longer use the description to refer to Gödel. The name "Gödel," on the other hand, has Gödel as its *semantic* referent: the name will always be applied to Gödel in the presence of correct information. Whether a term would be withdrawn in the presence of correct information (without changing the language) is a good intuitive test for divergence of semantic reference and speaker's reference (dis- regarding the cases in note 22).

28. There is another problem for any theory of semantic ambiguity. Donnellan says that if I say "Smith's murderer is insane," solely on the basis of the grisly conditions of Smith's body, my use of "Smith's murderer" is attributive (even if I in fact have a belief as to who the murderer is), but if I say it on the basis of the supposed murderer's behavior at the dock, my use is referential. Surely, however, my reasons can be mixed; perhaps neither consideration would have sufficed by itself, but they suffice jointly. What is my use then? A user of the unambiguous D- language would have to choose between "the" and "ze." It seems very implausible to suppose that the speaker is confused and uncertain about what sense he gives to his description; but what else can we say if we suppose that English is the ambig- uous D-language? (This problem arises even if the man at the dock is guilty, so that in fact there is no conflict. It is more obvious if he is innocent.)

A pragmatic theory of the referential–attributive distinction can handle such cases much more easily. Clearly there can be borderline cases between the simple and the complex use—where, to some extent the speaker wishes to speak of the semantic referent and to some extent he wishes to speak of something he believes to be the semantic referent. He need not sort out his motives carefully, since he thinks these things are one and the same!

Given such mixed motives, the speaker's reference may be partially to one thing and partially to another, even when the semantic reference is unambiguous. This is especially likely in the case of proper names, since divergences between speaker's referent and semantic referent are characteristically *misidentifications* (see note 26). Even if the speaker's referent of "Jones" in "Jones is raking the leaves" is Smith, to some extent I have said *of Jones* that he is raking the leaves. There are gradations, depending on the speaker's interests and intentions, as to what extent the speaker's reference was to Jones and to what extent it was to Smith. The problem is less common in the case of descriptions, where misidentification need not have occurred.

29. Of course these tests must be used with some caution. The mere fact that some language subdivides the extension of an English word into several subclasses, with their own separate words, and has no word for the whole extension, does not show that the English word was ambiguous (think of the story that the Eskimos have different words for different kinds of snow). If many unrelated languages preserve a single word, this in itself is evidence for a unitary concept. On the other hand, a word may have different senses that are obviously related. One sense may be metaphorical for another (though in that case, it may not really be a separate sense, but simply a common metaphor.) "Statistics" can mean both statistical data and the science of evaluating such data. And the like. The more we can explain relations among senses, and the more "natural" and "inevitable" the relationship, the more we will expect the different senses to be preserved in a wide variety of other languages.

The test, therefore, needs further exploration and refinement. It is certainly wrong to postulate an ambiguity without any explanation of some connection between the "senses" that explains why they occur in a wide variety of languages. In the referential–attributive case, I feel that any attempt to explain the connection between the referential and the attributive uses will be so close to the kind of pragmatic account offered here as to render any assumptions of distinct senses implausible and superfluous.

30. That is, the *concept* of truth conditions is somehow inappropriate for the semantics of English. The vague uneasiness expressed in these paragraphs expresses my own rather confused occasional doubts and is ancillary to the main theme. Moore's "paradox of analysis" may be a related problem.

Quine's philosophy of language characteristically is based on a naturalistic doubt about building any "rules" or "conventions" into a language that are not recoverable from actual linguistic practices, even if such rules may be necessary to stipulate the language. In this sense, the uneasiness expressed is Quinean in spirit. I find Quine's emphasis on a naturalistic approach to some extent salutary. But I also feel that our intuitions of semantic rules as speakers should not be ignored cavalierly.

31. Geach, in his book "Reference and Generality," emended ed. (Ithaca: 1970), and elsewhere, has argued vigorously against speaking of pronominalization as picking up a previous reference. I do not wish to argue the extent to which he is right here. I use the terminology given in the text for convenience, but to the extent Geach's views are correct I think the example could presumably be reformulated to fit his scheme. I think the views expressed in this paper are very much in the spirit of Geach's remarks on definite descriptions and speaker's reference in the book just cited. See Geach's discussion, e.g., on p. 8.

32. Donnellan, in "Speaker Reference, Descriptions, and Anaphora," thinks that the fact that pronouns can pick up a previous semantic reference somehow casts doubt on a view that makes speaker's reference a nonsemantical notion. I don't

see why: "he," "she," "that," etc., can, under various circumstances, refer to anything salient in an appropriate way. Being physically distinguished against its background is a property that may make an object salient; having been referred to by a previous speaker is another. In "Naming and Necessity," note 3, I suggested tentatively that Donnellan's "remarks about reference have little to do with semantics or truth conditions." The point would be put more exactly if I had said that Donnellan's distinction is not itself a semantical one, though it is relevant to semantics through pronominalization, as many other nonsemantical properties are.

Pronominalization phenomena are relevant to another point. Often one hears it argued against Russell's existential analysis of *indefinite* descriptions that an indefinite description may be anaphorically referred to by a pronoun that seems to preserve the reference of the indefinite description. I am not sure that these phenomena do conflict with the existential analysis. (I am not completely sure there are some that don't, either.) In any event, many cases can be accounted for (given a Russellian theory) by the facts that: (i) existential statements can carry a speaker's reference; (ii) pronouns can refer to the speaker's referent.

33. The use of "ze" in the unambiguous D-language is such that the semantic reference automatically coincided with the speaker's reference, but nevertheless, the notions are applicable. So are the notions of simple and complex uses of designators. However, speakers of the unambiguous D-language might be less likely ever to use "the" in a complex case: for, one might be inclined to argue, if such are their intentions, why not use "ze"?

34. Various moves might be tried, but none that I can think of seem to me to be plausible. It has been suggested to me that sometimes the respondent in a dialogue deliberately feigns to misunderstand an ambiguous phrase used by the first speaker, and that, given the supposed ambiguity of "her husband" in the ambiguous D-language, the first dialogue can be interpreted as such a case. For example, the following dialogue: "Jones put the money in a bank." "He put the money in one all right, but it wasn't commercial bank; he was so much afraid it would be discovered that he hid it near the river." It seems implausible to me that the first dialogue in the text fits into such a very jocular model. But notice further that the joke consists in a mock *confirmation* of the first speaker's assertion. It would be rather bizarre to respond, "He didn't put the money in the bank, and it wasn't a commercial bank." The first dialogue would have to conform to such a bizarre pattern on the hypothesis in question.

Alternatively, it might be suggested that B uses "he" as a pronoun of laziness for A's "her husband," taken in the supposed referential sense. This move seems to be excluded, since B may well be in no position to use "her husband" referentially. He may merely have heard that she is married to a cruel man.

35. I believe that Karttunen has advocated the view that the referential-attributive distinction arises from a scope ambiguity; I do not know whether this has been published. Since the referential–attributive "ambiguity" arises even in simple sentences such as "Smith's murderer is insane," where there appears to be no room for any scope ambiguity, such a view seems forced to rely on acceptance of Ross's

suggestion that all English assertive utterances begin with an initial "I say that," which is suppressed in "surface structure" but present in"deep structure."

For the view that derives the referential–attributive "ambiguity" from a distinction of restrictive and nonrestrictive clauses in "deep structure," see J. M. Bell, "What is Referential Opacity?" *The Journal of Philosophical Logic*, 2 (1973): 155–180. See also the work of Emmon Bach on which Bell's paper is based, "Nouns and Noun Phrases," in *Universals in Linguistic Theory*, ed. E. Bach and R. T. Harms (New York: 1968), pp. 91–122. For reasons of space I have not treated these views here. But some of my arguments that Donnellan's distinction is pragmatic apply against them also.

36. See p. 232 above; also see note 10 above.

37. The term is Donnellan's. See "Putting Humpty Dumpty Together Again," p. 204, footnote 5.

38. I believe that when Donnellan heard the present paper, he too mentioned considerations of this kind. The cases are mentioned briefly in Donnellan's paper, "Putting Humpty Dumpty together Again," *ibid*. Donnellan's paper "Speaker Reference, Descriptions and Anaphora" mentioned above also makes use of the existence of such incomplete descriptions but I do not find his arguments conclusive.

39. See the Santa Claus and Madagascar cases in "Naming and Necessity."

40. It seems likely that the considerations in this paper will also be relevant to the concept of a supposed "± Specific" distinction for indefinite descriptions, as advocated by many linguists.

Chapter 12

Demonstrative Reference   Howard Wettstein
and Definite Descriptions

The Fregean (or, more generally, descriptional) conception of singular
reference, according to which an object is referred to in virtue of its
unique possession of the properties associated with the referring expression, has, in the recent literature, been criticized by proponents of an
opposing conception inspired by John Stuart Mill's remarks on proper
names. Singular reference, on the Millian view, is thought of not on the
model of *describing* but on the model of *pointing*.[1]

In "Indexical Reference and Propositional Content" I defended an
account of reference by the use of indexical expressions, an account which
sides with Mill against Gottlob Frege with regard to its model of singular
reference. In this paper I shall extend the analysis to definite descriptions. I shall, in effect, be defending some theses of P. F. Strawson
and Keith Donnellan as against Bertrand Russell's theory of descriptions.
Indeed, my argument purports to establish a distinction between referential and attributive uses of definite descriptions, a distinction made
famous by Donnellan.[2] The version of this distinction I wish to defend,
and my argument in defense of it, differ, however, in crucial respects from
Donnellan's. My account preserves the intuitive appeal of Donnellan's
distinction, while it is, as I shall show, immune to a recent powerful
objection.

An Amended Referential–Attributive Distinction

What is the distinction between referential and attributive uses of definite
descriptions? Consider the referential use: there are contexts in which a

Reprinted from *Philosophical Studies* 40, pp. 241–257, by permission of Kluwer
Academic Publishers and Howard Wettstein. © 1981 Kluwer Academic Publishers.

speaker wishes to draw his audience's attention to an entity, perhaps one visually present to both speaker and audience, in order to go on and, for example, predicate something of it. It is irrelevant to the purposes of the speaker, in many such cases, how the attention of the audience is directed to the referent. Pointing with one's finger or uttering a demonstrative or proper name would do as well as some elaborate description. When a definite description is used in such a context, when it is used "referentially," it is, Donnellan says, "merely one tool for doing a certain job—calling attention to a person or thing—and in general any other device for doing the same job, another description or name, would do as well." By contrast, when a description is used attributively, "the definite description might be said to occur essentially, for the speaker wishes to speak about *whatever or whoever fits that description.*"[3]

To illustrate this distinction, in the case of a single sentence, consider the sentence, "Smith's murderer is insane." Suppose first that [a detective] come[s] upon poor Smith foully murdered. [He] might exclaim, "Smith's murderer is insane." I will assume ... that ... [he] does not know who murdered Smith (though this is not in the end essential to the case).[4] This, I shall say, is an attributive use of the definite description.

[By contrast, consider a situation] in which we expect and intend our audience to realize whom we have in mind when we speak of Smith's murderer and, most importantly, to know that it is this person about whom we are going to say something.

For example, suppose that Jones has been charged with Smith's murder and has been placed on trial. Imagine that there is a discussion of Jones's odd behavior at his trial. We might sum up our impression of his behavior by saying, "Smith's murderer is insane." If someone asks to whom we are referring by using this description, the answer here is "Jones." This, I shall say, is a referential use of the definite description.[5]

In the foregoing preliminary sketch of the distinction, I have, by design, failed to mention a supposed feature of referential use which is focal for both Donnellan and his critics. Donnellan maintains that the difference between the two uses of descriptions can be brought out by considering the consequences of the assumption that the definite description used fits nothing. Let us assume, then, that Smith was not murdered. If one says, "Smith's murderer is insane," using the description attributively (the detective case), then, depending on whether we adopt Russell's approach or Strawson's, we will say either that the statement made was false or that it has no truth-value.[6] If, however, we are using the description referentially (the courtroom case), then where the definite description is simply a means of identifying the person we want to talk about, it is quite possible for a correct identification to be made even though no one fits the description used. We were speaking about Jones even though he is not in fact Smith's murderer and, in the circumstances imagined, it was his behavior we were commenting upon. Jones might, for example, accuse us of saying false things of him in calling him insane, and it would be no defense, I should think, that our description, "the murderer of Smith," failed to fit him.[7]

Donnellan's view is that "using a definite description referentially, a speaker may *say something true* even though the description applies to nothing."[8]

Critics of Donnellan's distinction have often focused their attacks on the supposed feature of referential use just discussed. David Wiggins has argued that the distinction is flawed in that "Donnellan's [account] ... depends on the, for me, incredible idea that if I say 'The man drinking champagne is *F*' and the man I mean, though drinking water, is *F*, then *what I say is true*. (To say that the idea is not credible is not to say that *F* is not true of the man I mean.)"[9] Essentially the same point is made by Michael Lockwood:

> The question here is whether a name or definite description is required actually to apply to an individual in order to serve as a means of making that individual a subject of assertion. Donnellan holds that it is not—that a speaker can be said to have made a statement about an object he has in mind, in uttering a referring expression, even if it fails to qualify as what Kripke calls "the semantic referent"[10] of the term in question. But it seems to me that Donnellan is here quite unnecessarily riding roughshod over the common-sense distinction between what a speaker means and what he actually succeeds in saying ... genuine assertion (as opposed, say, to successful communication) calls, it seems to me, for a convergence between words and intention which, in the sort of case we are considering, is *ex hypothesi* lacking.[11]

My own inclination, at least for present purposes, is to sidestep this controversy, for it is clear that we need not decide this dispute in favor of Donnellan in order to preserve a referential–attributive distinction.[12]

There are two distinguishable issues here. First, can a description (or proper name, for that matter)[13] be used to refer to an item to which it does not apply? If I say, "Smith's murderer is insane," while observing Jones's odd behavior in the courtroom and if Jones is not Smith's murderer, have I succeeded in asserting the true proposition that Jones is insane? Donnellan thinks that I have succeeded in asserting this proposition, Lockwood and Wiggins hold that it is a necessary condition for referring to something that the expression used conventionally applies to the thing in question. A second question is this: is there a distinction to be drawn between referential and attributive uses of descriptions? Let us assume that Wiggins and Lockwood are correct: a description (or name) cannot be used to refer to an item to which it does not conventionally apply. This surely does not *preclude* a referential-attributive distinction, for we can still distinguish between cases in which a description, for example, "Smith's murderer," is used to refer to some particular individual the speaker has in mind (in which case the speaker succeeds in so referring, according to Wiggins and Lockwood, *only if* the item is the murderer of Smith) and cases in which the description may be paraphrased as "whoever murdered Smith." Thus even if Wiggins and Lockwood are correct and Donnellan wrong, nothing follows about the existence of a referential–attributive distinction.

Donnellan does himself a disservice in claiming that the referential–attributive distinction can best be brought out by considering cases in which the description fits nothing. These cases are controversial, but to rule against Donnellan with respect to them is not to rule against the referential–attributive distinction. Donnellan's making such cases central has, I think, diverted attention away from the heart of his thesis. Thus Castañeda writes of the referential–attributive distinction:

> I think, to put it disrespectfully, that it is too much ado about practically nothing. The fact at the bottom of all that fuss has nothing to do with definite descriptions. It is the fact that one can succeed in making a hearer think of something α by means of expressions that do not in reality as the language goes correspond with α.[14]

The Semantic Significance of the Distinction

The view that there are two uses of descriptions is not, I think, likely to meet widespread opposition. It is not implausible to maintain that descriptions are sometimes used to call attention to some particular entity the speaker has in mind and sometimes used to speak of whatever it is that has certain properties.[15] What is controversial is Donnellan's view (which I share) that the propositional content of referential and attributive utterances, as well as their truth conditions (in a sense to be explained below), differ.[16] It is often urged, contrary to Donnellan, that although there are two *uses* of descriptions, there is a single *semantic* account applicable to both uses, a semantic treatment in accordance with Russell's theory of descriptions, for example. According to a proponent of such a view, when one utters, "The F is G," *however* the description is used, the same proposition is asserted: there is one and only one F and it is G. To use Donnellan's example, whether our speaker who is present at Jones's trial says, "Smith's murderer is insane," in reaction to Jones's odd behavior (referential use) or whether he utters those words upon seeing Smith's brutally mutilated body, in which case he has no particular murderer in mind (attributive use), our speaker asserts the same thing—that there is one and only one murderer of Smith and he/she is insane. It is surely not obvious, it might be argued (against Donnellan), that what the speaker asserted (and the truth conditions thereof) should depend on whether he has Jones in mind (as Smith's murderer) or whether he has no idea who murdered Smith. Thus Kripke remarks, "I am tentatively inclined to believe, in opposition to Donnellan, that his remarks about reference have little to do with semantics or truth-conditions though they may be relevant to a theory of speech acts."[17] Kripke adds that in his view Donnellan's remarks require no modification of Russell's theory of descriptions.[18] Along similar lines, H. P. Grice, in "Vacuous Names," explicitly distinguishes "two ... modes of employment" of descriptions, what he calls "the type (1) non-identificatory" (corresponding to attributive) and "the type (2) identificatory" (corresponding to referential). Grice goes on to say that "the truth conditions for a type (2) statement, no less than for a type (1) statement, can be thought of as being given by a Russellian account of descriptions." He continues: "It is important to bear in mind that I am not suggesting that the difference between these ... represents a difference in the meaning or sense which a descriptive phrase may have on different occasions; on the contrary, I am suggesting that descriptive phrases have no relevant systematic duplicity of meaning; their meaning is given by a Russellian account."[19]

I shall maintain, contrary to Kripke and Grice, that the distinction has significance at the level of propositional content and truth conditions. I shall introduce my positive account by means of an argument that Russell's theory of descriptions fails as an account of the use of descriptions in natural language.

An argument quite similar to the one I shall present was briefly noted by Donnellan some time ago.[20] Donnellan, however, never gave a central place to this argument (he merely sketches it in passing in a footnote), nor did he fully appreciate its force.[21] I shall begin by considering the applicability of Russell's theory to cases of referential use. Then I shall consider Russell's theory in connection with cases of attributive use.

The great majority of the definite descriptions we actually utilize in ordinary discourse are what Donnellan has called "indefinite definite descriptions," that is, they are not uniquely denoting. Examples are "the table," "the murderer," "the man seated by the fire," "the next President." Consider an assertive utterance of a sentence containing such an indefinite definite description, for example, "The table is covered with books." The Russellian analysis of such an utterance would appear to be: one and only one thing is a table and it is covered with books. Strawson, in *Mind*,[22] argues that such utterances (some of which are undoubtedly true) present difficulties for Russell, since it is clear that it is not the case that *one and only one thing is a table* and is covered with books. In support of Russell, it might be argued that while Russell's account does require that there be a uniquely denoting description which figures in the speech act, it does not require that the description actually uttered be uniquely denoting. The description, for example, "the table," as uttered in a particular context, may be elliptical for a uniquely denoting description, say, "The (only) table in room 209 of Camden Hall at t_1." In uttering "The table is covered with books," as in uttering any "non-eternal sentence," the speaker, as Frege puts it, makes use of "certain accompanying conditions of utterance ... as a means of expressing the thought."[23] In our example, the speaker relies on the context to indicate how his description is to be made uniquely denoting.

This defense of Russell, however, will not do. When one says, for example, "The table is covered with books," the table the speaker has in mind can be more fully described in any number of ways, by the use of any number of nonsynonymous, uniquely denoting descriptions (for example, "the table in room 209 of Camden Hall at t_1," "the table at which the author of *The Persistence of Objects* is sitting at t_1," etc.). Since these more complete descriptions are not synonymous, it follows that each time we replace the indefinite definite description "the table" with a different one of these "Russellian" descriptions, it would seem that we obtain an expression for a *different proposition*, one that gets a different analysis via the theory of descriptions. For example, "The table in room 209 of Camden Hall at t_1 is covered with books" receives a different Russellian expansion than does "The table at which the author of *The Persistence of Objects* is sitting at t_1 is covered with books." The question now arises, which of these more complete (or Russellian) descriptions (or conjunction of such descriptions) is *the correct one*, the one that actually captures what the speaker intended by his use of the indefinite definite description "the table"? The question is important, for as noted, each of these non-equivalent descriptions determines a different Russellian analysis of the utterance.

With regard to this question, I wish to make two points. First, it is quite clearly wrong to suppose that, in many such cases, the circumstances of utterance put the listener in a position to select some one of these non-equivalent descriptions as the correct one, the one that actually captures what the speaker intended. Thus, even if one of these Russellian descriptions is *correct* (in the sense that only it captures what was intended), Russell's theory fails as an account of *what is communicated.*

Second, and more important, with regard to many such utterances none of these Russellian descriptions is *the correct one*. It is simply a mistake to view indefinite descriptions as elliptical for uniquely denoting descriptions. Let us begin with what appears to be an epistemological question: how are we to know *which* Russellian description is the correct one? Now it might be supposed that we could decide on one of these Russellian descriptions as the correct one by reference to the intentions of the speaker. In many cases, however, the speaker will have no such determinate intention. If the speaker is asked which Russellian description(s) was implicit in his utterance of "the table," he will not ordinarily be able to answer. "Although I meant to refer to that table," our speaker might well reply, "I don't think I meant to refer to it *as* the table in room 209 of Camden Hall at t_1 as opposed to, say, *as* the table at which the author of *The Persistence of Objects* is sitting at t_1. Nor did I intend to refer to it *as* the table in 209 *and* the table at which the author is sitting as opposed to, say, just *as* the table in 209."

At this point our concern is no longer merely the epistemological one: how are we to know which of these Russellian descriptions is the correct one? It now becomes difficult to attach sense to the idea the one of these Russellian descriptions could be correct. Surely it is implausible in the extreme to suppose that in fact one of these descriptions captures what the speaker intended but that we cannot, even with the help of the speaker himself, come to know which description that is.[24]

Russell's theory fails as a *general* account of definite descriptions in natural language, since in so many cases (at least in many cases of referential use) the indefinite definite descriptions we actually utter are not elliptical for the uniquely denoting descriptions that Russell's theory requires. This raises the following question. Consider an assertive utterance of a sentence containing an indefinite definite description, for example,

"The table is covered with books." Since the description actually uttered, "the table," applies to many things and since there is no implicit Russellian description, that is, one that fits only the table in question, how are we to account for the fact that the speech act is not at all indefinite or indeterminate? Put differently, in uttering this sentence the speaker predicates the property (being covered with books) of not just any table but of the table in question. But it is hard to see how this can be so if the phrase "the table" (which, after all, applies to many tables) is not a surrogate for a description which applies only to the table in question.

The same question arises with regard to indexical references, that is, references made by the use of "I," "he," "she," "it," and so forth. Consider an utterance of "It is covered with books" made in regard to some table. How is it that by my utterance of "it," which applies to just about anything, I succeed in asserting a determinate proposition about this particular table? It might be tempting to answer this question by viewing the indexical "it," as uttered in such a context, as a surrogate for some descriptive characterization of the table in question. If the indexical *were* a surrogate for, say, some Russellian description, we would certainly understand how a complete and determinate proposition gets asserted via an utterance of this sentence, which, from a semantic point of view, seems incomplete.

Indexicals, however, like indefinite definite descriptions, are not surrogates for Russellian descriptions. Indeed, the argument utilized above with regard to descriptions like "the table" applies mutatis mutandis to the case of indexicals. Given some utterance of "It is covered with books," there will be any number of replacements for "it" and no good reasons, at least in many cases, to choose one as the correct one.[25]

How, then, are we to account for the fact that in such cases a non-defective speech act is performed, a determinate assertion is made? Let us return to Frege's idea, mentioned above, that in uttering a non-eternal sentence, the speaker relies on the circumstances of utterance to supplement his words. The question is, how are we to characterize the circumstances of utterance? My answer is that the circumstances of utterance do help to provide us with an identification of the referent, but not by providing a more complete descriptive characterization of it. When one says, "The table is covered with books," for example, in the conspicuous presence of a single table, the context fails to reveal some Russellian description as lurking behind the utterance of "the table"; the context does reveal, however, *which* item is in question.

Thus the speaker may use an indefinite definite description, that is, an expression which applies to many things, to make a *determinate reference*, indeed, a "demonstrative reference," to some particular thing. We are now in a position to understand how a fully determinate assertion is made by the utterance of this semantically indeterminate sentence: the proposition is determinate since the speaker makes a *determinate reference* and goes on to predicate a property of the thing to which he has referred.

The account just given departs not only from the Russellian perspective on definite descriptions but also, in several respects, from the Fregean semantical perspective. First, Frege does not allow for determinate reference in the absence of a sense which uniquely determines the reference. We have in effect seen, however, that determinate reference is possible in the absence of such a sense. A speaker may refer, for example, by means of an indefinite definite description, an expression which lacks such a complete sense. And as we have in effect seen, it is simply not true that in such cases the speaker relies on various features of the circumstances of utterance to supplement the sense of his words so as to yield such a complete sense. (Just as the context does not provide a Russellian description, it does not provide the sense of such a description.)

Second, Frege takes the "thought" (or, for our purposes, proposition) expressed by the utterance of a sentence to be a sentential sense, indeed a *complete sentential sense*. Whatever else the force of "complete" is here, it surely precludes having as a subject constituent of a subject-predicate proposition the sense of an indefinite definite description. Only the "complete" sense of a uniquely denoting description can be such a subject constituent. As we have in effect seen, however, there are cases in which there is no such complete sense which can plausibly be taken to play the role of subject constituent and yet something determinate is asserted.

Following David Kaplan,[26] I shall call the (non-Fregean) proposition asserted when a description is used referentially (e.g. in the subject position of a subject-predicate assertion) a "singular proposition."[27] In order to sharply distinguish referential and attributive uses, note the unique role played in such a singular proposition by the item demonstrated. Consider the proposition asserted by a referential utterance of "Smith's murderer is insane," in which Jones, on the witness stand, is demonstrated. Jones, we shall assume, is both guilty and crazy. The proposition in question is true then, since Jones, the item demonstrated, satisfies the predicate. Now consider a counterfactual situation in which (1) Jones is insane but (2) Jones is not Smith's murderer and indeed (3) Smith's murderer is quite sane. With respect to such a counterfactual situation, the proposition we have been considering, namely, the proposition that *that one, Jones, is insane*, is again true. That is, the proposition expressed by the actual-world utterance would have been true had things turned out as described by (1), (2), and (3).

The "demonstrative" analysis just given to cases of referential use is surely not applicable to cases of attributive use. Although we can speak of a "referent" even in attributive cases, that is, the "semantic referent" (that person who in fact murdered Smith), the semantic referent is surely not demonstrated by the speaker's attributive use of the description. What is asserted by an attributive utterance is not anything like "*That one*, Jones, is insane" but is rather "One and only one person murdered Smith and he/she is insane" (or some Strawsonian variant). There is therefore an important sense in which the truth or falsity of this proposition, unlike that of the referential case, does not depend upon Jones and his properties. We can see this by evaluating this proposition in the counterfactual situation described by (1), (2), and (3) above. The proposition we are considering, roughly that one and only one person murdered Smith and is insane—unlike the singular proposition of the referential case—would have been *false* had things turned out as described by (1), (2), and (3). This proposition would have been false because in the counterfactual situation, despite Jones's insanity, one and only one person murdered Smith and that person is quite sane.

It might seem plausible that Russell's theory of descriptions, even if incorrect with regard to referential cases, supplies the correct account in attributive cases.[28] There is, however, a difficulty with Russell's theory even when restricted to cases of attributive use, a difficulty which will further illuminate the role of demonstrative reference in our use of definite descriptions.[29] The difficulty is this: the argument I have advanced that Russell's theory gives an inadequate account of cases of referential use applies mutatis mutandis to cases of attributive use. Consider an attributive utterance of a sentence containing an indefinite definite description: the detective, upon seeing Smith's mutilated body, exclaims, "The murderer is insane!" In many such cases of attributive use, the description uttered is not uniquely denoting, nor is there any uniquely denoting description which is implicit. As in the cases of referential use discussed above, there will be any number of ways to fill out the description so as to yield a Russellian description (e.g. "Harry Smith's murderer," "the murderer of Joan Smith's husband," "the murderer of the junior Senator from

New Jersey in 1975"), and, in many cases, nothing about the circumstances of utterance or the intentions of the speaker which would indicate that any one of these Russellian descriptions is the correct one.[30]

If a speaker (attributively) utters such an indefinite definite description, which, after all, applies to many things, and if there is no implicit Russellian description, how are we to account for the fact that his speech act was not at all indeterminate or incomplete? We have already answered this question for referential uses of descriptions: what accounts for such determinateness in referential cases is that the description which applies to many items is used to make a determinate demonstrative reference to one particular thing.

What of attributive uses of descriptions? It appears that we cannot here account for propositional determinateness in the way just discussed, that is, by appeal to demonstrative reference, for, as noted above, in attributive cases there is no demonstration of the (semantic) referent of the description.[31] Moreover, were we to try to account for propositional determinateness in attributive cases by appeal to determinateness of semantic reference, were we to say that what was asserted was determinate because insanity was predicated of *this* item (i.e. the semantic referent), it would follow that *which* proposition is asserted depends upon *which* item it is that is the murderer (which item it is that is the semantic referent). But what was asserted by an attributive utterance of "The murderer is insane" does not, of course, depend on who the murderer is. One fully understands the proposition without having any idea who murdered Smith. Were we to mistakenly take the murderer to be Brown and later discover it to be Jones, we would not thereby correct a mistaken impression of what was asserted by the utterance. Indeed, if understanding such a proposition required knowledge of which item was the murderer, the speaker himself would, at least in many cases, not understand his own utterance, for in attributive cases the speaker often has no belief about who the murderer is.

We return to our problem, someone's saying, "The murderer is insane," and using the description attributively. We have seen that (1) "the murderer" is not elliptical for some Russellian description and (2) no appeal to the referent of "the murderer" will account for propositional determinacy. Nevertheless, we can account for such determinacy by resorting to the notion of demonstrative reference (and the accompanying idea of the contribution of the context of utterance). For in uttering "The murderer is insane" in the presence of the mutilated body, the speaker relies on the context to reveal *whose* murder is in question. The speaker, that is, makes an *implicit* reference to the victim.

That there is an implicit reference made in cases like the one under discussion may be seen by comparing utterances of

(1) The murderer is insane.

(2) His murderer is insane.

When a speaker utters (2), part of what accounts for the fact that he has asserted a determinate proposition is that he has made an *explicit* reference by using the possessive pronoun "his," thus indicating which victim is in question. But this same indication can be accomplished, albeit implicitly, by simply uttering "The murderer is insane" in the presence of the body.

"Demonstrative" reference plays a role, then, even in some cases of the attributive use of descriptions. In this connection let us compare utterances of

(2) His murderer is insane.

(3) The murderer of the man on the couch is insane.

(4) The murderer of Smith is insane.

Examples (2), (3), and (4) reveal an important feature of the attributive use of descriptions which I will briefly explore. A description used attributively may contain indexical expressions, proper names, and finally other descriptions. Each of these kinds of singular term may be used *referentially* in the course of an attributive utterance of a description which contains them. Thus in uttering (2), the speaker uses the indexical "his" referentially; that is, the semantic account of indexicals sketched above applies here. "His," in this context, does not pick up new descriptive content; it is not a surrogate for the possessive form of some Russellian description. Similarly, in an attributive utterance of (3), the contained description "the man on the couch" is used *referentially*. To see that these expressions *are* being used referentially, we need only to apply our by now familiar argument once again: there is no uniquely correct way (and therefore no correct way) to fill out the description "the man on the couch" so as to make it uniquely denoting (and, similarly, no uniquely correct way to replace "his" in "his murderer" with [the possessive form of] some uniquely denoting description). Hence the description "the man on the couch" is not elliptical for a Russellian description. Despite its being an indefinite definite description, we can appeal to its *referent* to account for the fact that a determinate proposition was asserted.

How General Is the Distinction?

We have seen the need for a semantically significant referential–attributive distinction in the case of utterances containing *indefinite* definite descriptions. Is the distinction more generally applicable, to uniquely denoting descriptions, for example? Specifically, is there a (semantically distinct) referential use of uniquely denoting descriptions? (Clearly there is such an attributive use; indeed, on Russell's theory all utterances containing descriptions receive what is in effect an attributive analysis.) I wish to maintain that there is a referential use of uniquely denoting descriptions. The problem is that the argument I used to establish referential use in the case of indefinite definite descriptions is not applicable to the case of uniquely denoting descriptions. In the case of an indefinite definite description, the notion of demonstrative reference is needed in order to explain how a determinate proposition can be asserted by means of an utterance containing a semantically indeterminate (i.e. not uniquely denoting) description. But in the case of a uniquely denoting description, the description itself is semantically determinate, and so there is no need to appeal to the notion of demonstrative reference to explain how a determinate proposition is asserted.

How, then, can we establish that uniquely denoting descriptions have a referential use? Imagine a speaker making a demonstrative reference via an utterance of "the table" to a particular table in view, indeed the only table in view. Further imagine that he is speaking to someone who is confused and disoriented and who misunderstands him and either fails to have any idea which table he means or takes him to be speaking about a different table than the table in view. The speaker may try to make himself clear by adding further information to his description. Indeed, he may eventually add enough information so that his description is uniquely denoting. Since his sole interest is identifying for the listener the table he means, the speaker may very well not realize that the last description uniquely denotes, nor will he intend it to be taken in any radically different fashion than the earlier descriptions. We have then a continuum of descriptions, from "the table" to more complete but still indefinite definite descriptions and finally to a uniquely denoting description. *Ex hypothesi*, all of the descriptions except the last are, in effect, demonstratives. The last description, however, is, at least from the point of view of the speaker, indistinguishable from the earlier ones (except for the addition of one further bit of information). It surely seems implausible to suppose that the last description receives an entirely different sort of analysis than do the earlier ones, one, say, in accordance with Russell's theory of descriptions. If the indefinite definite descriptions receive a demonstrative analysis, then so does the uniquely denoting description.

It seems plausible, if not absolutely forced by the preceding, to generalize further. Any definite description can, in appropriate circumstances, be used referentially—even a description which the speaker knows to be uniquely denoting. Whether a description is indeed being used referentially or attributively is a matter of the intentions of the speaker. Does he intend to demonstrate an individual, or does he intend to use the description attributively?

We have, then, a general referential–attributive distinction of semantic significance. It is not quite the distinction that Donnellan originally formulated, for I have put to one side Donnellan's controversial view about reference via a conventionally inapplicable expression.[32] My version of this distinction does, however, preserve and elucidate what was, to my mind at least, at the heart of that distinction, namely, the difference between the use of a description to *point* to an individual entity and the use of a description to speak of whatever it is that uniquely has certain properties.[33]

Notes

1. Cf. Ruth Barcan Marcus's comment in "Dispensing with Possibilia," that proper names are "the long finger of ostension" (*Proceedings and Addresses of the American Philosophical Association*, 1975–76, vol. 49 [Newark, Del., 1976], p. 45).

2. See Keith S. Donnellan, "Reference and Definite Descriptions" [chapter 8 of this volume].

3. Ibid., p. 176; italics added.

4. It is not essential that the speaker not know or have a belief about who the murderer is. For even if he believes that Jones is the murderer, his use of the description will still be attributive just in case that belief is irrelevant to the speech act, that is, just in case what he communicates is that the murderer, whoever that is, is insane.

5. Donnellan, "Reference and Definite Descriptions," p. 176.

6. P. F. Strawson, in "On Referring" [chapter 6 of this volume], did not recognize an attributive use of descriptions (which occur in the subject position). A plausible application of Strawson's view to attributive cases, however, would be that in such

cases the speaker presupposes that *something or other* is Smith's murderer (as opposed to presupposing of some particular thing that *it* is Smith's murderer) and that the statement has no truth-value if this presupposition is unfulfilled. It should be noted that Donnellan takes no position on whether to prefer a Russell-type approach or a Strawson-type approach in cases of attributive use.

7. Donnellan, "Reference and Definite Descriptions," p. 177.

8. Ibid., p. 187; italics added.

9. David Wiggins, "Identity, Designation, Essentialism, and Physicalism," *Philosophia* 5 (1975): 1–30.

10. Very roughly, the semantic referent is the item to which the term conventionally applies. See Saul Kripke, "Speaker's Reference and Semantic Reference" [chapter 11 of this volume], for a detailed account of this and related notions and for Kripke's approach to the question of reference via a conventionally inapplicable expression.

11. Michael Lockwood, "On Predicating Proper Names," *The Philosophical Review* 84 (1975): 485 n. 21.

12. This point was brought to my attention by Lockwood in his "On Predicating Proper Names."

13. Donnellan makes the analogous claim for proper names in Keith S. Donnellan, "Proper Names and Identifying Descriptions," in *Semantics of Natural Language*, 2d ed., ed. D. Davidson and G. Harman (Dordrecht, 1972), pp. 356–379.

14. Castañeda, "On the Philosophical Foundations," p. 146 of the Theory of Communication.

15. While the view that there are two such uses is intuitively plausible, it appears to crucially involve the notoriously difficult notion of *having a particular item in mind*. It may be, then, that a complete account of the distinction awaits an analysis of this notion, an analysis which has not yet been successfully provided. On the other hand, if the assimilation of "referential use" to "demonstration" which I attempt in the present paper is correct, the notion of referential use may be no worse off in this regard than is the notion of demonstration. (The assimilation of referential use to demonstration was suggested in David Kaplan, "Dthat," *Syntax and Semantics*, vol. 9, ed. Peter Cole [New York, 1977]. Although the present paper was virtually completed before "Dthat," then unpublished, came into my hands, I am indebted to Kaplan for some of the present formulations.)

16. In this sense the distinction has semantic significance, but as Donnellan notes, this is not to say that descriptions are semantically ambiguous as between referential and attributive *senses*. Rather, a univocal description can be utilized in accordance with two radically different kinds of intentions. The distinction has semantic significance, since a referential utterance of the (univocal) description will make a different contribution to the truth conditions (of the utterance of the sentence as a whole) than will an attributive utterance of the description. (Cf. Donnellan's remark that we might say that sentences containing descriptions are pragmatically ambiguous ["Reference and Definite Descriptions," p. 186].)

17. Saul Kripke, "Naming and Necessity," in *Semantics of Natural Language*, 2d ed., ed. D. Davidson and G. Harman (Dordrecht, 1972), p. 343 n. 3.

18. In "Speaker's Reference and Semantic Reference," Kripke expands on these earlier remarks. He maintains that the arguments Donnellan advances in "Reference and Definite Descriptions" fail to support his claims concerning the referential–attributive distinction. Kripke's attack is, however, directed upon that aspect of Donnellan's view which I do not share, that is, Donnellan's view concerning reference via a conventionally inapplicable expression. Kripke, moreover, states that there are phenomena which may be suggestive of a (semantically significant) referential-attributive distinction. The phenomena he mentions are those which I investigate below, phenomena concerning "indefinite definite descriptions." (This is not, of course, to suggest that Kripke would agree with my findings.)

19. H. P. Grice, "Vacuous Names" [chapter 9 of this volume, p. 199].

20. See Keith S. Donnellan, "Putting Humpty Dumpty Together Again," *The Philosophical Review* 77 (1968): 204 n. 5.

21. Donnellan utilizes this sort of argument in Keith S. Donnellan, "Speaker Reference, Descriptions, and Anaphora," in *Syntax and Semantics*, vol. 9, ed. Peter Cole (New York, 1977), but the use he makes of it is, in my view, problematic. An account of Donnellan's argument there and my criticism of it are beyond the scope of this paper.

22. See Strawson, "On Referring," esp. pp. 147–148.

23. Gottlob Frege, "The Thought: A Logical Inquiry," in *Essays on Frege*, ed. E. D. Klemke (Urbana, 1968), p. 516.

24. My argument here, as well as in "Can What Is Asserted Be a Sentence?" and "Indexical Reference and Propositional Content" [both are in Wettstein, *Has Semantics Rested on a Mistake?* Stanford: Stanford University Press, 1991], has similarities to a line of reasoning used, for entirely different purposes, by Paul Benacerraf in "What Numbers Could Not Be," *The Philosophical Review* 74 (1965): 47–73.

25. See my "Indexical Reference and Propositional Content" for a more detailed discussion of indexical reference.

26. David Kaplan, "How to Russell a Frege-Church," *The Journal of Philosophy* 72 (1975): 716–729, and his "Dthat."

27. I speak here of the referential use of both indefinite definite descriptions and uniquely denoting descriptions. My view is that the demonstrative use of descriptions is not a phenomenon localized to indefinite definite descriptions. I defend this view in the next section of this paper, How General Is the Distinction?

28. See the concluding paragraph of Donnellan, "Reference and Definite Descriptions." As noted above, Donnellan does not commit himself to Russell's theory as an account of attributively used descriptions. He does, however, think it not implausible.

29. Frege's approach, as we saw, met with difficulty in cases of referential use of indefinite definite descriptions. That approach might appear better suited to cases

of attributive use, as might Russell's theory of descriptions. The difficulty about to be introduced militates against Frege's approach as well as against Russell's.

30. In "Putting Humpty Dumpty Together Again," p. 204 n. 5, Donnellan states that when a description is used *attributively*, it is plausible to maintain that we can look to the circumstances of utterance to "supply further qualifications on the description to make it unique. . . . Someone says, 'The next President will be a dove on Viet Nam,' and the context easily supplies the implicit 'of the United States.'" Contrary to Donnellan, such a defense of Russell is seldom, if ever, plausible. Even with regard to the case mentioned by Donnellan, it is not clear that "the context easily supplies the implicit 'of the United States,'" as opposed to, say, "of our country."

31. It might seem that since the description in question does not uniquely denote, there is no semantic referent. Surely the phrase "the murderer," considered in isolation, has no semantic referent. Nevertheless, we can speak here of a semantic referent: it is (roughly) the item that fits this description *as used on this occasion*. To anticipate, since in the context in question the force of "the murderer" is (something like) "the murderer of that one," the semantic referent is that individual (if there is one) who in fact murdered that person. (Cf. Kripke's mention of the "semantic reference *on a given occasion*" of ambiguous expressions, indexicals, etc., in "Speaker's Reference and Semantic Reference," p. 237.)

32. Moreover, Donnellan would not agree to my assimilation of referential use to demonstration, as is shown by some of his examples in "Speaker Reference, Descriptions, and Anaphora" (see esp. pp. 60–61). These examples indicate that the notion of "having a particular item in mind" bears much greater weight in Donnellan's treatment than it does here. (See also note 31 above.)

33. I am indebted to a number of people for comments on earlier versions. Special thanks are owed to Panayot Butchvarov, Peter A. French, R. A. Fumerton, Herbert Heidelberger, Dean Kolitch, Charles Landesman, Jr., Ernest LePore, and Richard Mendelsohn. My debt to the writings of Keith S. Donnnellan should be evident. The support of both the American Council of Learned Societies and the Graduate School of the University of Minnesota is gratefully acknowledged.

Chapter 13

Incomplete Definite Descriptions

Scott Soames

The treatment of definite descriptions in [1] is built around two fundamental themes of situation semantics—the context sensitivity of utterances and the partial nature of the information they encode. In emphasizing these themes, Barwise and Perry aim to replace a semantic paradigm in which a description ⌜the F⌝ is used to talk about a unique F-er *in reality as a whole* with one in which it is used to talk about a unique F-er *in some contextually determined situation*, or part of reality. This shift has important consequences for the analysis of so-called "incomplete definite descriptions," like "the table," "the cook," and "the murderer." Since the descriptive operands in these examples are satisfied by many objects, they do not determine referents for the descriptions when evaluated in the whole of reality. Nevertheless, these descriptions are often used in simple examples of the form (1) to make true statements.

(1) The F is G.

Whereas this is often seen as a serious problem for traditional analyses, it is just the sort of case for which situation semantics was designed. According to Barwise and Perry, what is required by the description in an utterance of an example of this sort is not that there be a unique F-er in the whole world, but only that there be a unique F-er in the relevant contextually determined situation.

This idea is presented in a framework in which the meaning of a sentence is taken to be a relation between contexts and interpretations. Intuitively, a context is a potential situation in which the sentence is uttered

Reprinted from *Notre Dame Journal of Formal Logic* 27, pp. 349–375, by permission of Scott Soames and University of Notre Dame Press. © 1986 University of Notre Dame Press.

by someone, to someone else, using words in some specific way. The interpretation of the sentence in the context is the type of situation that the utterance claims to be instantiated in reality.

In [1], Barwise and Perry use set theoretical models called "abstract situations" to play the role of potential situations. For example, the potential situation in which Perry is tired and Barwise is not (at 4 pm, July 17, 1986, Stanford, California) is represented by the abstract situation (2).

(2) $\left\{ \begin{array}{l} \langle l, \langle\!\langle \text{tiredness, Perry} \rangle, 1 \rangle\!\rangle \\ \langle l, \langle\!\langle \text{tiredness, Barwise} \rangle, 0 \rangle\!\rangle \end{array} \right\}$

    (where l is the spatio-temporal location: Stanford University-at-4pm-July-17-1986)

An abstract situation—i.e., a set of a certain sort—is said to be factual iff it corresponds to some real situation.[1] The meaning of a sentence is then seen as a relation between abstract situations representing potential contexts of utterance and sets of abstract situations that provide its truth-conditional interpretations in those contexts. In standard cases, an utterance of a sentence S in a context C is true iff some member of the interpretation of S in C is factual.

The structure of this account is notably similar to that found in versions of possible worlds semantics that incorporate Kaplan's distinction between character and content (see [5] and [6]). The most striking difference between the two frameworks is between the completeness of possible worlds (which determine truth-values for all object language sentences) and the partiality of abstract situations (which do not). It is this difference that Barwise and Perry attempt to exploit in their theory of descriptions.

In familiar, possible worlds treatments, a description, $\ulcorner$the $F\urcorner$, is associated with a partial function, f, from possible circumstances of evaluation to unique F-ers in those circumstances. The intension of (an attributive understanding of) an example like (1) is then defined to be the set of circumstances C such that for some (possible) object o, $f(C) = o$ and o "is G" in C. In general, $f(C)$ may vary with C, and the sentence may be taken as "saying" that the F (whoever it may be) is G.

If, in addition, a semantically referential interpretation is desired, it can be obtained by requiring f to be defined not on circumstances of evaluation, but rather on the circumstance given in the context (as is done by Kaplan's $\ulcorner dthat[\imath xFx]\urcorner$; see [4]–[6]). On this interpretation, the intension of (1), relative to a context C^*, is the set of circumstances C such that

$f(C^{*\prime}) = o$ and o "is G" in C (where $C^{*\prime}$ is the circumstance given in C^*). The sentence is then seen as "saying" that a particular individual, o, is G.[2]

In a nutshell, the Barwise–Perry theory of descriptions is just like this, except that circumstances are identified with abstract situations rather than possible worlds. ⌜The F⌝ is said to express a partial function, f, from abstract situations to unique F-ers in those situations; and examples like (1) are claimed to be semantically ambiguous, depending on which situations f is required to be defined on. The attributive understanding requires f to be defined on the abstract situations in the interpretation of the sentence (relative to the context). Thus, all these situations will contain unique F-ers, with (potentially) different objects playing this role in different situations. The referential interpretation requires f to be defined on a contextually supplied *resource situation*—typically, one that is given perceptually, or through preceding discourse.[3]

Formally, this means that contexts must be expanded to include resource situations tied to each referential occurrence of a description in a sentence.[4] For example, a context in which it is assumed that Jones murdered Smith may include the resource situation, RS, used to evaluate "the murderer of Smith."

(RS) $\{\langle l, \langle\!\langle\text{murderer-of, Jones, Smith}\rangle, 1\rangle\!\rangle\}$.

If f is the interpretation of the description in the context, then $f(\text{RS}) =$ Jones and the (referential) interpretation of (3) in the context is the set of abstract situations S such that $\langle l, \langle\!\langle\text{insane}, f(\text{RS})\rangle, 1\rangle\!\rangle$ is a member of S.

(3) The murderer of Smith is insane.

The basic structure of this theory is essentially the same as that of its possible worlds counterpart. What is new is its appeal to situations (rather than possible worlds), as models of partial (rather than total) information. The significance of this shift shows up in the analysis of incomplete definite descriptions—descriptions that have (unique) referents when evaluated in parts of reality, but not in the world as a whole.

According to Barwise and Perry, a description like "the murderer" can be used referentially in an utterance of

(4) The murderer is insane

to express the statement that Jones is insane, provided that the context includes a resource situation in which Jones is the only murderer (of anyone). Since situations are partial, the exploitation of such a resource situation carries no presumption that the world as a whole contains (or is assumed by the speaker to contain) only one murderer. Barwise and Perry see in this appeal to partiality a crucial advantage for situation semantics.

Traditional theories are often explained as though the whole world were accessible [to be used as a resource situation] and, indeed, as if this were the only accessible situation. To make this plausible, they choose for their paradigms those rare definite descriptions that are defined for this large situation, such as "the first child born in the 21st century" or "the author of *Waverly*." It is an advantage of our approach that we can naturally explain the fact that most definite descriptions manage to pick out individuals without finding describing conditions that are uniquely satisfied in the whole world. ([1], p. 153)

However, there is an apparent problem with this. Incomplete definite descriptions can be used attributively, as well as referentially. For example, coming across Smith, foully murdered, one might say "The murderer (whoever he may be) is insane." An account of incomplete descriptions must handle this kind of case, as well as the referential one. Thus, we cannot be sure that the partiality of situations is the key to analyzing descriptions until we have examined the attributive case more closely.

1 Attributive Incomplete Descriptions

There are two perspectives that might be taken on the problem posed by attributive interpretations of incomplete descriptions. For the traditional theorist, there is little alternative but to rely on contextual supplementation.[5] If C is a context in which (1) expresses a truth, then the interpretation of $\ulcorner$ The $F \urcorner$ in C must be a content that uniquely determines a referent when evaluated in the world in question. It is as if placing the description in the context transformed the operand from F, which is satisfied by many objects, to F', which is satisfied by only one.

In thinking of how this might work, one must distinguish two different ways in which a context might supplement a description. One way involves the addition of extra *descriptive* content to F. For example, an utterance of (4) in which 'the murderer' is understood attributively might be thought of as expressing one of the propositions in (5).[6]

(5a) The murderer of *the president of United Jersey Bank* is insane.

(5b) The murderer of *the man lying on the rug in front of me* is insane.

(5c) The murderer of *my neighbor's boss* is insane.

The problem with this suggestion is that there is often no way of extracting determinate descriptive content from the context. In the example at hand, the speaker may believe that the victim satisfies each of the italicized descriptions in (5a)–(5c), without his intention in uttering the sentence favoring any one of them (or any combination) over the others. Because of this it seems wrong to identify the information semantically encoded by his utterance of (4) with any proposition of the sort given in (5). Moreover, the speaker's remark may be true even if some of the underlined descriptions he associates with the victim do not in fact apply to him, and—worse—apply to someone else who has not been murdered. Thus, the strategy of relying on the context to complete the description by providing extra *descriptive* content seems to be fundamentally flawed.

There is, however, another way in which a context might supplement a description—namely, by contributing an object to the content of the description in the context. On this approach, the content of "the murderer" in the context of our example will be a "singular individual concept" involving the victim as one of its constituents. Thus, the content of "the murderer" in this context will be the same as that of "the murderer of him," or "the murderer of that one," with the victim as referent of the indexical. This analysis seems to fit the speaker's intentions quite well. The strategy for the traditional theorist must be to extend it to an appropriately broad range of cases in which incomplete definite descriptions receive attributive interpretations.[7]

The problem for the situation semanticist is different. Whereas the traditional theorist must rely on contextual supplementation of (attributive) incomplete descriptions to ensure that the truth-conditions of examples containing them are not too difficult to satisfy, the situation semanticist, who eschews such supplementation, must do something to ensure that the truth-conditions of such examples are not too easy to satisfy. I said earlier that, standardly, in situation semantics a sentence is true relative to a context iff its interpretation in the context contains at least one abstract situation which is factual. If this principle is retained for attributive examples like (1), then the truth-conditions of these examples will be assimilated to those of (6), since if any one of many Fs is G, the interpretation of (1) will always contain a factual situation whose unique F-er is G.

(6) An F is G.

To avoid this, the situation semanticist must find a way of semantically incorporating the uniqueness claim associated with the definite article, without destroying the apparent utility of partial situations in accounting for incomplete descriptions.

Barwise and Perry describe the problem as follows:

Consider the interpretation P of my utterance of "I am the cook."

$$P = \{e \mid d, c \ [\![\text{I AM THE COOK}]\!] \ e\}^8$$

If $e \in P$, then e will have just one person (me) doing the cooking at the relevant location $l = c(\text{COOK})$.[9] But any such e will be part of other e' which have more than one person cooking there. Such e' will not belong to P because there will be no person who is *the* cook. So P is not persistent. This raises a problem for our account of truth in the following way. Suppose my wife and I collaborate on cooking for a party. And suppose at a certain point in the party I say, "I am the cook," referring to l. Is what I have said true or not?

The answer is, "It depends on which situation I am describing." First, suppose someone comes up to me and says, "The food at this party is delicious! Who is the cook?" If I say, "I am the cook," I have clearly not described things accurately. I have claimed to be *the* person who did the cooking for the party. But suppose instead someone comes up to me eating a piece of my famous cheesecake pastry and says, "Who made this?" Then I may truly say that I am the cook.

The first case shows that the account we gave of truth for persistent statements does not work for nonpersistent statements. For in that case there is a factual situation, *part* of the situation referred to by the guest, where I am the unique cook. So there will be a factual (maybe even an actual c.o.e. [situation]) in P, and on our earlier account of truth, my statement would be true, whereas in fact it isn't. But surely nonpersistent statements can be true, for in the second case, what I said was true. A theory that did not allow this would be unfair to me. So we need an account of truth that can be applied to nonpersistent statements. ([1], pp. 159–160)

A persistent statement[10] is one whose interpretation is closed under the part-of relation on abstract situations—i.e., one whose interpretation I is such that for every $s \in I$, if s is a part (subset) of a larger situation s', then $s' \in I$. If the interpretation of such a statement contains a factual situation, then the statement not only holds in a part of reality, but continues to hold in all larger (containing) parts. Thus, for persistent statements there is no significant difference between the Barwise–Perry truth-characterization (T), and the alternative characterization (T′).

(T) S is true relative to C iff some member of the interpretation of S in C is factual.

(T') S is true relative to C iff the actual world (maximal factual situation) is a member of the interpretation of S in C. (If there is no maximal factual situation, one could require that the interpretation contain some factual s^*, together with all factual situations containing s^*.)

Since nonpersistent statements may hold in part of reality, while failing in reality as a whole, (T) and (T') are not equivalent for them. Moreover, (T) must be rejected, since the truth-conditions it provides for examples like (7a)–(7c) are obviously too weak. (These are characterized as nonpersistent in [1].)

(7a) The F is G

(7b) No F is G

(7c) Every F is G.

Although (T') might appear more promising, it makes no use of the partiality that distinguishes situations from possible worlds, and so is repugnant to the situation semanticist. In addition, adopting (T') would leave the situation semanticist in exactly the same position as the traditional theorist regarding incomplete, attributive descriptions. According to Barwise and Perry, this is unacceptable.

Notice also that the problem does not, as one might think, disappear for one who rejects our theory of situations for one big situation, Reality. For then almost none of our ordinary uses of definite descriptions and general NPs are accounted for. For example, if we required that the world were in the interpretation of an utterance, then neither of the true examples above [including the one involving an attributive use of "the cook"] would count as true. ([1], p. 160)

Having rejected (T) as providing truth-conditions that are too weak, and (T') as providing truth-conditions that are too strong, Barwise and Perry adopt a position they describe as descending from a view of J. L. Austin (see [1], pp. 160–161). According to this position, the context of utterance provides not only the basis for an interpretation of the sentence uttered, but also a situation that the speaker is using the sentence to refer to or talk about. The sentence is true relative to the context iff its interpretation in the context contains the actual[11] situation that the speaker is talking about.

Nonpersistent Truth: A nonpersistent sentence S is true relative to a context C iff there is an actual situation r such that the agent of C is using S to refer to r, and r is a member of the interpretation of S in C.

It is instructive to compare this approach to the strategy of contextual supplementation employed by the traditional theorist. The traditional theorist invokes implicit reference to contextually given objects to complete the contents of incomplete descriptions; Barwise and Perry leave the contents of these descriptions unsupplemented, but claim that the utterance as a whole carries implicit reference to a contextually determined situation. There are two contrasts here. One involves the entities doing the supplementing—objects for the traditional theorist vs situations for Barwise and Perry. The other involves what gets supplemented. For the traditional theorist it is the contents of (occurrences of) subsentential constituents. For Barwise and Perry, it is the utterance as a whole, which is associated with a new semantic parameter needed for its evaluation.

Although these differences are fundamental, there is one qualification that should be noted. Barwise and Perry do allow the contents (interpretations) of definite descriptions to be supplemented by implicit, contextually determined reference to spatio-temporal locations. Thus, in the example involving "the cook" quoted above, both utterances of the description involved reference to the particular location at which the cooking for the party was done. Although in some cases such reference might be enough to secure a unique referent for the description, Barwise and Perry were careful to construct their example so that the description remained incomplete even after this supplementation. Their claim that "almost none of our ordinary uses of definite descriptions and general *NP*s" are complete in the sense required by the traditional theorist seems to reflect a conviction that their example is typical, and that supplementation of descriptions by contextually determined locations leaves the central problem posed by incomplete definite descriptions unsolved.

2 Problems

The first, and most obvious, difficulty with the Barwise–Perry account is its failure to incorporate the results of contextual supplementation into a theory of propositional content. If *truth* is to be made dependent on a certain feature of the context, then *what is said* should be made similarly dependent. This is not done in [1].

For example, consider two different attributive utterances of (4), one made by x upon discovering Smith's body, the other made by y upon discovering Brown's body.

(4) The murderer is insane.

Let us suppose, for the sake of argument, that the utterances are made referring to distinct situations s and s'. Then, depending on the nature of s and s', Barwise and Perry can explain how these utterances might differ in truth value. But what about the assertions made, or beliefs expressed, by these utterances? In [1], Barwise and Perry adopt what amounts to a relational theory of the attitudes—one in which the objects of assertion and belief are the semantic interpretations of utterances. But then, since the interpretations of the two utterances are the same, we get the unacceptable result that they differ in truth-value while saying the same thing.

This difficulty is addressed in [2] (see especially pp. 128 and 158–160). There, Barwise and Perry introduce propositions as objects of the attitudes, and take the proposition expressed by a nonpersistent sentence S relative to a context C to consist of the interpretation, I, of S relative to C (i.e., a type, or class, of situations), plus the real (or actual) situation, r, that S is used to refer to in C. The proposition is then taken to claim that r is of type I.[12]

However, this does not solve the problem. For example, consider a case in which Smith has been murdered by the pathological Smyth (and only Smyth), and Brown has been murdered by the pathological Black (and only Black). In such a case, we want to say that x's assertion about Smith and y's assertion about Brown are true, even though x and y have no idea who the murderers are, and are using (4) attributively. Given the semantics of descriptions in [1], Barwise and Perry can get this result only if x (somehow) refers to a real (or actual) situation, s, in which Smyth is insane and (uniquely) murders Smith, and y (somehow) refers to a real (or actual) situation, b, in which Black is insane and (uniquely) murders Brown.[13] The analysis will then maintain that the proposition asserted by x consists of the interpretation of (4) plus s, while the proposition asserted by y consists of the interpretation of (4) plus b.

But this cannot be right. If it were, then Smyth would be a constituent of x's assertion on a par with Smith—since both are equally constituents of s, while being equally absent from the interpretation of (4). But Smyth is not a constituent of x's assertion in the way that Smith is. Intuitively, what x says is that Smith's murderer (whoever he may be) is insane. x does not say that Smyth is a murderer, or that Smyth is insane. This asymmetry is reflected in the fact that, intuitively, *what x said* (the proposition he asserted) will be true in a counterfactual circumstance E, iff in E, Smith is murdered by a single, insane, individual. Whether or not

Smyth is a murderer, or is insane, in E is irrelevant. Thus, the proposition expressed by x cannot be what the Barwise–Perry analysis requires.[14]

This point can also be made by systematically varying the contexts of utterance. For example, suppose x and y assertively utter (4) in contexts identical with the ones just mentioned, save for one crucial difference. In the new contexts Smith and Brown have been murdered by the pathological Smart and Beige, rather than Smyth and Black (though x and y do not know this). According to the Barwise–Perry analysis, the propositions asserted (and believed) in these contexts cannot be the same as those asserted (and believed) in the original contexts. But this is wrong; it is a mark of *attributive* uses of sentences that their propositional contents are not dependent in this way on the vicissitudes of actual reference.[15]

The failure to account for this fact is due to a fundamental feature of the Barwise–Perry analysis. On that analysis, the interpretation of (4) in x's context is (essentially) the same as its interpretation in y's context—namely, the type of situation s such that s contains a unique murderer, who is also insane in s. Since the victims, Smith and Brown, are not constituents of this interpretation, but are (intuitively) elements of the propositions asserted, the contexts must somehow succeed in introducing them. Unlike the traditional theorist, who sees the contexts as introducing the victims into the individual concepts expressed by the descriptions, Barwise and Perry maintain that what the contexts supply are single real (or actual) situations. The problem is to find situations containing the victims that do not also contain material extraneous to the assertions. This is impossible as long as the interpretation of (4) is the type of situation specified in [1], and the real (or actual) situation referred to is required to be of that type in order for the utterance to be true.[16]

This difficulty results (primarily) from taking single, real (or actual) situations (rather than individuals or properties) to be the entities that contextually supplement the contents of sentences containing incomplete attributive definite descriptions. An equally serious difficulty arises from the other main innovation of the Barwise–Perry analysis—namely, the decision to treat contextual supplementation not as augmenting the interpretations of (occurrences of) descriptions (and other subsentential constituents), but rather as associating the utterance as a whole with a new parameter required for its evaluation.[17] The key problem resulting from this decision involves cases in which *unsupplemented* descriptions place demands on situations that conflict with those arising from other constituents in the sentence. When this happens, the interpretation of the sentence (relative to a context) will be a type that cannot be satisfied by any real (or actual) situation. Utterances of this sort will then be characterized as false, no matter what situations are selected as their contextually determined referents.

In point of fact, however, many such utterances are true. Examples of this sort include the following[18]:

(8a) The cook is more experienced than the cook who prepared the main course.

(8b) The cook's father is a cook.

(8c) Everyone is asleep and is being monitored by a research assistant.

Each of these examples can be used attributively to express a truth in an appropriate context. A possible context for (8a) and (8b) might be one in which two cooks prepare the food for a party (at the same time and in the same kitchen)—one cooking the main course, the other the dessert. A guest who has no idea who cooked what might truly utter (8a), while munching some dessert. Another guest, agreeing with him, might truly utter (8b), on the basis of having heard earlier that the dessert chef is the son of a famous cook (working in the same kitchen preparing food for a second party).

Although these examples are true and attributive, they do not fit the Barwise–Perry analysis. According to that analysis, the interpretation of (8a) in the context is the type of situation s such that

(i) there is exactly one individual, o, who is a cook (at the relevant location) in s;

(ii) there is exactly one individual, o', who is a cook who prepared the main course (at the same location) in s; and

(iii) o is more experienced than o' in s.

Given that the locations of the cooks in (i) and (ii) are the same, we see that o must be identical with o'. (I here exploit the fact that a cook who prepares the main course is a cook.) But then, since there is no real (or actual) situation in which an individual is more experienced than himself, there is no real (or actual) situation of the type required by the interpretation of (8a) in the context. Thus, Barwise and Perry will wrongly predict it to be false. Analogous predictions will be made regarding (8b) and (8c), based on the facts that no one is his own father, and no one who is sleeping monitors anyone, in any real (or actual) situation.

The lesson here is that contextual supplementation works at the level of constituents of sentences or utterances, rather than the level of the sentences or utterances themselves. If contexts supplement the contents of these constituents (rather than introducing a new parameter of evaluation for entire utterances), then examples like those in (8a)–(8c) can easily be accommodated. Thus, the interpretation of "the cook" in the context for (8a) will be an individual concept applying to the unique individual who cooked the dessert at the party—a concept also expressed by "the cook of this" in a related context in which the demonstrative is accompanied by an appropriate demonstration. With this restriction of the description, the utterance no longer imposes impossible requirements on circumstances of evaluation, and can easily be true.[19]

The problem for Barwise and Perry is that they make no provision for this kind of contextual supplementation. This is not to say that they never allow contexts to supplement the interpretations of descriptions. As I noted earlier, they do allow supplementation of descriptions by contextually determined spatio-temporal locations. Because of this they have no more (and also no less) trouble with examples like (9) than the traditional theorist does.

(9) The cook (here) is more experienced than the cook there.

Their trouble lies with cases in which the supplementation required is not a matter of location alone. Thus, in constructing my counterexamples, I was careful to rely on contexts in which contextually determined locations were not enough to provide the interpretations needed. In so doing I was following the practice of Barwise and Perry themselves. When motivating their own account, they were careful to construct cases in which supplementation of descriptions by contextually determined spatio-temporal locations did not "complete" the descriptions, or provide them with unique referents. It was precisely in order to handle such cases that Barwise and Perry introduced their own "Austinian" theory of utterance supplementation by real (or actual) situations. What we have seen is that this theory does not handle the range of cases for which it was designed.

Barwise and Perry could, of course, expand their conception of the contextual supplementation of interpretations of incomplete definite descriptions to allow more than spatio-temporal locations to be provided. However, this would undercut their analysis of the very examples used to motivate their theory, as well as undermine the claimed superiority of their account over its traditional rivals. Once the situation semanticist avails himself of the kinds of contextual supplementation required by the traditional theorist, he loses any evident basis for relativizing the truth-value of nonpersistent utterances to real (or actual) situations referred to. Such an utterance may, instead, be characterized as true iff the set of real (or actual) situations in its (contextually supplemented) interpretation is both nonempty and persistent on the set of real (or actual) situations (i.e., contains all real (or actual) situations of which its members are parts).

Although this treatment of descriptions can be stated within situation semantics, it makes no use of the partiality of situations—treating it more as a bother to be circumvented than an asset to be utilized. For this reason it is not likely to appeal to the situation semanticist. Central to his program is the idea that a proper semantics for a variety of constructions requires switching from total truth-supporting circumstances (of the sort provided by possible worlds) to partial circumstances (of the kind given by situations). Initially it seemed that incomplete definite descriptions would be just the sort of expressions that would provide strong support for this idea. It now looks as if attributive descriptions do not support it at all.

This does not mean that there can be no substantive role for situations of any sort in the analysis of attributive definite descriptions. It is possible that a role might be salvaged, if the *individual concepts* expressed by (some) incomplete descriptions are analyzed as containing contextually determined situations, in roughly the manner discussed in note 17. One might try to deal with the problems noted there by taking ⌜the F⌝ as equivalent not to ⌜the F in that situation⌝, but rather to ⌜the F *relevant to* that situation⌝—where the demonstrative refers to a contextually given situation. For example, an attributive interpretation of an utterance of (4), made upon discovering Smith's body, could be seen as containing the information that the murderer relevant to a particular (perceptually given) situation s, containing the victim but not the murderer, is insane. Intuitively correct truth-conditions might then be forthcoming, on the assumption that in different possible circumstances different murderers are responsible for bringing s about. Whether or not such an approach can be made to work, and extended to a broad range of cases including those in note 7, is an open question. It should be noted, however, that the approach need not involve *replacing* possible worlds as circumstances of evaluation in a semantic theory, but rather can be seen as *adding* situations (of some sort) to the entities invoked by an essentially traditional theory.[20]

3 Beyond Situations and Attitudes

In discussing the Barwise–Perry treatment of descriptions, I have used both the general semantic framework given in [1] and the analysis of definite descriptions presented there. In [2], Barwise and Perry change the framework. Although they do not reanalyze definite descriptions, the thrust of their more general changes suggests the possibility of such a reanalysis. It is worth looking briefly at this possibility to determine whether it holds out any reasonable prospect of reviving their "Austinian" theory of utterance supplementation, and enhancing their ability to handle incomplete definite descriptions.

There are three basic changes in theoretical perspective introduced in [2]:

1. Types of situations are no longer identified with abstract situations, or sets of such; but rather are regarded as theoretical primitives to be thought of, roughly, as properties of real situations. The meaning of a sentence is seen as a relation which takes one from a type-of-situation in which it is uttered (a context) to the type-of-situation it describes in the context (its interpretation). This eliminates the need for abstract situations as basic entities of the theory.

2. Propositions are introduced, apparently in two varieties. The proposition expressed by a persistent utterance U is thought of as claiming that the type-of-situation T which is the interpretation of U, is realized—i.e., that some real situation or other is of type T. The proposition expressed by a nonpersistent utterance U includes both the type T and a particular real situation, s, referred to by U; the proposition is taken to claim that s is of type T. As before, utterances containing attributive definite descriptions are thought of as nonpersistent.

3. Higher-order properties are introduced in the interpretations of certain noun phrases, including $\ulcorner$an $F\urcorner$, $\ulcorner$no $F\urcorner$, and $\ulcorner$every $F\urcorner$.

It is this third change that is most important for the issues at hand.

In [1], the interpretation of indefinite descriptions closely paralleled that of definite descriptions. Thus, the interpretation of $\ulcorner$an $F\urcorner$ was taken to be a relation between abstract situations, s, and individuals, o, who "are F" in s. In [15], I argued that this account was inadequate, and suggested that the interpretations of examples like those in (10a)–(10b) involve attributions of second-order properties to first-order properties.

(10a) There are Fs

(10b) An F is G.

In (10a) the property of being instantiated is attributed to the property F; in (10b) the relation of co-instantiation is applied to the properties F and G. In [2] this suggestion is incorporated into the revised version of situation semantics.[21]

Barwise and Perry illustrate the new analysis with the following, complex example.

(11) "Hesperus" referred to a heavenly body$_i$ and "Phosphorus" referred to it$_i$ too.[22]

The interpretation of (11) is the type of situation **s** such that

in **s**: at p: co-instantiated, [**x**], [**y**]; yes

where p is a location that temporally precedes the location of utterance, and [**x**] is the type-of-object **x** such that

in **s**: at p: heavenly body, **x**; yes

and [**y**] is the type-of-object **y** such that

in **s**: at p: refers to, "Hesperus," **y**; yes

in **s**: at p: refers to, "Phosphorus," **y**; yes

Types-of-objects are theoretical constructs that play the role of (complex) properties of objects. For two such types to be co-instantiated is for there to be an object of which both are types. Thus, (11), which is seen as saying that there is a real situation in which [**x**] and [**y**] are co-instantiated, gets assigned the correct truth-conditions.

Barwise and Perry extend this "higher-order" analysis to "no" and "every," which are taken to stand for the disjointness and inclusion relations on types (see [2], pp. 146–147). Thus, (13b) and (14b) take their places alongside (12b) as interpretations of the corresponding (a) sentences— where [**x**] is the type-of-object **x** such that **x** is F in **s** at l ([**x**| in **s**: at l, F, **x**; yes]), and [**y**] is the type-of-object **y** such that **y** is G in **s** at l ([**y**| in **s**: at l, G, **y**; yes]).

(12a) An F is G.

(12b) [**s**| in **s**; at l, co-instantiated, [**x**], [**y**]; yes]

(13a) No F is G.

(13b) [s| in s: at l, disjoint, [x], [y]; yes]

(14a) Every F is G.

(14b) [s| in s: at l, included, [x], [y]; yes]

Moreover, the analysis cannot stop here. As I show in [16] and [17], the problems that force the higher-order analysis of indefinite descriptions apply with even greater force when definite descriptions are involved. Thus, the analysis of these expressions given in [1] must be replaced with a higher-order account. Although Barwise and Perry do not say anything about this in [2], it seems clear that something along the lines of (15a) and (15b) is needed.

(15a) The F is G.

(15b) [s| in s: at l, co-instantiated, [x], [y]; yes
               uniquely instantiated, [x]; yes]

In these examples, [x] and [y] represent the properties of being an F, and being a G, *in* s. For example, the interpretation of (13a) is the type of situation s in which *the property of being an F in* s bears the disjointness relation to *the property of being a G in* s. A real situation, r, is of this type only if it contains these properties as constituents, and they bear the disjointness relation (at the location in question). Of course, if the two properties really are disjoint (at the location), then there can be no individual who is both an F and a G (at the location) in r—i.e., there can be no individual o such that

in r: at l, F, o; yes
        G, o; yes.

However, if r is a real situation of type (13b), there may still be a real situation, r^*, of which r is a part, in which some individual is both an F and a G at the relevant location.

(16) in r^*: at l, disjoint, [x| in r: at l, F, x; yes], [y| in r: at l, G, y; yes]; yes
        in r^*: at l, F, o; yes
        in r^*: at l, G, o; yes

The reason this is possible is that there is no conflict between

(i) the existence of an individual that is both an F and a G in some part of reality; and

(ii) the disjointness of the properties of being F-in-a-certain-smaller-part-of-reality, and of being G-in-that-part-of-reality.

Thus, a real situation may be of the type (13b) even if larger situations containing it are not.[23]

On this analysis, utterances of (13a), (14a), and (15a) remain nonpersistent in a straightforward sense; their interpretations are types which may hold in parts of reality while failing to hold in larger, containing parts. Thus, they pose the same problems for theories of truth and propositional content that they did under the earlier analysis of [1]. In particular, one cannot maintain that an utterance of (15a) is true iff its interpretation is realized by some real situation or other, for to do so would be to fail to capture the uniqueness claim associated with the definite article. To avoid this, Barwise and Perry appeal to the "Austinian" theory of utterance supplementation, exactly as before.

Because of this, exactly the same problems arise as did earlier. For example, under the new analysis, the interpretation of an utterance of

(8b) The cook's father is a cook

must be something along the lines of (17), where [x] and [y] are:

[x| in s: at l, cook, x; yes]
[y| in s: at l, father-of, y, x; yes
              cook, y; yes]

(17) [s| in s: at l, uniquely instantiated, [x]; yes
              co-instantiated, [x], [y]; yes]

As before, this type can be realized by some real situation only if someone is his own father. Thus, Barwise and Perry wrongly predict that it cannot be true.

Next consider an attributive utterance of (4) made by Mary upon discovering Smith's body.

(4) The murderer is insane.

Under the new analysis, the interpretation of Mary's utterance is the type,

(18) [s| in s: at l, uniquely instantiated, [x]; yes
              co-instantiated, [x], [y]; yes]

where [x] and [y] are:

[x| in s: at l, murderer, x; yes]
[y| in s: at l, insane, y; yes]

In order for the utterance to be true, it must refer to some real situation r

of this type. Intuitively, this means that *the property of being a murderer (at l) in r* and *the property of being insane (at l) in r* must bear (in r) the higher-order properties and relations specified in (18). This can be the case only if r also contains a unique individual *o* such that for some individual *o'*, *o* is a murderer of *o'* (at l) in r, and *o* is insane (at l) in r. Let us suppose that Smyth really is the (unique) murderer of Smith (though Mary does not know this), and that Mary's utterance is true. Then the individuals *o* and *o'* in r must be Smyth and Smith, respectively. Since the proposition expressed by Mary's utterance is, on the Barwise–Perry analysis, a complex consisting of the type (18) together with the situation r, this means that Smyth and Smith are equally constituents of Mary's assertion. But this, as we have seen, is wrong.

There is, I believe, no way to avoid these problems short of abandoning the "Austinian" theory of utterance supplementation in favor of the more traditional account. This point can be illustrated by considering a particularly simple technique for dealing with the problem posed by attributive utterances of (4). Up to now, I have assumed that Barwise and Perry intend the first-order properties of objects that are the arguments of higher-order properties in the interpretations (12b)–(15b) to be indexed for particular situations. On this assumption, r will be of type (15b) only if in r, the property of being an *F* (at l) *in r*, and the property of being a *G* (at l) *in r*, bear the appropriate higher-order properties and relations. Suppose we drop this assumption of indexing. Then what is required for r to be of the appropriate type is for the property of being an *F* (at l) to be uniquely instantiated in r, and for the properties of being an *F* (at l), and being a *G* (at l), to be co-instantiated in r. With this amendment, it is possible for a real situation to be of type (15b) without *itself* containing any individual that is *F* or *G*. Thus, in the example involving Mary's utterance of (4), we no longer are forced to include Smyth in the proposition asserted.

However, this is no victory for the Barwise–Perry treatment of incomplete descriptions. For if the unindexed property of being an *F* is uniquely instantiated (in any real situation), then there must be exactly one individual *o* for whom there exists a real situation *r'* such that *o* is *F* in *r'*— i.e., if the property of being *F* really is uniquely instantiated, then there must be just one individual who is *F*, in reality as a whole.[24] Thus, under the amended analysis, utterances of (15a) are persistent, and the original motivation for the "Austinian" theory of utterance supplementation is eliminated. (Analogous points hold for (13a) and (14a).) Moreover, any semantically significant contextual supplementation of "incomplete" *NPs*,

$\ulcorner$the $F\urcorner$, $\ulcorner$no $F\urcorner$, and $\ulcorner$every $F\urcorner$, will have to proceed by augmenting the operand, F, exactly as in the traditional approach.

This result does not depend on abandoning indexing. What the problematic examples show is that the Barwise–Perry strategy of contextually supplementing attributive uses of incomplete definite descriptions (and other NPs) will not work. Unlike the traditional theorist, who appeals to contextually given objects to complete the contents of incomplete descriptions (and other NPs), Barwise and Perry leave the contents (interpretations) of subsentential constituents unsupplemented.[25] In place of such supplementation, they add a contextually determined situation, referred to by the utterance as a whole, to the proposition expressed. It is precisely this that causes the problems. Thus, Barwise and Perry have no choice but to modify their account to allow for contextual supplementation of the traditional sort.

For example, what is needed in the case of (8b) and (4) is for the types

[x| in s: at l, cook, x; yes]
[x| in s: at l, murderer, x; yes]

corresponding to the operands of the descriptions to be replaced by the contextually augmented types[26]:

[x| in s: at l, cook, x, o'; yes]
(where o' is the contextually indicated food)
[x| in s: at l, murderer-of, x, Smith; yes]
(where Smith is the indicated victim)

However, once this kind of contextual augmentation of interpretations is made generally available, the stated rationale for the "Austinian" theory of utterance supplementation evaporates.

That theory was developed to avoid the following dilemma: If utterances of (13a), (14a), and (15a) are potentially nonpersistent, then to characterize them as true iff their interpretations are realized by some real situation or other is to assign them truth-conditions that are too weak. On the other hand, if interpretations of these utterances are not contextually augmented, in the manner of the traditional approach, then to characterize them as true iff their interpretations are realized in reality as a whole is to assign them truth-conditions that are too strong. The "Austinian" theory was designed by Barwise and Perry to chart a middle course. The failure of the theory suggests an analysis in which these utterances are true iff they have contextually augmented interpretations that are both realized and persistent.

What this amounts to is simply the traditional theory, encoded in the (revised) framework of situation semantics. The central idea of the framework—namely, the partiality of the basic semantic objects—plays no role in the account. Thus, attributive descriptions, and other general *NP*s, do not support the idea that a proper semantics requires truth-supporting circumstances that are partial, in the manner of situations.

4   Attributive/Referential

This conclusion about attributive descriptions has implications for the analysis of referential uses as well. Once the interpretations of incomplete definite descriptions are allowed to be contextually augmented there is no longer such an evident need for partial "resource situations" in which to evaluate them. We have already seen that an attributive utterance of the description in (4), made upon discovering Smith's body, should be analyzed not as expressing the concept *unique murderer*, but rather as expressing the concept *unique murder of o* (where *o* is Smith).[27]

(4) The murderer is insane.

A unified treatment of descriptions will also assign this concept to referential uses of the description—for example, to utterances in which the murderer is present at the discovery of the body and the speaker wishes to assert of him that he is insane. If these different uses of (4) represent a genuine semantic ambiguity, then the proposition semantically expressed by the referential interpretation is the proposition that *i* is insane, where *i* is the unique individual who satisfies the contextually augmented description in the circumstance of the context—i.e., the unique individual who murdered Smith.

The point to notice is that there is no need for the circumstance of the context to be partial in order for the description to determine an object. If the individual concept semantically associated with the description in the context were simply that of being a unique murderer, then the referential interpretation would require a partial circumstance. However, the contextual augmentation of the concept eliminates this need, and allows a semantically referential interpretation to be defined (if such an interpretation is desired) using the world as a whole. Thus, semantically referential interpretations do not require partial circumstances of evaluation.[28]

Moreover, it is not obvious that there really are such interpretations. There are, of course, *referential uses* of descriptions of the sort noted by

Donnellan in [3]. However, these uses cannot be identified with *semantic interpretations*. Imagine, for example, a speaker using the description in (19) to identify a certain woman *w* he has in mind.

(19) The woman next to Jones drinking champagne is a famous philosopher.

Donnellan observes that in such a case it may be correct to characterize the speaker as having truly said of *w* that she is a famous philosopher—something that could also have been said by uttering "She is a famous philosopher" with appropriate contextual indication of *w* as the referent of "she." Donnellan goes on to point out that this characterization may be correct even if *w* is, in fact, drinking sparkling water rather than champagne. The reason it may be correct is that the description may successfully identify the person whom the speaker has in mind even when it fails to denote her semantically.

The mechanism that allows this is discussed by Kripke in his commentary on Donnellan's original paper [chapter 11 of this volume, pp. 237–238).

Two people see Smith in the distance and mistake him for Jones. They have a brief colloquy: "What is Jones doing?" "Raking the leaves." "Jones," in the common language of both is a name of Jones: it *never* names Smith. Yet, in some sense, on this occasion, clearly both participants in the dialogue have referred to Smith, and the second participant has said something true about the man he referred to if and only if Smith was raking the leaves (whether or not Jones was). How can we account for this? Suppose a speaker takes it that a certain object *a* fulfills the conditions for being the semantic referent of a designator, "*d*." Then, wishing to say something about *a*, he uses "*d*" to speak about *a*; say he says "$\phi(d)$." Then, he said, of *a*, on that occasion, that it ϕd; in the appropriate Gricean sense (explicated above), he *meant* that *a* ϕd. This is true even if *a* is not really the semantic referent of "*d*." If it is not, then *that a ϕs* is included in what he meant (on that occasion), but not in the meaning of his words (on that occasion).

There are three significant features of this account. First, it shows that the phenomenon of *referential use* is not limited to descriptions, but extends to other expressions, such as proper names, for which no relevant semantic ambiguity exists.[29] Second, it explains referential use in terms of a general process in which semantic information, the speaker's intentions, and background information are combined. Third, it accounts for how a person using the description in (19) might say something true about someone, *w*, even if the description fails to denote *w*. The reason this is possible is not that the description has a special semantics invoked for the occasion, but that there is a contextually recognized presumption that w fits the standard semantics of the description,[30] and that the speaker intends to exploit this presumption.[31]

This pragmatic account poses a dilemma for those who see referential *uses* of definite descriptions as reflexes of semantically referential *interpretations*. To insist that the *speaker's* assertion that w is a famous philosopher reflects the *semantic* content of (19), *even in contexts in which w does not satisfy the description*, is to ignore the distinction between semantic and pragmatic information, and to invite the multiplication of unmotivated semantic ambiguities, not only for descriptions, but also for names and other expressions.[32] However, to posit semantically referential interpretations *only* for cases in which the object fits the description is to complicate the semantics in a way that may be unnecessary. Surely, any pragmatic account capable of explaining the speaker's referential assertion in cases in which the description (or name) does not fit the object talked about will apply equally well to cases in which it does. Thus, if semantically referential interpretations are to be defended, more evidence than has so far been presented will have to be given.

Barwise and Perry do not provide it. In [1], they are more concerned with articulating a framework for stating referential interpretations than with marshalling evidence for them. The switch from abstract to real situations in [2] seems to entail a restriction of referential interpretations of descriptions to cases in which the description really applies to the object talked about—for if the resource situation is real, the constituent of it that satisfies the description must really have the properties required by the description. The question that remains unanswered is why such interpretations are needed, given that referential uses of names and descriptions that do not semantically apply to the intended individual must be treated pragmatically.[33]

5 Conclusion

In light of all this, it is reasonable to conclude that the semantics of definite descriptions do not call for partial circumstances of evaluation. This does not mean, of course, that they cannot be treated in a revised framework of situation semantics. However, it does mean that they fail to provide support for the central tenet of the program—namely, that a proper account of semantic information requires total circumstances of evaluation to be replaced by partial situations.

It is, of course, true that partial circumstances can be used to construct fine-grained semantic contents that are better candidates for objects of propositional attitudes than those provided by standard possible worlds accounts. However, this is also true of the semantic contents provided by other theories—in particular theories that identify the contents of sentences (in contexts), with structured, Russellian propositions (see [12], [13], [15]–[17]). Such propositions are complexes in which the contents of subsentential constituents are combined in a structure closely related to that of the sentences that express them. These propositions are not themselves circumstances of evaluation, but rather determine, without being determined by, sets of truth-supporting circumstances.

In earlier work ([15]–[17]) I argued that this conception of semantic content is superior to those developed using either partial or total truth-supporting circumstances. For example, I argued (using auxiliary assumptions common to the Russellian and situational frameworks) that the semantic contents of the following (a) and (b) examples must be distinguished, despite the fact that, intuitively, they are true in the same circumstances.[34]

(20a) t is F and t is G

(20b) t is F and t is G and something is such that it is F and it is G

(21a) t is an F and t is G

(21b) t is an F and t is G and an F is G

(22a) $t =$ the F and $t =$ the G

(22b) $t =$ the F and $t =$ the G and the $F =$ the G

As Salmon points out in [14], the arguments involving these examples can be extended to show that the (a) and (b) sentences in (23) and (24) must also have different contents.

(23a) tRt

(23b) tR itself (i.e., t self-Rs, or $[\lambda x(xRx)]t$)

(24a) t is F and t is G

(24b) t is F and G (i.e., $[\lambda x(F(x) \ \& \ G(x))]t$)

In each case, syntactic differences in sentences are paralleled by semantic differences in their contents. Accordingly, I see these results as confirming the basic intuition behind the structured propositions approach:

Semantic contents of sentences are not circumstances of evaluation, but rather are "syntactically" structured complexes which themselves undergo evaluation.

However, situation semanticists see things differently. While conceding that these examples must be assigned different contents, Barwise and Perry will take them as indicating that the initial conception of situations must be modified to allow the necessary distinctions. In particular, the principles in (25) will be given up in favor of their counterparts in (26).[35]

(25a) A situation in which o is F is one that supports the truth of the claim that something is F.

(25b) A situation in which o is F and o is G is one that supports the truth of the claim that an F is G.

(25c) A situation in which exactly one object o is F, and, moreover, o is G supports the truth of the claim that the F is G.

(25d) A situation in which o bears R to o is one that supports the truth of the claim that o bears R to itself, i.e., that o self-Rs.

(25e) A situation in which o is F and o is G is one that supports the truth of the claim that o is both F and G.

(26a) In order for a situation to support the truth of the claim that something is F it must be one in which the property of being F has the property of being instantiated; for this it is not sufficient for it to be a situation in which o is F.

(26b) In order for a situation to support the truth of the claim that an F is G it must be one in which the properties of being F, and being G, bear the co-instantiation relation; for this it is not sufficient for it to be a situation in which o is F and o is G.

(26c) In order for a situation to support the truth of the claim that the F is G it must be one in which the properties of being F, and being G, bear the co-instantiation relation, and the property of being F has the property of being uniquely instantiated; for this it is no sufficient for it to be a situation in which exactly one object o is F, and, moreover, o is G.

(26d) In order for a situation to support the truth of the claim that o bears R to itself (i.e., self-Rs) it must be one in which o has the property of self-Ring; for this it is not sufficient for it to be a situation in which o bears R to o.

(26e) In order for a situation to support the truth of the claim that o is F and G it must be one in which o has the compound property of being F-and-G; for this it is not sufficient for it to be a situation in which o is F and o is a G.[36]

These modifications in the notion of a situation raise the question of whether we ought to continue to regard them as a species of truth-supporting circumstance. They might even lead one to wonder whether the modified situational approach and the structured proposition approach are really notational variants of the same underlying view. Although important similarities exist, I do not think they are. It must be remembered that the appeal of partial circumstances of evaluation in situation semantics is not limited to the construction of fine-grained objects of the attitudes. Rather, partiality is supposed to be systematically significant in the analysis of a variety of constructions. Thus, it is of considerable theoretical importance to determine whether it really is. Initially it was thought that definite descriptions provided strong evidence for partiality. I have argued that, in fact, they do not; the analysis of definite descriptions is not facilitated by the kind of partiality that situation semantics provides.

Acknowledgment

I wish to thank the philosophy department, and the Syntax Research Center, of the University of California at Santa Cruz for the use of their facilities during the summer of 1985, when the initial work on this essay was done. I also wish to thank Nathan Salmon for valuable comments on the manuscript.

Notes

1. Intuitively, an abstract situation is factual just in case whenever it represents properties or relations as holding (or not holding) among specific objects at given locations, the properties and relations really do (do not) hold among those objects at those locations. In [1], Barwise and Perry express this by saying that factual situations *classify real situations* (parts of reality). More specifically, a factual abstract situation f classifies a real situation r iff whenever f represents properties or relations as holding (or not holding) among specific objects at given locations, r is a part of reality in which those properties and relations do (do not) hold among those objects at those locations. If, in addition, f specifies everything that holds (as well as everything that does not hold) in r, then Barwise and Perry call it actual, and claim that it (exactly) *corresponds* to r.

According to Barwise and Perry, every factual abstract situation is part of (i.e., is a subset of) some actual abstract situation; and for every finite set of factual abstract situations, there is an actual abstract situation of which each member is a part (subset). Nevertheless, they remain largely noncommittal on the question of which factual situations are actual. As a result, the distinctions between actual and factual, and between (exact) correspondence and classification, are put to little use. Thus, for my purposes it is sufficient to distinguish factual from nonfactual abstract situations. When I speak of a factual situation as corresponding to a real situation, I shall mean that the factual situation is a correct, but not necessarily complete, representation of the real situation.

2. The question of whether referential *uses* of definite description should be seen as reflecting semantically referential *interpretations* is a controversial one discussed in [3], [7], [18], and [11]. Although Barwise and Perry assume that such interpretations are needed, I will remain neutral on this point for the moment. Later, I will indicate why I think that such interpretations are not required.

3. In the semantics, these are, of course, abstract situations. However, [1] does not clearly specify whether or not they have to be factual. Thus, Barwise and Perry do not clearly indicate where they stand on the controversial question of whether the semantic interpretation of a description in a context may be an object that the description does not, in reality, apply to. Later, I will suggest a clarification of their stance based on changes in situation semantics discussed in [2].

4. In situation semantics a context is a certain kind of situation, which may contain extra resource situations as constituents. This contrasts with Kaplan's conception of a context in possible world semantics. In particular, a context for Kaplan contains a single world, which is used to evaluate all semantically referential descriptions in a sentence (constructed with the "*dthat*" operator). However, this difference may or may not be semantically significant. Whether or not it is depends on the treatment of incomplete definite descriptions, and the resolution of the question of whether resource situations can be nonfactual. The picture that I will argue for turns out to minimize the semantically significant differences between the two approaches.

5. I assume here that a speaker who uses "The murderer is insane" attributively may succeed in asserting a truth, and also that the sentence may semantically express that truth in the context of utterance—even though there is more than one murderer in reality as a whole. An alternative view might accept the pragmatic claim about what the speaker asserts, while rejecting the semantic claim about what the sentence expresses in the context (maintaining instead that the sentence semantically requires there to be a unique individual i for whom there is some i' or other such that i murdered i').

One point against this alternative is that although it recognizes that the speaker has said something true, it also seems to allow a straightforward sense in which he has asserted something untrue—namely the proposition that his sentence semantically expresses in the context. Intuitively, however, it does not seem as if, in this case, the speaker has said anything false. This contrasts with *referential* uses in which the description, $\ulcorner$the $F\urcorner$, employed by the speaker does not fit the intended referent. In such cases it may be quite natural to say that the speaker truly asserted of the intended referent that he is G, while mistakenly asserting that the F is G.

In what follows, then, I will assume that there is a range of cases in which attributive uses of $\ulcorner$The F is $G\urcorner$ semantically express truths relative to specific contexts of utterance, even though $\ulcorner$the $F\urcorner$, when taken in isolation from all contextual supplementation, fails to pick out a unique object. This is not to say that the alternative, purely pragmatic treatment does not deserve further investigation. Perhaps there are some cases for which it is correct. However, the semantic hypothesis seems quite natural for a range of cases, and should be pursued.

6. These examples are to be understood as expressing general propositions, with the italicized descriptions taken attributively.

7. See [18] and [11] for discussion. It should be pointed out that the strategy I have prescribed for the traditional theorist works best for examples like "the murderer" and "the cook," where an extra argument place is available to be filled by a contextually specified object. Examples like "the book" and "the table" are more challenging since the nature of the contextual supplementation is not as clear. In many cases, the supplementation may involve spatio-temporal locations; e.g., "the table there then." However, there seem to be cases in which the supplementation is more idiosyncratic—for example, uses of "the car" to express what might also be expressed by "our car." An important and vexing problem for the traditional theorist is that of finding significant semantic uniformity in the process of contextually supplementing the contents of incomplete descriptions.

8. This notation says that the interpretation P of the sentence in the context given by the "discourse situation" d with "speaker's connections" c is the set of abstract situations e "described by" the sentence in the context. Intuitively, a discourse situation is a situation in which a specified person is speaking certain specified words at a specified time and place to a specified audience. Speaker connections are facts indicating the objects, properties, and spatio-temporal locations that the speaker is using various of his words (including pronouns, proper names, and tense indicators) to refer to.

9. The spatio-temporal location at which the cooking is said to take place is specified in the context by one of the "speaker connections"—the one associated with the word "cook." In effect, the speaker simply has a location in mind that he wishes to talk about, and which is included in the interpretation of his utterance. (In the notation, "c" represents the speaker's connection function, which assigns appropriate contextually determined entities to the relevant words in the sentence.)

10. A statement, for Barwise and Perry, is an utterance of a sentence in a context.

11. See note 1 above for the distinction between actual and factual abstract situations. Although Barwise and Perry formulate their "Austinian" theory using the notion of an actual situation, they make no explicit use of the difference between actual and factual for that theory.

12. In [2] Barwise and Perry eliminate abstract situations as basic entities of the theory in favor of real situations and types of situations. Thus, they take the contextually determined situations referred to by utterances to be real situations, rather than the actual situations that exactly correspond to them. However, this theoretical change makes no significant difference to the "Austinian" theory of utterance supplementation. It may, therefore, be put aside for the present. In the next section the changes in basic theoretical stance proposed by Barwise and Perry will be looked at more closely.

13. Barwise and Perry provide no information regarding how reference to appropriate situations is determined. Although there are potential problems arising from this lacuna, none of my criticisms will depend on them.

14. The notion of a (persistent) statement being true in an alternative circumstance is modeled in [1], (pp. 60–61 and 139–141) by the notion of its being true in an alternative structure of situations. Where I is the interpretation of the statement, the statement is true in a structure, E, of situations iff some situation of type I is factual in E.

The introduction of propositions corresponding to nonpersistent statements would seem to involve an obvious extension of this idea. The proposition $\langle s, I \rangle$ expressed by a nonpersistent statement should be true in an alternative structure, E, of situations iff s is of type I and is factual in E. However, this leads to the intuitively incorrect truth conditions discussed above.

As stated, it also leads to the incorrect result that $\langle s, I \rangle$ may be false in a counterfactual circumstance in which Smyth is both insane and the unique murderer of Smith—where I is the interpretation of (4), and s has Smyth murdering Smith but no information about Smyth's sanity. Such a "proposition" might be assigned to an utterance of (4) in a case in which the speaker successfully refers to the actual situation in which Smyth murders Smith, but nevertheless expresses a falsehood due to Smyth's (actual) sanity.

Although various moves might be attempted to deal with one or another aspect of the truth-conditions problem, I see no way of completely solving it as long as the propositions expressed by nonpersistent statements are construed in the manner suggested by Barwise and Perry.

15. The problem can easily be extended to attributive utterances of (4) that are untrue. Suppose, for example, that x utters (4) in a context exactly like the original, save for the fact that, unknown to x, the victim has not been murdered, but rather has died of natural causes. There is no reason in this case to select a situation in which Smyth murdered Smith as the contextually determined referent of the utterance, especially if, as we may assume, Smyth is unknown to x. (In fact, we cannot select such a situation if the referent of the utterance must be real or actual.) However, if we do not select such a situation, then we fail to capture the apparent fact that *what x says* in the new context is the same as *what x says* in the original context.

Moreover, if we select, in the new context, a situation s' in which Smith has not been murdered at all, then it is hard to see how the resulting proposition $\langle s', I \rangle$ could be true in any counterfactual circumstance (structure of situations). Finally, assigning the utterance no referent in the context is unacceptable, since it leads to the incorrect conclusion that x and y say *the same thing* in contexts in which, unknown to them, the respective victims (Smith and Brown) have not been murdered.

16. The problem would, of course, remain even if the contextually specified situation were allowed to be factual, rather than real or actual. However, the insistence on the latter further emphasizes the difficulty, since actual situations are potentially more inclusive (bigger) than merely factual situations (see note 1). As a result, there is not much hope of excluding material extraneous to the assertions.

17. Though related, these two innovations of the Barwise–Perry analysis are distinct. One way of maintaining the first without the second would be to allow contextually determined situations to supplement the contents of incomplete descriptions. On this approach, an incomplete description ⌜the F⌝ can be thought of as containing indexical reference to a situation, in the manner of ⌜the F in that situation⌝. With the situation included as a constituent of the content of the description, the sentence as a whole can be evaluated in a total circumstance of evaluation, or possible world, as in the traditional account. For the most part, the problems illustrated above using utterances of (4) carry over to this approach as well (with the exception of the one noted in the penultimate paragraph of note 14). However, the approach does not fall prey to the refutation discussed below involving the sentences in (8a)–(8c).

The opposite is true of approaches that maintain the second innovation while dropping the first. One way to construct such an approach would be to let the contextually determined "referent" of an utterance be a type, R, of situation (or a set of abstract situations), rather than a single real (or actual) situation. For example, in the case of x's attributive utterance of (4), the "referent," R, might be the type of situation (or set of abstract situations) in which someone or other murdered the victim, Smith. The resulting proposition $\langle R, I \rangle$ could then be characterized as true in a circumstance (structure) iff the set of factual situations of the circumstance (structure) which were both of type R and of type I, was nonempty and persistent on the set of factual situations of the circumstance (i.e., contained all factual situations of the circumstance of which its members were parts).

This modification would, of course, change the account significantly. However, as the examples in (8a)–(8c) will show, it is still fundamentally inadequate.

18. Examples like (8a) have received considerable attention in the literature on "discourse referents." See, for example, [8], pp. 348–350, and [9], pp. 265–266.

19. It should be noticed that the examples in (8a)–(8c) which undermine the Barwise–Perry analysis are of the same sort as those originally used to motivate it. Thus, in discussing the key example used to motivate the "Austinian" approach to utterance supplementation, Barwise and Perry say the following:

First, suppose someone comes up to me and says, "The food at this party is delicious! Who is the cook?" If I say, "I am the cook" I have clearly not described things accurately. I have claimed to be *the* person who did the cooking for the party [when in fact two people collaborated]. But suppose instead someone comes up to me eating a piece of my famous cheesecake pastry and says, "Who made this?" Then I may truly say that I am the cook. ([1], p. 159)

Both here and in the examples in (8) the context can be seen as containing either an implicit or an explicit demonstration. Despite this, Barwise and Perry do not use the demonstration to restrict the interpretation of the description "the cook." Instead, they invoke reference to a contextually determined situation by the utterance as a whole. The examples in (8a)–(8c) show that this approach will not work. Since these examples illustrate the same phenomenon as the original example, the "Austinian" approach must be rejected, even for the cases that motivated it.

20. Although no full-fledged theory of this sort has been developed, suggestions along these lines are made in [8], pp. 348–350, [10], p. 18 note 16, and [11], pp. 42–43.

21. The point in [15] was not just that examples like those in (10a) and (10b) require a higher-order analysis, but that this change motivates an alternative semantic framework in which the semantic contents of sentences are structured, Russellian propositions, rather than types of truth-supporting circumstances. Barwise and Perry adopted the higher-order analysis, without accepting the alternative semantic framework. More on this below.

22. The subscripts indicate that the indefinite description is to be understood as the antecedent of the pronoun. For more on this example see [15], note 6, and [2], pp. 151–158.

23. This account is an interpretation of the very sketchy remarks by Barwise and Perry in [2]. It is supported in particular by their continued inclination to treat examples like those in (13–15) as nonpersistent, and by the remark on p. 144 that they now want to allow the possibility that a situation may be of a given type even though not all situations of which it is a part are of that type. An alternative (less likely) interpretation, which does not have these features, is discussed below.

24. Barwise and Perry assume that for any two real situations, s and s', there is a real situation, s'', of which both are parts. Thus if there were a real situation in which the property of being F had the property of being uniquely instantiated, and also real situations in which different objects were F, then there would be a real situation combining these. But such a situation is impossible, and so cannot be real.

25. Except for reference to contextually determined spatio-temporal locations.

26. Contextually augmented types incorporating the analysis of $\ulcorner$the $F\urcorner$ as $\ulcorner$the F relevant to that situation$\urcorner$ (discussed at the end of the previous section) could also be used here.

27. Or *unique murderer relevant to* s (where s is a perceptually given situation containing o).

28. This example is a particularly clear case in which contextual augmentation eliminates the need for partiality. However, it is meant to illustrate the admittedly programatic hypothesis that this sort of trade-off will hold generally.

29. Although Barwise and Perry posit a referential/attributive ambiguity in the semantics of definite descriptions, they do not do so for proper names. According

to them, each proper name n has the property expressed by ⌜being an n⌝ semantically associated with it. Although this property is not part of the interpretation of the name, it is supposed to constrain its reference. Barwise and Perry indicate that the property is to be understood metalinguistically, as something like having the name n, or being named n ([1], pp. 166–167).

Exactly what it is to have the name n, or to be named n, is not explained. However, they seem to have in mind some substantial, sociolinguistic condition. For one thing, the property of having the name n seems, on their account, not to be indexical—I do not have the name n in one context simply in virtue of the fact you happen to call me n in that context, while failing to have it in other contexts. For another thing, Barwise and Perry regard an utterance of ⌜He is n⌝ as providing substantive metalinguistic information to the hearer, in virtue of the fact that n is semantically associated with the property of having the name n (which constrains its reference). But this would be impossible if the property of having the name n relevant to a particular utterance of n were just the property of being the referent of that utterance. Finally, the examples given by Barwise and Perry involve an individual's having his given name, as well as certain special cases like "Wednesday" and "Christmas." All of this seems to point to a view in which having the name n is a matter of being associated with the name by some established convention of the linguistic community.

One question that arises for this view is how to account for private nicknames and temporary names—"Let's call him 'Bozo,'" or "Get lost Bozo." But whatever is said about this, the analysis does seem to have the right consequences for Kripke's Smith/Jones example. When the speaker sees Smith in the distance and mistakes him for Jones, his use of "Jones" semantically refers to Jones, not Smith. Moreover, although the speaker may succeed in saying something true about Smith, his words say something false about Jones. Thus, whatever may be the case for definite descriptions, Barwise and Perry need something like Kripke's pragmatic mechanism to account for referential uses of proper names.

30. As Donnellan points out, the speaker does not actually have to believe the presumption, so long as he recognizes that the conversational participants are willing to accept it, if only "for the sake of argument."

31. If Kripke's pragmatic account is accurate, then the speaker may have asserted more than one thing—the (false) proposition semantically expressed by his sentence in the context, and the true proposition determined by the pragmatic mechanism.

32. Kripke maintains that even quantified statements in a purely Russellian language can have referential uses [7], pp. 16–18 (this volume, pp. 241–242).

33. One piece of evidence for semantically referential interpretations given in [1], p. 147 involves the following example:

(3) The dog growled at the rabbit that sneezed.

Suppose Jim has been telling us about a situation. He has mentioned only one dog, Clarissa, and two rabbits: Hugh, who sneezed while eating Clarissa's food, and Fang. We would naturally take Jim's utterance of (3) to describe the event e:

in *e*: at *l*: growling at, Clarissa, Hugh; yes

where *l* is the location to which Jim was referring, a location temporally preceding that of the utterance. The definite descriptions contribute Clarissa and Hugh to the event described. Two factors enable them to do this:

1. the properties various parts of the expression designate;
2. the unique possession of those properties by Clarissa and Hugh in the situation built up by Jim's discourse.

In this example, Jim's discourse is taken to provide a resource situation for semantically referential interpretations of the descriptions in (3). Suppose, however, that Jim's story has been systematically false. In particular, suppose that Clarissa is really a wolf and that Hugh did not sneeze (also suppose that no other dog or sneezing rabbit is talked about). Then the discourse will not provide any *real* resource situation in which the descriptions are semantically defined. Thus, (3) will not semantically express the proposition that Clarissa growled at Hugh. However, *the speaker* may have asserted this. Moreover, all of this could occur without the speaker or his audience realizing that the story was false. But then, since pragmatic mechanisms explain the speaker's referential assertion in this case, why is a special semantic interpretation needed when the story happens to turn out true?

In fact, the problem goes much deeper. For many cases of this sort, in which a description is used in a discourse, no singular proposition is either asserted or expressed. For example, suppose I say: "*A student* came to my office before I arrived this morning and removed a book, I noticed something was wrong because when I got there the door was ajar, and the janitor said that he had not been in. What really bothers me is that *the student* must have a key to the building." I might say this having no idea about the identity of the intruder (but just thinking that whoever it is must be a student). In such a case there is no individual about whom I am talking, no assertion that he (or she) came to my office, removed a book, and has a key to the building, and no singular proposition toward which I bear a propositional attitude (the propositional attitude of being bothered that) if my remark turns out to be true.

34. In these examples, "*t*" stands in for a proper name, demonstrative, pronoun, or variable.

35. In [2] Barwise and Perry explicitly give up (25a,b) and adopt (26a, b), on the basis of arguments involving (20) and (21). Since the arguments involving (22–24) are exactly analogous, I am confident that they would give up (25c–e) and adopt (26c–e) as well. (The arguments involving (20–22) utilize the auxiliary assumption that a situation (circumstance) that supports the truth of each conjunct supports the truth of a conjunction, and vice versa.) In fact, Perry has accepted the argument involving definite descriptions in his comment on Soames [16], given at the Pacific Division Meetings of the American Philosophical Association, March 1985. That argument, it turns out, is based on an example slightly more complex than (22).

(i) $t = $ the $x : Fx$ & $t = $ the $x : Gx$ & the $x : Fx = $ the $x : Fx$ & $t = $ the $x : t = x$

(ii) (i) & the $x : Fx = $ the $x : Gx$

(Any two-place relation can be used in these examples in place of identity.)

36. In each of these cases (26a–e), the denial that situations of a certain type *support the truth* of a sentence, does not carry with it the claim that it is (metaphysically) possible for the sentence to be untrue when situations of the relevant type are real (or actual). For it may be that although r does not itself support the truth of S, it is connected by what Barwise and Perry call a "necessary constraint" to a situation r' which does—in which case the existence of r will guarantee that S is true, without, in the technical sense, *supporting the truth* of S.

References

[1] Barwise, J. and J. Perry, *Situations and Attitudes*. MIT Press, Cambridge, Massachusetts, 1983.

[2] Barwise, J. and J. Perry, "Shifting Situations and Shaken Attitudes," *Linguistics and Philosophy*, vol. 8 (1985), 105–161.

[3] Donnellan, K. S., "Reference and Definite Descriptions," *Philosophical Review*, vol. 75 (1966), 281–304 (chapter 8 of this volume).

[4] Kaplan, D., "Dthat," in *Syntax and Semantics*, vol. 9. P. Cole, (ed.). Academic Press, New York, 1978, pp. 221–243.

[5] Kaplan, D., "On the Logic of Demonstratives," in *Contemporary Perspectives in the Philosophy of Language*. P. A. French, T. E. Uehling, Jr., and H. K. Wettstein, (eds.). University of Minnesota Press, Minneapolis, 1979, pp. 401–412.

[6] Kaplan, D. (1989). "Demonstratives," in Joseph Almog, John Perry, and Howard Wettstein (eds.) *Themes from Kaplan*. New York: Oxford University Press, 1989, pp. 481–563.

[7] Kripke, S. A., "Speaker's Reference and Semantic Reference," in *Contemporary Perspectives in the Philosophy of Language*. P. A. French, T. E. Uehling, Jr., and H. K. Wettstein (eds.). University of Minnesota Press, Minneapolis, 1979, pp. 6–27 (chapter 11 of this volume).

[8] Lewis, D. K., "Scorekeeping in a Language Game," *Journal of Philosophical Logic*, vol. 8 (1982), 339–359.

[9] McCawley, J. D., *Everything that Linguists have Always Wanted to Know about Logic*. University of Chicago Press, Chicago, Illinois, 1981.

[10] Salmon, N. U., *Reference and Essence*. Princeton University Press, Princeton, New Jersey, 1981.

[11] Salmon, N. U., "Assertion and Incomplete Definite Descriptions," *Philosophical Studies*, vol. 42 (1982), 37–45.

[12] Salmon, N. U., *Frege's Puzzle*. MIT Press, Cambridge, Massachusetts, 1986.

[13] Salmon, N. "Tense and Singular Propositions," in Joseph Almog, John Perry, and Howard Wettstein (eds.) *Themes from Kaplan*. New York: Oxford University Press, 1989, pp. 331–392.

[14] Salmon, N. "Reflexivity," *Notre Dame Journal of Formal Logic* 27 (1986), 401–429; reprinted in Nathan Salmon and Scott Soames (eds.) *Propositions and Attitudes*. New York: Oxford University Press, 1988, pp. 240–274.

[15] Soames, S., "Lost innocence," *Linguistics and Philosophy*, vol. 8 (1985), 59–72.

[16] Soames, S. "Direct Reference and Propositional Attitudes," in Joseph Almog, John Perry, and Howard Wettstein (eds.) *Themes from Kaplan*. New York: Oxford University Press, 1989, pp. 393–419.

[17] Soames, S. "Direct Reference, Propositional Attitudes, and Semantic Content," in Nathan Salmon and Scott Soames (eds.) *Propositions and Attitudes*. New York: Oxford University Press, 1988, pp. 197–239.

[18] Wettstein, H. K., "Demonstrative Reference and Definite Descriptions," *Philosophical Studies*, vol. 40 (1981), 241–257 (chapter 12 of this volume).

Chapter 14

Context and Communication   Stephen Neale

14.1   Introductory Remarks

As we saw in ... Chapter 2 [of *Descriptions*], *prima facie* there is a case to be made for the view that descriptions may, on occasion, function more like referring expressions than quantifiers. Consequently, if Russell's theory is to serve as a *general* account of the semantics of descriptive phrases, an explanation of what is going on in such cases must be provided. And this means taking into account the powerful effects of *context* on the interpretation of utterances.

This breaks down into two distinct tasks. First, we need to graft onto the framework ... an account of context-sensitive expressions like indexicals and demonstratives, if only for the reason that definite descriptions —indeed quantifiers quite generally—may contain such expressions as *constituents*. Second, we need, at least in broad outline, a general framework within which to discuss the relationship between the genuinely semantical features of an expression ζ and those features of the use of ζ that issue, at least in part, from nonsemantical facts about the context of utterance and from constraints governing rational discourse. In particular, we need a framework within which we can provide a reasonably clear and precise characterization of the intuitive Gricean distinction between the *proposition expressed* by an utterance and the proposition (or propositions) the speaker seeks to communicate by it, what we might call *the proposition(s) meant* by the speaker.

From chapter 3 of Stephen Neale, *Descriptions*. Reprinted by permission of Stephen Neale and the Massachusetts Institute of Technology. © 1990 Massachusetts Institute of Technology.

In 14.2, I shall makes some preliminary remarks about the history and nature of the referential challenge to the Theory of Descriptions. In 14.3, I begin the examination of the effects of context on the interpretation of descriptions with the aid of a standard theory of indexicality. Section 14.4 is primarily an exegetical discussion of various strands of Grice's work on meaning and implicature, which will be put to use in 14.5.... (Grice's own machinery and terminology will be modified slightly to suit the present discussion, but this section can still be skipped by those familiar with Grice's program.) In 14.5, I attempt to spell out the details of the Gricean response to the referential challenge. In 14.6, I turn to the problems apparently raised by so-called incomplete descriptions like "the table."

14.2   The Referential Challenge

In the 1960s, several philosophers published papers in which they pointed to apparently *referential* "uses" or "functions" of definite descriptions. Marcus (1961), for example, noted a namelike use of descriptions. As she puts it, over a period of time a description may come to be used rather like a proper name (as "an identifying tag") its descriptive meaning "lost or ignored." Marcus suggests that "the evening star" and "the Prince of Denmark" are examples of this sort. Similarly, Mitchell (1962) distinguished between two "functions" of descriptions, one of which is to *identify* an individual in much the same way as a name does.[1] And Rundle (1965) argued for a genuinely referential interpretation of descriptions that could be put to use in modal contexts. According to Rundle, the *prima facie* ambiguity in a sentence like

(1)   The first person in space might not have been Gagarin

should be seen as the product of an ambiguity in the definite article: the definite description "the first man in space" is ambiguous between Russellian and referential interpretations.[2]

In 1966, Keith Donnellan published an influential paper in which he distinguished between what he called *attributive* and *referential* uses of descriptions; he then argued that Russell's theory did not provide an accurate account of sentences containing descriptions used referentially. To illustrate his distinction, Donnellan asks us to consider a sentence like

(2)   Smith's murderer is insane

as used in the following two scenarios:

(i) A detective discovers Smith's mutilated body and has no idea who has killed him. Looking at the body, the detective exclaims, "Smith's murderer is insane."

(ii) Jones is on trial for Smith's murder, and you and I are convinced of his guilt. Seeing Jones rant and rave in court, I say to you, "Smith's murderer is insane."

On Donnellan's account, in case (i) the description "Smith's murderer" is being used attributively; in case (ii) it is being used referentially. In the attributive case, Russell's analysis may well provide an accurate account of the proposition expressed. That is, in this situation the detective plausibly expresses the descriptive proposition that whoever it was that uniquely murdered Smith is insane. But in the referential case, Donnellan urges, the description functions like a referring expression not a quantifier phrase, and the proposition expressed is not faithfully captured by Russell's quantificational analysis. According to Donnellan, I will, by my use of "Smith's murderer," be *referring to* Jones, and hence I will be saying something *about him*, viz., that he (Jones, that man in the dock) is insane.[3]

Grice (1969) noted a similar distinction:

(1) A group of men is discussing the situation arising from the death of a business acquaintance, of whose private life they know nothing, except that (as they think) he lived extravagantly, with a household staff that included a butler. One of them says "Well, Jones' butler will be seeking a new position."

(2) Earlier, another group has just attended a party at Jones' house, at which their hats and coats were looked after by a dignified individual in dark clothes with a wing-collar, a portly man with protruding ears, whom they heard Jones addressing as "Old Boy," and who at one point was discussing with an old lady the cultivation of vegetable marrows. One of the group says "Jones' butler got the hats and coats mixed up." (This volume, p. 197)

Grice points to two important features of case (2) that are not shared by case (1). First, only in case (2) has some particular individual been "'described as,' 'referred to as,' or 'called,' Jones' butler by the speaker" (p. 197). Second, in case (2), someone who knew that Jones had no butler and who knew that the man with the protruding ears, etc. was actually Jones' gardener "would also be in a position to claim that the speaker had *mis*described that individual as Jones' butler" (p. 198).[4] As a preliminary convenience, let us take the first of these features to be characteristic of *referential* usage (a more useful and precise characterization will be provided in 14.5).

Unlike Donnellan, Grice did *not* feel that there was a problem for Russell here. On Grice's account, the intuitive distinction between case (1) and case (2) is quite consistent with the view that "descriptive phrases have no relevant systematic duplicity of meaning; their meaning is given by a Russellian account" (1969, p. 199). If one is to understand what is going on in case (2), Grice suggests, one needs to invoke an independently motivated distinction between what a speaker *says* (in a certain technical sense) and what he or she *means* (also in a technical sense)—or, as I shall put it in 14.4 and 14.5, between the *proposition expressed* and the *proposition(s) meant*.[5]

Those influenced by Donnellan have tended to see things rather differently. Despite some early equivocation, in the 1970s a very simple and exact claim emerged:

(A1) If a speaker *S* uses a definite description "the *F*" referentially in an utterance *u* of "the *F* is *G*," then "the *F*" functions as a referring expression and the proposition expressed by *u* is *object-dependent* (rather than descriptive).[6]

As I mentioned in Chapter 2 [of *Descriptions*], I shall take this claim (or pair of claims) to entail the view that there is a semantically distinct referential interpretation of definite descriptions. On this view, descriptions are *semantically ambiguous* between Russellian and "referential" interpretations, i.e., the definite article is lexically ambiguous.[7] One of the main aims of the present chapter is to compare the view that definite descriptions are ambiguous with the Gricean view that referential usage is a nonsemantical phenomenon.

For convenience, let us continue with the policy ... of treating as interchangeable the locutions (a) "the proposition expressed by *S*'s utterance *u* of ϕ," (b) "the proposition *S* expressed by *S*'s utterance *u* of ϕ," and (c) "the proposition *S* expressed by uttering ϕ," where *S* is the speaker, *u* is a particular dated utterance, and ϕ is a sentence of English. Let's now define what we might call *a basic case* of a referential use of a definite description "the *F*" as it occurs in a particular utterance *u* of "the *F* is *G*" made by a sincere speaker *S*. In the basic case four conditions obtain:

(a) There is an object *b* such that *S* knows that *b* is uniquely *F*;

(b) It is *b* that *S* wishes to communicate something about;

(c) "The *F*" occurs in an extensional context;[8]

(d) There are no pronouns anaphoric on this occurrence of "the *F*."

According to the "referentialist," if these four conditions are satisfied, the proposition expressed by u is true if and only if b is G. Thus the proposition expressed by u will be true on the referential interpretation if and only if it is true on the Russellian interpretation. So unless the referentialist can provide an argument that demonstrates beyond any doubt that one must entertain an object-dependent proposition about b in order to grasp the proposition expressed by u, he or she is forced to move away from the basic case in order to provide a convincing case for an ambiguity. (There is still, of course, an onus on the Russellian to explain how a referential use of a description can arise from general pragmatic principles.)

To the best of my knowledge, no one has ever provided the requisite argument for an ambiguity in the basic case. However, there are, in the literature, four quite distinct arguments for a non-Russellian interpretation that involve departing from the basic case in one way or another. The first such argument I shall call the "Argument from Misdescription." This argument involves toying around with conditions (a) and (b) in order to produce cases in which the Russellian and referential analyses yield propositions that differ in truth-value. The referentialist then urges that our ordinary intuitions favor the referential interpretation.

The second argument for a non-Russellian interpretation I shall call the "Argument from Incompleteness." This involves relaxing condition (a) in order that "the F" may be an "incomplete" definite description like "the table," which seems to resist Russell's analysis on account of not being uniquely-denoting. Again, an interpretation of such descriptions as referring expressions is supposed to get things right.

The third type of argument involves dispensing with condition (c) in order to examine sentences in which definite descriptions occur in nonextensional contexts, such as those created by modal and temporal operators and psychological verbs. Here a variety of interconnected considerations about scope, variable-binding, and opacity seem to have convinced some philosophers that the postulation of a referential (or otherwise non-Russellian) interpretation of descriptions will circumvent technical difficulties that arise for a unitary quantificational analysis. For example, it is sometimes claimed that so-called *de re* readings of sentences containing definite descriptions and nonetensional operators either lie beyond (or else stretch the plausibility of) Russell's theory because of semantical or syntactical constraints on quantification into nonextensional contexts.

Arguments that are based on such considerations I shall call versions of the "Argument from Opacity."

The fourth type of argument for an ambiguity involves dispensing with condition (d) in order to allow for pronouns that are anaphoric on "the *F*." It is then argued that certain anaphoric relations cannot be accounted for if the description is analyzed in accordance with Russell's theory. This argument comes in several different forms, some of which interact in interesting ways with versions of some of the other arguments. I shall call the general form of the argument the "Argument from Anaphora."

In this chapter, I shall address only the Arguments from Misdescription and Incompleteness. The Arguments from Opacity and Anaphora bring up questions about necessity, opacity, quantifier scope, syntactical structure, and variable-binding that we will not have the machinery to address [here].[9] Before looking at *any* of the arguments, however, we need to say a little about the role of context in the interpretation of utterances.

14.3   Context and the Propositions Expressed

Russell rarely invokes the intuitive distinction between sentences and *utterances* of sentences. However, we saw [in 2.2 of *Descriptions*] that once the philosophical underpinnings of the Theory of Descriptions are in focus, it is clear that Russell is concerned with the propositions expressed by particular utterances of sentences containing descriptive phrases; he is *not* primarily concerned with the more abstract notion of the linguistic meaning of sentence-*types*.

To facilitate discussion, let's distinguish between what we can call *meaning* and *value*; that is, between the *linguistic meaning of an expression* ζ, and the *semantical value of a particular dated utterance u of* ζ. Expressions have meanings; utterances of expressions have values....[10] [T]he semantical value of an utterance of a sentence ϕ is a *proposition*. The semantical value of an utterance of a subsentential expression α is whatever the utterance of α contributes to the identity of the proposition expressed by the utterance of the sentence ϕ of which α is a constituent. For the purposes of this chapter, it will be convenient to adopt Russell's talk of object-dependent propositions containing their "subjects" as constituents. (The reason is that this way of characterizing object-dependent propositions is utilized by several philosophers who have argued for a semantically distinct referential interpretation of definite descriptions. I will be addressing two of their official arguments later in this chapter, and working with the same conception of a proposition will make it easier to focus on the relevant issues and avoid orthogonal engagements. My use of this notion of a proposition should not be confused with any sort of commitment to its overall philosophical utility.)

On this account, the semantical value of an utterance of a *referring* expression is just the expression's *referent*. The characteristic property of an utterance of an *indexical* expression is that its semantical value depends, in a systematic way, upon the *context of utterance*. Thus the characteristic property of an utterance of an *indexical referring* expression is that its referent depends, in a systematic way, upon the context of utterance.

Consider the first person singular pronoun "I," as it occurs in the sentence "I am cold." If I utter this sentence right now, I will be the referent of my utterance of "I." But if you utter the very same sentence right now, you will be the referent of your utterance of "I." It is clear, then, that distinct utterances of "I" may receive distinct individuals as their respective semantical values. But this does not mean that the *linguistic meaning* of the expression-type "I" changes from occasion to occasion, or person to person. To know the linguistic meaning of the word "I" is to know something constant across utterances, roughly that the referent is the individual using the word. Similarly for "you": the referent is the addressee (or addressees).

The same distinction needs to be made for demonstrative noun phrases such as "this," "that," "that man," etc. Although different utterances of such expressions may have different *semantical values*, we are not forced to conclude that they have variable *linguistic meanings*. This is something that Russell apparently saw:

The word "this" appears to have the character of a proper name, in the sense that it merely designates an object without in any degree describing it ... the word "this" is one word, which has, *in some sense*, a constant meaning. But if we treat it as a mere name, it cannot have in any sense a constant meaning, for a name means merely what it designates, and the designatum of "this" is continually changing.... (Russell 1948, pp. 103–104)

Although Russell was close to distinguishing between meaning and value here, he does not seem to be guided by any general considerations reflecting the distinction between expression-types and particular utterances of expressions. Rather, he is concerned with the fact that demonstratives seem to be a bit like ordinary names (they refer without describing) and a bit like descriptions (they may be associated with different individuals on different occasions of utterance), but are really neither.[11] However, from the perspective I am adopting, the distinction should be seen as a reflex of the distinction between expression-types and particular utterances of expressions.

In simple formal languages like the first-order predicate calculus, there is neither room nor need to distinguish between meaning and value. Not until we introduce context-dependent expressions does the relevant gap open up. Following Strawson (1950), we might say that mastery of the linguistic meaning of an indexical referring expression consists in the mastery of some sort of *rule* or *recipe for referring* that takes into account the situation of utterance. The linguistic meaning of such an expression might be *identified* with this rule. For instance, since the referent of an utterance of "I" is simply whoever is speaking, the rule for "I" might be characterized as: *the referent is the individual speaking.* (To characterize the linguistic meaning of "I" in this way is not, of course, to say that "I" and "the individual speaking" have the same linguistic meaning.) And since the referent of an utterance of "you" is whoever is being addressed by the speaker, the rule for "you" might say something like: *the referent is whoever is being addressed.*

Such proposals have been implemented by taking the linguistic meaning of an indexical expression to be a function from contexts to semantical values.[12] On this account, a context C can be represented as an ordered n-tuple, the elements of which are features of the situation of utterance relevant to determining semantical value. For example, on a simple model, C might be represented as a quadruple $\langle s, a, t, p \rangle$, where $s =$ the speaker, $a =$ the addressee, $t =$ the time of utterance, and $p =$ the place of utterance. Following Lewis (1972), let's call the particular features that make up C "contextual coordinates." Using $[\![\zeta]\!]$ to represent the function that is the linguistic meaning of an expression ζ, we can formulate some elementary rules:

$[\![\text{I}]\!](\langle s, a, t, p \rangle) = s$

$[\![\text{you}]\!](\langle s, a, t, p \rangle) = a$

$[\![\text{now}]\!](\langle s, a, t, p \rangle) = t$

$[\![\text{here}]\!](\langle s, a, t, p \rangle) = p.$

In contrast to these "pure indexicals," Kaplan (1977) has suggested that genuinely demonstrative uses of the demonstrative pronouns "this" and "that," the personal pronouns "he," "she," "him," "his," and "her," and demonstrative descriptions like "this man," and "that woman," require accompanying "demonstrations," and that the rule for a genuine demonstrative specify that *the referent is the object of that demonstration.* To capture this we can construe a context as an ordered quintuple

$$\langle s, a, \langle d_1, \ldots, d_n \rangle, t, p \rangle$$

where $d_1, \ldots, d_n$ are the objects of any demonstrations $\delta_1, \ldots, \delta_n$ in the utterance.[13]

It is important to see that indexical pronouns like "I" and "you," demonstrative expressions like "this," "that," "this vase," and "that man," and demonstrative occurrences of personal pronouns like "he" and "she" are genuine referring expressions and hence subject to (R3), a fact that is sometimes overlooked because of their context-sensitivity. As Kaplan (1977) has emphasized, once we distinguish the situation of utterance from the actual or counterfactual situation at which the proposition expressed is to be evaluated for truth or falsity, the intrinsically rigid nature of demonstratives is plain to see. Suppose I point to someone and say to you

(1) That man is a spy.

The referent of my utterance of the demonstrative "that man" is the person I am demonstrating in the situation of utterance. However, we do not want to say that the definite description "the man I am demonstrating" determines the referent of (this particular utterance of) "that man." The proposition expressed by my (actual) utterance of (1) is true at some worlds in which I fail to point during my lifetime. And descriptions such as "the man I am talking about" or "the man I have in mind" will not do because the proposition expressed by my (actual) utterance of (1) is true at some worlds in which (e.g.) I never utter a word or think about anyone. It is clear, then, that a sentence of the form "that F is G" is semantically very different from a sentence of the form "the F is G." An utterance of the former expresses an object-dependent proposition; an utterance of the latter expresses an object-independent proposition.

Under certain reasonable assumptions to do with compositionality, a corollary of the distinction between the meaning of a referring expression b and the value (i.e., referent) of a particular utterance of b is a distinction between the meaning of a sentence "b is G" and the value of (i.e., the proposition expressed by) an utterance of "b is G." This comes out clearly when we turn to *understanding.* Suppose I have a room in which I keep nothing but a private vase collection. One day, I let a friend into the room and leave him there to browse. After a few minutes he calls out to me

(2) This vase is broken.

There is a clear sense in which I cannot grasp the proposition expressed by his utterance unless I establish the referent of "this vase." (This, of course follows from (R1), on the assumption that the demonstrative phrase "this vase" is a genuine referring expression; see above.) But there is an equally clear sense in which I know the *meaning* of the sentence uttered, simply by virtue of my knowledge of English—that is, by virtue of my knowledge of the meanings of the words of which the sentence is composed, and my ability to project the meanings of phrases on the basis of the meanings of their parts and their syntactical organization. We might say that although I do not know *which* proposition my friend has expressed, I know the *sort of* proposition he has expressed. He has said *of* some particular vase or other—which I have yet to identify—that it is broken. Another way of putting this is to say that although I do not come to entertain an object-dependent proposition concerning any particular vase, I come to entertain an object-independent proposition to the effect that one of my vases is broken.

(Consider the following nonlinguistic analogy. My friend says nothing while he is in the room, but after a few minutes I hear a crash. I deduce that he has broken one of my vases. It is in virtue of the fact that some particular vase broke that I heard what I heard, and that I came to believe what I came to believe. However, I only came to have an object-*in*dependent belief to the effect that one of my vases was broken, not an object-dependent belief concerning any particular vase.)

Precisely the same considerations apply in the case of pure indexicals. Suppose I return home at 7:30 P.M. and find the following message on my answering machine: "Guess what? I just flew in from London and I want to take you out for dinner tonight. I'll pick you up at eight." The voice is female and sounds familiar, but owing to the poor quality of the machine I cannot recognize it. Since I fail to establish the referent of "I," I fail to establish the proposition expressed. But I know the *sort of* proposition expressed: that's why I take a shower rather than start cooking.

It is important to see that quantifiers, including descriptions, may contain indexical expressions as constituents:

every *currently* registered Democrat
the *present* king of France
the first person *I* saw this morning
a woman who came to see *you*

the men who delivered *your* sofa
the girl who made *this vase*
most philosophers *I* have met
my mother
that woman's car.

Now it would be quite inappropriate to object to the Theory of Descriptions on the grounds that the implication of uniqueness is not honored by a sentence containing an indexical description. It is worth running through an example just to see how an indexical description like "my mother" works.... [F]or Russell the semantical value—what he would call the "meaning"—of an utterance of a referring expression "*b*" is just its referent; and the semantical value of an utterance of a sentence "*b* is *G*" is an object-dependent proposition. An utterance of a definite description, by contrast, will not take an object as its semantical value, because a description is a quantifier not a referring expression. The semantical value of an utterance of "the *F* is *G*" is a descriptive proposition to the effect that there is one and only one thing that is *F* and that one thing is *G*. There is no object for which the grammatical subject "the *F*" stands that is a genuine constituent of that proposition. Before looking at "my mother," let's look at "Stephen Neale's mother." An utterance of

(3) Stephen Neale's mother is English

expresses the proposition we can represent as

(4) [the x: x mother-of Stephen Neale] (x is English)

which invokes the relational property *being mother of Stephen Neale*, i.e., $(\lambda x)(x$ mother-of Stephen Neale).[14] But what property gets into the proposition expressed by an utterance of

(5) My mother is English

made by me? The same relational property. This does not mean that the relational description "Stephen Neale's mother," and the indexical description "my mother," have the same linguistic meaning. On the contrary, they have quite different rules of use. Only *I* can use the latter to invoke the property of being mother of *me*. However, you may use "My mother" to invoke the property of being mother of *you*. The fact that the denotation of "my mother" changes from speaker to speaker poses no threat to the Russellian implication of uniqueness. When I utter "My mother is English," unique motherhood is relative to *me*; when you utter it, it is relative to you.[15]

It is not, then, the *sentence* "the F is G" that carries any *particular* implication of uniqueness, but particular dated utterances of that sentence. The linguistic meaning of the sentence is just a rule for use that, among other things, specifies that the description is being used correctly only if there is, relative to the particular context $\langle s, a, \langle d_1, \ldots, d_n \rangle, t, p \rangle$, just one object satisfying the description in question. It is clear, then, that the Theory of Descriptions is not threatened by the existence of descriptions containing indexical components. Rather, this gives the Theory of Descriptions yet more expressive power (the importance of indexical descriptions will come out in 14.5 and 14.7).

In this section, I have made the common assumption that the proposition expressed by an utterance u of a sentence ϕ bears a tight relationship to the linguistic meaning of ϕ. To the extent that this relationship *is* tight, there is also a tight connection between understanding ϕ and understanding an utterance u of ϕ. But as we saw, there are several respects in which the linguistic meaning of ϕ may underdetermine the proposition expressed by u because of the various parameters left open by indexical expressions, parameters that must be pinned down by u's contextual coordinates.

Notice that knowledge of the language to which ϕ belongs together with knowledge of the relevant contextual coordinates will not necessarily put a hearer H in position to grasp the proposition expressed by u. The existence of lexical and structural ambiguity means that a particular string of sounds may satisfy the phonological criteria for being a tokening of sentence ϕ or of sentence ϕ^* ("Visiting relatives can be a nuisance"). Then there are the interpretive problems raised by (e.g.) names and pronouns. Consider an utterance of

(6) Nicola thinks she should become a banker.

H will need to assign referents to "Nicola" and to the pronoun "she," which may or may not be anaphoric on "Nicola."[16] H is surely seeking the reading that S *intended*. Indeed, if H assigns to "Nicola" a referent other than the one S had in mind, it is clear that H has not grasped the proposition expressed.[17]

For a referring expression "b" and a monadic predicate "—is G," the identity of the proposition expressed by a particular utterance of "b is G" is dependent upon the identity of the object b referred to by "b." The utterance expresses a true proposition just in case b is G. The proposition in question is object-dependent in the sense that it simply could not be expressed, or even entertained, if b did not exist.

The connection with contemporary talk of *truth conditions* can be made explicit by focusing on what it means to understand a proposition. To understand an object-dependent proposition, one must have identifying knowledge of the thing the proposition is about. In addition, one must know what property is being ascribed to that object. Thus we reach the position advanced by Wittgenstein, in the *Tractatus*, that understanding a proposition involves knowing what is the case if it is true.[18] And by extension we might therefore say that understanding an utterance (of a sentence) involves knowing its truth conditions—indeed its truth conditions in actual and counterfactual situations—and that a specification of the semantical value of an utterance (of a sentence) consists, at least in part, in a specification of its truth-conditions.

14.4 Propositions Expressed and Proposition Meant

It is clear that a hearer *H* may gather a lot more from an utterance than the proposition it expresses. Quite different thoughts may come to *H*'s mind. Let's begin with some trivial examples of the sort we shall *not* be concerned with. I am in a restaurant in San Francisco; the waitress asks me if I'd like an aperitif and I reply,

(1) I'd like a gin and tonic, please.

On the basis of certain acoustic properties of my utterance, the waitress may come to believe that I am English, or that I have a cold or hay fever. Such propositions are irrelevant to the communicative act performed, as are other propositions that are, in some sense, *made available* by my speech act but that may not spring immediately to mind, such as the proposition that I can speak English or the proposition that I am not dead.

Of considerably more importance for current concerns is the fact, emphasized by Grice (1961, 1967), that there are speech acts involving, in some communicatively *relevant* way, propositions other than the proposition strictly and literally expressed. A speaker may express a particular proposition by means of an utterance yet at the same time *communicate* something beyond this. Consider the following example due to Grice (1961). You are writing a letter of recommendation for one of your students who has applied for a position teaching philosophy at another institution. You write

(2) Jones has beautiful handwriting and is always very punctual.

The people who read this letter will surely conclude that you do not rate Jones very highly as a philosopher. And if so, you have succeeded in communicating a proposition to that effect. There is an intuitive distinction here between the proposition you expressed by the utterance and the proposition (or propositions) you sought to *convey* by it, what we might call the *proposition(s) meant*.

There is no temptation to say that the proposition that you do not rate Jones very highly as a philosopher is (or is a consequence of) the proposition expressed by your utterance. There is no specifiable method of correlating this proposition with the proposition determined by the linguistic meaning of (2) together with the contextual coordinates of the utterance. The sentence has a clear linguistic meaning based on the meanings of its parts and their syntactical arrangement, a meaning that has nothing to do with your assessment of Jones' philosophical abilities, even when the relevant contextual coordinates are plugged in. On the other hand, we might say that *you mean*, by your utterance of (2), that you do not rate Jones very highly. This is something that *you* have implied or suggested by uttering (2) in this particular context.

It is clear, then, that there may, on occasion, be a divergence between the proposition (or propositions) strictly and literally expressed by an utterance and the proposition(s) meant. (In the case we just considered, they might well be disjoint; in other case they might not be; see below.) Indeed, there seems little doubt that any plausible account of the way language works in communication will have to appeal to a distinction of this sort.

We have reached the familiar Gricean view, then, that at least three different notions need to be distinguished when talking about the "meaning" of a sentence ϕ as uttered by a speaker S on a given occasion: (i) the linguistic meaning of the sentence ϕ; (ii) the semantical value of ϕ relative to the context of utterance (the proposition expressed); and (iii) what S meant by uttering ϕ (the proposition(s) meant). But we need to get a lot clearer about the notion in (iii) and its relation to the notion in (ii) before we can use either with any confidence in our investigation.

In the simplest cases we might say that the proposition *expressed* is meant, and that in many such cases the proposition expressed *exhausts* the proposition(s) meant. But, of course, in Grice's letter of recommendation example this is not the case at all. How, then, might we characterize when a proposition is meant? One constraint that comes to mind is the following: For a particular utterance u of ϕ made by a speaker S to a hearer H, a proposition p is meant only if, on the basis of uttering ϕ, S *intends* H to entertain p. But we can go further than this. Borrowing from Grice's (1957, 1967) seminal work in this area, we might impose the following constraint on what it is for S to mean that p by uttering ϕ:

(G1) By uttering ϕ, S means that p only if for some audience H, S utters ϕ intending:
1. H to actively entertain the thought that p, and
2. H to recognize that S intends (1).

Consider the restaurant scene again, where the waitress learns from certain acoustic properties of my utterance of

(1) I'd like a gin and tonic, please

that I am English (or that I have a cold or hay fever). All *I mean* by my utterance is that I'd like a gin and tonic; I do *not* mean that I am English (or that I have a cold or hay fever). The first intention mentioned in (1) prevents such communicatively irrelevant propositions from being classed as part of what I mean because I do not *intend* the waitress to entertain the thought that I am English (or the thought that I have a cold or hay fever).

A modification of the same example will explain the role of the intention mentioned in (2). Suppose I do actually intend the waitress to realize that I have a cold (in order to get sympathy), or to realize that I am English (because I think I will get better service as a tourist), but I don't want her to realize that this is my intention. Intuitively, we don't want to say that *I mean* that I have a cold (or that I am English). The intention in (1) allows these propositions through. But I do not intend the waitress to *realize* that I intend her to think that I have a cold (or that I am English), so the intention in (2) prevents these propositions from being classed as a part of what I mean by my utterance.[19]

With the aid of this tentative constraint on when a proposition is meant, let's now turn to Grice's theory of *conversational implicature*. As Kripke (1977) and others have emphasized, several of Grice's proposals have a direct bearing on how we might characterize the uses of descriptions in various types of communicative settings. I shall therefore spend a little time going over certain features of Grice's general picture before putting it to use in the area of main interest.

On Grice's (1967) account, conversation is a characteristically purposeful and cooperative enterprise governed by what he calls the *Cooperative Principle*:

(CP) Make your conversational contribution such as is required, at the
      stage at which it occurs, by the accepted purpose or direction of the
      talk exchange in which you are engaged.

Subsumed under this general principle, Grice distinguishes four categories
of more specific maxims and submaxims enjoining truthfulness, informativeness, relevance, and clarity.

Maxim of Quantity: Make your contribution as informative as is
required (for the current purposes of the exchange). Do not make your
contribution more informative than is required.

Maxim of Quality: Try to make your contribution one that is true.
Specifically: Do not say what you believe to be false; do not say that for
which you lack adequate evidence.

Maxim of Relation: Be relevant.

Maxim of Manner: Be perspicuous. Specifically: Be brief and orderly;
avoid ambiguity and obscurity.

    Of central concern to us is Grice's claim that there is a systematic cor-
respondence between the assumptions required in order to preserve the
supposition that the Cooperative Principle and attendant maxims are
being observed and a certain class of propositions meant, what Grice calls
conversational implicatures. The letter of recommendation case discussed
earlier is a good example of a case that seems to involve a deliberate and
flagrant violation of the Cooperative Principle, or at least one or more of
the maxims. On Grice's account, by writing "Jones has wonderful handwriting and is always very punctual," (in this context) you appear to have
violated the maxim enjoining relevance—since Jones is one of your students, you must know more of relevance than *this*. Furthermore, you
know that more information than this is required in this particular context. Not surprisingly, the reader is naturally led to believe that you are
attempting to convey something else, perhaps something you are reluctant
to express explicitly. This supposition is plausible only on the assumption
that you think Jones is no good at philosophy. And this is what you have
conversationally implicated. In general, a speaker S conversationally implicates that which S must be assumed to believe in order to preserve the
assumption that S is adhering to the CP and maxims.[20]
    Grice contrasts this case with one in which there is supposed to be "no
obvious violation" of the Cooperative Principle. Suppose H is standing

by an obviously immobilized car and is approached by *S*. *H* says to *S*, "Where can I buy some gas?" *S* replies, "There is a gas station around the next corner." If *S* did not think, or think it possible, that the gas station was open and had gas for sale, his remark would not be properly relevant; thus he may be said to conversationally *implicate* that it is open and has gas for sale. That is, *S* implicates that which he must be assumed to believe in order to preserve the assumption that he is adhering to the CP, in particular, the maxim enjoining relevance.

On Grice's account, a necessary condition for an implication to count as a conversational implicature is that it be *cancellable*, either explicitly or contextually, without literal contradiction, or at least without linguistic transgression.[21] For instance, in the letter case you might have continued with "Moreover, in my opinion he is the brightest student we have ever had here." This addition might be odd, but it would not give rise to any literal contradiction. Notice that it might well be the case that in this example only what is implicated is meant (i.e., backed by your communicative intentions). You may have no idea what Jones' handwriting is like because he has only shown you typed manuscripts of his work (or because he has never shown you anything), and you may have no opinion as to whether or not he is punctual. Here the proposition implicated *supplants* the proposition expressed with respect to being meant.[22] The truth-values of the proposition expressed and the proposition(s) implicated may of course differ. Jones may have quite atrocious handwriting, and you may know this; but given the relevance of the proposition implicated, you may care very little whether the proposition expressed is true. That is, the primary message (what you *meant*) may not be calculable at the level of the proposition expressed but only at the level of the proposition implicated, in the sense that it is the latter that has the backing of your communicative intentions. (In the stranded motorist case, the propositions implicated seem to *supplement* (rather than supplant) the proposition expressed.)

Although cancellability is taken by Grice to be a necessary condition of an implication's being classed as a conversational implicature, rather more importance is attached to derivability.[23]

... the final test for the presence of a conversational implicature ha[s] to be, as far as I [can] see, a derivation of it. One has to produce an account of how it could have arisen and why it is there. And I am very much opposed to any kind of sloppy use of this philosophical tool, in which one does not fulfil this condition. (Grice 1981, p. 187)

Let's call this the *Justification Requirement*. On Grice's account, whenever there is a conversational implicature, one should be able to reason
somewhat as follows:

(a) S has expressed the proposition that p.

(b) There is no reason to suppose that S is not observing the CP and
maxims.

(c) S could not be doing this unless he thought that q.

(d) S knows (and knows that I know that he knows) that I can see that he
thinks the supposition that he thinks that q is required.

(e) S has done nothing to stop me thinking that q.

(f) S intends me to think, or is at least willing to allow me to think,
that q.

(g) And so, S has implicated that q.

In each of the cases we have considered, it is possible to justify the
existence of the implicature in question in this sort of way.[24]

So far, we have only looked at cases involving what Grice calls *particularized* conversational implicature. The presence and content of a particularized conversational implicature depend in a very transparent way
upon facts about the particular context of utterance. Of rather more
philosophical interest are those implicatures the presence and general
form of which seem to have very little to do with the particular details of
a given context of utterance, so-called generalized conversational implicatures. It is tempting to characterize the syntactician as that philosopher
of language whose job it is to provide a finite, systematic characterization
of a proprietary body of intuitions concerning such things as syntactical
well-formedness, i.e., grammaticality. Analogously, we might view the
semanticist as that philosopher of language who does the same thing for
intuitions of truth, falsity, entailment, contradiction, and so on. In effect,
the semanticist's aim is to construct a theory that will, among other
things, yield predictions in accord with these intuitions. But great care
must be taken when appealing to semantical intuitions. An initial judgment of truth or falsity, or of entailment or contradiction, might have to
be reevaluated in the light of further considerations or a little tutoring
of one form or another. For instance, what at first sight may seem like a
semantical entailment may, upon further reflection, turn out to be something quite different.[25]

Grice (1961, 1967) argues that there has been a tendency among some
linguistically oriented philosophers to overcharacterize the linguistic

meanings of certain linguistic expressions. Let ζ be such an expression. According to Grice, certain conversational implicatures that typically attach to uses of ζ have been treated, mistakenly, as part of ζ's meaning. Semantical claims about certain "intentional" verbs (e.g., "seem," "try," "intend," "know," and "remember") and about the linguistic counterparts to some of the formal devices of quantification theory (e.g., "and," "or," "if ... then ...," "the," and "a") were some of Grice's philosophically important targets. Indeed, for Grice, conversational implicature is a powerful philosophical tool with which to investigate the logical forms of certain philosophical claims and also clarify the relationship between formulae of quantification theory and sentences of natural language.

For example, *pace* Strawson (1952, p. 79ff.), it is at least arguable that many of the apparently divergent implications that seem to be present when the English word "and" is used to conjoin sentences are not attributable to any sort of lexical ambiguity in the word but can be understood as conversational implicatures of one form or another, there being no difference in meaning between "and" and the & of classical logic.[26] Compare the following sentences:

(1) The moon goes around the earth and the earth goes around the sun

(2) Jack and Jill got married and Jill gave birth to twins

(3) The President walked in and the troops jumped to attention.

One feature of & is that it is commutative (p & q is equivalent to q & p). This does not seem to create a problem for the view that the occurrence of "and" in (1) has the force of &. But in (2) the conjuncts describe events and, in the normal course of things, someone who uttered this sentence would be taken to imply that Jack and Jill got married *before* Jill gave birth to twins. Indeed, if the order of the conjuncts is reversed, so is the implication. And in (3) there seems to be an implication not just of temporal priority but of causal connection.

On the basis of facts like these, one might be led to the view that "and" is at least three ways ambiguous. Now the fact that the truth of "p and$_{(3)}$ q" guarantees the truth of "p and$_{(2)}$ q," which guarantees the truth of "p and$_{(1)}$ q" might well make one wonder whether the postulation of such ambiguity is not a little extravagant. Indeed, on Grice's account, there is another, perhaps preferable avenue that might be explored. It is good methodological practice, Grice (1967) suggests, to subscribe to what he calls *Modified Occam's Razor: Senses are not to be multiplied beyond necessity.* Given the viability of a broadly Gricean distinction between the proposition expressed and the proposition(s) meant, if a pragmatic explanation is available of why a particular expression appears to diverge in meaning in different linguistic environments (or in different conversational settings) then *ceteris paribus* the pragmatic explanation is preferable to the postulation of a semantical ambiguity.

As Grice observes, pragmatic explanations of what is going on in (2) and (3) do seem to be available. The implication of temporal sequence might be explicable in terms of the fact that each of the conjuncts describes an event (rather than a state) and the presumption that the speaker is observing the Maxim of Manner, in particular the submaxim enjoining an orderly delivery.[27] And the implication of causal connection in (3) might be explicable in terms of the presumption that the speaker is being relevant. Again the conjuncts describe events and it is natural to seek some sort of connection between them since the speaker has mentioned them both in the same breath. The idea, then, is that these implications are cases of *generalized* conversational implicature. I am not going to present a serious defense of the view that "and" *always* means & (even if restricted to cases where it conjoins pairs of sentences rather than pairs of noun phrases or pairs of verb phrases); I just want to outline the form a pragmatic explanation of the alleged ambiguity is supposed to take.[28]

The reasons for preferring pragmatic explanations over the postulation of semantical ambiguities are, of course, economy and generality. A pragmatic explanation is, in some sense, *free*: the machinery that is appealed to is needed anyway. In any particular case, this may not in itself constitute an overwhelming objection to a theory that posits an ambiguity; but in the case of "and" the generality lost by positing several readings is considerable. Grice makes three relevant observations here. First, there is the fact that implications of (e.g.) temporal priority and causal connection attach to uses of the counterparts of "and" across unrelated languages. One could, of course, posit parallel ambiguities in these languages; but the phenomenon is more readily explained as the product of general pragmatic considerations. Second, it is not unreasonable to assume that implications of the same sorts would arise even for speakers of a language containing an explicitly truth-functional connective &. Third, the same implications that attach to a particular utterance of p & q would attach to an utterance of the two sentence sequence $p.q$. It seems clear, then, that on *methodological* grounds the pragmatic account of the temporal and causal implications in (2) and (3) is preferable to an account that makes essential use of a semantical ambiguity. Of course, there may well be uses of the English word "and" that resist a truth-functional semantics, but I do not take myself to be arguing for the view that the word has just one meaning; my purpose is to illustrate Grice's point that where semantical and pragmatic accounts handle *the same range of data*, the pragmatic account is preferable.

It will be convenient now to focus on an example of generalized conversational implicature that involves the use of the determiner "some." (This will put us on course for a detailed discussion of the determiner "the" in the next section.) Suppose two journalists S and H are discussing a recent demonstration in a notoriously repressive country. There was some violence at the demonstration and several of the demonstrators were killed, allegedly by the police. S was present at the demonstration and he knows that some of the deaths were accidental because he saw two demonstrators accidentally run over by a car full of other demonstrators. H knows that S dislikes the repressive regime, but he also knows that S is a very honest reporter. When H quizzes S about the deaths, S says,

(4) Some of the deaths were accidental.

In this situation, S would very likely be taken to endorse the truth of, or at least entertain the possibility of the truth of (5):

(5) Some of the deaths were not accidental.

But we don't want to say that "some Fs are Gs" entails "some Fs are not Gs," or even that (4) entails (5). Nor do we want to say that "some" is ambiguous, that on one reading "some Fs are Gs" entails "some Fs are not Gs" and that on another it does not. At least, not if a pragmatic explanation is available of how (4) may be used to convey a proposition that differs from the proposition it would be taken to express on its standard quantificational reading.

And of course a pragmatic explanation *is* available. Intuitively, the proposition expressed by (4) is "weaker" than the one expressed by

(6) All of the deaths were accidental.

And since in a typical communicative setting it would be more appropriate (informative, straightforward, relevant) to make the stronger claim (if it were believed true), a speaker who makes the weaker claim (in such a setting) will, *ceteris paribus*, conversationally implicate that he or she does not subscribe to the stronger claim. Now if S does not subscribe to the view that all of the deaths were accidental, S must be willing to entertain the possibility that some of the deaths were not accidental.[29] Using a Gricean justification schema,

(a) S has expressed the proposition that some of the deaths were accidental.

(b) There is no reason to suppose that S is not observing the CP and maxims.

(c) S could not be doing this unless he were willing to entertain the possibility that some of the deaths were *not* accidental. (Gloss: On the assumption that S is adhering to the Maxim of Quantity, if he thought that *all* of the deaths were accidental he would have said so. Therefore S is willing to entertain the possibility that some of the deaths were not accidental. (On the assumption that S is adhering to the Maxim of Quality, he does not think that *none* of the deaths were accidental, since he has said that some of them *were*.))

(d) S knows (and knows that I know that he knows) that I can see that he thinks the supposition that he is willing to entertain the possibility that some of the deaths were not accidental is required.

(e) S has done nothing to stop me thinking that he is willing to entertain the possibility that some of the deaths were not accidental.

(f) S intends me to think, or is at least willing to allow me to think, that he is willing to entertain the possibility that some of the deaths were not accidental.

(g) And so, S has implicated that he is willing to entertain the possibility that some of the deaths were not accidental.

It seems to me that we should resist the temptation to formulate *pragmatic rules* with which to derive certain standard cases of generalized conversational implicature. For instance, it might be suggested that a pragmatic theory contain a rule like the following:

(7) $[\text{some } x: Fx] (Gx) \gg \Psi [\text{some } x: Fx] \neg (Gx)$

where $\gg$ stands for something like "conversationally implicates unless there is good evidence to the contrary," and Ψ stands for something like "the speaker is willing to entertain the possibility that." In one very important respect, nothing could be further from the spirit of Grice's theory than the construction of such an avowedly singular pragmatic rule. For Grice, the conversational implicatures that attach to a particular utterance must be justifiable given the CP and maxims, construed as quite *general* antecedent assumptions about the rational nature of conversational practice. It is important not to be misled by Grice's intuitive distinction between particularized and generalized implicatures into thinking that instances of the latter do not have to satisfy the Justification Requirement. To label a certain range of implicatures "generalized" is not to bestow upon them some special status, it is simply to acknowledge the fact that the presence of the implicatures is relatively independent of the details of the particular conversational context.

We now have enough of a framework in place to begin addressing the issues raised by so-called referential uses of descriptions.

14.5   The Referential Challenge Revisited

As I mentioned in 14.2, we can, I believe, ascribe to those who see the need for a semantically distinct referential interpretation of definite descriptions the following thesis:

(A1)   If a speaker S uses a definite description "the F" referentially in an utterance u of "the F is G," then "the F" functions as a referring expression and the proposition expressed by u is *object-dependent* (rather than descriptive).

But what does it mean to say that a definite description is being used *referentially* on a given occasion? (Or, to use the alternative terminology of Kripke (1977) and Donnellan (1979), what does it mean to say that a particular use of a definite description is *accompanied by speaker reference*?).

This question is addressed by Donnellan (1979). Consider S's utterance u of the sentence "The strongest man in the world can lift at least 450lbs." Donnellan claims, quite rightly in my opinion, that it is not enough for S's use of "the strongest man in the world" to be classified as referential that there exist some object b such that S knows (or believes) that b is the strongest man in the world. On such an account, the referentialist would be committed to the fantastic view that whenever S knows (or thinks he or she knows) who or what satisfies some description or other, S can no longer use that description nonreferentially. This would, indeed, be a peculiar consequence: the existence or nonexistence of a particular semantical ambiguity in a speaker's idiolect would be based solely on the speaker's epistemological history.[30]

Donnellan also claims, again correctly in my opinion, that it is not enough for S's use of "the strongest man in the world" to be classified as referential that there exist some object b such that the grounds for S's utterance are furnished by the object-dependent belief that b is the strongest man in the world and the object-dependent belief that b can lift 450lbs.[31] What is characteristic of a referential use, Donnellan suggests, is the nature of "the intentions of the speaker toward his audience" (p. 50).

In the light of the discussions in 14.2 and 14.4, we might suggest that a speaker S uses a definite description "the F" referentially in an utterance u of "the F is G" if and only if there is some object b such that S means by u that b is G. But this is not quite strong enough. Suppose it is common knowledge between S and H that the tallest man in the world, whoever he is, is spending the weekend with Nicola. Suppose that there is no individual b such that either S or H believes of b that b is the tallest man in the world; however, it is common knowledge between S and H that the tallest man in the world (whoever he is) is very shy and that Nicola will take him with her wherever she goes this weekend. S and H are at a party on Saturday and it is a matter of some interest to S and H whether Nicola is present. S overhears a conversation during which someone says "The tallest man in the world is here." S goes over to H and says "The tallest man in the world is here" intending to communicate that *Nicola* is here. In this example there clearly is some object b (viz., Nicola) such that S means by u that b is here; but equally clearly, S's utterance does not involve a referential use of "the tallest man in the world." We seem to need something more like this:

(A2) A speaker S uses a definite description "the F" referentially in an utterance u of "the F is G" iff there is some object b such that S means by u that b is the F and that b is G.[32]

The debate between the Russellian-Gricean and the referentialist can now be summarized as follows. The referentialist endorses (A1) and (A2); the Russellian (to the extent that he or she believes that it is possible to provide a clear account of referential usage) endorses (A2) and (A3):

(A3) If a speaker S uses a definite description "the F" referentially in an utterance u of "the F is G," "the F" still functions as a quantifier and the proposition expressed by u is the object-independent proposition given by [the x: Fx] (Gx).

In short, then, the Russellian-Gricean sees referential usage as an important fact about *communication* to be explained by general pragmatic principles, not something of *semantical* import. Let us now examine this position.

As Evans (1982) observes, there are two rather different cases of referential usage to take into account, according as the putative referential description is supposed to be functioning like a *name* or like a *demonstrative*. Suppose that you and I both know Harry Smith and it is common knowledge between us that Harry is the present Chairman of the Flat Earth Society. Harry calls me up and informs me that he will be arriving in San Francisco next Saturday. Later that day I see you in the street and I say,

(1) The Chairman of the Flat Earth Society is coming to San Francisco next Saturday

fully intending to communicate to you the object-dependent proposition that Harry Smith is coming to San Francisco next Saturday, rather than (or rather than *just*) a descriptive proposition concerning the unique satisfier of a certain descriptive condition. I utter (1) intending you (a) to actively entertain the (object-dependent) proposition that Harry Smith is coming to San Francisco next Saturday, and (b) to recognize that I intend you to actively entertain that proposition (see (G1)). And I feel confident that these intentions can be fulfilled because I believe (i) that you have identifying knowledge of Harry Smith, (ii) that you take Harry Smith to uniquely satisfy the description "the Chairman of the Flat Earth Society," and (iii) that you can infer from the fact that I have used this description that I wish to convey something to you about Harry Smith. There would appear to be no barrier, then, to saying that (part of) what *I mean* by my utterance of (1) is that Harry Smith is coming to San Francisco next Saturday; the object-dependent proposition that Harry Smith is coming to San Francisco next Saturday is (one of) the *proposition(s) meant*.

Now it is clear that I might have conveyed to you that Harry Smith is coming to San Francisco next Saturday by uttering (2) instead of (1):

(2) Harry Smith is coming to San Francisco next Saturday.

Consequently, one might consider interpreting the description (as it occurs in this utterance) as something akin to a proper name. Let's say that in this case the description is used *referentially$_N$* ("N" for "name").

Let's now turn to a rather different example of the sort exploited by Donnellan (1966). We are at a party together; in one corner of the room is a man, x, wearing a top hat; I notice that x is trying to attract your attention, so I say to you,

(3) The man wearing a top hat is trying to attract your attention

fully intending to communicate to you an object-dependent proposition (about x), rather than (or rather than *just*) a descriptive proposition concerning the unique satisfier of the descriptive condition. I utter (3) intending you (a) actively to entertain the (object-dependent) proposition that x is trying to attract your attention, and (b) to recognize that I intend you actively to entertain that proposition. And I feel confident that these intentions can be fulfilled because I believe (i) that you have identifying knowledge of x, (ii) that you take x to uniquely satisfy the description "the man wearing a top hat," and (iii) that you can infer from the fact that I have used this description that I wish to convey something to you about x. There would appear to be no barrier, then, to saying that (part of) what *I mean* be my utterance of (3) is that x is trying to attract your attention; the object-dependent proposition that x is trying to attract your attention is (one of) the *proposition(s) meant*.

Now it is clear that I might have conveyed to you the same object-dependent proposition by uttering

(4) That man is trying to attract your attention

accompanied by some sort of demonstration or gesture. Consequently, one might consider interpreting the description (as it occurs in this utterance) as something akin to a demonstrative. Let's call this a *referential$_D$* use of a description ("*D*" for "demonstrative").[33]

The question for the semanticist here is whether we need semantically distinct non-Russellian interpretations of the descriptions in (1) and (3) in order to make sense of the scenarios just constructed.

There are good methodological reasons to resist a complication of the semantics of the definite article in this way. The first thing to remember is that the phenomenon of referential usage is not something peculiar to definite descriptions. Consider the following example adapted from Wilson (1978). You and I both see Harris lurking around at the party; we both know (and know that the other knows) that Harris is a convicted embezzler; later in the evening I see Harris flirting with your sister so I come up to you and say,

(5) A convicted embezzler is flirting with your sister

fully intending to communicate to you the object-dependent proposition that Harris is flirting with your sister. I utter (5) intending you (a) to actively entertain the (object-dependent) proposition that Harris is flirting with your sister, and (b) to recognize that I intend you to actively entertain that proposition. There would appear to be no barrier, then, to saying that (part of) what *I mean* by my utterance of (5) is that Harris is flirting with your sister; the object-dependent proposition that Harris is flirting with your sister is (one of) the *proposition(s) meant*.

It is clear that I might have conveyed to you that Harris is flirting with your sister by uttering (6) instead of (5):

(6) Harris is flirting with your sister.

We appear to have here something approximating a referential$_N$ use of an *indefinite d*escription (modifications to (A2) would capture this).

It is, of course, open to the referentialist to claim that indefinite descriptions are also ambiguous between Russellian and referential *interpretations*.[34] But the Gricean-Russellian will claim that some sort of important communicative generalization is being missed by proceeding in this way. Indeed, as Sainsbury (1979) emphasizes, the case for an ambiguity in the definite article weakens considerably once it is realized that sentences containing all sorts of quantifiers may be used to convey object-dependent propositions. Suppose it is common knowledge that Smith is the only person taking Jones' seminar. One evening, Jones throws a party and Smith is the only person who turns up. A despondent Jones, when asked the next morning whether his party was well attended, says,

(7) Well, everyone taking my seminar turned up

fully intending to inform me that only Smith attended. The possibility of such a scenario, would not lead us to complicate the semantics of "every" with an ambiguity; i.e., it would not lead us to posit semantically distinct quantificational and referential interpretations of "everyone taking my seminar."

We find a similar situation with plural quantifiers.[35] Suppose that Scott Soames, David Lewis, and I are the only three people in Lewis's office. Soames has never played cricket and knows that I know this. In addition, Soames wants to know whether Lewis and I have ever played cricket, so I say

(8) Most people in this room have played cricket

fully intending to communicate to Soames that Lewis and I have both played cricket. There is surely no temptation to complicate the semantics of "most" with an ambiguity, no temptation to posit a semantically distinct referential interpretation of "most people in this room." The natural thing to say is that given his background beliefs and given the quantificational proposition expressed by my utterance in the context in question, Soames was able to *infer* the truth of a particular object-dependent proposition (or two object-dependent propositions). I was thus able to convey an object-dependent proposition by uttering a sentence of the form "most Fs are Gs". (Similar cases can be constructed using "all senators," "many Americans," "few Stanford women," "five of us," "a convicted embezzler," "some politicians," "the man wearing a top hat," "the women who work for Martha," and so on.)

Thus the Gricean-Russellian views the referential use of definite descriptions as an instance of a more general phenomenon associated with the use of quantified noun phrases. Of course, definite descriptions are particularly susceptible to referential usage because of their own particular semantics. As Klein (1980) points out, if S is observing the Maxim of Quality, S will typically believe that one and only one object satisfies the description used. (The complications introduced by so-called *incomplete* descriptions like "the table," "the cat" and so on are discussed in 14.7.) And quite often S will believe this because S knows of some particular object b that b is uniquely F. The beginnings of an explanation of the quite general phenomenon of communicating object-dependent propositions using quantified sentences surely lie in the fact that the grounds for a quantificational assertion are very often object-dependent beliefs of one form or another. (By (A1), object-dependent grounds do not suffice for referential usage, of course.) I know that some Britons are currently residing in the U.S.A. One reason I know this is that I know that I am British and that I am currently residing here, and I know that John McDowell is British and that he is currently residing here. Thus the grounds for my asserting

(9) Some Britons are currently residing in the U.S.A.

are furnished by object-dependent beliefs about John McDowell and about me. Similar remarks apply to the cricket case discussed a moment ago. Add to this the context of utterance, shared background assumptions, the sorts of inferential abilities we all possess, and the sorts of Gricean considerations that appear to govern rational discourse, and the way is open for a quite general explanation of how it is that we manage to convey object-dependent propositions using quantificational sentences, including, of course, sentences containing descriptions.

Consider the referential$_N$ use of "the Chairman of the Flat Earth society" in (1) again. Echoing Grice, we might say that

(a) S has expressed the proposition that [the x: Fx](Gx).

(b) There is no reason to suppose that S is not observing the CP and maxims.

(c) S could not be doing this unless he thought that Gb (where "b" is a name). Gloss: On the assumption that S is observing the Maxim of Relation, he must be attempting to convey something beyond the general proposition that whoever is uniquely F is G. On the assumption that S is adhering to the Maxim of Quality, he must have adequate evidence for thinking that the F is G. I know S knows that b is the F, therefore S thinks that Gb.

(d) S knows (and knows that I know that he knows) that I know that b is the F, that I know that S knows that b is the F, and that I can see that S thinks the supposition that he thinks that Gb is required.

(e) S has done nothing to stop me thinking that Gb.

(f) S intends me to think, or is at least willing to allow me to think, that Gb.

(g) And so, S has implicated that Gb.

On a referential$_D$ use of "the F," (c) might be replaced by

(c') S could not be doing this unless he thought that Gb (where "b" is a demonstrative.) Gloss: On the assumption that S is observing the Maxim of Relation, he must be attempting to convey something over and above the general proposition that whoever is uniquely F is G. On the assumption that S is adhering to the Maxim of Quality, he must have adequate evidence for thinking that the F is G. It is not plausible to suppose that he has just general grounds for this belief; therefore he must have object-dependent grounds. I can see that there is someone b in the perceptual environment who could be taken to satisfy the description "the F," and I can see that S can see this. Therefore the grounds for his assertion that the F is G are plausibly furnished by the belief that Gb.[36]

Although a description "the F" does not itself refer to any individual, following Kripke (1977) let us say that in situations like those just discussed *the speaker S refers* to an individual, the individual S is interested in communicating a proposition about.

We have reached the situation, then, in which we appear to have a perfectly good explanation of referential uses of definite descriptions that does not appeal to any sort of semantical ambiguity. The Russellian and the ambiguity theorist agree that when a description is used referentially, (one of) the proposition(s) *meant* is object-dependent; they just provide different explanations of this fact. The referentialist complicates the semantics of "the"; the Russellian appeals to antecedently motivated principles governing the nature of rational discourse and ordinary inference. As far as accounting for the data we have considered, a stalemate appears to have been reached.

But general methodological considerations lend support to the Russellian. Modified Occam's Razor enjoins us not to multiply senses beyond necessity, i.e., to opt for a theory that (*ceteris paribus*) does not have to appeal to a semantical ambiguity. The similarity with the case of "and" (discussed in 14.4) is striking. First, the phenomenon of referential usage is not something specific to English, nor even to Indo-European languages. Second, as already noted, the phenomenon is not even specific to definite descriptions, it arises with quantifiers quite generally. Third, as Kripke (1977) has pointed out, there is no good reason to suppose that speakers of a language who are taught explicitly Russellian truth conditions for sentences containing definite and indefinite descriptions would not come to use such phrases referentially. Furthermore, speakers of a version of first-order logic without descriptions might still succeed in referring to particular individuals by using existential quantifications of the form "there is exactly one F and whatever is F is G." Indeed, as Kripke (chapter 11, this volume, p. 241) observes, on occasion one can even get away with this sort of thing in English:

(10) Exactly one person is drinking champagne in that corner and I hear he is romantically linked with Jane Smith.

On methodological grounds, then, if attention is restricted to basic cases (14.2), a unitary Russellian theory seems to be preferable to a theory that posits a semantical ambiguity.[37]

14.6 The Argument from Misdescription

Up to now, discussion of referential usage has been restricted to what I earlier called *basic cases*. I want now to turn to the first of several arguments that are often appealed to by some of those who reject (A3) in favor of (A1), the Argument from Misdescription. This argument comes in two forms. What I shall call the "standard" form of the argument is due to Donnellan (1966) and goes something like this. Consider a referential$_D$ use of "Smith's murderer." Now suppose Smith was not in fact murdered but died of natural causes. On Russell's account, the definite description "Smith's murderer" will be nondenoting, therefore the proposition expressed will be false (it is not the case that there exists some unique x such that x murdered Smith). But this, Donnellan claims, is just incorrect. For suppose the man S *meant*, viz., Jones, *is* insane. Then, surely S will have said something true of that man. The moral we are supposed to draw is that "... using a definite description referentially, a speaker may say something true even though the description applies to nothing" (p. 207). And the conclusion we are encouraged to accept is that when a description is used referentially, it is the object S wishes to convey something about rather than the descriptive condition used to get at this object that is of semantical relevance. The proposition expressed is therefore object-dependent rather than descriptive.[38]

The problem with this argument is that it relies on the existence of a clear intuition that the proposition expressed is still true despite the fact that neither Jones nor anyone else satisfies the description "Smith's murderer." But this is simply not so. We feel an uneasy tension when we are presented with such cases. As several authors have noted, we want to say that S did something right but *also* that S did something *wrong*. After all, the description he used *failed to fit* the person S wanted to "talk about," and to that extent the speech act was defective.[39]

The referentialist can say nothing useful here, but the Russellian can provide a theoretical explanation of the aforementioned tension: What has been left out by the referentialist is the Gricean distinction between the proposition expressed and the proposition(s) meant. Indeed, one of the earliest overt defenses of the Theory of Descriptions in the face of the Argument from Misdescription was the one sketched by Grice (1969) himself. According to Grice, "what, in such a case, a speaker has *said* may be false, what he *meant* may be true" (p. 199). The proposition expressed by an utterance of "the F is G" is still descriptive, but the speaker may exploit the fact that both speaker and hearer are willing to entertain the idea that some particular individual b is uniquely F in order to communicate an object-dependent proposition about b. Again, the proposition that b is G may well be part of what is *meant* but it is not the proposition expressed, nor is it implied by it.[40] Applied to Donnellan's example, the proposition expressed by my utterance of "Smith's murderer is insane" is false; but the proposition I intended to communicate is true (if Jones is indeed insane). Thus the Russellian-Gricean has, if only in a rudimentary way, an account of the conflicting pretheoretic intuitions we typically have when presented with cases involving misdescription. The possibility of misdescription does not advance the case for a semantically referential interpretation in the least; indeed, the unitary Russellian analysis has the edge here.

More or less the same is true with what we can call the *inverted* form of the Argument from Misdescription, due to Hornsby (1977). Consider again a referential$_D$ use of "Smith's murderer is insane." Now suppose that the man I *meant* was not insane, and moreover that he did not murder Smith. But suppose that the man who did murder Smith is insane. On Russell's account, the proposition expressed is true, since the unique individual who murdered Smith is insane. But according to Hornsby this is a mistake. I was talking about that man there in the dock, and since he is not insane my utterance cannot be true. We should conclude, Hornsby suggests, that on this occasion, "Smith's murderer" functions as a genuine referring expression.

The problem with this form of the argument is that it relies on the existence of a clear intuition that the proposition expressed is false, despite the fact that the unique individual that does in fact satisfy "Smith's murderer" is insane. But this is simply not so. As with the standard form of the argument, we feel an uneasy tension when we are presented with such cases, a tension the Russellian-Gricean can explain.[41]

I doubt these sorts of considerations can be worked up into knock-down arguments against a semantically distinct referential interpretation. However, as Salmon (1982) argues, related counterfactual considerations cast serious doubt on the viability of a referential interpretation. Occurrences of "Smith's murderer" that are semantically referential will be rigid designators. Consequently, if I utter the sentence "Smith's murderer is insane" in a context C, with the intention that "Smith's murderer" refer to Jones, then the proposition expressed by my utterance is true with respect to any counterfactual situation in which Jones is insane, even those in which Jones does not murder Smith, those in which Smith is not murdered, those in which Smith does not exist, and those in which there are no murders. And this, Salmon maintains, is quite unacceptable.

Salmon's argument can also be inverted. If I utter the sentence "Smith's murderer is insane" in a context C, with the intention that "Smith's murderer" refer to Jones, then the proposition expressed by my utterance is false with respect to any counterfactual situation in which Jones exists but is not insane, even those in which Smith is murdered and the person who murdered him is insane. I must admit I am sympathetic to Salmon's reaction to such results, but I am not sure that it is possible to arrive at judgments of truth or falsity that are not to some extent shaped by either one's initial position on the debate or one's views about the bearers of truth or falsity.[42] My own conclusion—a conclusion I am perfectly happy with—is that cases involving misdescription simply provide no evidence for a semantically referential interpretation of descriptions.

14.7 The Argument from Incompleteness

In 14.3, we established that the propositions expressed by utterances containing indexical descriptions like "my mother" or "the philosopher I most admire" are partially determined by context. But it is not just overtly indexical descriptions that are context-sensitive. This can be illustrated with the help of the following passage from Strawson's "On Referring":

Consider the sentence, "The table is covered with books." It is quite certain that in any normal use of this sentence, the expression "the table" would be used to make a unique reference, i.e. to refer to some one table. It is a quite strict use of the definite article, in the sense in which Russell talks on p. 30 of *Principia Mathematica*, of using the article "strictly, so as to imply uniqueness." On the same page Russell says that a phrase of the form "the so-and-so," used strictly, "will only have an application in the event of there being one so-and-so and no more." Now it is obviously quite false that the phrase "the table" in the sentence "the table is covered with books," used normally, will "only have an application in the event of there being one table and no more." (chapter 6, this volume, pp. 147–148)

There is an important truth in this passage. A speaker may use a definite description when, strictly speaking, it is quite clear that there is no object that uniquely satisfies it. And, on the face of it, this seems to pose a problem for Russell. If I say to you right now

(1) The table is covered with books

I would not normally be understood as committing myself to the existence of one and only one table. But a naïve application of the Theory of Descriptions appears to have precisely this unwelcome consequence. And since there does not seem to be any good reason for doubting that a determinate proposition is expressed by an utterance of (1), *prima facie* the Russellian is under some obligation to specify its content. By contrast, a theory that postulates a semantically distinct referential interpretation of descriptions seems to provide a natural account of what is going on in (1): the description functions as a referring expression.

Let's call a description "the F" that appears to have a legitimate application even if there is more than one F an *incomplete* or *improper* description.[43]

The first thing to notice about incompleteness is that it is neither a necessary nor a sufficient condition for referential usage, an observation made explicit by Peacocke. That incompleteness is not necessary:

If you and I visited the Casino at Monte Carlo yesterday, and saw a man break the bank ... and it is common knowledge that this is so, then the description

"The man who broke the bank at Monte Carlo yesterday"

as it occurs in a particular utterance *today* of

"The man who broke the bank at Monte Carlo yesterday had holes in his shoes"

may well be satisfied by just one object in the universe, but it is here [referential]. (chapter 10, this volume, pp. 208–209)

That incompleteness is not sufficient:

[Suppose] two school inspectors [are] visiting an institution for the first time: one may say to the other, on the basis of the activities around him, "The headmaster doesn't have much control of the pupils." Here there is no object such that the school inspector has said of it that it doesn't have much control over the pupils. One cannot say that the headmaster is such an object, since what the inspector (*actually*) said would be true even if someone else were headmaster. (p. 209)[44]

Whenever we find some phenomenon associated with the use of definite descriptions, we should look for corresponding phenomena associated with the uses of other quantifiers. This tactic served us well in 14.5 when we examined how someone might convey an object-dependent proposition while expressing (only) an object-independent proposition, and it serves us equally well here. Suppose I had a dinner party last night. In response to a question as to how it went, I say to you

(2) Everyone was sick.

Clearly I do not mean to be asserting that everyone in existence was sick, just that everyone *at the dinner party I had last night* was. In some fashion or other, this is discernible from the context of utterance.[45] Similar examples can be constructed using "no," "most," "just one," "exactly eight," and, of course, "the" (as it occurs with both singular and plural complements). Indeed, the problem of incompleteness has nothing to do with the use of definite descriptions *per se*; it is a quite general fact about the use of quantifiers in natural language.[46] What is needed, then, is not just an account of incomplete descriptions, but a quite general account of incomplete quantifiers. It seems unlikely, therefore, that incompleteness raises any special problems for a quantificational analysis of descriptions that do not have to be faced in any event by quantificational analyses of other quantifiers.[47]

There are two main approaches to incompleteness in the literature, what we might call the *explicit* and the *implicit* approaches. According to the explicit approach, incomplete quantifiers are *elliptical* for proper quantifiers. As Sellars puts it, the descriptive content is "completed" by context. According to the implicit approach, the context of utterance delimits the domain of quantification and leaves the descriptive content untouched.[48] Consider sentence (2) again. On the explicit approach, the quantifier "everybody' (as it is used on this occasion) is elliptical for "everybody at the dinner party I had last night," or some such "narrower" quantifier. On the implicit approach, the domain of quantification is understood as restricted to some favored class of individuals (or to some favored part of the world).[49]

On the assumption that one (or both) of these approaches (or something very similar to one or other of them) will play a role in any complete theory of natural language quantification, any theory that treats definite descriptions as quantifiers is at liberty to appeal to either when incompleteness arises. Consider again Strawson's example

(1) The table is covered with books.

On the explicit approach (taken by, e.g., Sellars 1954), a particular utterance of "the table" might be elliptical for (e.g.) "the table *over there*."[50] On the implicit approach, the domain of quantification might be restricted to (e.g.) objects in the immediate shared perceptual environment. The mere fact that we find incomplete descriptions in discourse does not *by itself* then, give us any reason to abandon Russell's quantificational analysis of descriptions.[51]

Nonetheless, some philosophers have argued that there are intrinsic problems with one or other of these approaches to incompleteness, and that instead of being contextually completed, some occurrences of incomplete descriptions simply have to be provided with semantically referential interpretations.

Let's suppose that an incomplete description is elliptical for a proper (i.e., uniquely-denoting) description recoverable from the context of utterance. As a general account of incomplete descriptions, this type of proposal has come under fire from Donnellan (1968), Hornsby (1977), Wettstein (1981), and Récanati (1986).[52] In his brief discussion of incomplete descriptions, Donnellan is quite willing to accept the elliptical proposal for descriptions used nonreferentially:

> Without considering the two uses of descriptions, the reply [to Strawson's comments cited above] one is inclined to make on Russell's behalf is that in the loose way of everyday speech the context is relied upon to supply further qualifications on the description to make it unique. This seems a plausible reply when considering attributive uses. Suppose someone says, "The next President will be a dove on Viet Nam," and the context easily supplies the implicit "of the United States" (1968, p. 204, note 5).

But Donnellan does not think that this will work for incomplete descriptions used referentially:

> But where one has a very "indefinite" [i.e., incomplete] definite description, with many things in the world satisfying the actual description, the reply is not so plausible. There are commonly, I believe, referential uses. A speaker wants to refer to some object and uses an "indefinite" definite description. Asked to make his description more precise, he may have to think about how best to do it. Several further descriptions may come to mind, not all of which are actually correct. Which, then, shall we say is the full but implicit one? Once we see the function of a referential description, however, we need not suppose that there is any one description recoverable from the speech act that is supposed uniquely to apply to the object referred to. The audience may through the partial description and various clues and cues know to what the speaker refers without being in possession of a description that uniquely fits it and which was implicit all along in the speaker's speech act. (ibid.)

Donnellan is not, then, arguing *from* incompleteness *to* referentiality; rather he seems to be claiming that the method of contextual supplementation is implausible *if the description in question is being used referentially*. Wettstein (1981) suggests that we have here the basis of a knock-down argument for a semantically distinct referential interpretation of descriptions. For according to Wettstein, in many cases where an incomplete description is used there will simply be *no* adequate way of contextually deriving a complete description. And the only plausible way out, he suggests, is to concede that in such a case the description is functioning as a *demonstrative* referring expression and that consequently the proposition expressed is object-dependent rather than descriptive. On this account, then, the description takes as its semantical value the object the speaker intended to communicate something about (in the sense of 14.5).

To fix ideas, let's consider Wettstein's argument as applied to one of his own examples. Suppose, on a particular occasion of utterance, "the table" is taken to be elliptical for "the table in room 209 of Camden Hall at [time] t_1." According to Wettstein, this proposal is unworkable because there are a number of nonequivalent ways of filling out the descriptive condition to make it uniquely applicable and no principled way to choose between the resulting descriptions. For instance, "the table on which Wettstein carved his name at [time] t_2" might well be satisfied by, and only by, the unique object that satisfies the descriptive condition "table in room 209 of Camden Hall at t_1." Since it is the descriptive condition rather than the denotation that makes it into the proposition expressed, on Russell's account the particular choice of uniquely-denoting description seems to be crucial: a different description means a different proposition. And this apparently leaves the Russellian with the embarrassing task of deciding which of these nonequivalent descriptions is the correct one.

According to Wettstein, it is "implausible in the extreme" to suppose that the situation of utterance somehow enables the hearer to recover the correctly completed description, viz., the one the speaker intended. In many cases, there will simply be no such indication. Moreover, in many cases it doesn't even make sense to ask which of a batch of nonequivalent, codenoting descriptions is *the correct one*. What criterion would one use in deciding which description is the correct one? The one that figures in the speaker's intentions?

In many cases ... the speaker will have no such determinate intention. If the speaker is asked which Russellian description(s) was implicit in his utterance of "the table" he will not ordinarily be able to answer. "Although I meant to refer to that table" our speaker may well reply, "I don't think I meant to refer to it *as* the table in in room 209 of Camden Hall at t_1 as opposed to, say, *as* the table at which the author of *The Persistence of Objects* is sitting at t_1. Nor did I intend to refer to it *as* the table in 209 *and* the table at which the author ... as opposed to, say, just *as* the table in 209." (chapter 12, this volume, p. 263)

If we can't, even by enlisting the help of the speaker, determine which complete description the incomplete description is elliptical for, Wettstein argues, it doesn't make sense to say that there *is* some such correct, complete description.

According to Wettstein, the entire problem can be sidestepped by endorsing the neo-Russellian conception of an object-dependent proposition and treating the description as a referring expression that contributes just an object to the proposition expressed. In short, the description is to be viewed as a device of *demonstrative reference*. Embarrassing questions about the complete descriptive content are then circumvented, as it is the *object itself*, rather than any particular descriptive condition, that makes it into the proposition expressed. We can call this the Argument from Incompleteness for a referential interpretation of descriptions.

The first sign that something is amiss here is the fact that the argument seems to go through just as well with other quantifiers and with descriptions used *non*referentially. Consider again the sentence

(2) Everyone was sick

uttered in response to a question about last night's dinner party. On the explicit approach, the quantifier "everyone" (as it is used on this occasion) might be viewed as elliptical for "everyone at my dinner party last night," "everyone who ate at my house last night," or some other quantifier of the form "every *F*" that denotes everyone who came to the dinner party I had last night. Since the descriptive content is different in each case, the precise character of the proposition expressed depends upon which of these codenoting quantifiers is selected. It is clear, then, that Wettstein has put his finger on a very important fact about elliptical analyses of incomplete quantifiers (and perhaps ellipsis quite generally); but it is beginning to look as though no real support for a referential interpretation of descriptions is going to come out of this.

Ironically, this becomes much clearer when we take into account Wettstein's own remarks on incomplete descriptions used *non*referentially. Consider the case of the detective who comes across Smith's body and has no idea who killed him. Rather than uttering "Smith's murderer is insane" or "The man who murdered Smith is insane," the detective simply says,

(3) The murderer is insane.

According to Wettstein,

As in the cases of referential uses ... there will be any number of ways to fill out the description so as to yield a Russellian description (e.g., "Harry Smith's murderer," "the murderer of Joan Smith's husband," "the murderer of the junior senator from New Jersey in 1975") and in many cases there will be nothing about the circumstances of utterance or the intentions of the speaker which would indicate that any of these Russellian descriptions is the correct one. (ibid., p. 266–267)

As Wettstein observes, here he is in conflict with Donnellan, who suggests that the elliptical proposal *will* work for descriptions used nonreferentially. Indeed, Wettstein concedes, on Russellian grounds, that the objection he has raised cannot be overcome by treating *this* occurrence of "the murderer" as a device of demonstrative reference: "One fully understands the proposition without having any idea who murdered Smith" (p. 267). We seem to be stuck:

[1] "the murderer" is not elliptical for some Russellian description, and [2] no appeal to the referent of "the murderer" will account for propositional determinacy. (1981, p. 267)

Given his endorsement of [1], Wettstein then makes a very odd suggestion. Although this occurrence of the description "the murderer" is not referential, Wettstein suggests that demonstrative reference still plays a role in a proper characterization of its content:

For in uttering, "the murderer is insane" in the presence of the mutilated body, the speaker relies on the context to reveal *whose* murder is in question. The speaker, that is, makes an *implicit* reference to the victim. (ibid.)

Recall that Wettstein's own account of descriptions used referentially is supposed to be immune to the problem of codenoting, nonequivalent descriptions that he has raised for the Russellian. The reason, of course, is that Wettstein explicitly endorses the neo-Russellian conception of an object-dependent proposition: it is the object itself (rather than any descriptive condition or sense) that gets into the proposition expressed. But on this conception of an object-dependent proposition, in the example we are considering there is simply no difference between saying that there is an "implicit reference" to the victim and saying that the incomplete description "the murderer" is elliptical for a uniquely denoting description, such as "the murderer of *that man*" (where "that man" refers to the victim), or "the murderer of *him*" (where "him" refers to the victim), or "*his* murderer" (where "his" refers to the victim), all of which contribute the same thing to the proposition expressed, viz., the descriptive condition *murderer-of-b* where *b* is the victim himself rather than some description of *b*. Wettstein is just mistaken in claiming that "the murderer" is "not elliptical for some Russellian description" (ibid.); the proposition expressed by (3) is given by (4):

(4) [the *x*: *x* murdered *b*] (*x* is insane).

It is unclear why Wettstein thinks the description in (4) is non-Russellian. One possibility is that he has conflated (a) the notion of a *referential description* (i.e., a description that is interpreted referentially), and (b) the notion of *a description containing a referential component*. An alternative diagnosis is that he is unwilling to countenance descriptions containing relational predicates like "murderer-of-*b*," where "*b*" is a referential term. But this is certainly not a constraint the *Russellian* is obliged to work under.[53] If "*R*" is a binary relational predicate, "*b*" is a name, and "*x*" is a variable, then "*Rbx*" is an open sentence, and "[the *x*: *Rbx*]" is a perfectly good definite description [see (2.6) of *Descriptions*]. Perhaps Wettstein is just unwilling to allow the Russellian access to descriptions containing context-sensitive elements such as demonstratives or indexicals. But again, there is no reason to constrain the Russellian in this way (14.3). (As Grice (1970) observes, one of Russell's (1905) own examples of a definite description is "my son.") To the extent that one countenances indexical and demonstrative referring expressions—and Wettstein certainly does—if "*b*" is an indexical or demonstrative, then "[the *x*: *Rbx*]" is a perfectly good Russellian description, albeit one with an indexical or demonstrative component. I submit, then, that if descriptions may contain overtly referential components (including indexical and demonstrative components), then there is nothing to prevent the ellipsed elements of incomplete descriptions from being referential. And this is very different from saying that the *description* is interpreted referentially.[54]

The completion of incomplete descriptions with referential components is implicit in Evans' discussion of incompleteness:

... travelling in a car through the United States, I might pass through a town whose roads are particularly bumpy, and in consequence say "They ought to impeach the mayor." I do not intend my audience to identify the object spoken about as one of which he has information; I intend merely that he take me to be saying that the mayor of this town, through which we are passing, ought to be impeached, and this statement is adequately represented quantificationally. (1982, p. 324)

Evans is surely right to claim that in his example there is no intention to identify any individual—and hence no temptation to regard this particular utterance of the incomplete description "the mayor" as referential. Moreover, Evans suggests that he (the speaker) *would* be able to complete the description in a uniquely appropriate way, and supplies a plausible completion using referential rather than descriptive material. As the neo-

Russellian would put it, it is the *town itself* rather than some descriptive characterization of the town that gets into the descriptive condition and thereby into the proposition expressed.

There is no reason, of course, why descriptions used referentially should not also be completed using referential material, thus avoiding the problem raised by nonequivalent codenoting descriptions. As Soames (1986) remarks, this suggestion is very natural for descriptions such as "the Mayor" or "the murderer," where an additional argument place can be made available for a particular individual specified by the context of utterance. But with examples like "the table" (which Strawson originally used to attack Russell, and upon which Wettstein fastens in mounting his own attack) it is true that there is no natural argument position to be made available. However, the contextual coordinates (14.3) of an utterance provide further nondescriptive material. One way of construing Sellars's (1954) original proposal for dealing with "the table" is that reference is made to the spatial coordinate. On Sellar's account, an utterance of "the table" is treated as elliptical for (e.g.) "the table *over here*," or "the table *over there*," both which of course contain indexicals sensitive to the spatial coordinate p rather than additional descriptive material.[55] Wettstein's own list of complete descriptions for which "the table" might be viewed as elliptical includes only sentences containing descriptions completed with additional *descriptive* material ("the table in room 209 of Camden Hall at t_1," "the table at which the author of *The Persistence of Objects* is sitting at t_1," and so on). This is the weak point in his discussion. The semanticist who regards (utterances of) incomplete quantifiers —including incomplete descriptions—as elliptical for complete quantifiers is under no obligation to treat the ellipsed material as free of referring expressions and indexicals.

An account of how incomplete descriptions are to be treated is not required solely to ward off the Argument from Incompleteness. First, incompleteness affects descriptions used *non*referentially, so a general account of the phenomenon cannot be based on a referential interpretation. Second, incompleteness affects quantifiers more generally, not just definite descriptions. And to that extent, appeals to contextual coordinates and ellipsed material are independently required by any adequate theory of natural language quantification.[56]

It should be noted that the problem of incompleteness can also emerge with descriptions used *anaphorically*, as in (5) and (6):

(5) I bought *a donkey* and a horse last week. For some reason *the donkey* will not eat anything.

(6) *Three women* and *a man* arrived in a large truck. *The women* got out and began dancing in the road while *the man* played the accordian.

In these cases, it is plausible to suppose (as Evans (1977) has argued) that the descriptions in question are completed using material from the clause containing their antecedents.

14.8   Concluding Remarks

We have seen in this chapter that the Theory of Descriptions is not threatened by the fact that context plays important and complex roles in the way sentences containing descriptions are understood. First, index-icality is a pervasive feature of natural language, and the fact that quantifiers, including definite descriptions, may contain indexical components does nothing to undermine either the schematic theory of quantification [presented in chapter 4, this volume, 4.2–4.6] or the place of the Theory of Descriptions within that theory. Second, the fact that a speaker may use a definite description to convey an object-dependent proposition poses no threat to this picture; in particular it provides no support for the view that descriptions are ambiguous between Russellian and referential interpretations. Again, the phenomenon is one that is not specific to descriptions but something we find with quantifiers quite generally. Once one takes into account (a) a very natural distinction between the proposition expressed and the proposition(s) meant, (b) the nature and role of context, (c) communicative aims or goals, and (d) our abilities to make certain elementary inferences, the general form of an explanation of this phenomenon comes clearly into view. Finally, no support for a referential interpretation of descriptions can be derived from the fact that quantifiers may be superficially incomplete.

Notes

1. Mitchell (1962, pp. 84–85) writes:

Definite descriptions occurring as the subjects of sentences, have at least two distinct functions, which may be illustrated by two sets of examples:

(1) (a) "The Prime Minister presides at Cabinet meetings"
    (b) "The Sovereign of Great Britain is the head of the Commonwealth"
    (c) "The man who wrote this unsigned letter had a bad pen"

(2) (a) "The Prime Minister has invited me to lunch"
   (b) "The Queen made a tour of the Commonwealth"
   (c) "The author of *Waverley* limped."

It is not difficult to see that the grammatical subjects of the sentences quoted in List 1 are not used—as proper names, for instance, are used—to refer uniquely. For "The Prime Minister" and "the Sovereign" we can substitute, without change of meaning, "Whoever is Prime Minister" and "Whoever is Sovereign.". . . With the sentences in List 2 the case is different. The subject phrases serve to identify individuals, and what is predicated in each case is predicated of the individuals so identified.

2. Construed as a general account of such readings, this position has been falsified by Cartwright (1968) and Kripke (1977), both of whom produce examples whose *de re* readings are not correctly captured by referential interpretations. For discussions, see 4.2 and 4.4 [of *Descriptions*].

3. It is tempting to think of Donnellan as simply labeling Mitchell's distinction (see, e.g., Davies, 1981). However, I do not think this is quite right. First, Mitchell seems to think that his two "functions" of descriptions are tied to the particular sentences used, whereas Donnellan argues that the same sentence may be used with either an attributive or a referential "reading" of the description it contains. Second, Mitchell's (1c)—see note 1—is very like the sorts of examples Donnellan uses to illustrate his attributive use in that the proposition expressed seems to be "about" an individual only under a description. However, (1a) and (1b) seem to be "about" a particular role or position that may be filled by different individuals on different occasions. Thus I am not much inclined to see Mitchell's non-identificatory function as a genuine precursor of Donnellan's attributive use. In particular, it seems to me that an utterance of (1b) could be true even if there were not, at the time of utterance, a Sovereign of Great Britain. Suppose the Queen dies and for various complex reasons a constitutional crisis ensues that somehow prevents Prince Charles or anyone else from taking the throne. A true utterance of (1b) might still be made.

François Récanati has pointed out to me that something very close to Donnellan's distinction can be found in the work of the seventeenth-century French philosopher Antoine Arnauld, author of the *Port-Royal Logic*. See Dominicy (1984), pp. 123–127.

4. Grice also echoes the point, made by Mitchell (1962) and Donnellan (1966), that in case (1), one may legitimately insert "whoever he may be" after the definite description. In view of certain worries pointed out by Searle (1979), I have not emphasized this characteristic of case (1).

5. This is also the view of Hampshire (1959), Geach (1962), Kripke (1972, 1977), Wiggins (1975, 1980), Castañeda (1977), Sainsbury (1979), Searle (1979), Klein (1980), Davies (1981), Evans (1982), Salmon (1982), Davidson (1986), and Soames (1986). There are important differences of detail in these proposals, but at the same time there is a consensus that the phenomenon of referential usage does not warrant the postulation of a semantical ambiguity in the definite article. (My indebtedness to the detailed discussions by Kripke, Sainsbury, Searle, and Davies will become clear as this chapter unfolds.)

6. This way of characterizing the alleged semantical significance of referential usage is explicit in (e.g.) Peacocke (1975), Hornsby (1977), and Kaplan (1978); it also seems to be what Donnellan (1978) has in mind. As both Kripke (1977) and Searle (1979) emphasize, for those who advocate a *semantical* distinction between Russellian and referential descriptions, there is still the problem of providing an account of *when*, exactly, a definite description *is* referential (see 14.5). The importance of this fact seems to be recognized by Donnellan (1978).

7. The argument implicit in this remark is unpacked in note 37. In places, Donnellan (1966) suggests that he is highlighting a "pragmatic" rather than a semantical ambiguity. But as Searle (1979) points out, it is unclear what a "pragmatic ambiguity" is supposed to be:

"I went to the bank" is semantically ambiguous. "Flying planes can be dangerous" is syntactically ambiguous. But what is a pragmatic ambiguity? Is "You are standing on my foot" supposed to be pragmatically ambiguous because in some contexts its utterance can be more then just a statement of fact? If so, then every sentence is indefinitely "pragmatically ambiguous." If we had a notion of "pragmatic ambiguity" we would also have a notion of "pragmatic univocality" but in fact neither notion has any clear sense at all. (Searle, 1979, p. 150, note 3)

All things considered, it seems to me that the (semantical) ambiguity thesis is held by Rundle (1965), Donnellan (1966, 1968, 1979), Stalnaker (1972), Partee (1972), Peacocke (1975), Hornsby (1977), Kaplan (1978), Devitt (1981), Wettstein (1981, 1983), Récanati (1981, 1986, 1989), Fodor and Sag (1982), and Barwise and Perry (1983), among others. Récanati (1989) explicitly denies that his view entails a semantical ambiguity; I disagree. For discussion, see note 37.

A parallel semantical thesis for *indefinite* descriptions appears to be held by (e.g.) Partee (1972), Chastain (1975), Donnellan (1978), Wilson (1977), Fodor and Sag (1982), Barwise and Perry (1983), and Stich (1986), among others. For discussion, see King (1988) and Ludlow and Neale (1991).

8. An expression ζ occurs in a nonextensional context just in case ζ is within the scope of a nonextensional operator.... [A] unary, sentential, sentence-forming operator O is extensional just in case the truth-value of "$O(\phi)$" depends only upon the truth-value of the embedded sentence ϕ. Thus, the contexts created by modal operators and attitude verb frames are nonextensional.

9. [See chaps. 4 and 5 of *Descriptions* for a fuller discussion of the latter two arguments. Ed.]

10. I was tempted to borrow Kaplan's (1977) technical terms "character" and "content." However, any suggestion of commitment to Kaplan's intensional machinery is best avoided by using different terminology. I have, however, drawn on Kaplan's informal remarks on indexicals and demonstratives in which his character/content distinction is introduced.

11. In the period with which I am primarily concerned (1905–1919) Russell came to view the class of genuine names as restricted to just (e.g.) "this" and "that," which makes his (albeit later) talk of demonstratives as not "mere" names rather misleading in the present context.

12. See (e.g.) Montague (1968), Lewis (1975), and Kaplan (1977).

13. Further contextual coordinates may be required to capture other essential features of context. For discussion, see Lewis, (1975) p. 175.

14. $(\lambda X)\zeta$ represents a function from objects of the type over which X ranges to objects of the same type as ζ. The Russellian could take the semantical value of a description [the x: Fx] to be the function denoted by (λP) ([the x: Fx] (Px)), i.e., as a function from properties to propositions. See Montague (1970, 1973).

15. We can construct analogous cases for a description such as "your mother," which contains an element sensitive to the addressee coordinate a; "that man's mother," which is sensitive to the demonstration coordinate d; "the current U.S. President," sensitive to the temporal coordinate t; and "the woman who was just sitting here," sensitive to the temporal and spatial coordinates t and p.

16. It is open to argue that (6) is actually ambiguous according as the pronoun is to be given an anaphoric or nonanaphoric (e.g., demonstrative) reading (see Evans (1977, 1980) for discussion). The general form of the problem the hearer is faced with is the same.

17. As argued by Sperber and Wilson (1986), even if we anchor indexicals, assign referents, and fully disambiguate an utterance, very often H will *still* not be able to properly characterize the proposition expressed because of vagueness, ellipsis, and so on. As they put it, sentence meaning *radically* underdetermines the proposition expressed.

18. Wittgenstein, *Tractatus Logico-Philosophicus*, 4.024.

19. Part of Grice's project involves providing an analysis of meaning that does not presuppose any linguistic or otherwise semantical concepts, so (G1) is not a genuine Gricean condition because ϕ is implicitly understood to be a *sentence*. More appropriate would be the following:

(G2) By producing u, S means that p only if for some audience H,
       S produced u intending:
       1. H actively to entertain the thought that p, and
       2. H to recognize that S intends (1)

where u is any piece of behavior the production of which is a candidate for meaning something. For the purposes of this essay, (G1) will suffice because (a) I am not attempting any sort of reductive analysis, and (b) the examples I am most concerned with all involve linguistic utterances. In cases where u is an utterance of the sentence ϕ, I see no harm (for present purposes) in treating as interchangeable the locutions "by producing u, S means that p" and "by uttering ϕ, S means that p."

Grice's attempts to provide necessary and sufficient conditions for utterer's meaning make use of a third intention designed to rule out cases where some feature of the utterance in question makes it completely obvious that p. Grice was worried by cases like the following: (i) Herod presents Salome with the head of St. John the Baptist on a charger; (ii) in response to an invitation to play squash, Bill displays his bandaged leg. According to Grice, we do not want to say that Herod *meant* that St. John the Baptist was dead. Nor do we want to say that Bill *meant* that his leg was bandaged. (We may well want to say that he meant that he could not play squash, or even that he had a bad leg, but not that his leg was bandaged.) Thus Grice suggests the addition of a third clause, the rough import of which is that S intend H's recognition of S's first intention to function as a reason for H to actively entertain the thought that p. Candidate conditions of the form of (G2) are therefore superseded by conditions of the form of (G3):

(G3) By producing u, S means that p only if for some audience H,
       S produced u intending:
       1. H to actively entertain the thought that p,
       2. H to recognize that S intends (1), and
       3. H's recognition that S intends (1) to function, at least in part, as a reason for (1).

It is not clear to me that the additional constraint in (3) is necessary. The same degree of manifestness seems to be present in certain cases involving properly linguistic utterances. Consider an utterance of, e.g., "I can speak English," or an utterance of "I can speak in squeaky voice" said in a squeaky voice (I owe this example to Neil Smith), or an utterance of "I am over here" bawled across a crowded room at someone known to be looking for the utterer (this example is due to Schiffer (1972)). In none of these cases is there a temptation to say that the speaker did not *mean* what he or she said. As I have stated it, I am not sure whether clause (3) really blocks such cases, but in any event, in the light of the similarities between these cases and those that worried Grice, I do not feel the need for an additional constraint on utterer's meaning, such as (3), that is supposed to prevent (e.g.) Herod from meaning that St. John the Baptist was dead, or Bill from meaning that his leg was bandaged. On this matter, see also Schiffer (1972) and Sperber and Wilson (1986).

20. Grice's wording suggests that a particular maxim or submaxim concerns only what is said (e.g., "Do not say what you believe to be false") while another concerns, perhaps, what is *meant* (e.g., "Be relevant"). (I owe this observation to Deirdre Wilson.) However, except for those submaxims under Manner (perhaps) that apply only to what is said, I think we must interpret Grice as allowing a violation of a maxim at the level of what is said to be over-ridden by adherence to that maxim at the level of what is implicated. This seems to me to be the only way to make sense of his account of flouting; i.e., blatantly violating a maxim at the level of what is said but adhering to it at the level of what is implicated does not involve a violation of the CP.

A variety of complications for Grice's theory are discussed by Sperber and Wilson (1981, 1986) and Wilson and Sperber (1981, 1986), who utilize some of Grice's insights in their *relevance*-based approach to utterance interpretation. Since writing the body of this chapter, I have come to believe (mostly through conversations with Dan Sperber) that my own discussion might well have been facilitated had I made use of Sperber and Wilson's theory rather than Grice's.

21. Consider an utterance of "She is poor and she is honest. Moreover, I don't think she's honest." The linguistic transgression here is not of the order of an outright contradiction; rather it is more like an instance of Moore's paradox. Nor

will contradiction ensue in cases involving an attempted cancellation of what Grice calls *conventional* implicature. Unlike conversational implicatures, conventional implicatures arise regardless of context and are (at least in part) attributable to linguistic convention. To borrow one of Grice's (1961) examples, there is no truth-conditional difference between "She is poor and honest" and "She is poor but honest," but we are still inclined to say that these sentences differ in meaning. On Grice's account, an assertion of the latter would involve an additional "non-central" speech act indicating the speaker's (or perhaps someone else's) attitude towards the propositional content of the central speech act (i.e., the assertion that she is poor and honest), an attitude of unexpectedness or contrast. This Grice calls a *conventional* implicature.

There are complex issues involved in spelling out Grice's remarks on this topic, in particular the extent to which the precise content of a given conventional implicature is conversationally determined, i.e., established by recourse to the maxims of conversation and not just to linguistic meaning. As Grice (1961, p. 127) observes, in the example just discussed there is no prospect of characterizing the conventional implicature as a "presupposition" in any interesting sense of this much-abused term: even if the implicature were false, i.e., even if there were no reason on Earth to suppose that poverty and honesty contrasted in any way, what is asserted could still be false, say if she were *rich* and honest. I am here indebted to discussion with Paul Grice.

22. In such a case, Grice would say that you "made as if to say" that p, and implicated that q, as long as you had no intention of inducing (or activating) in your interlocutor the thought that p.

23. Cancellability cannot be a sufficient condition because of ambiguity. Consider the following exchange. A and B meet in the street:

A: Where are you going?
B: I am going down to the bank to get some money.
A: Who do you bank with?
B: I'm sorry, I don't understand.
A: You said you were going down to the bank to get some money.
B: And so I am; I keep my money buried in a chest down by the river.

One might be tempted to argue that B's first utterance carries with it the implication that B is about to visit some sort of financial institution, and that his third utterance succeeds in cancelling this implication. Of course, no one would be tempted to argue that "bank" is unambiguous in English; but since Grice wanted to account for certain alleged ambiguities of philosophical importance in terms of conversational implicature rather than lexical (or syntactical) ambiguity, he cannot (and does not) take cancellability as a sufficient condition for implicature.

24. As pointed out by (e.g.) Sperber and Wilson (1986), since q is simply introduced without explanation in step (c), this schema cannot be construed as a characterization of any sort of method for actually *calculating* implicatures, but only as a method for establishing whether or not a particular implication qualifies as a conversational implicature.

25. As Chomsky has emphasized, the syntactician is in a very similar position with respect to intuitions concerning well-formedness (grammaticality). And as Rawls (1971) has pointed out, more or less the same considerations carry over from syntax to ethics.

26. I shall restrict attention to cases where "and" conjoins sentences for the simple reason that it seems unlikely, to me at least, that all occurrences of "and" that conjoin (e.g.) noun phrases can be analysed in terms of logical conjunction. While a sentence like

(i) Russell and Whitehead lived in Cambridge

might be analysable in terms of the conjunction of (ii) and (iii),

(ii) Russell lived in Cambridge

(iii) Whitehead lived in Cambridge

such a proposal is quite unsuitable for

(iv) Russell and Whitehead wrote *Principia Mathematica*.

We have here yet another problem raised by sentences involving plural noun phrases that admit of collective readings.

27. The results of some psycholinguistic experiments suggest that an "order-of-mention" strategy is applied fairly blindly in the earlier stages of language acquisition by children confronted with utterances containing the words "before" and "after." In particular, children appear to grasp "*A* before *B*" and "After *A*, *B*" before they grasp "Before *B*, *A*" and "*B* after *A*." See Clark (1971) and Johnson (1975).

28. Even if it is possible to treat the temporal and causal implications that attach to utterances in which "and" is conjoining sentences in terms of conversational implicature, Carston (1988) points out that it is not at all clear how to extend the proposal to sentences like

(i) Tell me a secret and I'll tell you one

(ii) Shout at me again and I'll quit

in which "and" seems to have the force of "if ... then."

Carston proposes a way of holding onto the idea that "and" is unambiguous while at the same time allowing for a difference between the proposition expressed by "*p* and *q*" and "*p* & *q*" on the grounds that linguistic meaning underdetermines the proposition expressed. Carston's approach may well inherit the positive characteristics of Grice's approach without inheriting many of its problems.

29. According to (e.g.) Gazdar (1979), an utterance of a sentence of the form "some *F*s are *G*s" gives rise to a generalized conversational implicature to the effect that the speaker knows that some *F*s are not *G*s. But as Soames (1982, pp. 533–537) points out, it is more plausible to suppose that the generalized implicature is really that the speaker does not know whether all *F*s are *G*s, an additionally particularized implicature to the effect that the speaker knows (or believes) that some *F*s are not *G*s, arising if the speaker can be presumed to know

whether or not all *F*s are *G*s. In order to avoid getting immersed in the details of this type of example, I have deliberately refrained from saying that the speaker conversationally implicates that some of the deaths were not accidental, or that the speaker believes (or knows) that some of the deaths were not accidental, opting instead for talk of the speaker implicating that he or she is willing to entertain the possibility that some *F*s are not *G*s.

30. Furthermore, as Martin Davies has pointed out to me, parity of reasoning would require that if *S* knew of *a, b, c, d*, and *e* that they were all of the *F*s in existence, *S* could not use "all *F*s" as a quantifier. The real force of this point will emerge once we turn to referential uses of other quantifiers.

31. The existence of certain object-dependent beliefs on the part of the speaker is sometimes taken to suffice for a "referential" or "specific" use of an *indefinite* description in the literature on this topic (see, e.g., Fodor and Sag (1982)). In my opinion, this leads to considerable confusion. For discussion, see Ludlow and Neale (1991).

32. Although there are counterexamples to (A2), I shall ignore them in what follows. The type of patching that is required would take us too far astray, and after all, I am only trying to provide the referentialist with a workable account of referential usage that can be utilized in conjunction with (A1), I am not trying to present a watertight conceptual analysis. The conjunction of (A1) and (A2) provides the referentialist with *a far more plausible position* than does the conjunction of (A1) with any alternative characterization of referential usage I have seen. (As Kripke (1977) and Searle (1979) observe, Donnellan's (1966) positive characterizations of referential and attributive usage lead to a classification that is neither exclusive nor exhaustive and problematic borderline cases can easily be constructed (on this point, see also Davies, 1981). No doubt the sorts of considerations that Kripke and Searle adduce could also be used to undermine (A2), but it still seems to me to provide the referentialist with the most reasonable position available.)

33. In conversation, it has more than once been suggested that the distinction between referential$_D$ and referential$_N$ uses is pedantic since the claim made by the referentialist is just the broad claim that descriptions used referentially function as referring expressions. But the distinction can only seem pedantic to those who presuppose a neo-Russellian conception of an object-dependent proposition. To someone who is as sensitive as Evans to the important differences between names and demonstratives, the distinction between referential$_D$ and referential$_N$ uses of descriptions will be vital if a semantically distinct referential interpretation turns out to be necessary. I do not want to presuppose any particular account of object-dependence; my reasons for adhering to the distinction concern satisfaction of the Justification Requirement.

34. Such an ambiguity is argued for by Chastain (1975), Wilson (1978), Donnellan (1979). Fodor and Sag (1982), Barwise and Perry (1983), and Stich (1986). For problems with this view, see King (1988) and Ludlow and Neale (1991). As Kripke (1977) points out, many of the considerations that favor a unitary Russellian account of definite descriptions carry over *mutatis mutandis* to indefinite descriptions.

35. This point is made by Sainsbury (1979), Davies (1981), and Blackburn (1984). The example I have used is based on an example due to Davies.

36. To the extent that such schemata seem to be adequate for many cases involving referential uses of descriptions, and to the extent that purely descriptive grounds for an assertion that the F is G are the exception rather than the rule, we might view such schemata as having the status of interpretive heuristics. More or less this suggestion is made by Klein (1980), though he does not distinguish between referential$_N$ and referential$_D$ uses.

37. This view has been contested by Récanati (1989) on the grounds that one can endorse (A1) and (A2) without being committed to an ambiguity in the definite article. I am baffled by this claim. Récanati explicitly assumes something akin to a three-way Gricean distinction between (a) the linguistic meaning of a sentence ϕ, (b) the proposition expressed by a particular utterance u of ϕ by a speaker S, and (c) the proposition(s) S meant by u. By analogy with the semantics of indexical and demonstrative referring expressions, Récanati suggests that a difference in the proposition expressed by distinct utterances of "the F is G" does not correspond to distinct linguistic meanings of this sentence (or two linguistic meanings of the description "the F" or two linguistic meanings of the definite article "the").

To fix ideas, let's return to the semantics of demonstratives. If I point to Récanati and say

(i) That man is French

I express a true object-dependent proposition about Récanati. If I point to David Lewis and utter (i) I express a false object-dependent proposition about Lewis. Of course, we do not have to say that (i) is ambiguous. It has a unique linguistic meaning; but because it contains an indexical component sensitive to a contextual coordinate, it may be used on different occasions to express different object-dependent propositions. In cases in which the proposition expressed exhausts the proposition(s) meant, we get the following picture (F1):

(F1)   linguistic meaning (LM): $[\![$ that F is G $]\!]$

        semantic value/proposition expressed (PE): $Gb, Gc, \ldots Gz$
                                                          $|$ $|$ $|$
        propositions(s) meant (PM): $Gb, Gc, \ldots Gz$

where each chain represents a distinct utterance of "that F is G."

I have assumed until now that the referential use of a description "the F" may be captured in one of two ways, which might be pictured as follows:

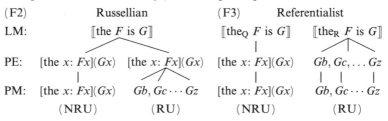

(F2)   Russellian   (F3)   Referentialist

LM: $[\![$ the F is G $]\!]$ $[\![$ the$_Q$ F is G $]\!]$ $[\![$ the$_R$ F is G $]\!]$

PE: [the x: Fx](Gx)   [the x: Fx](Gx)   [the x: Fx](Gx) $Gb, Gc, \ldots Gz$
           $|$ $|$ $|$ $|$ $|$ $|$
PM: [the x: Fx](Gx) $Gb, Gc \cdots Gz$ [the x: Fx](Gx) $Gb, Gc \cdots Gz$

         (NRU)   (RU)   (NRU)   (RU)

where "NRU" and "RU" signify nonreferential and referential usage, respectively. For the Russellian "the F is G" has one linguistic meaning, represented as ⟦the F is G⟧; for the referentialist it has two linguistic meanings, represented as ⟦the$_Q$ F is G⟧ and ⟦the$_R$ F is G⟧.

Underlying the picture of the referentialist's position given in (F3) is the following argument: (i) if a particular utterance u of "the F is G" expresses the object-independent proposition that whoever or whatever is uniquely F is also G, and a distinct utterance u^* of "the F is G" expresses the object-dependent proposition that b is G, then the sentence "the F is G" is semantically ambiguous, i.e., the sentence has two (or more) linguistic meanings (in the sense of 14.3); (ii) if the sentence "the F is G" is ambiguous and the predicate "is G" is unambiguous, then the definite description "the F" is ambiguous, i.e., the description has two (or more) linguistic meanings; (iii) if the description "the F" is ambiguous and the predicate "F" is unambiguous, then the definite article "the" is ambiguous, i.e., the article has two (or more) linguistic meanings.

It appears to be Récanati's view that descriptions can be treated on the model of indexicals and demonstratives, i.e., on the model of (F1) rather than (F3). That is, the sentence "the F is G" does *not* have two linguistic meanings; rather, it is "indexical" and expresses either an object-dependent or an object-independent proposition according as the description is used referentially or nonreferentially. Récanati is, then, advocating the following picture:

(F4)   LM: ⟦the F is G⟧

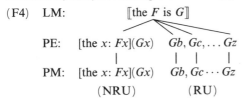

PE: [the x: Fx](Gx) $Gb, Gc, \ldots Gz$
         | | | |
PM: [the x: Fx](Gx) $Gb, Gc \cdots Gz$
            (NRU)   (RU)

I find this proposal puzzling. The word "I" is unambiguous because it always refers to the speaker; a simple sentence of the form "I am G" is unambiguous because it always expresses an *object-dependent* proposition about the speaker. The demonstrative expression "that F" is unambiguous because it always refers to the object of the speaker's demonstration and a simple sentence of the form "that F is G" is unambiguous because it always expresses an *object-dependent* proposition about the object of the speaker's demonstration. On Récanati's proposal, not only may different utterances of "the F is G" express different *object-dependent* propositions, but other utterances of this same sentence may express the *object-independent* proposition that whatever is uniquely F is G. It all depends on whether the description is used referentially or nonreferentially.

It seems to me highly artificial to say that "the F is G," "the F" and "the" are "unambiguous" on this proposal. On some occasions of use "the F" *refers* (or is supposed to *refer*) to some contextually determined individual and the proposition expressed by "the F is G" is object-dependent, whereas on other occasions of use "the F" does *not* refer (and is not even intended to refer), and the proposition expressed is a complex quantificational affair. Since two utterly distinct *types* of proposition may be expressed, I fail to see how a theory with such flexibility can fail to be a theory that is postulating a semantical ambiguity. Despite Récanati's remarks to the contrary, it seems to me that his claim that "the F" is unambiguous within his theory is close to being on a par with the claim that the noun "bank" is unambiguous: on some occasions it is used for ground alongside a river and on others it is used for a type of financial institution.

Of course, even if Récanati is right that one can endorse (A1) and (A2) without postulating a genuine lexical ambiguity, a unitary Russellian theory of descriptions is still simpler than a theory that allows the proposition expressed to be either object-independent or object-dependent depending upon the context of utterance. Furthermore, the putative coherence of such a theory would not demonstrate that (A1) is true and (A3) is false. (There are also problems internal to Récanati's own positive proposal that I shall not address here.)

38. The general observation that one may succeed in conveying something about an individual by using a description that the individual does not satisfy is due to Hampshire (1959), p. 203. (See also Geach, 1962, and Linsky, 1963, 1966.) Indeed, Hampshire's brief discussion of descriptions (pp. 201–204) appears to anticipate quite a lot of subsequent discussion that appeals to misdescription and the distinction between the proposition expressed and the proposition(s) meant.

39. See (e.g.) Kripke (1977), Sainsbury (1979), Searle (1979), Davies (1981), Evans (1982), and Blackburn (1984). As pointed out by Kripke and Searle, we find a similar tension in cases where a proper name is misapplied. To borrow Kripke's example, suppose two people A and B see Smith in the distance but mistake him for Jones. A says "Jones is up early." B replies "Yes, he's hard at work too." Devitt (1981) points out some further troubling features of this sort of example that suggest that the distinction between the proposition expressed and the proposition(s) meant will not clear up all of its complexities.

40. Responses to the Argument from Misdescription in the same vein are also presented by Wiggins (1975), and in rather more detail by Kripke (1977), Sainsbury (1979), Searle (1979), and Davies (1981). For remarks that anticipate the Gricean response to the Argument from Misdescription, see Hampshire (1959), pp. 201–204, and Geach (1962), p. 8.

41. Up to now, I have considered only cases in which the speaker is genuinely mistaken about who or what satisfies the description that is being employed. But as Donnellan (1966) points out, one might perfectly well use a description "the F" referentially without being sure that the individual one has in mind is the F; indeed, as Hampshire (1959), Donnellan (1966), Grice (1981), and others have pointed out, conceivably one might use the description "the F" while being quite sure that it does *not* apply to the individual one has in mind, or to any individual at all. The possibility of such cases does not force us to alter the general picture that has emerged so far, though it certainly adds interesting complications in providing an exact specification of when a description is being used referentially.

If the hearer is intended to reason as before, then such cases are no different from the ones we have been considering, except that [the $x: Fx](x = b)$, and very likely [the $x: Fx](Gx)$, will no longer furnish the speaker's grounds for his or her utterance. On the other hand, the speaker may be well aware that the hearer does not believe that *b* is the *F*, yet still think it possible to comunicate a singular proposition to the effect that *b* is *G* by uttering "the *F* is *G*." (For example, Donnellan considers a case in which both speaker and hearer are aware that the description "the king" does not strictly apply to the individual being referred to because that individual is a usurper; but they continue to use this description because they are fearful of reprisals. Another example: it may become the practice of the members of a certain group of individuals to use the description "the *F*" when they wish to say something about a certain individual. Of course, at a certain point one might well be inclined to treat this description as a name on a par with "The Holy Roman Empire" or "The Evening Star.") A variety of interesting cases can be constructed by tinkering with speakers' and hearers' beliefs about the satisfiers of descriptions and with beliefs about each others' beliefs, but the complexities involved do not seem to provide any insurmountable problems for the Russllian. Indeed, as Kripke (this volume, p. 251, note 22) points out, if anything, the fact that many of these cases—for instance, Donnellan's king/usurper case—look a lot like cases involving irony or "inverted commas" seems to actually *weaken* the case for a semantical ambiguity. After all, we want a pragmatic account of irony, not an account that appeals to distinct literal and ironical meanings of expressions. (Once again, these considerations seem to carry over *mutatis mutandis* to other quantifiers, especially indefinite descriptions. On this matter, see Ludlow and Neale (1991).)

42. Wettstein (1984) suggests that Salmon's argument turns on the mistaken assumption that a sentence relativized to a context of utterance *C* can be evaluated for truth or falsity at a possible world *w*, when in fact truth or falsity are properly predicated of the proposition expressed. But if Salmon is assuming a standard possible worlds semantics, it is unclear to me what technical or philosophical error Wettstein claims to have discovered in Salmon's discussion.

43. There seems to be no generally agreed upon label. Such phrases are known variously as *incomplete, improper, imperfect,* or *indefinite* definite descriptions.

44. According to Devitt (1981), incomplete descriptions "... are ones that are unsuitable for attributive use because only someone with crazy beliefs would use them: it is obvious that they do not denote" (p. 521). Peacocke's example is a clear counterexample to Devitt's claim, as are the examples from Donnellan (1968) and Evans (1982) quoted below.

45. This point is made by Quine (1940), Sellars (1954), Sainsbury (1979), Davies (1981), and Blackburn (1984).

46. Following Barwise and Cooper (1981), let's say that a quantifier $[Dx: Fx]$ is *persistent* just in case the following is a valid inference:

$[Dx: Fx](Gx)$
$[\text{every } x: Fx](Hx)$
_____
$[Dx: Hx](Gx)$

for arbitrary *G* and *H*. Strictly speaking, the particular problem concerning incompleteness that I am addressing surfaces only with nonpersistent quantifiers, though a derivative problem surfaces for persistent quantifiers. A precise generalization does not seem to be possible here because of complex issues to do with predication, but very roughly we can say the following. For nonpersistent quantifiers the problem is that $[Dx: Fx](Gx)$ might be false while $[Dx: Fx \& Hx](Gx)$ is true; for persistent quantifiers the problem is that $[Dx: Fx](Gx)$ might be true while $[Dx: Fx \& Hx](Gx)$ is false.

47. There seems to be an even more general issue here. As (e.g.) Sellars (1954) and Sperber and Wilson (1986) have stressed, in many cases the linguistic meaning of a sentence—or sentence fragment—radically underdetermines the proposition it is used to express on a given occasion. We have already considered the sort of contextual supplementation that is required where an utterance contains overtly indexical or demonstrative components; but context-sensitivity does not end there. Suppose I ask S how old he is and he replies, "Twenty-five." We want to say that S has expressed the proposition that he is twenty-five years old. Or take the sentence "This cup is mine." Here there is no obvious ellipsis, but depending upon the context of utterance I might use this sentence to express the proposition that (e.g.) this cup is owned by me, or that it is being drunk from by me, or that it is being used by me, or that it has been assigned to me.

48. One could, of course, maintain that incompleteness is of no consequence once one takes into account the distinction between the proposition expressed and the proposition(s) meant. The idea here would be that my utterance of "everybody was sick" expresses the manifestly false proposition that everybody was sick, but in the particular conversational setting it is very clear that I am attempting to *convey* the proposition that everybody who came to the dinner party I had last night was sick (standard forms of Gricean reasoning explaining the leap from the proposition expressed to the proposition meant). I know of no knock-down argument against this approach to incompleteness, but in view of the fact that context-dependence is such a ubiquitous feature of the use of natural language, it seems likely that the explicit and implicit methods yield predictions more in accordance with our intuitive ascriptions of truth and falsity.

49. When all is said and done, the explicit and implicit methods might turn out to be notational variants of one another. For remarks that suggest otherwise, see Davies (1981) and Soames (1986).

50. For similar suggestions, see also Quine (1940), Vendler (1967), Lewis (1973), Cresswell (1973), and Grice (1981).

51. As noted at the outset, the problem of incompleteness affects plural as well as singular descriptions. In what follows, I shall restrict attention to singular descriptions, though nearly everything I shall have to say ought to carry over *mutatis mutandis* to plurals.

52. Even Kripke (1977) and Evans (1982), both of whom are very sympathetic to a unitary Russellian interpretation of descriptions, suggest that incompleteness may be just enough of a problem for the Russellian to warrant the postulation of a referential interpretation.

53. This has been noted by, e.g., Sellars (1954), Grice (1970, 1981), Evans (1982), Salmon (1982), and Soames (1986). After the bulk of the present chapter was completed, Nathan Salmon drew my attention to a recent paper by Blackburn (1988) in which the same point is made in the context of a discussion of Wettstein's argument.

54. To be more precise, saying that a Russellian description "[the x: Rbx]" may contain a referential component "b" is very different from saying that the description is referential (in the intended sense) *as long as R is not the identity relation*. A phrase of the form "[the x: $x = b$]" is technically a Russellian definite description; but the claim that referential uses of descriptions do not require distinctive non-Russelian interpretations would indeed be hollow if the Russellian position could be maintained only by employing the identity relation to concoct descriptions of this form (e.g., "[the x: $x =$ that]"). There is nothing in the present work to suggest that descriptions of this form are required to account for referential usage. I am here indebted to Martin Davies.

55. The coordinates of a simple context $\langle s, a, \langle d_1, \ldots, d_n \rangle, t, p \rangle$ will not systematically supply a correct completion. Consider the incomplete description "the President." Suppose we are in the middle of a conversation right now somewhere in the U.S.A. and I say to you

(i) The President is very ill.

The fact that the utterance takes place in the U.S.A. does not guarantee that the description "the President" is elliptical for "the U.S. President." For suppose our entire conversation has been about the health of French politicians and I was in fact "talking about" the French President.

It may, at this stage, be tempting to add further coordinates to the formal notion of a context to cover such things as the *topic of discourse* and so on (see, e.g., Lewis, 1975). Husserl (1913, p. 85) suggests that "When a contemporary German speaks of "the Emperor," he means the present German Emperor." A literal reading of this remark suggests that one's nationality is the relevant coordinate! In 14.4, I argued that we should not expect to be able to provide a formal specification of those features of context that play a role in the calculation of (e.g.) conversational implicatures. (This is not to say, of course, that one cannot attempt to provide a specification of the sorts of principles hearers bring to bear on the interpretation process.) For essentially the same reason, I think it quite unlikely that an expansion of the formal notion of a context will be of much help in pinning down those factors that, on a given occasion of utterance, may play a role in the full specification of the content of an incomplete description. The important point to note here is that there is absolutely no requirement that a semantical theory be able to provide an account of which contextual features will be drawn upon in order to complete an incomplete description in any given scenario. It is enough if a semantical theory provide the general mechanisms with the aid of which actual complete contents can be specified.

56. In addition to the referential use of descriptions, it is possible to isolate several others.

Appositive Use. Searle (1979), and Barwise and Perry (1983) observe that descriptions may be used *appositively*, as in

(i) John Smith, the man who threw strawberry ice cream at the Pope, was today sentenced to 50 years hard labor.

This example does not seem to present any sort of additional problem for Russell that will not have to be faced in any event by a semantical theory of apposition. One approach to (i) that might be explored is an analysis in terms of the conjunction of (ii) and (iii):

(ii) John Smith was today sentenced to 50 years hard labor

(iii) John Smith was the man who threw strawberry ice cream at the Pope.

Another approach that might be explored is to treat the subject of (i) as a complex definite description "[the x: $x =$ John Smith & x threw ice cream at the Pope]." Of course, these suggestions need to be investigated in detail before we can feel comfortable with either of them. Unlike the former proposal, the latter seems to carry over naturally to an example like

(iv) The sculptor John Smith died today.

Predicative Use. No new problems are presented by an example like

(v) John Smith is the man who threw strawberry ice cream at the Pope.

Indefinite Use. Tom Wasow has noted examples such as

(vi) Look it up in the dictionary!

(vii) Let's go to the beach.

These examples are (perhaps) best seen as idiomatic.

References

Barwise, J., and R. Cooper. (1981). Generalized Quantifiers and Natural Language. *Linguistics and Philosophy* 4, 159–219.

Barwise, J., and J. Perry. (1983). *Situations and Attitudes*. Cambridge, Mass: MIT Press.

Blackburn, S. (1984). *Spreading the Word: Groundings in the Philosophy of Language*. Oxford: Clarendon Press.

Blackburn, W. (1988). Wettstein on Definite Descriptions. *Philosophical Studies* 53, 263–278.

Carston, R. (1988). Implicature, Explicature, and Truth-Theoretic Semantics. In R. Kempson (ed.) *Mental Representations*. Cambridge: Cambridge University Press, 155–181.

Cartwright, R. (1968). Some Remarks on Essentialism. *Nôus* 2, 229–246.

Castañeda, H. C. (1977). Philosophical Foundations of the Theory of Communication. In P. A. French, T. E. Uehling, Jr., and H. K. Wettstein (eds.) *Contem-*

porary Perspectives in the Philosophy of Language. Minneapolis: University of Minnesota Press.

Chastain, C. (1975). Reference and Context. In K. Gunderson (ed.) *Minnesota Studies in the Philosophy of Science, vol. VII: Language, Mind and Knowledge*. Minneapolis: University of Minnesota Press, 194–269.

Clark, E. (1971). On the Acquisition of the Meaning of "before" and "after." *Journal of Verbal Learning and Verbal Behavior* 10, 266–275.

Cresswell, M. (1973). *Logics and Languages*. London: Methuen.

Davidson, D. (1986). A Nice Derangement of Epitaphs. In R. Grandy and R. Warner (eds.), *Philosophical Grounds of Rationality, Intentions, Categories, Ends*. Oxford: Clarendon Press, 157–174.

Davies, M. (1981). *Meaning, Quantification, Necessity*. London: Routledge and Kegan Paul.

Devitt, M. (1981). Donnellan's Distinction. In P. A. French, T. E. Uehling, Jr., and H. K. Wettstein (eds.) *Midwest Studies in Philosophy VI*. Minneapolis: University of Minnesota Press, 511–524.

Dominicy, M. (1984). La Naissance de la Grammaire Moderne: Langage, Logique, et Philosophie à Port Royal. Bruxelles: Pierre Mardags Editeur.

Donnellan, K. (1966). Reference and Definite Descriptions. *Philosophical Review* 77, 281–304 (this volume, chapter 8).

Donnellan, K. (1968). Putting Humpty Dumpty Back Together Again. *Philosophical Review* 77, 203–215.

Donnellan, K. (1979). Speaker Reference, Descriptions, and Anaphora. In Peter Cole (ed.) *Syntax and Semantics, vol. 9: Pragmatics*. New York: Academic Press, 47–68.

Evans, G. (1977). Pronouns, Quantifiers, and Relative Clauses (I). *Canadian Journal of Philosophy* 7, 467–536. (Reprinted in Evans (1985), 76–152.)

Evans, G. (1980). Pronouns. *Linguistic Inquiry* 11, 337–362.

Evans, G. (1982). *The Varieties of Reference*. Oxford: Clarendon Press.

Evans, G. (1985). *The Collected Papers*. Oxford: Clarendon Press.

Fodor, J., and I. Sag. (1982). Referential and Quantificational Indefinites. *Linguistics and Philosophy* 5, 355–398.

Gazdar, G. (1979). *Pragmatics: Presupposition, Implicature, and Logical Form*. New York: Academic Press.

Geach, P. (1962). *Reference and Generality*. Ithaca, NY: Cornell University Press.

Grice, H. P. (1957). Meaning. *Philosophical Review* 66, 377–388.

Grice, H. P. (1961). The Causal Theory of Perception. *Proceedings of the Aristotelian Society*, suppl. vol. 35, 121–152.

Grice, H. P. (1967). Logic and Conversation. (William James Lectures.) In *Studies in the Way of Words*. Cambridge, Mass: Harvard University Press, 1989.

366   Stephen Neale

Grice, H. P. (1969). Vacuous Names. In D. Davidson and J. Hintikka (eds.) *Words and Objections*. Dordrecht: Reidel, 118–145 (this volume, chapter 9).

Grice, H. P. (1970). Lectures on Logic and Reality. University of Illinois at Urbana. (Lecture VI published as Grice (1981).)

Grice, H. P. (1981). Presupposition and Conversational Implicature. In P. Cole (ed.) *Radical Pragmatics*. New York: Academic Press, 183–198.

Hampshire, S. (1959). *Thought and Action*. New York: Viking Press.

Hornsby, J. (1977). Singular Terms in Contexts of Propositional Attitude. *Mind* 86, 31–48.

Husserl, E. (1913). *Logische Untersuchungen, Zweiter Band*, 2nd ed., Halle: Niemeyer. English tr. By J. N. Findlay, London: Routledge and Kegan Paul.

Johnson, H. (1975). The Meaning of "before" and "after" for Preschool Children. *Journal of Experimental Child Psychology* 19, 88–99.

Kaplan, D. (1977). Demonstratives. In J. Almog, J. Perry, and H. Wettstein (eds.) *Themes from Kaplan*. New York: Oxford University Press, 1989, 481–563.

Kaplan, D. (1978). Dthat. In P. Cole (ed.) *Syntax and Semantics, vol. 9: Pragmatics*. New York: Academic Press, 221–243.

King, J. (1988). Are Indefinite Descriptions Ambiguous? *Philosophical Studies* 53, 417–440.

Klein, E. (1980). Defensible Descriptions. In F. Henry (ed.) *Ambiguities in Intensional Contexts*. Dordrecht: Reidel, 1981, 83–102.

Kripke, S. (1977). Speaker's Reference and Semantic Reference. In P. A. French, et al. (eds.) *Contemporary Perspectives in the Philosophy of Language*. Minneapolis: University of Minnesota Press, 6–27 (this volume, chapter 11).

Kripke, S (1972). Naming and Necessity. In D. Davidson and G. Harman (eds.) *Semantics of Natural Language*. Dordrecht: Reidel, 253–355, and 763–769.

Lewis, D. (1972). General Semantics. In D. Davidson and G. Harman (eds.) *Semantics of Natural Language*. Dordrecht: Reidel, 169–218.

Lewis, D. (1973). *Counterfactuals*. Cambridge, Mass: Harvard University Press.

Lewis, D. (1975). Adverbs of Quantification. In E. Keenan (ed.) *Formal Semantics of Natural Language*. Cambridge: Cambridge University Press, 3–15.

Linsky, L. (1963). Reference and Referents. In C. E. Caton (ed.), *Philosophy and Ordinary Language*. Urbana: University of Illinois Press, 74–89.

Linsky, L. (1966). *Referring*. London: Routledge and Kegan Paul.

Ludlow, P., and S. Neale. (1991). Indefinite Descriptions: In Defense of Russell. *Linguistics and Philosophy* 14, 171–202.

Marcus, R. B. (1961). Modalities and Intensional Languages. *Synthese* 27, 303–322.

Mitchell, D. (1962). *An Introduction to Logic*. London: Hutchison.

Montague, R. (1968). Pragmatics. In R. Thomason (ed.) *Formal Philosophy: Selected papers of Richard Montague*. New Haven: Yale University Press, 1974, 95–118.

Montague, R. (1970). English as a Formal Language. In R. Thomason (ed.) *Formal Philosophy: Selected papers of Richard Montague*. New Haven: Yale University Press, 1974, 188–221.

Montague, R. (1973). The Proper Treatment of Quantification in Ordinary English. In R. Thomason (ed.) *Formal Philosophy: Selected papers of Richard Montague*. New Haven: Yale University Press, 1974, 247–270.

Partee, B. (1972). Opacity, Coreference and Pronouns. In D. Davidson and G. Harman (eds.) *Semantics of Natural Language*. Dordrecht: Reidel, 415–441.

Peacocke, C. (1975). Proper Names, Reference, and Rigid Designation. In S. Blackburn (ed.) *Meaning, Reference, and Necessity*. Cambridge: Cambridge University Press, 109–132 (this volume, chapter 10).

Quine, W. V. O. (1940). *Mathematical Logic*. Cambridge, Mass: Harvard University Press, revised edition, 1951.

Rawls, J. (1971). *A Theory of Justice*. Cambridge, Mass: Harvard University Press.

Récanati, F. (1981). On Kripke on Donnellan. In H. Parret, M. Sbisa, and J. Verschueren (eds.), *Possibilities and Limitations of Pragmatics*. Amsterdam: John Benjamins, 595–630.

Récanati, F. (1986). Contextual Dependence and Definite Descriptions. *Proceedings of the Aristotelian Society* 87, 57–73.

Récanati, F. (1989). Referential/Attributive: A Contextualist Proposal. *Philosophical Studies* 56, 217–249.

Rundle, B. (1965). Modality and Quantification. In R. J. Butler (ed.), *Analytical Philosophy, Second Series*. Oxford: Blackwell, 27–39.

Russell, B. (1948). An Inquiry into Meaning and Truth. *Harmondsworth: Penguin*.

Russell, B. (1905). On Denoting. *Mind* 14, 479–493 (this volume, chapter 1).

Sainsbury, R. M. (1979). *Russell*. London: Routledge and Kegan Paul.

Salmon, Nathan. (1982). Assertion and Incomplete Definite Descriptions. *Philosophical Studies* 42, 37–45.

Searle, John. (1979). Referential and Attributive. *The Monist* 62: 140–208. (Reprinted in *Expression and Meaning*. Cambridge: Cambridge University Press, 1983, 137–161.)

Schiffer, S. (1972). *Meaning*. Oxford: Clarendon Press.

Sellars, W. (1954). Presupposing. *Philosophical Review* 63, 197–215.

Soames, S. (1982). How Presuppositions are Inherited: A Solution to the Projection Problem. *Linguistic Inquiry* 13, 483–545. (Reprinted in Steven Davis (ed.) *Pragmatics: A Reader*. New York: Oxford University Press, 1991, 428–470.)

368 Stephen Neale

Soames, S. (1986). Incomplete Definite Descriptions. *Notre Dame Journal of Formal Logic* 27, 349–375 (this volume, chapter 13).

Sperber D., and D. Wilson (1981). Irony and the Use-Mention Distinction. In P. Cole (ed.) *Radical Pragmatics*. New York: Academic Press, 295–318.

Sperber D., and D. Wilson (1986). *Relevance*. Cambridge, Mass: Harvard University Press.

Stalnaker, R. (1972). Pragmatics. In D. Davidson and G. Harman (eds.) *Semantics of Natural Language*. Dordrecht: Reidel, 380–397.

Stich, S. (1986). Are Belief Predicates Systematically Ambiguous? In R. J. Bogden (ed.) *Belief*. Oxford: Clarendon Press, 119–147.

Strawson, P. F. (1950). On Referring. *Mind* 59, 320–344 (this volume, chapter 5).

Strawson, P. F. (1952). *Introduction to Logical Theory*. London: Methuen.

Vendler, Z. (1967). Singular Terms. In *Linguistics in Philosophy*. Ithaca, NY: Cornell University Press.

Wettstein, H. (1981). Demonstrative Reference and Definite Descriptions. *Philosophical Studies* 40, 241–257 (this volume, chapter 12).

Wettstein (1983). The Semantic Significance of the Referential-Attributive Distinction. *Philosophical Studies*, 44. (Reprinted in *Has Semantics Rested on a Mistake?* Stanford: Stanford University Press, 1991, 50–58.)

Wiggins, D. (1975). Identity, Designation, Essentialism, and Physicalism. *Philosophia* 5, 1–30.

Wiggins, D. (1980). "Most" and "All": Some Comments on a Familiar Programme, and on the Logical Form of Quantified Sentences. In M. Platts (ed.), *Reference, Truth, and Reality*. London: Routledge and Kegan Paul, 318–346.

Wilson, D. and D. Sperber (1981). On Grice's Theory of Conversation. In P. Werth (ed.), *Conversation and Discourse*. London: Croon Helm, 155–178.

Wilson, D. and D. Sperber (1986). On Defining Relevance. In R. Grandy and R. Warner (eds.), *Philosophical Grounds of Rationality, Intentions, Categories, Ends*. Oxford: Clarendon Press, 243–258.

Wilson, G. (1978). On Definite and Indefinite Descriptions. *The Philosophical Review* 87, 48–76.

Chapter 15

Descriptions, Indexicals, and Belief Reports: Some Dilemmas (But Not the Ones You Expect)

Stephen Schiffer

1 Introduction

I am going to state what I take to be a couple of dilemmas for certain theorists. The first is a dilemma for theorists who hold both that certain sentences containing pronouns or demonstratives express object-dependent propositions and that a certain version of Russell's theory of descriptions can account for all uses of definite descriptions.[1] The second is a dilemma for a certain view about the semantics of belief reports which is common among those who hold that sentences containing certain kinds of singular terms express object-dependent propositions, and this dilemma is generated by a partial solution to the first dilemma.

So my dialectic involves the following players. To begin, there are three theses which, for reasons that will become clear, I shall call *the hidden-indexical theory of belief reports, the hidden-indexical theory of descriptions,* and *the direct-reference theory of indexicals.* Next, there is a dilemma for one who holds the direct-reference theory of indexicals in conjunction with the hidden-indexical theory of descriptions. After that comes a partial resolution of that dilemma, and that partial resolution is used to create a dilemma for one who holds the hidden-indexical theory of belief reports. Finally, I speculate fleetingly, but with much hand waving, about the complete resolution of these dilemmas. I begin by setting up the three theses.

Reprinted from *Mind* 104, pp. 107–131, by permission of Stephen Schiffer and Oxford University Press. © 1995 Oxford University Press.

2 Three Theses

2.1 The Hidden-Indexical Theory of Belief Reports

Elsewhere,[2] I have argued that if, as is widely held, natural languages have compositional semantics, then the best account of the logical form of belief reports is one I call the *hidden-indexical theory*. Several philosophers have proposed versions of the hidden-indexical theory,[3] but my favoured version—stated first in its naive form—proceeds as follows. The theory begins by holding that the relation expressed by "believes" in sentences of the form "*A* believes that *S*" is a three-place relation, $B(x, p, m)$, holding among a believer x, a mode-of-presentation-less proposition p, and a mode of presentation m under which x believes p.[4] Thus, it is possible for x to believe p under one mode of presentation m while believing not-p under a second mode of presentation m', and while suspending judgment altogether under a third mode of presentation m''. By a "mode-of-presentation-less" proposition I mean, quite roughly, a proposition that contains the objects and properties the belief is about unaccompanied by any modes of presentation of them. Such a proposition might be a mere "singular proposition," like the ordered pair ⟨Fido, doghood⟩, but it could also be whatever set-theoretic construction an extreme direct-reference theorist has in store for "Whoever murdered Smith is insane."

So much for the relation's second term. Its third term is a mode of presentation under which the believer believes the proposition believed. This propositional mode of presentation is determined by modes of presentation of the objects and properties the proposition is about. Here it is not supposed that we have some antecedent understanding of what these modes of presentation are. Rather, our understanding of the notion of a mode of presentation is *functional*: a mode of presentation of an object or property is whatever can play a role in determining a propositional mode of presentation, and a propositional mode of presentation is whatever can play the role defined by the mode-of-presentation place in the belief relation. Thus, it remains to be determined what sorts of things in fact play the mode-of-presentation role—that is to say, it remains to be determined what modes of presentation *are*—but I cannot attempt here to resolve this difficult issue. Suffice it to say that my own view is that most of the things that have been proposed as modes of presentation are incapable of playing the mode-of-presentation role. I make an exception, however, for conceptual, or functional, roles of mental representations. It is possible, I believe, to have a conception of conceptual roles which simply allows satisfaction of the mode-of-presentation role to be built into certain conceptual roles, and these could serve as modes of presentation, at least in the context of the hidden-indexical theory.

The crux of the hidden-indexical theory is its account of the logical form of particular occurrences of belief-ascribing sentences. As applied to the sentence

(1) Ralph believes that no woodchuck is a groundhog,[5]

the naive version of the theory holds that the logical form of an utterance of this sentence may be represented as

$\exists m[\Phi^*m$ & B(Ralph, the proposition that no woodchuck is a groundhog, $m)]$,

where Φ^* is an implicitly-referred-to and contextually-determined *type* of propositional mode of presentation, where by this I mean a *property* of modes of presentation of propositions. This type of mode of presentation will be made up, as it were, of contextually-relevant types of modes of presentation of the constituents of the proposition that no woodchuck is a groundhog. There will be a type of mode of presentation for the first occurrence of the property of being a woodchuck (= the property of being a groundhog), a type of mode of presentation for the second occurrence of that property, and types of modes of presentation for the other constituents of the proposition. In a limiting case, the type of mode of presentation may be vacuous, so that the speaker's import in uttering "*A* believes that *S*" is merely that *A* believes the proposition that *S* under some mode of presentation or other, while in an opposite sort of limiting case the type of mode presentation to which the speaker refers may determine a unique particular mode of presentation. Between these two limits lies reference to a substantial type of mode of presentation which fails to determine a unique mode of presentation. This theory is aptly called the *hidden*-indexical theory because the reference to the mode-of-presentation type is not carried by any expression in the belief ascription. In this sense, it is like the reference to a place at which it is raining which occurs in an utterance of "It's raining." And the theory is aptly called the hidden-*indexical* theory, because the mode-of-presentation type to which reference is made in the utterance of a belief sentence can vary from one utterance of the sentence to another.

Let me say a little about what recommends the theory. To begin, there are reasons for taking that-clauses in sentences of the form "*A* believes

that *S*" to be referential singular terms.[6] Then there are reasons for taking
their referents to be propositions of some stripe or other, where by this I
mean abstract, mind- and language-independent entities that have truth
conditions, and have their truth conditions both essentially and absolutely.[7] The reasons for taking that-clauses to refer to propositions are
pretty good (see Schiffer (1992, pp. 504–506)), but I cannot now go into
them; so I shall concentrate on what can be said to motivate the hidden-
indexical theory to someone who agrees that that-clauses refer to propositions of some kind or other. The point of the theory is then well illustrated
by the example already used, an utterance of (1) ("Ralph believes that
no woodchuck is a groundhog").

One wants to recognize that an utterance of (1) is true, while at the
same time recognizing that an utterance of

(2) Ralph doesn't believe that no woodchuck is a woodchuck

could also be true. This would be impossible if, as the extreme direct-
reference theory holds, "believes" in these sentences expressed a two-place
relation and both that-clauses referred to the same proposition, as they
would if "woodchuck" and "groundhog" in those that-clauses simply referred to the single property they both express. Now, one famous way of
accounting for the truth of these two utterances is Frege's way: take the
two that-clauses to have different references. Specifically, take the occurrences of "woodchuck" and "groundhog" to introduce into the propositions to which the that-clauses refer distinct modes of presentation of
the single property they both express. But it is implausible that this
should be required to account for the truth of both utterances. In the
first place, the that-clause in (1), "that no woodchuck is a groundhog," cannot
be making a context-independent reference to a mode-of-presentation-
containing proposition, for the predicate "believes that no woodchuck is
a groundhog" can be univocally and correctly predicated of people—say,
you and Helen Keller—who think of the property of being a woodchuck/
groundhog in radically different and non-overlapping ways. And in the
second place, no context-dependent reference can be required, for a
speaker can make a true statement in uttering (1) even though she is not in
a position to refer to any specific mode of presentation that Ralph has for
the property of being a woodchuck/groundhog. Indeed, it will generally
be difficult for a speaker to refer to specific modes of presentation if, as I
have already suggested, the best account of modes of presentation identi-

fies them with conceptual roles of mental representations, for ordinary speakers do not have suitable epistemic access to these things.[8]

Although a speaker may not know any relevant *specific* mode of presentation under which Ralph believes that no woodchuck is a groundhog, she may know a relevant *type* of mode of presentation. For example, she may know that Ralph believes that no woodchuck is a groundhog under some propositional mode of presentation that requires thinking of woodchuckhood first under a mode of presentation associated with Ralph's use of "woodchuck" and then under a mode of presentation associated with Ralph's use of "groundhog." Thus, we can see how the naive hidden-indexical theory captures the attractive features of both the extreme direct-reference theory of belief ascription and the Fregean theory while at the same time avoiding the pitfalls of both theories. With the extreme direct-reference theory, the hidden-indexical theory sees the that-clauses in (1) and (2) as referring to the same mode-of-presentation-less proposition, while, with the Fregean theory, it recognizes that both utterances are true. This is possible because the two utterances involve implicit references to distinct mode-of-presentation types.

But the hidden-indexical theory in the form I have just stated it cannot be right, and this is why I have called it the *naive* hidden-indexical theory. For, as so far stated, the theory requires the belief ascriber to be referring to a *particular* mode-of-presentation type, and this is implausible. To see the problem, pretend that we are having a casual conversation about the French Riviera, when Stella, a nonphilosopher who likes to drop names, says to us,

(a) Jean Luc Godard believes that Brigitte Bardot is selling her villa in St. Tropez and moving to Liverpool.

If the naive hidden-indexical theory is correct, there is a certain mode-of-presentation type Φ such that Stella, in uttering (a), is referring to Φ, and this is so by virtue of her implicitly stating, and thus meaning, the proposition

(b) that there is something x such that x is of the type Φ and Jean Luc Godard believes *that Brigitte Bardot is selling her villa in St. Tropez and moving to Liverpool* under x.

Here Φ is a particular type of propositional mode of presentation, and it will incorporate particular types of modes of presentation for each of the constituents of the proposition to which (a)'s that-clause refers—Brigitte

Bardot, the selling relation, Bardot's villa, the in relation, St. Tropez, conjunction, the moving-to relation, and Liverpool. Yet it seems clear that there is no definite such Φ, that Stella was not implicitly stating a definite substitution instance of (b). After all, you are the audience and you understood her utterance perfectly well. If she stated a substitution instance of (b), you should be able to say what it is. But you cannot; just try to do it. If you try, you will find that there is a large collection of mode-of-presentation types that are equally good candidates for entering into Stella's statement, none of which is sufficiently salient to enable us to peg it as the one to which she was definitely referring.[9]

So the naive version of the hidden-indexical theory cannot be right. The question then is whether some other version of the theory might be right, and it is apt to seem that the needed adjustment is fairly minor. Simply restate the hidden-indexical theory so that it allows for the belief ascriber to be making an *indeterminate* reference to a type of mode of presentation. The details of how we might do this are perhaps negotiable, but the general idea seems tolerably clear. Suppose you call Ernie Lepore in New Brunswick and ask him where Jerry Fodor is. "He's here," Ernie replies. To what does the utterance of "here" refer? To New Brunswick? To Rutgers University? To Douglass Campus? To Davison Hall? To Ernie's office? The example is underdescribed, but even if I fully describe it, there need not be a definite answer. Almost certainly, Ernie's utterance of "here" does not refer to some definite region of space. The word is being used to make a vague or indeterminate reference. There are many admissible ways of sharpening the reference, and thus of sharpening the proposition Ernie meant, and it is reasonable to hold that his utterance is true just in case it is true under all admissible sharpenings, false just in case it is false under all admissible sharpenings, and neither true nor false if it is true under some sharpenings while false under others.[10] Since no place is being definitely referred to, there is no proposition Ernie definitely meant. But he *sort-of-meant*, or vaguely meant, all the propositions that could be used to precisify his indeterminate statement, and the truth value of the statement could be thought of as determined in the supervaluational way crudely suggested.

Likewise, it might seem, with respect to Stella's utterance of (a). She was not making a determinate reference to any particular type of mode of presentation, but she was making a vague or indeterminate reference to any number of contextually relevant types of modes of presentation of which she and her audience were mutually aware. In other words, there are many admissible ways of sharpening her implicit indeterminate reference, and thus of sharpening the proposition she meant. Although she was not *determinately* stating anything, she was making an indeterminate statement, and this statement is true just in case it is true under all admissible sharpenings of her implicit reference, false just in case it is false under all admissible sharpenings, and neither true nor false if it is true under some sharpenings while false under others. All we need to do to get a correct version of the hidden-indexical theory, the suggestion goes, is to restate it in a way that allows for the speaker's hidden-indexical reference to be indeterminate. As I said, it is negotiable how exactly the improved version of the hidden-indexical theory is to be stated, but the foregoing vague characterization of the direction of improvement is good enough, I dare say, to make us wonder later whether even the improved version can be right.

2.2 The Hidden-Indexical Theory of Descriptions

A Donnellan-inspired view of definite descriptions one might have is that they are ambiguous in the sense that, when used attributively, Russell was right about the nature of the proposition expressed, whereas, when used referentially, a definite description functions as a *directly-referential* singular term in the sense that the proposition expressed is an object-dependent proposition that would not exist if the definite description's referent did not exist.

Opposed to this is a Grice/Kripke-inspired line which holds that there is no ambiguity: the theory of descriptions gives the right account of what is *strictly and literally stated* for *all* uses of definite descriptions. True, in the "referential" cases, the speaker uttering "The F is G" *means* an object-dependent proposition, but, the claim continues, not only is that compatible with her also making a description-theoretic statement, it is also the case that we can give Gricean pragmatic explanations of why speakers often mean object-dependent propositions when they are making description-theoretic statements.

But what do we mean here by "the theory of descriptions"? Russell's theory of descriptions is about the nature of the proposition stated by an utterance of a sentence of the form "The F is G." To a first approximation, it says that in uttering "The F is G" the literal speaker states the proposition *that the F is G*, where this proposition is true in a possible would w just in case in w there is exactly one F and it is G, and is false in w otherwise. But of course this is very much a first approximation, since it is clear that in uttering "The dog is chewing your hat" the literal speaker is not stating something that entails that there is exactly one dog in the universe.

A better approximation to a reasonable version of the description theory is given by what we may call the *naive hidden-indexical theory of descriptions*. It holds that the meaning rule for "The *F* is *G*" is:

Utter "The *F* is *G*" only if there is a property *H* such that you mean that the *F* and *H* is *G*.

This is aptly called the *hidden*-indexical theory of descriptions, because nothing in "The *F* is *G*" expresses the implicitly meant property *H*, and it is aptly called the hidden-*indexical* theory of descriptions because different completing descriptions can be meant on different occasions of utterance. And the theory is aptly called *naive* for the same reason the naive hidden-indexical theory of belief ascription was naive: it is implausible that utterances of "incomplete" descriptions will have determinate completers.

Imagine that you and I are in the audience awaiting a talk by the eminent philosopher Ferdinand Pergola. The professor arrives, and you say to me "I'll be damned! The guy's drunk." Even before your utterance it was mutually evident to us that we had knowledge of the professor under *numerous* shared definite descriptions—*the author of Smells and Tickles, the only man within sight wearing a yellow jacket and red golf pants, the man we are waiting to hear, the man now staggering up to the podium*, and the list, in any realistic situation, will go on and on.[11] Now, if the naive hidden-indexical theory of descriptions is correct, then there is some contextually-salient property *H* such that in uttering "The guy's drunk," you implicitly stated, and thus meant, *that the H guy was drunk*, where *the H guy* was one of those shared definite descriptions. Yet it is doubtful that you meant any such thing, for it is hard to see how you could have the meaning intentions such an act would require. Imagining myself as your audience, I do not see how I could have identified any one definite description, however complex, as *the one* that figured in the proposition you asserted. And yet, it would seem that I understood your utterance perfectly well, and it ought to be a consequence of any acceptable theory of meaning that if a speaker, speaking literally, meant *p* in uttering *u*, then one who understood his utterance perfectly well took him to have meant *p* in uttering *u*. It seems clear that in our example you *could not* mean what the naive theory requires you to mean, because no *one* of the numerous shared definite descriptions is sufficiently salient to make it mutually evident to us that you meant a proposition containing it.

But why not say that one uttering "The F is G" means that *the most salient F is G*? Two problems. (1) This suggestion presupposes that the description *the most salient F* will be the most salient of the candidate definite descriptions, but that is simply false: the fact that the notion of salience occurs in a description does not make that description the most salient description. When the speaker utters "The F is G," the description *the most salient F* is at best just one of any number of definite descriptions that might be meant, and it need not be the most salient description. For example, when a speaker attributively utters "The murderer must be insane," what she intuitively means is that *Smith's murderer*—or *the murderer of that person*—must be insane, and not that the most salient murderer must be insane. (2) The description *the most salient F* is itself incomplete: most salient in what respect? I strongly suspect that when this is spelled out the intended description will amount to the circular *the F to which I am referring in this utterance of "the F."*

Once again, it is apt to seem that only a minor revision is required (cf. Blackburn 1988). Simply revise the hidden-indexical theory of descriptions so that it allows for the speaker to be making an *indeterminate* statement. As before, the details are negotiable, but the general idea is tolerably clear. In the Pergola example, you did not definitely mean any general proposition in uttering "The guy is drunk," but you *sort-of-meant*, or vaguely meant, several general propositions, one for each definite description that could be used to sharpen what you vaguely meant. And your indeterminate statement might reasonably be held to be true just in case it is true under every admissible sharpening of what you meant, false just in case it is false under every such admissible sharpening, and neither true nor false if it is true under some admissible sharpenings while false under others. To be sure, the theorist recognizes that the speaker in our example was also using "the guy" referentially, and thus meant an object-dependent proposition involving Pergola along with all the description-theoretic propositions she indeterminately meant. But, to repeat, he holds that there are Gricean pragmatic explanations available to explain why the speaker would mean the object-dependent proposition in the course of making her indeterminate description-theoretic statement.

Let us call the improved version of the naive hidden-indexical theory of descriptions simply the *hidden-indexical theory of descriptions*. I shall assume it is what a theorist holds—or at least should hold—when he says that a certain version of Russell's theory of descriptions can account for all uses of definite descriptions.[12]

2.3   The Direct-Reference Theory of Indexicals

Here I can be both brief and conservative. The thesis is that, certain qualifications aside, single-word indexicals are directly-referential singular terms. By single-word indexicals (*indexicals*, for short) I mean at least pronouns such as "I," "you," "he," "she," and "it," as well as demonstratives such as "this" and "that." The qualifications pertain to such things as the use of pronouns as variables, and I shall ignore them. By saying that indexicals are directly-referential singular terms, I mean that the propositions stated by utterances of sentences containing indexicals are object-dependent propositions involving the referents of the tokens of those indexicals—propositions, that is, which would not exist if those referents did not exist.

3   A Dilemma

There we have our three theses, which, as I said in section 1, are importantly related in the following way: there is a dilemma for one who holds both the hidden-indexical theory of descriptions and the direct-reference theory of indexicals, and a certain preferred solution to that dilemma itself creates a dilemma for one who holds the hidden-indexical theory of belief reports. The first dilemma is that one who holds the hidden-indexical theory of descriptions seems not to be in a position to hold the direct-reference theory of indexicals. Since I have proposed that the hidden-indexical theory of descriptions should be held by anyone who wishes to extend the theory of descriptions to all uses of definite descriptions, the dilemma should confound anyone who combines the Russellian line on descriptions with the direct-reference line on indexicals.[13]

The reason I think that one who holds the hidden-indexical theory of descriptions is in no position to hold the direct-reference theory of indexicals is not that the two theses are incompatible; rather, it is that one who holds the theory of descriptions seems not to have a good basis for preferring the direct-reference theory of indexicals to a certain other theory of them, one I shall call the *hidden-indexical description theory of indexicals*.

In considering this theory, it is well to begin with its *naive* version. The naive hidden-indexical description theory of indexicals holds that the meaning rule for "α is G," where "α" is an indexical, is:

Utter "α is G" only if, for some suitably constrained property F, you mean that the F is G.

The "suitably constrained" idea is that indexicals put constraints on the meant property: "he" constrains it to entail being male, "you" constrains it to entail being an audience, "it" has an empty constraint, and so on. Given that this is the meaning rule, it would follow that it is a description-theoretic proposition of the form *the F is G* which is strictly and literally stated in an utterance of "α is G." Anyway, we know that, for reasons of semantic indeterminacy, no one can take the naive theory seriously for very long. So in this way we reach the *hidden-indexical description theory of indexicals*, which is simply the naive theory suitably corrected to allow for a literal utterance of "α is G" to be making an indeterminate description-theoretic statement. I hasten to add, on the theorist's behalf, that this hardly precludes the utterer of "α is G" from also meaning an object-dependent proposition involving the referent of "α." Indeed, mimicking the hidden-indexical theorist of descriptions, the theorist will tell us that we can give neat Gricean explanations of how his theory predicts that one uttering "α is G" will also mean an object-dependent proposition. This is after all to be expected, since the hidden-indexical description theory of indexicals in effect tells us that indexicals are disguised incomplete descriptions, where these in turn obey the hidden-indexical theory of descriptions. "He," for example, is simply synonymous with "the male."

Now I can state why the hidden-indexical theorist of descriptions appears to have no good basis for preferring the direct-reference theory of indexicals to the hidden-indexical description theory of them. It is because:

(1) If the hidden-indexical theory of descriptions is correct, then in uttering a sentence containing a referentially used incomplete definite description a literal speaker performs an indeterminate (or determinate) description-theoretic act of meaning.

(2) If in uttering a sentence containing a referentially used incomplete definite description a literal speaker performs a description-theoretic act of meaning,[14] then so does a literal speaker who utters a sentence containing a referentially used indexical.

(3) But if the indexical speaker performs a description-theoretic act of meaning, then there is no evident way one can nonarbitrarily choose between the direct-reference theory of indexicals and the hidden-indexical description theory of indexicals.

Each of these premises requires justification.

Re (1). In the way that I have informally presented proposals about the literal meanings of sentences as speaker-meaning prescriptions, I have tacitly assumed the correctness of this premise. But now that push has come to shove, it is best that I be painstakingly explicit, and defend, however briefly, at least some of what one might sensibly seek to question.

According to a familiar way of thinking, to know the meaning of a sentence is to know two things: the kind of act of speaker meaning conventionally correlated with the sentence and something that constrains the propositional content of that speech act. In the case of declarative sentences, to which our concern may harmlessly be limited, the relevant sort of speaker meaning is a speaker's meaning that such-and-such is the case. The literal speaker of a sentence is one who, in uttering the sentence, means a proposition within the constrained range, as one who utters "It's snowing" might mean that it is snowing in Manhattan at the time of utterance. I assume that acts of speaker meaning require complex propositional attitudes, but I do not assume any analysis, Gricean or otherwise, of them.

Now, the objection I anticipate may be put thus: To know the meaning of a declarative sentence is to know how it constrains what can be strictly and literally *said* or *stated* in its utterance. But one can *say* (or state) *p* in uttering a sentence without meaning *p*. Thus, the correct way of stating the hidden-indexical theory of descriptions is as a thesis about the *semantic content* of a literal utterance of "The *F* is *G*," what would be *said* in a literal utterance of it, and thus what is determinative of its truth conditions: a literal statement made in the utterance of "The *F* is *G*" is an indeterminate (or determinate) description-theoretic statement of the kind already described. One can perform such a *statement* in uttering, say, "The guy is drunk," even though the only thing one *means* is an object-dependent proposition involving the person to whom one is referring in uttering "the guy."

A small initial point by way of reply is that while one can of course mean *p* without saying/stating *p*, it is very hard to see what could intuitively count as saying/stating p without meaning p. If in uttering "The shirt is dirty" one is implicitly saying that one's tuxedo shirt is dirty, then surely one may be said also to mean that one's tuxedo shirt is dirty. To be sure, if I say sarcastically "God's gift to philosophy has arrived" to communicate that a certain person has arrived, then I have not *meant* that God's gift to philosophy has arrived. But nor have I *said* that. I was speaking figuratively, not literally.

The deep issue here is not about the use of semantic idioms in ordinary language. It is really about the way a sentence must be related to a form of proposition in order for that form of proposition to give the sentence's meaning. It is eminently reasonable to suppose that the link must be formed via practices that connect utterances of the sentence with speech acts whose contents fall under the form of proposition. Now, what kind of speech act? The problem with saying that it is *saying/stating* that such and such is that in the quasi-technical sense in which these terms are now generally used in semantics, it is not possible to say/state p in uttering σ unless σ already means a form of proposition to which p belongs. Thus, one cannot *explain* σ's meaning that form of proposition by claiming that it is conventionally correlated with *saying/stating* propositions of the form. The moral is that if we are to have any sort of informative account of sentence meaning (and such an account need not be reductive), then the meaning-constitutive practices that give sentences their meanings in a population of speakers must correlate sentences with kinds of speech acts that do not themselves presuppose the notion of sentence meaning. *Speaker meaning*, itself a quasi-technical notion, is designed to do precisely the job in question. For those who find it useful to understand sentence meaning in terms of speaker meaning, the favoured notion of saying/stating holds, roughly speaking, that to say that p was *said/stated* in the utterance of a sentence is to say, first, that the speaker meant p in uttering the sentence, and, second, that the meaning of the sentence requires the literal speaker to mean some proposition of a type to which p conforms. (This is easily modified to recognize indeterminacy.)

I do not expect these brief remarks to be persuasive to those theorists who suppose a sentence's having a certain meaning consists merely in the sentence's being correlated with that meaning by the language's "semantic rules," while those rules make no demands on what a literal speaker might mean in uttering the sentence. (Is it then merely a serendipitous *coincidence* that there is a tendency for a speaker to mean p

in uttering σ when σ itself means p?) But I shall be content to raise a dilemma for those of my targeted theorists who find premise (1) plausible.

Re (2). To help see the plausibility of this premise, let us return to the Pergola example, but let us have it that the speaker, instead of saying "The guy is drunk," now says "He is drunk." Clearly, there is no property H such that the speaker definitely meant that the H male was drunk. But if the speaker uttering "The guy is drunk" indeterminately meant various propositions of the form *the H guy is drunk*, then the speaker uttering "He is drunk" indeterminately meant various propositions of the form *the H male is drunk*. For the two cases have *exact psychological parity with respect to those psychological facts on which the relevant speaker meaning would have to supervene*. If you ask the speaker what she meant in uttering "The guy is drunk," you will not get a report that favours the description theory: the speaker will almost certainly offer up an object-dependent proposition involving Pergola, the intended referent of her utterance of "the guy." If a *theorist* is to be justified in discovering an indeterminate description-theoretic act of meaning in the utterance of "The guy is drunk," it will have to be on the basis of the fact that the speaker intended it to be mutual knowledge between her and her audience that certain definite descriptions applied to Pergola and that certain of these were essential to the communicative act in that the speaker would not have uttered her sentence if she had thought those descriptions were not mutually known to be instantiated. If we are warranted in ascribing an indeterminate description-theoretic act of meaning to the speaker when she utters "The guy is drunk," then it will have to be solely on the basis of these psychological facts. But these very same facts also obtain when the speaker utters "He is drunk." For example, in neither case would the speaker have produced her utterance if she had not thought that just one man was staggering up to the podium to give a talk. Moreover, these psychological facts pertaining to contextually-relevant definite descriptions apply to *any* utterance of an indexical-containing sentence, and I shall assume that this is clear to you on reflection. For example, it should be obvious that if I point to a building and say "That's where Michele works," then the situation with respect to communicatively relevant definite descriptions that are mutually believed to apply to the referent is exactly the same as in the Pergola example.[15]

The most likely way for the hidden-indexical theorist of descriptions to challenge this premise is to deny that the description-theoretic act of

meaning performed by one uttering a description supervenes on propositional attitudes of a kind shared by one uttering a sentence containing an
indexical. In particular, the theorist might take the unGricean stance that
what a speaker means in uttering a sentence may partly supervene on the
meaning of the sentence uttered. This could conceivably allow one to hold
that what was meant in the utterance of "The guy is drunk" was different
from what was meant in the utterance of "He is drunk," even though the
speakers' propositional attitudes in uttering the sentences were relevantly
the same.

I do not think this is a good tack for the hidden-indexical theorist of
descriptions to take. A speaker of course succeeds in meaning what she
does in uttering a sentence thanks in part to the sentence's meaning, but
here meaning what she does depends, conceptually, not on the sentence's
meaning, but on the intentions with which the sentence is uttered. The
hidden-indexical theorist can hardly deny this, for he is intent on claiming
that in using a definite description referentially, the speaker means an
object-dependent proposition, even though that act of meaning is not required by the meaning of the sentence uttered. One might try saying that
sometimes speaker meaning supervenes partly on sentence meaning and
sometimes it does not, but an appropriate sorting principle is needed if
this is to be anything other than self-serving wishful thinking, and it is
probably a pretty bad idea to be committed to finding such a principle.

Re (3).   It goes without saying that the indexical speaker typically means
an object-dependent proposition. Suppose that she is also performing an
indeterminate description-theoretic act of meaning. The problem then is
that these speaker-meaning facts seem equally well explained by two incompatible explanatory hypotheses, one involving the direct-reference
theory of indexicals, the other the hidden-indexical description theory of
indexicals. The two hypotheses are:

The direct-reference hypothesis: The literal speaker of "α is G" is stating
an object-dependent proposition while also indeterminately meaning
various description-theoretic propositions.

The hidden-indexical hypothesis: The literal speaker of "α is G" is
indeterminately stating various description-theoretic propositions while
also meaning an object-dependent proposition.

Thus, there are two possible ways of explaining what is going on in, say,
our imagined utterance of "He is drunk." (i) "He" is a directly-referential

singular term and thus the literal speaker states, and hence means, an object-dependent proposition. But for such-and-such fairly obvious reasons, it is impossible to have the intentions and beliefs such an act requires without also having the psychological states which the hidden-indexical theorist of descriptions must hold constitute indeterminately meaning various description-theoretic propositions containing definite descriptions the speaker and her audience mutually know to be relevant to the speaker's communicative intentions. (ii) "He" is synonymous with "the male," understood in the way of the hidden-indexical theory, and thus the literal speaker indeterminately (or determinately) states, and hence indeterminately (or determinately) means, one or more description-theoretic propositions. The further fact that the speaker also means an object-dependent proposition involving the referent of "he" is explained in the same Gricean way that the hidden-indexical theorist of descriptions explains referential uses of incomplete descriptions.

How is the hidden-indexical theorist of descriptions to be in a position nonarbitrarily to prefer the direct-reference theory of indexicals to the hidden-indexical description theory of them when both theories equally well explain all the speaker-meaning facts? Well, he can try to deny either (a) that the speaker-meaning facts exhaust all the relevant evidence or (b) that the two competing hypotheses do explain the speaker-meaning facts equally well.

As regards (a), perhaps the most promising tack for our theorist to pursue is to claim that he has a direct intuition of the possible-worlds truth conditions of what is strictly and literally stated in an utterance of "α is G." For example, concerning the ongoing example, he might claim to have a direct intuition that the speaker, in uttering "He is drunk," is making a statement that is true with respect to any counterfactual situation just in case *Pergola* is drunk in that situation.

Now, I am inclined to concede that we have such an intuition, but, as we shall presently see, this may be due to the fact that the *only* thing the speaker means in uttering "He is drunk" is an object-dependent proposition involving Pergola. The direct-intuition reply becomes unconvincing when the theorist concedes that there are always *two* acts of meaning taking place, one involving an object-dependent proposition, the other involving object-independent description-theoretic propositions. For how is he then to know that he is not confusing what is merely meant with what is stated? Howard Wettstein has in effect argued that he has a direct intuition that an object-dependent proposition is stated in a referential utterance of "The F is G," for he has a direct intuition that in such an utterance a *determinate* statement is made, and it is clear that the only thing determinately meant in such a case is an object-dependent proposition (Wettstein 1979, 1981, 1983). But a defender of the hidden-indexical theory of descriptions would rightly reply that this is an unreliable intuition if, as he claims, there are *two* acts of meaning taking place— an indeterminate description-theoretic act of meaning and a determinate object-dependent act of meaning. Wettstein's intuition can then be explained by his focusing on one of the two kinds of propositions meant. But if this is a good response to Wettstein, as I think it is, then it is equally a good response to the hidden-indexical theorist of descriptions who claims to have a direct intuition that an object-dependent proposition provides the semantic content of an utterance of "α is *G*."[16]

As regards (b), our theorist might argue that indexicals do not have purely attributive uses, but that they ought to if the hidden-indexical hypothesis is correct. There are, however, two problems with this response, even pretending that we have an adequate grasp of what an "attributive" use is supposed to be. In the first place, indexicals arguably do have attributive uses. For example, upon encountering a huge footprint in the sand, you might exclaim, "He must be a giant!" and arguably what you would mean is *that the man whose foot made the print, whoever he is, must be a giant.* In the second place, there is evidently an explanation of why, given that the hidden-indexical hypothesis is correct, purely attributive uses of indexicals are uncommon. It is the same explanation of why it is unusual to find purely attributive uses of maximally incomplete descriptions such as "the guy" or "the table." For such expressions there is generally no way of raising meaning-candidate complete definite descriptions to contextual saliency except in the presence of a contextually-salient reference candidate. I cannot in just any circumstances say "The dog has fleas" and intend my audience to grasp a proposition of the form *the H dog has fleas* which I even vaguely mean, for without prior fanfare there is no way my utterance can raise relevant completers to contextual saliency. But if we are in Central Park and your kid is hugging some mangy mongrel, then my utterance of "The dog has fleas" *will* raise relevant completers to contextual saliency.

4   A Partial Solution

Evidently, there is reason to hold that indexicals are directly referential, that the hidden-indexical version of Russell's theory of descriptions is correct, and that the former two theses cannot reasonably be held together.

Something has got to give. What is it? I doubt that it is the third thesis; I do not think you can reasonably hold that indexicals are directly referential if you hold the hidden-indexical theory of descriptions. I recognize, however, that these are complex issues on which there is plenty more to be said. I also recognize that an adequate pursuit of these issues would take us too far afield. I propose, then, provisionally to assume that the two theses are not cotenable and to see, however tentatively, where we might go from there.

Most philosophers of language nowadays think that indexicals are directly-referential singular terms, and this is something they would give up only as a last resort. This strikes me as a pretty good intuition, so let us take it as a starting point. Thus, in uttering "He's drunk" in our little scenario, the speaker is stating an object-dependent proposition involving Pergola. Is there anything else the speaker means, either determinately or indeterminately? In particular, does she also indeterminately mean each of a bunch of description-theoretic propositions involving complete definite descriptions the speaker and her audience mutually believe to apply to the referent of "he"? I think that many readers would have answered no if the question had been asked at the start of this paper. They would have said that the relevant psychological facts simply do not imply that any description-theoretic propositions are even vaguely, or indeterminately, meant. This has strong intuitive support. If you ask the speaker what she meant in uttering "He's drunk," it is very unlikely that she would mention any description-theoretic propositions. To be sure, she might well say that she meant that the guest speaker was drunk, or that the guy staggering up to the podium was drunk, but she would be using those descriptions to refer to Pergola; she would not be intending any "de dicto" readings of those self-ascriptive meaning reports wherein the that-clauses refer to description-theoretic propositions. The fact that the speaker would not have spoken as she did had she not believed that certain definite descriptions were mutually believed by her and her audience to apply to the referent of "he" does not support the hypothesis that those descriptions enter into even vaguely-meant propositions. They are not part of anything that is meant. They are simply part of the psychological baggage that goes with meaning an object-dependent proposition involving the referent of "he." It is not possible for one uttering "He's drunk" to mean an object-dependent proposition involving Pergola without bringing certain contextually-salient definite descriptions into play, for without the presupposition that Pergola satisfies such descriptions, there is no way the speaker could hope to have him identified as the referent. In general, it would seem that in meaning an object-dependent proposition involving a thing, the speaker must rely on the audience's coming to believe various object-independent propositions containing definite descriptions which that thing satisfies.[17] This does not show that it is impossible to mean an object-dependent proposition without also *meaning*, determinately or indeterminately, various description-theoretic propositions. If we could say that, in addition to meaning her object-dependent proposition, the speaker was also vaguely meaning lots of description-theoretic propositions relevant to her assertion, then you might as well say that among the things she meant was that she believed that Pergola was drunk and that she had good reasons for that belief. In any act of communication the speaker will expect numerous propositions to get conveyed to her audience, and many of these are such that the speaker would not have spoken as she did if she had thought that those propositions were either false or not going to be conveyed. But this does not show that those propositions are in any relevant sense *meant*. Meaning requires special audience-directed intentions, and we must not confusedly elevate psychological presuppositions of an act of meaning into further acts of meaning. The psychological facts manifest when the speaker utters "He is drunk" simply do not imply that she even vaguely meant any description-theoretic proposition.

If so, then the same holds for when, in the same circumstances, the speaker says, "The guy is drunk" instead of "He is drunk." For speaker meaning supervenes on the speaker's propositional attitudes, and the relevant propositional attitudes are precisely the same in the two cases. And if the speaker does not even indeterminately mean a description-theoretic proposition, then she also does not indeterminately state such a proposition.[18]

So I am inclined to conclude that we have no reason yet to reject the direct-reference theory of indexicals, but that we should reject the hidden-indexical theory of descriptions. However, before rushing to conclude that this forces one to recognize a strong attributive/referential distinction wherein a sentence of the form "The *F* is *G*" can be used literally to state either a description-theoretic proposition or else an object-dependent proposition, we should notice that our partial resolution of the first dilemma itself creates a dilemma for one who holds the hidden-indexical theory of belief reports.

5 Another Dilemma

The dilemma for the hidden-indexical theorist of belief reports is that she will find it difficult to stay a hidden-indexical theorist if she accepts the fate just proposed for the two other hidden-indexical theories—the hidden-indexical theory of descriptions and the hidden-indexical description theory of indexicals. For if, as I have argued, the utterer of "He is drunk" or "The guy is drunk" does not have propositional attitudes which entail that she indeterminately means any description-theoretic proposition, then the utterer of "*A* believes that *S*" does not have propositional attitudes which entail that she indeterminately means any proposition involving a type of mode of presentation. And what is not meant is not stated. The two sorts of cases appear to be precisely on a par.

Stella utters (a) ("Jean Luc Godard believes that Brigitte Bardot is selling her villa in St. Tropez and moving to Liverpool"), and according to the hidden-indexical theory the only statement she makes is an indeterminate statement involving various contextually-pertinent mode-of-presentation types. But if you ask Stella what she said in uttering (a), she will tell you that what she said, and all that she said, was that Jean Luc Godard believes that Brigitte Bardot was selling her villa in St. Tropez and moving to Liverpool. She would not recognize herself as having even vaguely said that there is something that is both Φ and such that Jean Luc Godard believes *that Brigitte Bardot is selling, etc.* under it, for various contextually-relevant mode-of-presentation types Φ. Notice how unlike this is from a paradigmatic case of vague reference, such as Stella's utterance of "It is raining here." In this case, Stella *will* recognize her statement as involving an indeterminate reference to a place, and this would be so even if Stella had merely said "It's raining" and the indeterminate reference to a place were implicit. None of this, however, implies that when Stella utters (a) she will not acknowledge that she expected her audience to think of Godard as thinking of Bardot, St. Tropez, Liverpool, etc. in certain sorts of ways, and would not have spoken as she did if she had thought those sorts of ways were not mutually known by her and her audience to apply. But this sort of counterfactual relevance no more implies meaning here than it did in the case of indexicals. To suppose otherwise is to confuse psychological states that perforce accompany what one means with separate acts of meaning. The psychological states involved in Stella's utterance seem not to yield the acts of meaning required by the hidden-indexical theory, which means that that theory seems not to be right. I am inclined to think that this pill has to be swallowed, but if so, then where do we go from here?

6 Towards a Radical Resolution

Suppose, as I have suggested but certainly have not proved, we should reject the hidden-indexical theory of belief reports and the hidden-indexical theory of descriptions. Then there are two pressing questions to be resolved. How should we accommodate the semantics of definite descriptions? And how should we accommodate the semantics of belief reports?

If we had stopped after the partial resolution of the first dilemma, it would have been reasonable to suppose that we had an argument to show that the Donnellanesque view of sentences of the form "The F is G" was right: utterances of them have two kinds of semantic contents. But having to deal with the question about belief reports may move the entire semantic discussion onto another plane. For if the hidden-indexical theory of belief reports is false for the proposed reason, then that suggests that belief reports do not involve contextually-determined references to modes of presentation or to types of modes of presentation, and this would mean that the semantics of those sentences cannot appeal to modes of presentation. Without this appeal, we have no reason not to treat the logical form of "A believes that S" as being what at face value it appears to be: a two-place verb linking two arguments. But this is where the trouble appears. For what are we to make of the proposition referred to by the that-clause in, say, "Ralph believes that no woodchuck is a groundhog"? According to traditional compositional semantics, the reference of the that-clause is determined by its syntax and the references that its component words have in the that-clause. Yet if we follow this course to its logical conclusion, we will end up wrongly counting "Ralph believes that no woodchuck is a groundhog, but does not believe that no woodchuck is a woodchuck" as false.

It seems to me that a radically new sort of view may be called for: radical with respect to the determination of that-clause reference, radical with respect to the nature of the propositions to which that-clauses refer, and radical with respect to classical conceptions about compositional semantics. I do my best to sketch such a view in a recent paper, "A Paradox of Meaning" (1994). Its crucial idea is that the propositions to which that-clauses refer and which provide the semantic contents of utterances are noncompositionally-determined hypostatizations of our that-clause-invoking linguistic and conceptual practices. On currently prevalent accounts of propositions, propositions are compositionally-determined, structured entities, made up either out of the objects and properties our beliefs are about or out of modes of presentation of those objects and properties. These propositions are compositionally determined in that there are compositional rules that will build all of the propositions to which our that-clauses can refer out of some stock of propositional building blocks, the basic constituents of propositions. These propositional building blocks will be the referents words have in that-clauses, and the proposition to which a that-clause refers will be determined, in accordance with a compositional semantics, by the that-clause's syntax and the references its words have in the that-clause. On the view that I propose, however, propositions are mere shadows of the sentences contained in that-clauses. We get the proposition that no woodchuck is a groundhog by, as it were, allowing ourselves automatically to move from the sentence "No woodchuck is a groundhog" to the singular term "that no woodchuck is a groundhog," which we then indefeasibly take to refer to (the proposition) that no woodchuck is a groundhog. This is why we can trivially move back and forth between "No woodchuck is a groundhog" and its pleonastic equivalent "That no woodchuck is a groundhog is true" (more colloquially, "It is true that no woodchuck is a groundhog"). When suitably elaborated and supplemented, this picture of how the notion of a proposition enters our conceptual scheme makes it possible to see how the proposition that no woodchuck is a groundhog might not be compositionally determined, and therefore not a structured entity made up out of propositional building blocks. If, as I speculate, it is not compositionally determined, then we cannot account for the reference to it by "that no woodchuck is a groundhog" in the standard compositional way that sees the reference of a that-clause as determined by its syntax and the references its words have in it. Indeed, if the propositions to which our that-clauses refer are noncompositionally determined, then our languages will lack compositional semantics. In the work just mentioned I try to explain why this is not something to fear, and I offer an account of that-clause reference that is consistent with the referent of a that-clause being a noncompositionally-determined proposition.

I suspect that if we rethink semantics in this deflationary way, then we will have an alternative to the hidden-indexical theory of belief reports. We will be in a position to hold that the that-clauses in "Ralph believes that no woodchuck is a groundhog" and "Ralph believes that no wood-chuck is a woodchuck" refer to distinct propositions *without having to appeal to "modes of presentation" and without having to find distinct objects to be the referents of "woodchuck" and "groundhog" as they occur in those that-clauses.*

I suspect we will also find ourselves with other options for answering our still unanswered question about definite descriptions than that provided by Donnellan's ambiguity thesis. This is inevitable, for on the deflationary view in question, there will be *no* standard semantics for definite descriptions, which is to say, no treatment of them in conformity with a compositional meaning theory. But to elaborate this further would require an extended discussion of how sentences get their meanings and of the individuation of noncompositionally-determined propositions, topics explored in "A Paradox of Meaning."

Acknowledgment

I am indebted to comments by Kent Bach, Paul Boghossian, Jennifer Church, Mark Crimmins, Hartry Field, Greg Fitch, Graeme Forbes, David Kaplan, Bernie Kobes, Stephen Neale, Christopher Peacocke, François Récanati, Marga Reimer, Nathan Salmon, Gabriel Segal, and Scott Sturgeon.

Notes

1. It should eventually be clear that I could have constructed this dilemma with proper names thrown in with pronouns and demonstratives, but I want to keep the argument as uncluttered as possible.

2. See Schiffer (1977, 1978, 1987, 1992).

3. See, e.g., Crimmins and Perry (1989); Crimmins (1992); Richard (1990); Fodor (1990).

4. Actually, I should say that believing is a four-place relation, its fourth place being a time at which x believes p under m. But I suppress temporal references for simplicity of exposition.

5. I borrow the groundhog/woodchuck example from Edward Zalta (unpublished).

6. For present purposes, I count a that-clause as a referential singular term even if it is understood on an analogy with a Russellian treatment of extensional occurrences of definite descriptions, the "denotation" of the that-clause being the proposition uniquely characterized by the that-clause.

7. The proposition that no woodchunk is a groundhog has its truth condition in every possible world, and, unlike sentences and other representations, it has its truth condition absolutely, not relative to a language or anything else.

8. But might not the speaker's reference be fixed by some such description as *the mode of presentation Ralph associates with "woodchuck"*? It is not clear that it can. First, on any reasonable way of individuating modes of presentation, Ralph will associate several modes of presentation with each expression he uses. At best, the speaker would have to have in mind some particular sort of *maximal* mode of presentation associated with "woodchuck," something like a complete "dossier." But then how plausible is it that an ordinary speaker would have such a sophisticated description in mind? Second, the notion of a mode of presentation here invoked, and even the notion of a *way of thinking of a thing*, is a quasi-technical notion, and it is far from clear what suitable commonsense notion might replace it.

9. Might this be a case where the type of mode of presentation is vacuous, so that what Stella means is merely that Godard believes, under some mode of presentation or other, *that Brigitte Bardot is selling her villa in St. Tropez and moving to Liverpool*? No. For suppose that Godard merely overheard someone in the booth behind him at Maxim's, whose voice he failed to identify but which in fact was Bardot's, say that she was selling her villa in St. Tropez and moving to Liverpool, and thus formed the belief, of that unrecognized person, that she was selling her villa, etc. This fact would not make Stella's utterance of (a) true, but it would if she merely meant what was just proposed.

10. The notion of an "admissible sharpening/precisification" is a technical notion. A vague statement will have certain conditions under which it is definitely true, certain conditions under which it is definitely false, and certain borderline conditions—conditions under which it is neither definitely true nor definitely false. (For simplicity, I ignore "higher-order vagueness," e.g., a statement's being neither definitely definitely true nor definitely not definitely true.) An admissible sharpening of a vague statement s may be thought of as a precise statement that (a) is either definitely true or definitely false and (b) is definitely true when s is definitely true, and definitely false when s is definitely false. Thus, a vague statement will have many admissible sharpenings, and it itself will be true when true on all admissible sharpenings, false when false on all admissible sharpenings, and neither true nor false when true on some admissible sharpenings while false on others. See, e.g., Fine (1975).

11. A slightly different variant of this example occurs in Schiffer (1981). Note that, strictly speaking, what enters into the meaning-candidate propositions are not "definite descriptions," but rather *individual concepts*, where an individual concept is the property of having a certain property uniquely. Note, too, that particulars can occur in these properties, so that "the thing that's R to α" and "the thing that's R to β" might express the same individual concept even thought "α" and "β" are distinct singular terms.

12. I recognize that there are other ways a Russellian might try to go, but for the purposes of this paper I shall simply assume without argument—what I in fact

believe—that the hidden-indexical theory is the best way to extend the theory of descriptions to "incomplete" definite descriptions. Some of these other ways would entail analogous dilemmas, but nothing turns on my restriction, since I shall be content to have stated a dilemma for the hidden-indexical version of the theory of descriptions.

13. Once I construct the dilemma, it will be evident that the details of the hidden-indexical theory of descriptions are unimportant. For example, an analogous dilemma could be constructed for one who accepts the naive hidden-indexical theory of descriptions. Yet it is important to state the dilemma in terms of the most plausible version of the description theory, and how exactly we set up the dilemma will affect its resolution. After writing this paper, I noticed that George M. Wilson stresses a similar dilemma (1991).

14. I shall take it as assumed that a description-theoretic act of meaning can be indeterminate.

15. Might there not be some demonstrative utterances wherein the speaker does not expect his audience to believe contextually-relevant description-theoretic propositions along with the primarily intended object-dependent proposition? Why cannot the reference be achieved not by getting the audience to believe an object-independent proposition but simply by getting her in the right *perceptual* state? Two comments. (i) As a simple matter of fact, *I* cannot think of any such case. Consider a paradigm perceptual/demonstrative utterance: my saying to you "This is attractive," where "this" refers to one among several swatches. It is difficult to see how reference could be achieved without the expectation that the audience will believe the swatch to satisfy some such description as *the swatch to which the speaker is pointing* or *the last swatch to be displayed*. (ii) If there are indexical utterances that do not bring contextually-salient definite descriptions into play, then there will certainly be referential uses of definite descriptions wherein no description-theoretic proposition can be said to be even indeterminately meant ("The swatch is attractive"). But then we shall have what appear to be serious and literal utterances of sentences of the form "The *F* is *G*" wherein no description-theoretic act of meaning is even remotely in the offing, and so much the worse for the hidden-indexical theory of descriptions.

16. It might seem that the direct-intuition line could gain support from the behaviour of indexicals in modal contexts. For example, "That guy might have been sober" seems not to have a reading on which it is both true and "that guy" does not refer to some intended actual-world referent. But the same can be said of "The guy might have been sober," and of course the description theorist can use scope distinctions to account for such *de re* occurrences of singular terms.

17. But see note 15 for a possible qualification.

18. Does this mean that a speaker cannot be making an indeterminate description-theoretic statement when she uses an incomplete definite description *attributively*? Not at all; for in such a case the speaker's propositional attitudes will be critically different from those in the referential case. (I am hardly denying the possibility of meaning indeterminacy!) Thus, you utter "The murderer is insane"

and mean that *that* guy is insane. In this referential case, various contextually-salient definite descriptions will be more-or-less essential to your communicative intentions in the now familiar way—*the person everyone thinks murdered Smith, the prisoner in the dock, the lunatic now raving before us*, etc.—but you do not indeterminately mean as many description-theoretic propositions to the effect that *the Φ is insane*. This is because those propositions enter as psychological baggage carried by your primary intention to communicate an object-dependent proposition involving the referent of your utterance of "the murderer." But now suppose we have the familiar *attributive* utterance of "The murderer must be insane," which you produce upon first seeing Smith's hideously mutilated corpse. In this case, you arguably do not intend to communicate any object-dependent proposition involving the murderer. Your primary intention is to communicate a completion of the description-theoretic proposition *the murderer of . . . must be insane*, but it may be genuinely indeterminate whether you mean *that the murderer of Smith must be insane* or *that the murderer of the person whose mangled corpse lies before us must be insane*. In this case, you *do* perform an indeterminate description-theoretic act of meaning, but that is because your propositional attitudes are relevantly different from those in the referential case.

References

Blackburn, William K. 1988: "Wettstein on Definite Descriptions." *Philosophical Studies*, 53, pp. 263–278.

Crimmins, Mark 1992: *Talk About Belief*. Cambridge, Mass.: MIT Press.

Crimmins, Mark and Perry, John 1989: "The Prince and the Phone Booth: Reporting Puzzling Beliefs." *The Journal of Philosophy*, 86, pp. 685–711.

Fine, Kit 1975: "Vagueness, Truth, and Logic." *Synthese*, 30, pp. 265–300.

Fodor, Jerry 1990: "Substitution Arguments and the Individuation of Belief," in *A Theory of Content*. Cambridge, Mass.: MIT Press.

Richard, Mark 1990: *Propositional Attitudes*. Cambridge: Cambridge University Press.

Schiffer, Stephen, 1977: "Naming and Knowing" in P. A. French, T. E. Uehling, and H. K. Wettstein, eds., *Midwest Studies in Philosophy*. Minneapolis, Minnesota: University of Minnesota Press.

———1978: "The Basis of Reference." *Erkenntnis*, 13, pp. 171–206.

———1981: "Indexicals and the Theory of Reference." *Synthese*, 69, pp. 43–100.

———1987: "The 'Fido'-Fido Theory of Belief," in James E. Tomberlin, ed., *Philosophical Perspectives* I. Atascadero, California: Ridgview.

———1992: "Belief Ascription." *The Journal of Philosophy*, 89, pp. 492–521.

———1994: "A Paradox of Meaning." *Nôus*, 28:3, pp. 279–324.

Wettstein, Howard 1979: "Indexical Reference and Propositional Content." *Philosophical Studies*, 36, pp. 91–100.

————1981: "Demonstrative Reference and Definite Descriptions." *Philosophical Studies*, 40, pp. 241–257 (chapter 12, this volume).

————1983: "The Semantic Significance of the Referential-Attributive Distinction." *Philosophical Studies*, 44, pp. 187–196.

Wilson, George M. 1991: "Reference and Pronominal Descriptions." *The Journal of Philosophy*, 88, pp. 359–387.

Zalta, Edward (unpublished): "Modes of Presentation and Fregean Senses." Available at: http://mally.stanford.edu/publications.html

Bibliography

This bibliography is organized by topic. In many cases, however, a paper addresses a number of relevant topics simultaneously. Thus it is inevitable that there be some arbitrariness in categorizing a paper under one heading rather than another. The reader wishing to research a given topic should therefore not limit herself to the most obvious classification, but should examine papers listed under other relevant headings.

Origins

Blackburn, Simon and Alan Code. (1978). The Power of Russell's Criticism of Frege: "On Denoting" pp. 48–50. *Analysis* 38, 65–77; reprinted in A. D. Irvine and G. A. Wedeking (eds.), *Russell and Analytic Philosophy*. Toronto: University of Toronto Press, 1993.

Cartwright, Richard. (1987). The Origins of Russell's Theory of Descriptions. In *Philosophical Essays*. Cambridge, Mass.: MIT Press, 95–133.

Cassin, Chrystine E. (1970). Russell's Discussion of Meaning and Denotation: A Re-examination. In E. D. Klemke (ed.), *Essays on Bertrand Russell*. Chicago: University of Illinois Press, 256–272.

Coffa, J. Alberto. (1988). *The Semantic Tradition from Frege to Carnap*. New York: Cambridge University Press. Chapter 6, "On Denoting."

Dau, Paolo. (1986). Russell's First Theory of Denoting and Quantification. *Notre Dame Journal of Formal Logic* 27, 133–166.

Frege, Gottlob. (1967). *The Basic Laws of Arithmetic*, trans. Montgomery Furth. Los Angeles: University of California Press. Part 1, Section 11.

Geach, Peter. (1958–59). Russell on Meaning and Denoting. *Analysis* 19; reprinted in *Logic Matters*. Berkeley: University of California Press, 1972, 27–41.

Hylton, Peter. (1990a). *Russell, Idealism, and the Emergence of Analytic Philosophy*. New York: Oxford University Press.

————. (1990b). The Significance of "On Denoting." In C. Wade Savage and Anthony Anderson (eds.), *Rereading Russell*. Minneapolis: The University of Minnesota Press.

Jones, E. E. Constance. (1910). Russell's Criticisms of Frege's Theory of Sense and Reference. *Mind* (New Series) 19, 378–386.

———. (1910–11). A New Law of Thought. *Aristotelian Society Proceedings, New Series* 11, 166–186.

Kremer, Michael. (1994). The Argument of "On Denoting." *Philosophical Review* 103, 249–297.

Makin, Gideon. (1996). Why the Theory of Descriptions? *Philosophical Quarterly* 46, 158–167.

Meinong, Alexius. (1960). The Theory of Objects. In Roderick Chisholm (ed.), *Realism and the Background of Phenomenology*. Glencoe, Illinois: Free Press.

Quine, Willard van Orman. (1966). Russell's Ontological Development. *Journal of Philosophy* 63; reprinted in David Pears (ed.), *Bertrand Russell*. New York: Doubleday, 1972, 291–304.

Russell, Bertrand. (1903). *The Principles of Mathematics*. London: George Allen and Unwin.

———. (1905). The Existential Import of Propositions. *Mind* (New Series) 14, 398–401; reprinted in Douglas Lackey (ed.), *Essays in Analysis*. New York: George Braziller, 1973, 98–102.

———. (1908). Mathematical Logic as Based on the Theory of Types. *American Journal of Mathematics* 30, 222–262; reprinted in Jean Van Heijenoort (ed.), *From Frege to Gödel, A Sourcebook in Mathematical Logic, 1879–1931*. Cambridge, Mass.: Harvard University Press, 1967, 156–182.

———. (1911). Knowledge by Acquaintance and Knowledge by Description. *Proceedings of the Aristotelian Society* 11, 108–128; reprinted in *Mysticism and Logic*. London: George Allen and Unwin, 1917.

———. (1912). *The Problems of Philosophy*. New York: Oxford University Press.

———. (1944). My Mental Development. In Paul Arthur Schilpp (ed.) *The Philosophy of Bertrand Russell*. Evanston, Illinois: Northwestern University Press.

———. (1956). *Logic and Knowledge*, R. C. Marsh (ed.). London: George Allen and Unwin.

———. (1956). Mr. Strawson on Referring. *Mind*, 66, 385–389.

———. (1959). *My Philosophical Development*. London: George Allen and Unwin.

———. (1967). *The Autobiography of Bertrand Russell, 1872–1914*. Boston: Little, Brown and Company.

———. (1985). *The Philosophy of Logical Atomism*, David Pears, ed. La Salle, Illinois: Open Court; also in Russell (1956), 41–56. Originally published in 1918.

———. (1994). On Fundamentals. In Alasdair Urquhart (ed.), *The Collected Papers of Bertrand Russell, Vol. IV: Foundations of Logic 1903–5*. London: Routledge, 360–413. Written in June 1905.

Schilpp, Paul Arthur (ed.). (1944). *The Philosophy of Bertrand Russell*. Evanston, Illinois: Northwestern University Press.

Searle, John. (1958). Russell's Objections to Frege's Theory of Sense and Reference. *Analysis* 18, 137–143.

Urquhart, Alasdair. (1994–95). G. F. Stout and the Theory of Descriptions. *Russell* 14, 163–171.

Whitehead, A. N. and Bertrand Russell. (1927). *Principia Mathematica, Vol. I,* 2nd Ed. Cambridge: Cambridge University Press.

Descriptive Pronouns and Pronominal Descriptions

Chierchia, Gennaro. (1995). *Dynamics of Meaning.* Chicago: University of Chicago Press.

Donnellan, Keith. (1979). Speaker Reference, Descriptions, and Anaphora. In Peter Cole (ed.), *Syntax and Semantics.* New York: Academic Press.

Evans, Gareth. (1977). Pronouns, Quantifiers, and Relative Clauses (I). *Canadian Journal of Philosophy* 7, 467–536; reprinted in Evans (1985).

———. (1977). Pronouns, Quantifiers, and Relative Clauses (II). *Canadian Journal of Philosophy* 7, 777–797; reprinted in Evans (1985).

———. (1980). Pronouns. *Linguistic Inquiry* 11, 337–362; reprinted in Evans (1985).

———. (1985). *The Collected Papers.* New York: Oxford University Press.

Groenendijk, J. and M. Stokhof. (1991). Dynamic Predicate Logic. *Linguistics and Philosophy* 14, 39–100.

Heim, Irene. (1982). *The Semantics of Definite and Indefinite Noun Phrases.* Dissertation, University of Massachusetts at Amherst; published by Garland Press, New York, 1989.

———. (1990). E-Type Pronouns and Donkey Anaphora. *Linguistics and Philosophy* 13, 137–177.

Hintikka, Jaakko and Jack Kulas. (1985). *Anaphora and Definite Descriptions.* Dordrecht: D. Reidel.

Kadmon, Nirit. (1990). Uniqueness. *Linguistics and Philosophy* 13, 273–324.

Kamp, Hans. (1981). A Theory of Truth and Semantic Representation. In J. Groenendijk et al. (eds.), *Truth, Interpretation, and Information.* Dordrecht: Foris, 1–43.

Moltmann, Friederike. (1999). E-Type and Dynamic Approaches to Unbound Anaphoric Pronouns. *Journal of Philosophical Logic* (forthcoming).

Neale, Stephen. (1990). *Descriptions.* Cambridge, Mass.: The MIT Press. Chapters 5 and 6.

———. (1990). Descriptive Pronouns and Donkey Anaphora. *Journal of Philosophy* 87, 113–150.

Simons, Mandy. (1996). Pronouns and Definite Descriptions: A Critique of Wilson. *Journal of Philosophy* 93, 408–420.

Soames, Scott. (1989). Review of Gareth Evans, *The Collected Papers. Journal of Philosophy* 86, 141–156.

Wilson, George. (1984). Pronouns and Pronominal Descriptions: A New Semantical Category. *Philosophical Studies* 45, 1–30.

———. (1991). Reference and Pronominal Descriptions. *Journal of Philosophy* 88, 359–387.

The Description Theory of Names

Braun, David. (1995). Katz on Names without Bearers. *Philosophical Review* 104, 53–76.

Donnellan, Keith. (1972). Proper Names and Identifying Descriptions. In Donald Davidson and Gilbert Harman (eds.), *Semantics of Natural Language*. Dordrecht: D. Reidel, 356–379.

Evans, Gareth. (1979). Reference and Contingency. *The Monist* 62, 161–189; reprinted in Evans (1985).

Frege, Gottlob. (1980). On Sense and Meaning. Trans. Max Black. In Peter Geach and Max Black (eds.), *The Philosophical Writings of Gottlob Frege*, 3rd Ed. Oxford: Basil Blackwell.

Katz, Jerrold J. (1990). Has the Description Theory of Names Been Refuted? In George Boolos (ed.), *Meaning and Method: Essays in Honor of Hilary Putnam*. New York: Cambridge University Press, 31–61.

———. (1994). Names without Bearers. *Philosophical Review* 103, 1–39.

Kripke, Saul. (1972). Naming and Necessity. In Donald Davidson and Gilbert Harman (eds.), *Semantics of Natural Language*. Dordrecht: D. Reidel, 253–355, 763–769; reprinted, with Preface, as *Naming and Necessity*, Cambridge, Mass.: Harvard University Press, 1980.

Linsky, Leonard. (1963). Reference and Referents. In C. Caton (ed.), *Ordinary Language*. Urbana, Illinois: University of Illinois Press, 74–89.

———. (1967). *Referring*. London: Routlege and Kegan Paul.

———. (1977). *Names and Descriptions*. Chicago: University of Chicago Press.

Loar, Brian. (1976). The Semantics of Singular Terms. *Philosophical Studies* 30, 353–377.

———. (1980). Names and Descriptions: A Reply to Michael Devitt. *Philosophical Studies* 38, 85–89.

Plantinga, Alvin. (1978). The Boethian Compromise. *American Philosophical Quarterly* 15, 129–138.

Salmon, Nathan. (1981). *Reference and Essence*. Princeton: Princeton University Press.

Searle, John. (1958). Proper Names. *Mind* 67, 166–173.

———. (1981). *Intentionality*. New York: Cambridge University Press.

Descriptions as Quantifiers

Barwise, Jon and Robin Cooper. (1981). Generalized Quantifiers and Natural Language. *Linguistics and Philosophy* 4, 159–219.

Chierchia, Gennaro and Sally McConnell-Ginet. (1990). *Meaning and Grammar*. Cambridge, Mass.: The MIT Press. Chapter 9 ("Generalized Quantifiers").

Chomsky, Noam. (1975). Questions of Form and Interpretation. *Linguistic Analysis* 1, 75–109.

Davies, Martin. (1981). *Meaning, Quantification, Necessity*. London: Routledge and Kegan Paul.

Dummett, Michael. (1973). *Frege: Philosophy of Language*. London: Duckworth. Chapter III.

Evans, Gareth. (1982). *The Varieties of Reference*. New York: Oxford University Press. Chapter 2, Section 2.4, "Definite Descriptions."

Harman, Gilbert. (1972). Deep Structure as Logical Form. In Donald Davidson and Gilbert Harman (eds.), *Semantics of Natural Language*. Dordrecht: D. Reidel, 25–47.

Lewis, David. (1979). Scorekeeping in a Language Game. *Journal of Philosophical Logic* 8, 339–359.

Linsky, Bernard. (1992). The Logical Form of Descriptions. *Dialogue* 31, 677–683.

May, Robert. (1985). *Logical Form: Its Structure and Derivation*. Cambridge, Mass.: The MIT Press.

Ostertag, Gary. (1998). A Scorekeeping Error. *Philosophical Studies* 52.

Prior, A. N. (1963). Is the Concept of Referential Opacity Really Necessary? *Acta Philosophica Fennica* 16, 189–198.

———. (1962). Nonentities. In R. J. Butler (ed.), *Analytical Philosophy, Second Series*. Oxford: Barnes and Noble, Inc., 120–132; reprinted in *Papers in Logic and Ethics*, P. Geach and A. Kenny (eds.). Amherst: University of Massachusetts Press, 109–121.

Sharvy, R. (1969). Things. *The Monist* 53, 488–504.

Stanley, Jason and Timothy Williamson. (1995). Quantifiers and Context Dependence. *Analysis* 55.4, 291–295.

Indefinite Descriptions

Chastain, Charles. (1975). Reference and Context. *Minnesota Studies in the Philosophy of Science, Vol. VII*. Minneapolis: University of Minnesota Press, 194–269.

Fodor, Janet and Ivan Sag. (1982). Referential and Quantificational Indefinites. *Linguistics and Philosophy* 5, 355–398.

Higginbotham, James. (1987). Indefiniteness and Predication. In E. Reuland and A. ter Meulen (eds.), *The Representation of (In)definiteness*. Cambridge, Mass.: The MIT Press, 43–70.

King, J. (1988). Are Indefinite Descriptions Ambiguous? *Philosophical Studies* 53, 417–440.

Ludlow, Peter and Stephen Neale. (1991). Indefinite Descriptions: In Defense of Russell. *Linguistics and Philosophy* 14, 171–202.

Wilson, George. (1977). On Definite and Indefinite Descriptions. *Philosophical Review* 87, 48–76.

Referential/Attributive

Atlas, Jay David. (1989). *Philosophy without Ambiguity*. New York: Oxford University Press.

Bach, Kent. (1981). Referential/Attributive. *Synthese* 49, 219–244; reprinted in Stephen Davis (ed.), *Pragmatics*. New York: Oxford University Press, 1990, 17–32.

———. (1988). *Thought and Reference*. New York: Oxford University Press.

———. (1994). Ramachandran vs. Russell. *Analysis* 54.3, 183–186.

Barwise, Jon and John Perry. (1983). *Situations and Attitudes*. Cambridge, Mass.: The MIT Press.

Bezuidenhout, Anne. (1997). Pragmatics, Semantic Underdetermination, and the Referential/Attributive Distinction. *Mind* 106, 375–409.

Blackburn, William K. (1988). Wettstein on Definite Descriptions. *Philosophical Studies* 53, 263–278.

Devitt, Michael. (1974). Singular Terms. *Journal of Philosophy* 71, 183–205.

———. (1981). Donnellan's Distinction. *Midwest Studies in Philosophy VI*. Minneapolis: University of Minnesota Press, 511–524.

Donnellan, Keith. (1968). Putting Humpty Dumpty Back Together Again. *Philosophical Review* 77, 203–215.

———. (1982). *The Varieties of Reference*. New York: Oxford University Press. Chapter 9, Section 9.3 ("The information-invoking use of definite descriptions").

Ganeri, Jonardon. (1995). Contextually Incomplete Descriptions—a New Counterexample to Russell? *Analysis* 55.4, 287–290.

Gauker, Christopher. (1997). Domain of Discourse. *Mind* 106, 1–32.

Grice, H. P. (1975). Logic and Conversation. In Peter Cole (ed.), *Syntax and Semantics, vol 3: Speech Acts*. New York: Academic Press, 113–128; reprinted, with changes, in Grice (1989).

———. (1981). Presupposition and Conversational Implicature. In P. Cole (ed.), *Radical Pragmatics*. New York: Academic Press, 183–198.

———. (1989). *Studies in the Way of Words*. Cambridge, Mass.: Harvard University Press.

Loar, Brian. (1976). The Semantics of Singular Terms. *Philosophical Studies* 30, 353–377.

Neale, Stephen. (1992). Paul Grice and the Philosophy of Language. *Linguistics and Philosophy* 15, 509–559.

Patton, Thomas E. (1997). Explaining Referential/Attributive. *Mind* 106, 245–261.

Ramachandran, Murali. (1994). A Strawsonian Objection to Russell's Theory of Descriptions. *Analysis* 53.4, 209–212.

———. (1995). Bach on Behalf of Russell. *Analysis* 55.4, 283–287.

———. (1996). The Ambiguity Thesis versus Kripke's Defense of Russell. *Mind and Language* 11, 371–387.

Récanati, François. (1989). Referential/Attributive: A Contextualist Proposal. *Philosophical Studies* 56, 217–249.

———. (1993). *Direct Reference: From Language to Thought*. New York: Basil Blackwell. Part II.2, "Referential/Attributive."

———. (1996). Domains of Discourse. *Linguistics and Philosophy* 19, 445–475.

Reimer, Marga. (1992). Incomplete Descriptions. *Erkenntnis* 37, 347–363.

———. (1992). Demonstrating with Descriptions. *Philosophy and Phenomenological Research* 52, 877–893.

———. (1993). Russell's Anticipation of Donnellan's Distinction. *Australasian Journal of Philosophy* 71, 70–77.

Sainsbury, R. M. (1979). *Russell*. London: Routledge and Kegan Paul.

Salmon, Nathan. (1982). Assertion and Incomplete Definite Descriptions. *Philosophical Studies* 42, 37–45.

———. (1991). The Pragmatic Fallacy. *Philosophical Studies* 63, 83–97.

Schiffer, Stephen. (1992). Belief Ascription. *Journal of Philosophy* 89, 499–521.

Searle, John. (1979). Referential and Attributive. *The Monist* 62, 140–168; reprinted in *Expression and Meaning*, New York: Cambridge University Press, 1983, 137–161.

Sellars, Wilfrid. (1954). Presupposing. *Philosophical Review* 63, 197–215.

Soames, Scott. (1994). Donnellan's Referential/Attributive Distinction. *Philosophical Studies* 73, 149–168.

Stalnaker, Robert. (1972). Pragmatics. In Donald Davidson and Gilbert Harman (eds.), *Semantics of Natural Language*. Dordrecht: D. Reidel, 176–186.

———. (1974). Pragmatic Presuppositions. In Milton Munitz and Peter Unger (eds.), *Semantics and Philosophy*. New York: New York University Press, 197–230; reprinted in Stephen Davis (ed.), *Pragmatics*. New York: Oxford University Press, 1990, 471–481.

Strawson, P. F. (1954). Reply to Mr. Sellars. *Philosophical Review* 63, 216–231.

Wettstein, Howard. (1984). The Semantic Significance of the Referential–Attributive Distinction. *Philosophical Studies* 44, 187–194; reprinted in *Has Semantics Rested on a Mistake?* Stanford: Stanford University Press, 1991, 50–58.

Wilson, George. (1991). Reference and Pronominal Descriptions. *The Journal of Philosophy* 88, 359–387.

Descriptions as Singular Terms

Bacon, John. (1965). An Alternative Contextual Definition for Descriptions. *Philosophical Studies* 16, 75–76.

Burge, Tyler. (1974). Truth and Singular Terms. *Journal of Philosophy* 8, 309–325; reprinted in Karel Lambert (ed.), *Philosophical Foundations of Free Logic*, New York: Oxford University Press, 1991, 189–204.

Gödel, Kurt. (1944). Russell's Mathematical Logic. In Paul Arthur Schilpp (ed.), *The Philosophy of Bertrand Russell*. Chicago: Northwestern University Press, 447–469; reprinted in Paul Benacerraf and Hilary Putnam (eds.), *Readings in the Philosophy of Mathematics*, 2nd Ed., New York: Cambridge University Press, 1983, 447–469.

Grandy, Richard. (1972). A Definition of Truth for Sentences Containing Intensional Definite Description Operators. *Journal of Philosophical Logic* 1, 137–155; reprinted in Karel Lambert (ed.), *Philosophical Foundations of Free Logic*. New York: Oxford University Press, 1991, 171–188.

Kalish, Donald, Richard Montague, and Gary Mar (1980). *Logic: Techniques of Formal Reasoning*, 2nd Ed. New York: Harcourt Brace Jovanovitch, 1980. Chapters VI ("'THE'") and VIII ("'THE' again: A Russellian Theory of Descriptions").

Kaplan, David. (1970). What is Russell's Theory of Descriptions? In Wolfgang Yourgrau et al. (eds.), *Physics, Logic, and History*. New York: Plenum Press; reprinted in David Pears (ed.), *Bertrand Russell*. New York: Doubleday, 1972, 227–244.

Kaplan, David. (1978). Dthat. In Peter Cole (ed.), *Syntax and Semantics*. New York: Academic Press, 221–243.

―――. (1989). Demonstratives. In Joseph Almog, John Perry, and Howard Wettstein (eds.), *Themes from Kaplan*. New York: Oxford University Press, 481–563.

―――. (1978). On the Logic of Demonstratives. *Journal of Philosophical Logic* 8, 81–98; reprinted in Nathan Salmon and Scott Soames (eds.), *Propositions and Attitudes*. New York: Oxford University Press, 66–82.

Stephen Neale. (1995). The Philosophical Significance of Gödel's Slingshot. *Mind* 104, 761–825.

Scott, Dana. (1967). Existence and Description in Formal Logic. In Ralph Schoenman (ed.), *Bertrand Russell, Philosopher of the Century*. Boston: Little, Brown and Co, 181–200; reprinted in Karel Lambert (ed.), *Philosophical Foundations of Free Logic*. New York: Oxford University Press, 1991, 28–48.

Smiley, Timothy. (1981). The Theory of Descriptions. *Proceedings of the British Academy* 67, 321–337.

Taylor, Barry. (1985). *Modes of Occurrence*. Oxford: Basil Blackwell. Chapter 2, "States of Affairs."

Descriptions and Modality

Linsky, Leonard. (1977). *Names and Descriptions*. Chicago: University of Chicago Press.

———. (1983). *Oblique Contexts*. Chicago: University of Chicago Press.

Marcus, Ruth Barcan. (1963). Modalities and Intensional Languages. In *Boston Studies in the Philosophy of Science, Vol I*. Dordrecht: Reidel, 77–116; reprinted in *Modalities*. New York: Oxford University Press, 1993.

Marti, Genoveva. (1994). Do Modal Distinctions Collapse in Carnap's System? *Journal of Philosophical Logic* 23, 575–593.

Neale, Stephen. (1990) *Descriptions*. Cambridge, Mass.: The MIT Press. Chapter 4 ("Scope, Substitutivity and Opacity").

———. (1993). Term Limits. *Philosophical Perspectives* 7, 89–123.

Quine, Willard Van Orman. (1953). Three Grades of Modal Involvement. *Proceedings of the XIth International Congress of Philosophy* 14: 65–81; reprinted in *The Ways of Paradox*, 2nd Ed., Cambridge, Mass.: Harvard University Press, 1976.

———. (1960). *Word and Object*. Cambridge, Mass.: The MIT Press.

Smullyan, Arthur F. (1948). Modality and Description. *Journal of Symbolic Logic* 13, 31–37; reprinted in L. Linsky (ed.) *Reference and Modality*. New York: Oxford University Press, 1971, 35–43.

Thomason, Richmond H. and Robert Stalnaker. (1968). Modality and Reference. *Noûs* 2, 359–372.

Descriptions and Mass Terms

Sharvey, R. (1980). A More General Theory of Definite Descriptions. *Philosophical Review* 89, 607–624.

Useful Anthologies

Davis, Steven. (1990). *Pragmatics*. New York: Oxford University Press. (Includes important essays by Grice, Stalnaker, Carston, Récanati, and Sperber and Wilson. Essential further reading for anyone interested in the pragmatic dimension of Russell's theory of descriptions; interested readers should also consult the papers by Récanati and Bezuidenhout in the Referential/Attributive section, above.)

Lackey, Douglas. (1973). *Essays in Analysis*. Now York: George Braziller. (Unfortunately out of print. Especially useful for its coverage of Russell's transition from the *Principles* to "On Denoting.")

Lambert, Karel. (1991). *Philosophical Foundations of Free Logic*. New York: Oxford University Press. (Rather specialized, but the papers by Scott, Grandy, and Burge are essential reading for those who desire a complete picture of the singular-term interpretation of *Principia* *14.01 and *14.02.)

Index